LITERARY LANDSCAPES
OF THE
BRITISH ISLES

LITERARY LANDSCAPES
OF THE
BRITISH ISLES

A Narrative Atlas

DAVID DAICHES & JOHN FLOWER

PADDINGTON PRESS LTD
NEW YORK & LONDON

Third Printing

Library of Congress Cataloging in Publication Data
Daiches, David, 1912–
  Literary landscapes of the British Isles.

  Includes index.
   1.   Literary landmarks—Great Britain.   2.   Authors,
English—Homes and haunts.   3.   Literary landmarks—
Great Britain—Maps.   4.   Great Britain—Description and
travel—1971–   I.   Flower, John R., joint author.
II.   Title.
PR109.D34   820'.9'941   78–11446
ISBN 0 7092 0150 8
ISBN 0 448 22205 1 (U.S. and Canada only)

Created in association with Lund Humphries Publishers Ltd.,
London, England.
Filmset in England by S.X. Composing Ltd., Rayleigh, Essex, and
Vantage Photosetting Co. Ltd., Hants.
Map processing by Y. Kahn.

Printed and bound in the United States
Designed by Colin Lewis

Grateful acknowledgement is made to the literary estate of
Virginia Woolf, the Hogarth Press and Harcourt Brace
Jovanovich, Inc. for permission to reprint passages from
Mrs. Dalloway, The Years, Jacob's Room, "Street Haunting—A
London Adventure" (from *The Death of a Moth*) and *The Diary
of Virginia Woolf.*

In the United States
PADDINGTON PRESS
Distributed by
GROSSET & DUNLAP

In the United Kingdom
PADDINGTON PRESS

In Canada
Distributed by
RANDOM HOUSE OF CANADA LTD.

In Southern Africa
Distributed by
ERNEST STANTON (PUBLISHERS) (PTY.) LTD.

In Australia and New Zealand
Distributed by
A. H. & A. W. REED

CONTENTS

LIST OF MAPS

INTRODUCTION

THERE IS A STORY of a Malaysian professor of English, a great lover of Wordsworth, who on visiting England for the first time and seeing some dandelions growing on a bomb site as his taxi took him from the station to his hotel, stopped the taxi, got out, and kneeling down by the dandelions recited Wordsworth's poem about the daffodils. I thought of this story not long ago when, rambling round Ullswater, I came across a clump of daffodils in precisely the spot where Wordsworth and his sister Dorothy had seen them. Does it matter if when you read Wordsworth's poem you think of the daffodils as dandelions growing on a London bomb site? In a sense, of course, any great work of literary imagination has its own life and can be appreciated without a knowledge of the precise places and objects associated with its composition. Yet in another sense it is surely true that, at least in certain kinds of works by certain kinds of writers, a knowledge of those precise places and objects may add to appreciation and enjoyment and even to understanding. Quite apart from the fact that certain novels require that the reader understand the topography involved in the plot if he is to follow the action adequately, there is the added excitement that comes from recognition of known places. This is a very human kind of emotion, akin to the emotion that drives people to make pilgrimages to places where great geniuses have lived and worked, yet at the same time different from that emotion for it is concerned with new perceptions into the life of the literary work rather than with what might be called the tourist's view of literary shrines.

The fact is that a sense of place plays a profound part in the emotional structure of most people, not only of writers, and the various ways in which that sense can be recognized, developed, related to other kinds of awareness and in general cultivated can help to make our lives more interesting. It would surely be a needless puritanism that would deny to readers the satisfactions and insights provided by topographical aids to reading and especially by linking place with time so as to understand more clearly the total ambiance within which a writer's imagination moved.

It was out of reflections of this kind that the idea of this book first developed. We began by wondering whether it might not be helpful to readers of English literature if we could illustrate, both in essays and in maps, ways in which a sense of place was important in the literary imagination of some major writers. The more we worked on it the more various the ways in which we saw how topography could assist literary understanding. There are, for example, the simple biographical facts about where a writer was born and grew up and how his native region nourished his imagination and reveals itself in his work. (This applies, in different ways, to Wordsworth and Emily Brontë and Hardy, among others.) There is the environment in which a writer lived and worked and which reveals itself directly or indirectly in his writing: thus we consider the London of Chaucer, of Shakespeare, of Dr. Johnson, of Dickens, of Virginia Woolf. There are works which depend for their full understanding on the reader's precise awareness of where specific characters are at different times – Joyce's *Ulysses*, for example, and Virginia Woolf's *Mrs. Dalloway* and, in a rather different way, Robert Louis Stevenson's *Kidnapped*. There is a geography of the imagination, such as the medieval image of Troy and the ancient classical world in general, reflected in Chaucer among other writers. There is the appeal of foreign countries to certain writers at specific moments of history, such as that of France to the early Romantic poets at the time of the outbreak of the French Revolution or the appeal of Italy and Greece for Byron. There are changes in a landscape, such as the blackening of much of the face of England as a result of the Industrial Revolution, which haunted the imagination of so many writers. There are towns which play important parts in the work of particular writers, such as Bath in the eighteenth and early nineteenth centuries (Smollett, Sheridan, Fanny Burney, Jane Austen, Dickens) and Edinburgh from the late fifteenth century onwards (William Dunbar, Robert Fergusson, Robert Louis Stevenson) and occasions when a sense of townscape is an important part of a writer's equipment (as in *Mrs. Dalloway*). And then there is what might be called the simple reference element: information about where writers were born, lived, had special associations, are particularly remembered, and so on (as in the Gazetteer section, which will be of special interest to those eager to visit places associated with particular writers).

The approach is thus both flexible and selective. We cannot hope to deal with all the writers of the British Isles to whom a sense of place was important nor to give topographical information about all English literature in a comprehensive encyclopedic manner. We have no single definition of the way in which a sense of place may be relevant or in which a work or an author can be illuminated by topographical and cartographical aids. But in exploring different aspects of literature and topography and of literature and geography, we have come to realize how manifold these are and how fascinating it is to investigate at least some of them. We hope our readers share our sense of discovery and fascination.

D.D.

CHAUCER'S WORLD

Chaucer's London

LONDINIUM, THE ROMAN walled town, developed and flourished as a port and trading centre during the first four centuries A.D. It re-emerged as London after the confusion of the Anglo-Saxon invasions, the natural advantages of its site (at the head of tidewater navigation on the Thames, easily accessible from the Continent by sea, and at the lowest practical point for crossing the Thames) reasserting themselves. By the eighth century it had redeveloped enough for Bede to describe it as the market-place of many peoples coming by land and sea. By the year 1000 London was unquestionably the largest town in England, though not formally the capital of the country, since the idea of a capital city had not yet fully emerged and the centre of government moved from place to place with the king's court. It is not described in the Domesday Book, compiled in 1086–7 after the Norman conquest by order of William the Conqueror, but we know from a customs document of about 1000 of its extensive trading with the Continent.

William built the Tower of London at the eastern end of the city and his follower Ralph Baynard built Castle Baynard near the western end, where the Fleet River flows into the Thames. Henry I gave London its charter early in the twelfth century, giving Londoners control not only of their own city but also of Middlesex in which it lay. In the reign of his successor, Stephen, Londoners asserted their right to their own communal government independent of the Crown, but Stephen's strong successor, Henry II, soon put an end to that. The Londoners reasserted themselves in Richard I's reign, but not for long; one result of London's self-assertion, however, was the permanent establishment of the office of mayor by 1193.

We have a vivid picture of London at this time from William Fitz Stephen, in the preface to his biography of Thomas à Becket written in 1183. He describes the Tower—"exceeding great and strong, whose walls and bailey rise from very deep foundations"—and "the two strongly fortified castles" on the west (Castle Baynard and the nearby Montfichet's Tower). He described the Thames as "teeming with fish". The city contained thirteen great conventual churches and 126 parish churches. "Merchants from every nation that is under heaven" brought "their trade in ships". West of the city wall populous suburbs connected the city with the incomparable royal palace at Westminster; these suburban houses had their gardens "planted with trees, spacious and fair, adjoining one another". North of the city the vast forest of Middlesex, with its wooded thickets, its wild beasts and plentiful game, enhanced the beauty of London by contrast.

Fitz Stephen was especially proud of the city's public cook shops: "there daily according to the season, you may find viands, dishes roast, fried and boiled, fish great and small, the coarser food for the poor, the more delicate for the rich, such as venison and birds, both big and little". Two centuries later we recognize a similar scene in the account of London street cries at the end of the Prologue of *Piers Plowman*:

> Cokes and here knaves cryede "Hote pyes, hote!
> Goode gees and grys, ga we dyne, ga we!"
> Taverners till them told the same:
> "Whit wyn of Oseye and wyn of Gascoyne,
> Of the Reule and of the Rochele, the roost to defy!"*

It was in Fitz Stephen's time that the first stone London Bridge was built (begun in 1176 and finished in 1209): the previous bridge had been of wood. It was an outstanding piece of medieval engineering, and lasted until early in the nineteenth century. (The next London Bridge, opened in 1831, only lasted until 1969, when it was pulled down and transported piece by piece to the United States.) The medieval London Bridge, known equally to Chaucer, Shakespeare and Dr. Johnson, had twenty stone arches and a drawbridge, with a gatehouse at each end and the Chapel of St. Thomas of Canterbury in the centre. Chaucer's pilgrims, on their way to St. Thomas's shrine at Canterbury, must have looked in at the chapel as they crossed the bridge from London to the Tabard Inn at Southwark.

The Normans changed the face of London by their prolific building of churches and monasteries. In the thirteenth century further changes resulted from the establishment in London of various orders of friars. The Blackfriars (Dominicans) first settled in Holborn near the present Lincoln's Inn and in 1276 moved to the vicinity of Castle Baynard, thus giving their name to the London district still known as Blackfriars. The Greyfriars settled in London soon after their arrival in England in 1224, and built their friary and church north of St. Paul's (the old St. Paul's of the eleventh to thirteenth centuries) where the General Post Office is now situated and where the name Grey-friars Passage still reminds us of them. The Whitefriars (Carmelites) came to London in 1241 and made their home between what is now Fleet Street and the Thames. The Austin Friars settled just south of the city wall in Broad Street Ward in 1253: the name is still preserved in the area, between London Wall and Throgmorton Street. By Chaucer's time (*c.* 1340–1400) the homes of these four orders had long been established as London land-marks. By this time, too, London had long been the hub of the country's transport system, as is made clear by the so-called Gough map of about

---

*Cooks and their boys cried, "Hot pies, hot!/Good geese and pigs. Come and eat!"/Innkeepers cried their wares in the same way:/"White wine from Alsace, and wine of Gascony,/Of La Reole and Rochelle to digest your roast."

"London, thou art the flour of Cities all," wrote William Dunbar. This fifteenth-century manuscript illustration showing the Duc d'Orleans imprisoned in the Tower, with London Bridge and the densely packed buildings and spires in the background, gives a good impression of what London was like throughout the Middle Ages.

1360 which shows the road system of fourteenth-century London. From London, roads ran north to Stamford and York (partly the old Roman Ermine Street), west to Oxford and Gloucester and to Reading and Bristol, southwest to Winchester and Exeter, south over London Bridge to Canterbury and Dover. (Oddly enough, this last road, important both as the Pilgrim's Way and as the road to Dover and the Continent, is not shown on Gough's map.)

Chaucer's London was a walled city, separated from Westminster to the west by an ill-paved thoroughfare, the Strand, which was flanked by great

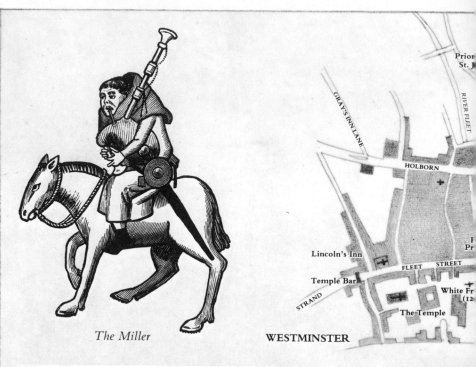

Prior
St. J

GRAY'S INN LANE

RIVER FLEET

HOLBORN

Lincoln's Inn

F
Pr

FLEET STREET

Temple Bar

White Fr
(12

STRAND

The Temple

The Miller

WESTMINSTER

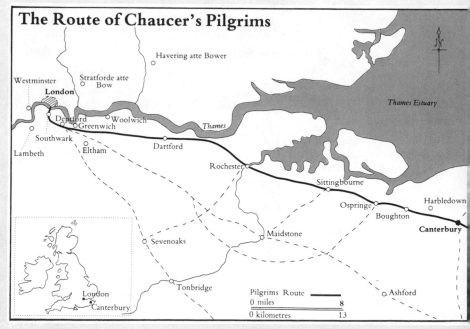

The Route of Chaucer's Pilgrims

Havering atte Bower

Westminster

Stratforde atte Bow

London

Thames Estuary

Deptford Woolwich
Greenwich   Thames

Southwark   Dartford

Lambeth   Eltham

Rochester

Sittingbourne

Ospringe   Harbledown

Boughton

Canterbury

Sevenoaks   Maidstone

London
Canterbury

Tonbridge

Ashford

Pilgrims Route

0 miles   8

0 kilometres   13

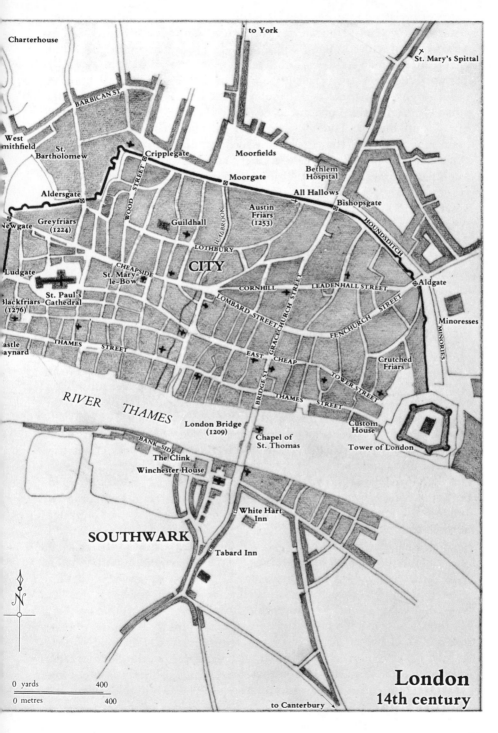

Charterhouse

to York

+ St. Mary's Spittal

BARBICAN ST.

West
Smithfield

St.
Bartholomew

Cripplegate

Moorfields

Bethlem
Hospital

Moorgate

All Hallows

Bishopsgate

Aldersgate

WOOD STREET

Newgate

Greyfriars
(1224)

Guildhall

WALBROOK

Austin
Friars
(1253)

HOUNDSDITCH

LOTHBURY

Ludgate

CHEAPSIDE

St. Mary-
le-Bow

CITY

Aldgate

Blackfriars
(1276)

St. Paul's
Cathedral

CORNHILL

LEADENHALL STREET

GRACECHURCH STREET

Castle
Baynard

THAMES

STREET

LOMBARD STREET

FENCHURCH STREET

Minoresses

MINORIES

EAST

CHEAP

Crutched
Friars

BRIDGE ST.

THAMES

STREET

TOWER STREET

RIVER

THAMES

London Bridge
(1209)

Chapel of
St. Thomas

Custom
House

Tower of London

BANK SIDE

The Clink

Winchester House

SOUTHWARK

White Hart
Inn

Tabard Inn

N

0 yards   400

0 metres   400

to Canterbury

London
14th century

13

houses of prelates and noblemen. Westminster was the main seat of royal power, but the seat of commercial power was London which, though tiny by comparison with modern London, was the biggest city in England with a population which has been estimated at about thirty-five thousand. Its area was little more than the square mile of the present City of London. It was roughly semicircular in shape, with the river itself as the base of the semicircle, having the Tower at its eastern end and the Fleet River (which flowed south into the Thames) at its western. The Thames was, in a sense, the missing section of the city wall, which ran north from the Tower by Aldgate and Houndsditch (really a ditch, running outside the wall on its eastern side, originally part of the city defences running all round the walls), west by Bishopsgate, Moorgate, Cripplegate, then south by Aldersgate, Newgate and Ludgate. These last two gates faced west; Aldersgate faced north at the northwestern end of the wall; Cripplegate also faced north, as did Moorgate to the east of it. Beyond Moorgate in medieval times lay a marshy moor. "When the great marsh which washes the walls of the city on the north side is frozen over," wrote Fitz Stephen, "the young men go out in crowds to divert themselves upon the ice." It was not drained until the end of the sixteenth century; meanwhile because of its marshiness (the existence of the wall preventing drainage to the Thames) it was "burrowed and crossed with deep stinking ditches and noysome common sewers". These gates were all real gates, closed at night, and each had a small gate-house above it; it was in the gatehouse at Aldgate that Chaucer lived from 1374 to 1386 during his period first as controller of customs and subsidy on wools, skins and hides in the port of London and then as controller of the petty customs on wines. The world of Chaucer's personal life and daily personal activities centred mostly on London, where he was born in the early 1340s. It was here that he spent his early days and a considerable part of his maturity, and here where he retired shortly before his death in 1400. This "personal" world also included places outside London: Hatfield, Yorkshire, where, as we know from the household accounts of Elizabeth, countess of Ulster (wife of Prince Lionel) whom he served as a youngster, he received clothing from the countess's wardrobe in May 1357; various places in Kent, for which county he was appointed justice of the peace in 1385 and elected Knight of the Shire in 1386 and where he settled some years earlier on leaving London; Somerset, where he served as deputy forester of the royal forest of North Petherton towards the end of his life, though how far his duties required him to live there we cannot say; and Windsor, where in 1390 he was given a special commission to oversee the repairs of St. George's Chapel during his tenure as clerk of the king's work. He must have been especially familiar with the stretch of the Thames from Greenwich to Woolwich, since in that same year, 1390, he was appointed a member of a commission to look after the walls, bridges, sewers and ditches along that part of the river.

But fourteenth-century London remained Chaucer's true home. The main room of Chaucer's gatehouse at Aldgate had two windows, one looking out on open country to the east and north and the other looking into the city with all its teeming life. But though he must have been intimately acquainted with all aspects of city life, it has little direct reflection in his poetry. We get a glimpse of the closing of the city gates in that memorable account in *Troilus and Criseyde* of Troilus waiting in vain at the gates of Troy for the return of Criseyde:

> The warden of the yates gan to calle
> The folk which that wuthoute the yates were,
> And bad hem dryven in hire bestes alle,
> Or all the nyght they moste bleven [remain] there.

In "The Nun's Priest's Tale" there is a reference to the attacks on Flemings in London during the Peasants' Revolt of 1381. (There were many Flemish weavers in Chaucer's London: Edward III encouraged them to come to England, and they and other foreign workers were to be found in considerable numbers in London, always vulnerable to an outbreak of popular xenophobia.) Langland gives us more vivid glimpses of London than Chaucer does, as in the passage already quoted from *Piers Plowman*. But if one wants a sustained colourful picture of late medieval London, one must go to lesser poets, like the unknown author of *London Lickpenny*:

> In to London I gan me by,
> of all the lond it beareth the prise.
> "Hot pescods," one gan cry,
> "Strabery rype, and chery in the ryse."
> One bad me come nere and by some spice,
> pepar and saffron they gan me bede [offer],
> clove, grayns, and flowre of rise.
> For lacke of money I might not spede. . . .

> Then into Chepe I gan me drawne,
> where I sawe moche people.
> One bad me come ner, and by fine cloth of lawne,
> Paris thred, coton, and vmple [?].

> I seyde there vpon I could no skyle [had no knowledge],
> I am not wont there to in dede.
> One bad me by an hewre my hed to hele.
> For lacke of money I might not spede. . . .

> Then I hied me into estchepe,
> one cried ribes of befe, and many a pie.

Pewtar potts they clatteryd on a heape,
there was harpe, pipe and sawtry.
"Ye by cokke," "Nay by cokke," some began to cry.
Some sang of Jenken and Julian, to get them selves mede.
Full fayne I wold hadd of that mynstralsie,
but for lacke of money I cowld not spede.

Chaucer's London was noisy, crowded, unsanitary, and vulnerable to plague; but it was washed by a still clean Thames and surrounded by fields, woods, gardens and pastures. The address to London written perhaps by William Dunbar a century after Chaucer sums up its pre-eminence in the whole late medieval period:

London, thou art of townes A *per se*.
  Soveraign of cities, someliest in sight,
Of high renoun, riches, and royaltie;
  Of lordis, barons, and many goodly knyght;
  Of most delectable lusty ladies bright;
Of famous prelatis in habitis clericall;
  Of merchauntis full of substaunce and myght;
London, thou art the flour of Cities all. . . .

Thy famous Maire, by princely governaunce,
  With sword of justice the rulith prudently.
No Lord of Parys, Venyce, or Floraunce
  In dignytie or honoure goeth to hym nye.
  He is exampler, lode-ster, and guye [guide];
Principall patrone and roose orygynalle,
  Above all Maires as maister moost worthy;
London, thou art the flour of Cities all.

Touring with Chaucer's Pilgrims

ON THE SOUTH SIDE of the River Thames, one of London's suburbs outside the city walls, was Southwark, the "south work" or bridgehead at the south end of London Bridge. At Southwark the roads from the south of England converged for the crossing of the Thames, and that is why early on it became noted for its inns, of which the two most famous are the Tabard, where Chaucer's pilgrims assembled at the start of their journey, and the White Hart, referred to by Shakespeare in *2 Henry VI* and, centuries later, that same inn where Mr. Pickwick first met Sam Weller: the Tabard survived until 1875 and the White Hart till 1889. Its geographical position made Southwark the natural starting point for a journey from the London area to anywhere in the south of England. The road to Dover (the gateway

*Chaucer's Canterbury Pilgrims setting out from the Tabard Inn. In the centre
is the Host (arms outstretched). The Knight is at the head of the procession
(right foreground) and Chaucer himself is at the rear (left foreground).
Engraving by William Blake c. 1809.*

to France and the gateway to England from France) started here. For its
first fifty-six miles or so the Dover Road was also the Pilgrims' Way,
which led to Canterbury, the oldest centre of Christianity in England and
regarded as especially sacred (and so a most important place of pilgrimage)
after the murder of Thomas à Becket there in 1170.

The pilgrims assembled at the Tabard Inn on April 16, supposedly in the
year 1387, and set out at sunrise ("whan that day bigan to sprynge"—about
4.45 A.M.) the following day. A little way past "the waterying of Seint
Thomas" they drew lots to determine the order in which they should tell
their stories. This was a little brook at the second milestone on the Dover
Road. The Knight and the Miller have already told their stories by "halfway pryme" (7.30 A.M.) when the Host, before inviting the Reeve to begin
his tale, notes that they are within sight of Deptford and Greenwich. The
natural place for the pilgrims to have passed the night would have been
Dartford. It is presumably the next evening when the Host, calling on the
Monk for his tale, says "Loo, Rouchestre stant heer faste by": at Rochester
they would spend their second night. The Summoner promises to tell two
or three tales "er I come to Sidyngborne", and it is at Sittingbourne where
we may presume the pilgrims spend their third night. This would mean
that they had gone fifteen miles the first day, fifteen the second, and ten
the third. They are now sixteen miles from Canterbury and could make it
in a day, but they may well have done only six miles on the fourth day to
spend the night, as many pilgrims did, at Ospringe. We are told that the
Canon and his Yeoman overtake the company at Boghtoun under Blee
(modern Boughton), which is five miles from Ospringe. This must have
been early on the fifth day, for it is still morning when the Host tries to
rouse the drunken cook at the "litel toun which that ycleped is Bobb-up-

and-doun", the modern Harbledown, just east of Canterbury, which the pilgrims can be assumed to have reached soon afterwards.

In the Prologue to *The Legend of Good Women* Alceste enjoins the poet to present the finished work to the queen "at Eltham or at Sheene". There were royal residences at Eltham, which is seven miles from London, in Kent, close by the Pilgrims' Way, and at Sheene, now Richmond, lying westward up the Thames in Surrey. (Henry VII, who was Earl of Richmond 'in Yorkshire, changed its name to Richmond in 1500.) Several other English places are mentioned in the course of *The Canterbury Tales*. The Wife of Bath came not from the city itself but from "Biside Bathe": the medieval town of Bath was entirely confined within its ancient walls, and the lady probably lived in the little parish of St. Michael-without-the-Walls (or *juxta Bathon*), which had grown up outside the north gate. The Prioress, who spoke French "after the scole of Stratford atte Bowe" (east of London, north of the Thames) presumably came from the nearby Benedictine nunnery of St. Leonard. The Merchant was particularly anxious that the sea should be guarded between Middleburg on the Dutch coast, and the English port of Orwell, at the mouth of the River Orwell opposite Harwich. The Shipman was from Dartmouth, in Devonshire, a port known for the intrepidity and tendency to privateering of its seamen. The Clerk was still pursuing his studies at Oxford, which, together with its sister university town of Cambridge, Chaucer must have known, though he studied at neither. The clerk Nicholas of "The Miller's Tale" is also from Oxford, but the clerks John and Aleyn in "The Reeve's Tale" are from Cambridge. The Reeve is from Norfolk, and perhaps the Miller is too for they are presented as close enemies of long standing.

Chaucer Overseas: The Country of His Mind

THE INTERMITTENT WAR between France and England known as the Hundred Years' War had begun a few years before Chaucer's birth. Chaucer served in the English army in France and was taken prisoner near Reims in 1359–60; he was released for a ransom in March 1360, and during peace negotiations later that year he was sent back to France with official correspondence. He was now in the service of King Edward III, who employed him on embassies abroad. He was in Italy from December 1372 till May 1373, negotiating on commercial matters with the Genoese, and he also visited Florence. Further missions to France followed. In May 1378 he went with the retinue of Sir Edward de Berkeley to negotiate with Bernabò Visconti, Lord of Milan, and with Sir John Hawkwood on various royal affairs. Though these visits to France and Italy were on official government business, there is no doubt that Chaucer took the opportunity

Chaucer fought in the Hundred Years' War and was held prisoner in 1359–60.
Pictured here is the fighting at Brest, from the fourteenth-century
Chroniques d'Angleterre.

to satisfy his own curiosity about people and places and also that he used
every possible occasion to increase his knowledge of what had been going
on in French and Italian literature. England, France and Italy Chaucer thus
knew from direct personal experience. But there was another world
which his literary imagination inhabited, and it in turn can be divided into
two parts, which can be called respectively the world of contemporary
adventure and the world of historical fiction.

Chaucer's world of contemporary adventure was largely the world of
crusades and pilgrimages. The attempt by Christian European armies to
recover Jerusalem and the Holy Land from the Moslems had begun when
the First Crusade had been preached by Pope Urban II at the Council of
Clermont in 1095. By Chaucer's day the ideal of the Crusades, which had
always been tainted with a variety of material motives and cursed by
feuding among the Christian princes who led the expeditions, had become
thoroughly tarnished, but it had not disappeared, and the very fact that the
ideal of knighthood was in decline and the Crusades had in the long run
been more harmful to Christendom than to the Moslem world led to a
nostalgic idealization of knight errantry and a great appetite for accounts
of knightly adventures against the infidel in Spain, North Africa and the
Middle East. An inhabitant of Chaucer's world of contemporary adventure, the Knight of *The Canterbury Tales*, is presented as someone who has
actually fought in the desultory campaigns against the infidel which were

"At Alisaundre he was whan it was wonne . . ." Chaucer's *"worthy Knyght"*
from William Caxton's edition of The Canterbury Tales *(1493)*.

still, in a very general way, thought of as part of a Crusade; while the story
he tells belongs to Chaucer's other imaginative world, that of historical
fiction concerned with the ancient world. Chaucer is quite specific about
the geography of his Knight's adventures:

> At Alisaundre he was whan it was wonne.
> Ful ofte tyme he hadde the bord bigonne
> Aboven alle nacions in Pruce;
> In Lettow hadde he reysed and in Ruce,
> No Cristen man so ofte of his degree.
> In Gernade at the seege eek hadde he be
> Of Algezir, and riden in Belmarye.
> At Lyeys was he and at Satalye,
> Whan they were wonne; and in the Grete See
> At many a noble armee hadde he be.
> At mortal batailles hadde he been fiftene,
> And foughten for oure feith at Tramassene
> In Lystes thries, and ay slayn his foo.
> This ilke worthy knyght hadde been also
> Somtyme with the lord of Palatye
> Agayn another hethen in Turkye.

20

To identify the places here named and to associate them with the events to which Chaucer is referring and some knowledge of which he takes for granted in his audience, is to learn about the geographical imagination of late fourteenth-century Europe.

Alisaunder is Alexandria in Egypt, which had been ruled by the Mamelukes (a Moslem military oligarchy descended from Circassian or Turkish slaves converted to Islam) since 1250. Attempts to mount a Crusade against the Mamelukes had deteriorated into sporadic piracy when Pierre I de Lusignan, king of Cyprus, gave a new impetus to the crusading movement by his passionate appeals made personally on a tour of the courts of Europe between 1362 and 1365. The English King Edward III expressed polite interest but did nothing, but there were English knights among the many other men-at-arms who joined Pierre's expedition which sailed from Rhodes in September 1365 in 165 ships. Their objective was kept secret, but it turned out to be Alexandria, an ill-defended port of great wealth. The crusading forces succeeded in scaling the city walls and entering the city, where they engaged in massacre and pillage. King Pierre wanted to hold Alexandria, as the key to all Egypt, but the crusaders were more interested in immediate loot than in permanent conquest, and sailed away with their plunder. Chaucer's Knight, we assume, would have been on the side of Pierre in wanting to hold the city rather than make off with the spoils, as he is presented as a wholly idealistic crusader. Egypt was a target for the Crusaders not simply because it was a country of infidels, but because it was a key to the traditional crusading objectives in the Holy Land; two unsuccessful invasions of Egypt with these objectives in mind had been made in the thirteenth century.

Pruce and Lettow are Prussia and Lithuania, and the Knight's activities here show that he had also been involved on what might be called the northern crusading front—the operations of the Knights of the Teutonic Order in defending the frontier of Christianity against the pagan Lithuanians and Tartars. The Tartars were part of the Mongolian hordes that had overrun much of the east before reaching Hungary and Germany. In Chaucer's time they still dominated much of Russia (which Chaucer calls Ruce). The Teutonic Knights had moved from the Mediterranean to establish their centre in Marienburg in 1309 in order to apply the techniques they had learned in crusading in the Middle East against the enemies of Christianity in the north and in so doing to colonize Prussia. Chaucer's Knight was therefore one of the many foreign volunteers who served with the Teutonic Knights in their more or less continuous warfare on the bounds of Christendom in eastern Europe; he may be assumed to have served in the mid-1380s, which was a particularly active time on this front, and to have returned to England immediately afterwards (the supposed date of *The Canterbury Tales* is 1387).

Gernade is Granada, the region and city in the south of Spain that was still occupied by the Moors in Chaucer's day. The Moors had overrun most of the Iberian peninsula in the eighth century, and the Umayyid caliphate of Cordoba was a great Moslem cultural centre between 756 and 1031. Portugal became an independent Christian kingdom in the twelfth century, and Spain was gradually reconquered by Christian armies advancing from the north. By Chaucer's time only Granada remained unconquered: the Moors were not driven out until 1492. Algezir, the modern Algeciras, was a major Moorish stronghold which fell to Alfonso of Castile in 1344 after a long siege in which volunteers from all over Christian Europe participated. The Knight must have been there as a young man, and as he had also "ridden in Belmarye" he must have been involved in a number of campaigns against the Moors in the Mediterranean, for Belmarye was a Moorish kingdom in North Africa, while Tramassene, where we learn the Knight had also fought, is the modern Tlemcen in Western Algeria. Indeed, the Knight is presented as having served the Christian cause all over the Mediterranean, for in addition to participating in campaigns in Spain and North Africa he had been at Lyeys and at Satalye and had been with "many a noble armee" in the Grete See (Mediterranean). This refers to a campaign in Asia Minor undertaken by King Pierre de Lusignan in 1361, before his propaganda tour in Europe and his subsequent attack on Alexandria. Satalye, which Pierre captured from the Saracens, is the ancient Attalia, on the southern coast of Asia Minor, and had long been a threat to Cyprus. The Knight seems also to have been with Pierre when he captured Lyeys (Lyas or Ayas in Armenia the Lesser, which is ancient Cilicia) from the Turks in 1367. It is less certain what Chaucer meant by Palatye, with whose lord the Knight had served "agayn another hethen in Turkye", but it is probably the Turkish Balat, on the site of the ancient Miletus.

Going on a crusade was a way of engaging in travel and adventure, and so was going on a pilgrimage, which in the Middle Ages represented the nearest equivalent to our going off on a holiday, either to another part of our own country (as the pilgrims went to Canterbury) or, more excitingly, abroad, as the Wife of Bath had done:

> And thries hadde she been at Jerusalem;
> She hadde passed many a straunge strem;
> At Rome she hadde been, and at Boloigne,
> In Galice at Seint-Jame, and at Coloigne.

Jerusalem had been captured by the original Crusaders in 1099, but the Latin Kingdom of Jerusalem which they established fell to Saladin in 1187. Forty years of crusading failed to recapture it for the Christians, but finally in 1229 the Emperor Frederick II acquired by treaty with the sultan of Egypt control of Nazareth, Bethlehem and Jerusalem together with a strip of territory connecting Jerusalem with the port of Acre and the coastal towns which already were in Christian possession. The Saracens recaptured Jerusalem in 1244, and henceforth it remained in Moslem hands, though Christian pilgrims like the Wife of Bath were allowed entry. Rome was naturally a great Christian centre of pilgrimage; a late fourteenth-century guidebook to the city, entitled *Stacions of Rome*, gives a full account of what the pilgrims ought to see there; this included St. Peter's, for a visit to which many thousands of years of remission of Purgatory could be obtained, and a fantastic number of relics, including the two tablets of the Law which Moses brought down from Sinai and the clothes worn by Christ. Boloigne is probably Boulogne-sur-Mer and not Bologna, which Chaucer spells in exactly the same way. There was a fragmentary image of the Virgin there which was venerated by pilgrims. At Cologne pilgrims visited the shrine of the Three Kings. More important than either of these was the shrine of Saint James at Compostella, in "Galice" (Galicia) in northern Spain. There was a legend that after the death of the Apostle James his body was placed secretly in a boat which had neither rudder nor helmsman, and that the boat, by divine providence, eventually landed on the shores of Galicia; there the disciples laid the body on a great stone, which at once softened like wax and shaped itself into a sarcophagus fitted to the body. The famous basilica of St. James was built to contain the tomb, which was covered by the great altar: it was one of the most noted sights in the Christian world in Chaucer's day and a popular place of pilgrimage.

The Wife of Bath introduces us not only to the late medieval world of lay pilgrimages, but also to the world of the cloth industry. She was a skilled weaver:

> Of clooth-makyng she hadde swich an haunt [skill]
> She passed hem of Ypres and of Gaunt.

Ypres and Ghent were centres of the Flemish wool trade, and in the fourteenth century many Flemish weavers settled in England. If the Wife of Bath really surpassed the weavers of Ypres and Ghent, she must have been skilled indeed, but perhaps Chaucer is being ironical, for the cloth made in Bath did not enjoy a high reputation.

A knight who had been on a Crusade and a civilian who had been on a pilgrimage to distant lands not only acquired merit but became persons of enormous interest who could cater to the inexhaustible medieval appetite for travellers' tales. And anyone who had seen the Mediterranean world, with its twin contacts both with the fabled wealth and magic of the East and the wonders of the classical world of ancient Greece and Rome, had also entered the world of the medieval literary imagination, which played such an important part in Chaucer's writings.

Chaucer's imaginative world also embraced the ancient world of the medieval literary imagination. We see it perhaps most vividly in his

SCOTLAND

IRLAUNDE

WALYS

ENGELOND

York
• Hull
Stamford
Gloucester• •Canterbrigge
Bristol• •Oxford •Harwich
N. Petherton• •Bath •London
•Canterbury
Dartmouth Dover•
Calais•
Boulogne• •Gaunt
•Crécy FLAUNDRE
•Rouen
Paris•
•Reims

Marier

HOLY

•Coloigne

BOHEMIA

BRITAIGNE
OR
ARMORIC

NORMANDY

MAINE

ANJOU

Poitiers•

FRANCE

BURGOYNE

ROMAN

HUNGARY

Bordeaux•

•Limoges

AQUITANE

•Compostella

•Lyon
KINGDOM ALPS
OF ARLES
ALPS
Montpelliers• •Avignon

EMPIRE

Padowe•

Milan•
Genoa•
Venyse•
•Bologna
•Florence

Pyrenees

CASTILE

ARAGON

PAPAL
STATES
•Rome

Lisbon•

•Cordoba
•Granada

GRANADA

•Malaga •Cartagena

SARDINIA

Algezir•

•Tramyssene

•Cartage
Tewnes•

AFFRIKE

Grete

| 0 miles | 300 |
| 0 kilometres | 500 |

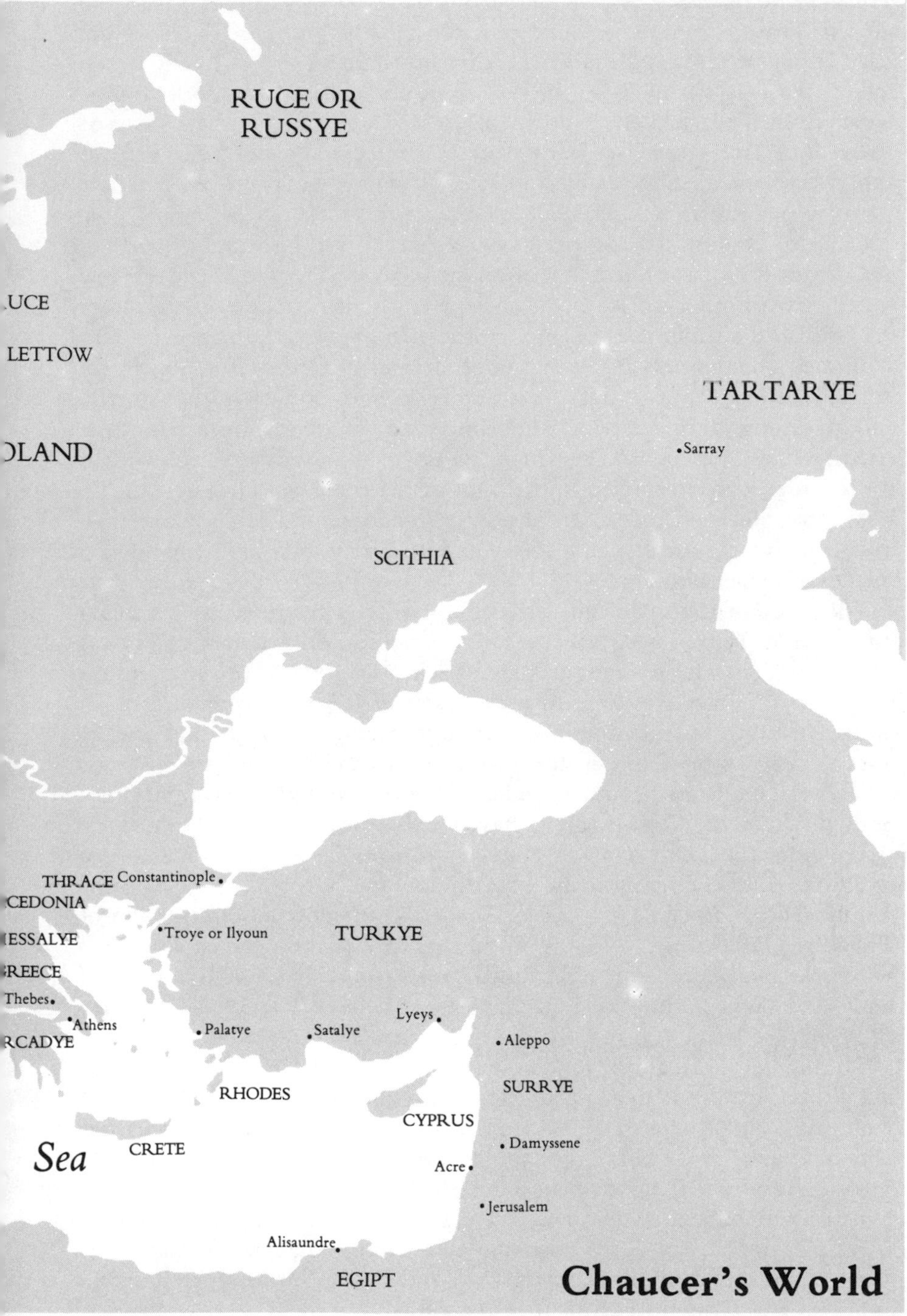

RUCE OR
RUSSYE

.UCE

LETTOW

TARTARYE

OLAND

•Sarray

SCITHIA

THRACE Constantinople•
CEDONIA

TURKYE

ESSALYE   •Troye or Ilyoun

REECE

Thebes•
                                        Lyeys•
      •Athens
RCADYE   •Palatye   •Satalye   •Aleppo

                                        SURRYE
              RHODES

                      CYPRUS

Sea   CRETE   •Damyssene
                          Acre•

                          •Jerusalem

              Alisaundre•

              EGIPT   Chaucer's World

25

Troilus and Criseyde, where he takes from Boccaccio a story set during the siege of Troy; although he concentrates on the psychological details of the story of the two lovers, he sets the action firmly in an environment which reflects the way the medieval literary mind looked back on the Homeric world, which reached them through late Latin retellings of the story of Troy. The late twelfth-century *trouvère* (minstrel of northern France) Jean Bodel divided the subject matter of medieval romance into the "Matter of France" (exemplified chiefly in the *Chanson de Roland*), the "Matter of Britain" (the stories of King Arthur and his knights) and the "Matter of Rome the Great". This last included stories of the siege of Troy together with other stories of the ancient world, of Thebes, of Alexander the Great and of Julius Caesar among others. In medieval romances dealing with these themes we can see the world of ancient Greece not as a clearly defined historical period but as a group of legends about Greek historical and mythological figures who were conceived of as feudal lords with their retainers (like Theseus in "The Knight's Tale"). Any love story dealt with in this context was interpreted in the light of the medieval ideal of Courtly Love, that idealized code of male service to adored and often inaccessible mistresses which is one of the most extraordinary developments of the medieval European mind.

The story of the siege and destruction of Troy haunted the medieval imagination. Troy was a great city, a city of heroes and warriors, and it was destroyed after a long siege through a trick. *Fuit Ilium*, Troy *was* and no longer is: this fact was a permanent lesson in the impermanence of all human institutions and all human greatness. Medieval readers and writers got the Trojan story from the fourth-century Latin writer Dictys Critensis (Dictys of Crete) and the somewhat later Dares Phrygius (Dares of Phrygia), both of whom claimed actually to have been at the siege and told the story as eyewitnesses. The story was worked up from these sources in the late twelfth-century French romance, the *Roman de Troie*, and the thirteenth-century Latin *Historia Destructionis Troiae* (History of the Destruction of Troy) by Guido delle Colonne. Virgil's picture of the siege of Troy was known in the Middle Ages, but mostly as the source for the love story of Dido and Aeneas, mediated through the French romance, the *Roman d'Enéas*.

The medieval imagination sided with Troy against Greece in looking at the Trojan war, and many countries of western Europe actually traced their origins to Trojans who fled from Troy after its destruction. This was how Rome was said to have been founded too, and the cultured men of the Middle Ages saw themselves nearer both in history and in imaginative sympathy to ancient Rome than to ancient Greece. After all, they themselves still used Latin as the language of learning; their main land communications were still the Roman roads, steadily declining from the state in which the Romans left them in the fifth century; Roman aqueducts throughout Europe were still pointed to as relics of a great engineering nation capable of feats beyond anything the medieval world could achieve. Most of all, Rome was the centre of medieval Christianity. It was the conversion of the Roman emperor Constantine that made possible, almost at a stroke, the Christianization of Europe, so the Roman Empire was seen as a divinely ordained institution for converting pagans on a mass scale. It was for this reason that it was the Roman Empire, not the Roman Republic, that the medieval imagination liked to linger on. Dante put Brutus and Cassius, who conspired to murder the potential founder of the Roman Empire, in the lowest circle of Hell. The Holy Roman Empire, in spite of the famous quip that it was neither holy, nor Roman nor an empire, represented to the medieval mind what the Roman tradition meant in European history.

When, therefore, Chaucer set his *Troilus and Criseyde* against the background of the Trojan War, he was setting it in a context both familiar and sympathetic to his readers. His Troy is, of course, medievalized, with medieval architecture and medieval customs curiously altering the classical atmosphere. Sallies out from the city walls against the besieging Greeks occur almost daily and provide constant opportunity for the performance of knightly deeds. And the love story of the hero and heroine is told most precisely in terms of the medieval convention of Courtly Love.

"The Knight's Tale" was based by Chaucer on the much longer narrative poem by Boccaccio, *La Teseide*, which in turn was quarried from the *Thebaid*, an epic of legendary Theban history by the first-century Roman poet Statius. (Chaucer also knew and admired Statius, and drew on his work independently.) Here we have a more widely ranging world of the medieval historical and geographical imagination, again seen in terms of medieval customs and institutions, so that Theseus is presented as "Duke" of Athens:

> Whilom, as olde stories tellen us,
> Ther was a duc that highte Theseus;
> Of Atthenes he was lord and governour,
> And in his tyme swich a conquerour,
> That gretter was ther noon under the sonne.
> Ful many a riche contree hadde he wonne;
> What with his wisdom and his chivalrie,
> He conquered al the regne of Femenye,
> That whilom was ycleped Scithia,
> And weddede the queene Ypolita,
> And broghte hire hoom with hym in his contree
> With muchel glorie and greet solemonytee, . . .
> And certes, if it here to long to heere,
> I wolde have toold yow fully the manere

How wonnen was the regne of Femenye
By Theseus and by his chivalrye;
And of the grete bataille for the nones
Betwixen Atthenes and Amazones;
And how asseged was Ypolita,
The faire, hardy queene of Scithia; . . .

This is romantic geography indeed! "Femenye" is the land of the warlike
women, the Amazons, which the early Greek historian Herodotus had
identified as Scythia. Chaucer goes on to tell how, urged by a group of
weeping women, Theseus attacked Thebes and killed its tyrant Creon,
bringing back with him to Athens two wounded Theban knights, both of
royal blood. It was while in prison in Athens that the knights caught a
glimpse through their prison window of Ypolita's beautiful younger sister
Emily, and so the story of two young men in love with the same girl is set
on foot. There is even less attempt here than in *Troilus and Criseyde* to give
any impression of an actual historical classical city. The Athens and Thebes
of the Knight's Tale are medieval cities, and the clothes, customs, ceremonies, methods of fighting, and so on, belong to the medieval world of
chivalry and Courtly Love. Yet at the same time the language manages to
convey (as in the lines quoted) a sense of the mystery and otherness of a lost
ancient world.

Even more exotic and mysterious is the setting of "The Squire's Tale", a
story of wonder and romance set in "Sarray, in the land of Tartarye". It
was there that

Ther dwelte a kyng that werreyed [made war on] Russye,
Thurgh which ther dyde many a doughty man.
This noble kyng was cleped Cambyuskan, . . .

Sarray has been identified with modern Tzarev, near Volgograd in southern
Russia, which was founded by Batu Khan in the thirteenth century and
became the capital of the Tartar empire. There were many travellers'
accounts of journeys in the Mogul Empire in circulation in western Europe
in the thirteenth and fourteenth centuries, some of which were probably
known to Chaucer. But this is not important, for the "Sarray, in the land of
Tartarye" of "The Squire's Tale" is a country of pure romance, chosen,
one might almost say, simply for the flavour of its name. The Squire himself
is presented as "a lovyere and a lusty bacheler" of twenty years of age, a
lover of song and dance, courteous, lively and romantic. He was a good
horseman:

And he hadde been sometyme in chyvachie [engaged in feats
of horsemanship]
In Flaundres, in Artoys, and Pycardie, . . .

We are told specifically that the Squire went on the Flemish crusade "in hope to stonden in his lady grace", unlike his father the Knight, who had engaged in his crusades out of religious idealism. The personal romantic reasons for the Squire's engaging in this expedition presumably obscured from him the general sordidness of the motives of those who planned it. This was the so-called crusade of Henry Le Despenser, Bishop of Norwich, in 1383, "backed entirely by political and commercial interests, not by any pious zeal", as a modern scholar has put it. Perhaps the disparity between the Squire's youthful romanticism and the real aims of the crusade in which he engaged in order to find favour with his lady is a measure of the romantic unreality of his geography, which is a country of the mind or the imagination purely, for all the specificness of the names.

Most of the other *Canterbury Tales* are more realistically localized, in contemporary England or Italy. "The Franklin's Tale", which is a version of an old and widely disseminated folktale, is said by the Franklin to be a "Breton lay", that is, one of the traditional Celtic stories associated with the Celtic inhabitants of ancient Britain and Brittany. While this may or may not be the true origin of the story (he may have got it through Boccaccio) Chaucer certainly takes pains to set it "In Armorik, that called is Britayne". Armorica was the medieval name for Brittany and the name evoked echoes of Celtic history. Yet for all the romanticism of the story the location is geographically precise, so much so in fact that F. N. Robinson, in his classic edition of Chaucer, refers the reader to *A Yachtsman's Guide to the Coasts of Brittany* for further information about it. This is an interesting case where a region known to the author and a literary region with its own imaginative geographical suggestion come together to combine what Chaucer himself called "experience" and "auctoritee".

The Wife of Bath   The Pardoner

SHAKESPEARE'S LONDON

IN ACTUAL EXTENT, Shakespeare's London covered little more ground than Chaucer's, comprising essentially what is now known as the City. It took the form roughly of a semicircle, bounded on the south by the River Thames, on the east by the Tower of London and on the west by the Fleet Ditch. When Shakespeare arrived there from Stratford about 1588, he would have entered the city by its western gate, Newgate. The city was still surrounded by walls in which there were gates—Aldgate, which led eastward through Whitechapel and Mile End to Bow, through still rural country ("I remember at Mile-end Green, when I lay at Clements' Inn", said Justice Shallow in *2 Henry IV*); Bishopsgate, the principal entrance from the north and way to the great north road; Moorgate, also on the north wall, leading into Moorfields, soon to be drained and laid out in walks—which were still locked at night. There were two roads from Stratford to London, the one more generally taken running through Oxford and the other, slightly longer, via Banbury: both roads met at Uxbridge, and Shakespeare, on his first and many subsequent journeys to London from Stratford, must have come in from the west along the Uxbridge Road by Shepherd's Bush, past the gibbet at Tyburn (now Marble Arch), along what is now Oxford Street to the village of St. Giles in the Fields (which was then literally a village in the fields), and thence eastward to Holborn and by the churches of St. Andrew and St. Sepulchre to Newgate. From Newgate in the west to Aldgate in the east you could cut across the centre of the city by Cheapside, Cornhill and Leadenhall Street. The road from north to south lay from Bishopsgate along Grace-church Street to London Bridge, which was the gateway to the south: this road crossed the east–west road at the junction of Cornhill and Leadenhall Streets.

Westminster lay adjacent to London on the west, and though there were open fields between the two they were united by the common highway, the Thames, London's principal thoroughfare on which (according to John Stow, writing in 1598) over two thousand wherries and other small boats plied for hire. There were great houses fronting on the river both in London and in Westminster, the most palatial being the Savoy, in the Strand, Westminster, originally built in 1245 by Peter of Savoy, Earl of Richmond, burned down by Wat Tyler and his followers in 1381, and rebuilt early in the sixteenth century. These great houses had their private stairs on to the river with their own boats, but there were also numerous public stairs from which the watermen plied, crying "Eastward Ho!" and "Westward Ho!" to indicate to potential passengers the way they were

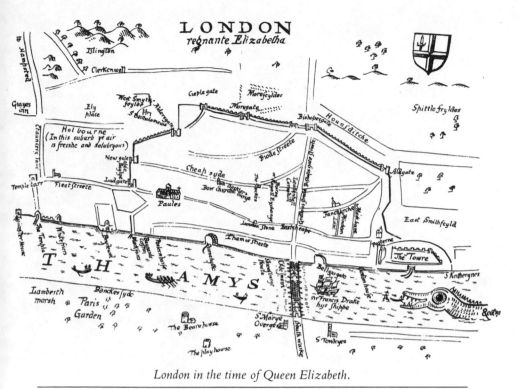

London in the time of Queen Elizabeth.

going. Watermen also took people north and south across the river, for there was only one bridge, London Bridge, a bridge, wrote Fynes Moryson in 1617,

worthily to be numbered among the miracles of the world, if men respect the building and foundation laid artificially and stately over an ebbing and flowing upon 21 piles of stone, with 20 arches, under which barks may pass, the lowest foundation being (as they say) packs of wool, most durable against the force of water . . .; or if men respect the houses built upon the bridge, as great and as high as those of the firm land, so as a man cannot know that he passeth a bridge, but would judge himself to be in the street.

On the south bank was the borough of Southwark with its theatres and bear garden and houses of prostitution (all safely outside the jurisdiction of the puritanical city fathers of London, in whose eyes all three were equally immoral).

In Shakespeare's time London probably had a population approaching two hundred thousand inhabitants, more than twelve times as many as in any other town in England. "London," wrote Frederick, Duke of Württemberg, in 1592 after a visit to the city, "is a large, excellent and mighty city of business, and the most important in the whole kingdom; most of the

31

Höfnagel's TudorWedding *(1590) depicts a feast on the Southwark side of the Thames at Bermondsey. The Tower of London can be glimpsed in the background.*

inhabitants are employed in buying and selling merchandise, and trading in almost every corner of the world, since the river is most convenient and useful for this purpose, considering that ships from France, the Netherlands, Sweden, Denmark, Hamburg and other kingdoms, come almost up to the city, to which they convey goods and receive and take away others in exchange." The duke also commented on the magnificent apparel of the inhabitants and their proud bearing.

The houses, wrote Moryson, "are very narrow in the front towards the street, but are built five or six roofs high, commonly of timber and clay with plaster, and are very neat and commodious within. . . . But withal understand that in London many stately palaces, built by noblemen upon the river Thames, do make a very great show to them that pass by water; and that there be many more like palaces, also built towards land, but scattered and great part of them in back lanes and streets, which if they were joined to the first in good order, as other cities are built uniformly, they would make not only fair streets, but even a beautiful city, to which few might justly be preferred for the magnificence of the building."

The narrow, crowded and dirty streets made the smooth and clear

Thames all the more valued as a highway. Coaches were few in Queen Elizabeth's reign, for the streets could barely accommodate them, but at the very end of the century they began to increase in numbers, to the annoyance and confusion of the inhabitants. "In every street, carts and coaches make such a thundering as the world ran upon wheels," wrote Thomas Dekker in 1606. "At every corner men, women and children meet in such shoals, that posts are set up of purpose to strengthen the houses, lest with jostling one another they should shoulder them down." Fortunately, the city possessed a large number of gardens and open spaces. Tension between the court and the citizenry, between noblemen and merchants, and between both court gallants and sober citizens on the one hand and volatile 'prentices on the other was always liable to precipitate some kind of street fighting, and the cry of "Clubs!" could be counted on to bring 'prentices violently to the rescue.

Shakespeare's London was a lively, colourful, dangerous and crowded city. The crowding and the inadequate sanitation—a channel in the centre of the streets served as an open sewer—caused frequent outbreaks of plague during all the years Shakespeare lived in London, 1593 and 1603 being especially bad years. The theatres would be closed during times of plague, and the actors would have to tour the provinces.

There were over a hundred churches in Elizabethan London, the most famous being St. Paul's Cathedral. The central aisle of St. Paul's, known as "Paul's Walk", was a popular meeting place for all sorts of people (act III, scene i of Ben Jonson's *Every Man out of His Humour*, is actually set there). In Paul's Walk, wrote Dekker, "at one time, in one and the same rank— yea, foot by foot and elbow by elbow—shall you see walking the Knight, the Gull, the Gallant, the Upstart, the Gentleman, the Clown, the Captain, the Applesquire, the Lawyer, the Usurer, the Citizen, the Cheater, the Puritan, the Cut-throat, the High-men, the Low-men, the True-men and the Thief—of all trades and professions some, of all countries some." "Paul's Walk is the land's epitome," wrote John Earle in 1628. St. Paul's Churchyard was the headquarters of the book trade: some publishers and booksellers had their houses as well as shops within the churchyard, and others had stalls fixed against the cathedral walls.

There were many prisons in Shakespeare's London, in addition to the Tower, frequently referred to in his English history plays: these included the Cage, the Cripplegate, the Fleet, Ludgate and Newgate. In Southwark alone there were five: the Clink, the Compter (or Counter, popular name for a debtor's prison: Falstaff refers to it in *The Merry Wives of Windsor* as especially hateful to him), the Marshalsea, the King's Bench and the White Lion. Taverns were very numerous. The Boar's Head in Eastcheap, frequented by Prince Hal and Falstaff, was a real tavern (though there is no evidence that the historical Prince Henry ever drank there); other taverns in Cheapside were the Mitre (not to be confused with Dr. Johnson's Mitre

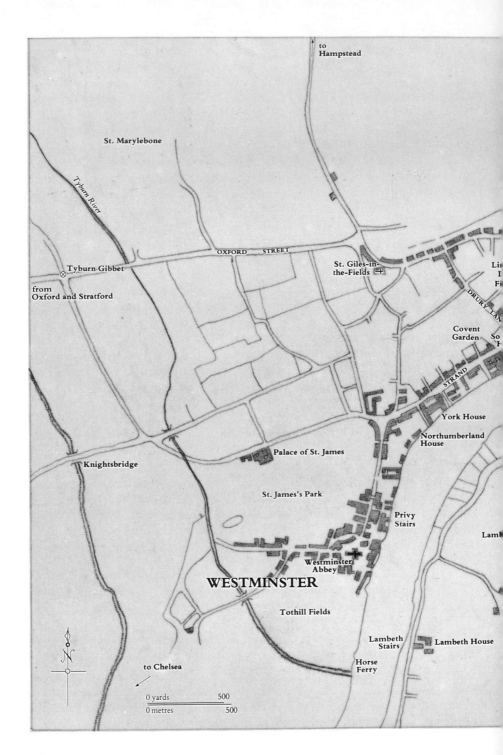

to
Hampstead

St. Marylebone

Tyburn River

OXFORD   STREET

Tyburn Gibbet

St. Giles-in-
the-Fields

Li
I
Fi

DRURY LAN

from
Oxford and Stratford

Covent
Garden

So
H

STRAND

York House

Northumberland
House

Palace of St. James

Knightsbridge

St. James's Park

Privy
Stairs

Lam

Westminster
Abbey

WESTMINSTER

Tothill Fields

Lambeth
Stairs

Lambeth House

to Chelsea

Horse
Ferry

0 yards   500

0 metres   500

Finsbury Fields

The Theatre (1576)

Curtain Theatre (1577)

Priory of St. John

Charterhouse

Gray's Inn

HOLBORN

River Fleet

LONG LANE

Cripplegate

Moorfields

Spital Fields

St. Andrew

W. Smithfield

St. Sepulchre

Aldersgate

Moorgate

Bishopsgate

Newgate

Fleet Prison

FLEET STREET

Ludgate

Whitefriars

St. Paul's Cathedral

CHEAPSIDE

Mitre

CITY

LOTHBURY

St. Helen

Mermaid

St. Mary-le-Bow

CORNHILL

LEADENHALL ST.

Temple Stairs

Blackfriars Theatre

THAMES

GRACECHURCH ST.

Aldgate

RIVER THAMES

THAMES STREET

Boar's Head

EAST CHEAP

E. Smithfield

BRIDGE ST.

TOWER STREET

Paris Garden

Swan Theatre (1595)

BANKSIDE

Bear Garden

Clink Prison

Billingsgate

Rose Theatre (1587)

Globe Theatre (1599)

Pike Garden

Winchester House

St. Mary Overie

London Bridge

Tower of London

SOUTHWARK

Marshalsea Prison

St. George's

King's Bench Prison

to Mile End, Whitechapel and Bow

London
Late 16th century

"Without the city are some theatres . . .," wrote the German traveller Paul Hentzner in 1598. One of them was the Swan, shown here as sketched by Johannes deWitt in 1596.

in Fleet Street) and the Mermaid, where Shakespeare, Ben Jonson and other poets and dramatists regularly met.

> What things have we seen
> Done at the Mermaid! heard words that have been
> So nimble and so full of subtle flame . . .

So Francis Beaumont wrote in his "Epistle to Ben Jonson". There were taverns of many varieties for all sorts of people. "If these houses have a box-bush, or an old post," wrote Donald Lupton in 1632, "it is enough to show their profession. But if they be graced with a sign complete, it's a sign of good custom. In these houses you shall see the history of Judith, Susanna, Daniel in the lion's den, or Dives and Lazarus painted upon the wall. . . . It is the host's chiefest pride to be speaking of such a gentleman, or such a gallant that was here, and will be again ere long."

The first regular public playhouse in England was known simply as the Theatre and was built in 1576 by the actor James Burbage and his brother-in-law John Brayne. The following year the theatre known as the Curtain

36

THE GLOBE THEATRE,

On the Bankside.

As it appeared in the reign of King James I.

was built. Both playhouses were situated in Shoreditch, a northern suburb, to be outside the jurisdiction of the civic authorities, who tended to regard theatrical performances as promoters of immorality and idleness. The Rose was built in 1587 on the Bankside in Southwark in the district known as the Liberty of the Clink. It was owned by the theatrical manager Philip Henslowe, whose papers and so-called diary tell us so much about the Elizabethan theatrical world. The Swan (c. 1595) was built by Francis Langley, also on the Bankside in Southwark. This was the theatre sketched by the Dutchman Johannes de Witt when he visited London in 1596, the only known view of an Elizabethan playhouse. (In spite of this evidence, scholars disagree about many of the details of the structure and pattern of the Elizabethan playhouse.)

The Globe was built in 1599 by Cuthbert and Richard Burbage (sons of James) under rather peculiar circumstances. The owner of the land on which the original Theatre stood refused to renew the lease for the building, so the two Burbages, having inherited the Theatre on the death of their father in 1597, had the building pulled down and the materials removed to the other

37

side of the Thames, on the Bankside near Maiden Lane, where they were used in building the new Globe. The Burbages retained half of the ownership of the Globe and divided the other half among five members of the dramatic company known as the Chamberlain's Men, Shakespeare being among the five. The seven co-owners were known as "housekeepers": they were each responsible for a proportionate share of the ground rent and the costs of maintenance and in return received a share of the gate receipts. Shakespeare was thus both a member of and actor and "sharer" in the Chamberlain's Men, which became the King's Men in 1608/9, and a joint proprietor of the Globe, which remained the exclusive home of the Chamberlain's Men and King's Men until 1609, when the company acquired the Blackfriars theatre, formerly used by the Children of the Chapel, as a winter home, retaining the Globe for summer use. The alternating use by the King's Men of both the Globe and the Blackfriars lasted until the closing of the theatres by the Puritans in 1642. But after 1613 it was no longer the same Globe, for the original Globe was destroyed by fire in that year and rebuilt in 1614. The precise form and structure of the Globe has long been a matter of dispute among scholars.

The star of the Chamberlain's Men and King's Men was Richard Burbage, and he must have played the part of *Hamlet* at early performances of the play at the Globe, Shakespeare, according to one tradition, playing the part of the ghost. However, there is no precise evidence for the date of the play nor for its early performances. Oddly enough, the first recorded performance of Shakespeare's *Hamlet* (there was an earlier play of the same name) was on board H.M.S. *Dragon* at Sierra Leone on September 5, 1607.

The audiences at the Blackfriars, a more expensive and exclusive "private" theatre, were less of a cross-section of the public than those at the "public" Globe. A German traveller called Paul Hentzner visited England in 1598 and wrote (in Latin) an account of his impressions, including his view of the London public theatres:

Without the city are some theatres, where English actors represent almost every day comedies and tragedies to very numerous audiences; these are concluded with variety of dances, accompanied by excellent music and excessive applause of those that are present. . . . At these spectacles and everywhere else, the English are constantly smoking the Nicotian weed which in America is called Tobaca – others call it Paetum – and generally in this manner; they have pipes on purpose made of clay, into the farther end of which they put the herb, so dry that it may be rubbed into powder, and lighting it, they draw the smoke into their mouths, which they puff out again through their nostrils, like funnels, along with it plenty of phlegm and defluxion from the head. In these theatres, fruits, such as apples, pears and nuts, according to season, are carried about to be sold, as well as wine and ale.

The Globe audiences probably represented a wider range of citizens than have attended theatres in Britain since that time. The cost of admission was low, to attract as large a number as possible. The "groundlings", who stood on the ground in the orchestra where there were no seats, were made up for the most part of shopkeepers, craftsmen and members of what might be called the lower bourgeoisie. There were also the apprentices, rowdy young men given to exhibitionism and liable to create disturbances out of sheer exuberance of spirit, but genuine lovers of the theatre, and usually well educated. There were also gentlemen of various degrees, professional men, courtiers, and members of the nobility. They would occupy two-penny or threepenny seats in the gallery. The higher members of the nobility would present themselves conspicuously in seats at the side of the stage itself or in shilling "rooms". Women were among the audience, often the respectable wives of tradesmen, a fact which surprised foreign visitors to London. The capacity of the Globe was probably about two thousand or a little more, and a typical audience would consist of at least one thousand people. Puritan enemies of the theatre insisted that people came there to make assignations and carry on immoral activities; but although a minority may have done this, there can be no doubt what-ever that the large bulk of the audience came to enjoy the play. No body of drama as stimulating and sophisticated as the Elizabethan and Jacobean could have existed without the discriminating enthusiasm of the bulk of the audience.

As for Shakespeare himself, by 1592 he was established in London as an actor and playwright. In 1595 we find him living in St. Helen's, Bishopsgate, but in 1599 he is in Southwark and in 1604 or perhaps a little later in Cripple-gate (by the north wall, west of Moorgate). He bought a house in Blackfriars in 1613, probably as an investment rather than for his own use. By now he had retired to Stratford and paid only occasional visits to London.

DR. JOHNSON'S LONDON

"SIR," DR. JOHNSON REMARKED to Boswell on July 5, 1763, "if you wish to have a just notion of the magnitude of this city, you must not be satisfied with seeing its great streets and squares, but must survey the innumerable little lanes and courts. It is not in the showy evolutions of buildings, but in the multiplicity of human habitations which are crowded together, that the wonderful immensity of London consists." The London that Johnson loved—and of which he said on September 20, 1777, "When a man is tired of London he is tired of life; for there is in London all that life can afford"—was not the London of great public edifices which had arisen in the rebuilding after the Great Fire of 1666, but the crowded London of huddled streets where houses and shops had been quickly rebuilt after the fire on the same sites where the earlier wooden buildings had stood. They were now of brick, for an act for the rebuilding of London passed in 1667 had specified that everything should now be of brick or stone, and even fixed the height for buildings in different kinds of streets: four storeys high for detached houses in principal streets, three storeys in lesser streets, and two storeys in the narrower lanes and alleys. This and subsequent regulations meant a certain standardization in the structure and appearance of the houses of Georgian London.

The best account of London in the years immediately preceding the fire emerges from the pages of the diary of Samuel Pepys, which he began to keep on January 1, 1660. Pepys was as much a Londoner as Johnson. Latham and Matthews, in the introduction to their classic edition of Pepys's Diary, make the point succinctly:

London was the centre of Pepys' civilisation. It was at that time unchallenged in its eminence among English cities. The metropolitan area held about half-a-million inhabitants – perhaps five-eights of the total urban population of the country. . . . Yet, from the point of view of the people living in it, London was not over-large. All that Londoners needed for a full life was there, yet contained in a space so small that it was easy to escape for an hour's airing to fields or river walks. It had taverns, clubs, shops and (after the Restoration [in 1660]) public playhouses. Its musical life – at a time when music held a high place in English culture – was the best in the country. It housed scholars, writers, artists and publishers. In its churches and conventicles was offered an inviting variety of sermon and service. Above all, it was the centre of English political life – the home of royalty, of parliament, of high finance and of the governing *élite*.

As in Shakespeare's day, the main means of communication between the

City of London and Westminster was by boat along the Thames. Pepys talks of going from London to Westminster, indicating that (unlike Dr. Johnson in the next century) he considered them separate, although they were contiguous. Pepys' London changed radically after the Great Fire, but even before then it differed from Shakespeare's in its larger number of public buildings, notably the Palace of Whitehall in Westminster, designed by Inigo Jones for James I on the site of a former residence of the archbishops of York which had been occupied and beautified by Wolsey, acquired and reconstructed by Henry VIII on Wolsey's disgrace, and largely destroyed by fire in 1615. James I did not live to see the completion of his new palace, and only the existing banqueting hall was finished by the time of the outbreak of the Civil War in 1642. But in Charles II's time the palace was complete and became the very symbol both of a self-indulgent royalty and of government. Pepys's position as Clerk of the Acts to the Navy Board took him regularly to Whitehall from his house (the Clerk of the Navy's official lodgings) in Seething Lane in the City. He generally made the journey by water, as on August 1, 1660: "Up very early, and by water to White-hall to my Lord's lodging (W. Howe being now ill of the goute at Mr. Pierces) and there talked with him about the affairs of the Navy and how I was now to wait today at the Privy Seale." Sometimes, however, Pepys went by coach, and he several times describes the congestion produced by coaches in narrow streets.

The Great Fire of London began about two o'clock in the morning on September 2, 1666, in Pudding Lane, near Fish Street Hill, not far from London Bridge, and it raged for four days and nights before a change of wind halted it during the nights of the 4th–5th. Over 32,000 houses were said to have been destroyed, an area of about 436 acres was levelled and about 100,000 people were made homeless. Pepys recorded the beginning of the fire on Sunday, September 2:

Some of our maids sitting up late last night to get things ready against the feast today, Jane called us up, about 3 in the morning, to tell us of a great fire they saw in the City. So I rose, and slipped on my nightgown and went to her window, and thought it to be on the back side of Markelane at the furthest; and being unused to such fires as fallowed, I thought it far enough off, and so went to bed again and to sleep. . . . By and by Jane comes and tells me that she hears that above 300 houses have been burned down tonight by the fire we saw, and that it was now burning down all Fishstreet by London Bridge. . . . So I down to the water-side and there got a boat and through bridge, and there saw a lamentable fire. . . .

Pepys was up early on the 7th "and, blessed God, find all well, and by water to Paul's wharfe. Walked thence and saw all the town burned, and a miserable sight of Pauls church, with all the roofs fallen and the body of the Quire fallen into St. Fayths [the crypt under the choir of the cathedral]—

41

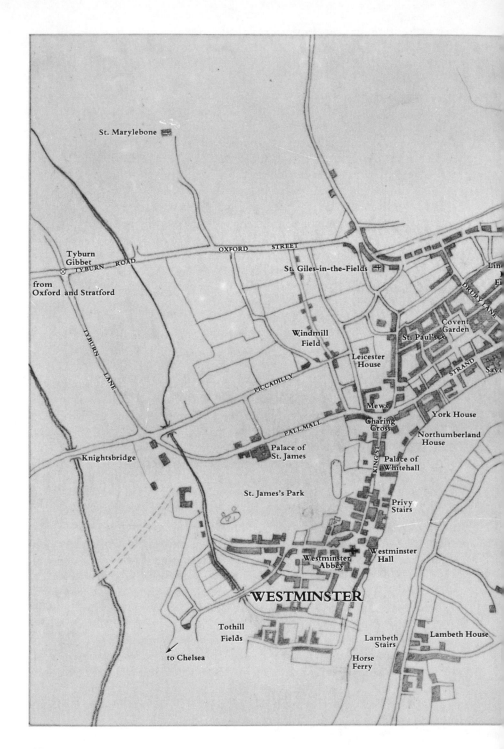

St. Marylebone

Tyburn
Gibbet

OXFORD   STREET

TYBURN   ROAD

St. Giles-in-the-Fields

Lin
Fi

from
Oxford and Stratford

DRURY LANE

TYBURN   LANE

Windmill
Field

Covent
Garden

St. Paul's

Leicester
House

PICCADILLY

STRAND

Sav

Mews

PALL MALL

Charing
Cross

York House

Northumberland
House

Knightsbridge

Palace of
St. James

KING ST.

Palace of
Whitehall

St. James's Park

Privy
Stairs

Westminster
Abbey

Westminster
Hall

WESTMINSTER

Tothill
Fields

Lambeth
Stairs

Lambeth House

to Chelsea

Horse
Ferry

Finsbury Fields

Charterhouse

Gray's
Inn

HOLBORN

Lincoln's
Inn

St. Andrew

St. Sepulchre

Newgate

Fleet
Prison

FLEET STREET

Ludgate

Essex
House
del
ase

Temple

Temple
Stairs

RIVER

THAMES

Cripplegate

WOOD STREET

Aldersgate

Guildhall

St. Paul's
Cathedral

CHEAPSIDE

WATLING ST.

St. Mary-le-Bow

LOTHBURY

CITY

Moorfields

Moorgate

Bishopsgate

Spital
Fields

ROUNDSDITCH

CORNHILL

GRACECHURCH ST.

LEADENHALL ST.

Aldgate

to Mile End White Chapel and Bow

Paul's
Wharf

Paris
Garden

Bear Garden

BANK SIDE

Clink
Prison

London Bridge

Lambeth Marsh

SOUTHWARK

HIGH STREET

St. Mary Overie

Marshalsea
Prison

St. George's

King's Bench
Prison

THAMES STREET

EAST CHEAP

MARK LANE

SEETHING LANE

Navy Office

Trinity
House

Pudding Lane
(site of the Great Fire)

Custom
House

Tower of London

Maximum extent of Great Fire ⎯ ⎯

0 yards   500

0 metres   500

London
c. 1660 (before the Great Fire)

"So I went down to the water-side . . . and there saw a lamentable fire"
—*Samuel Pepys*

Paul's school also—Ludgate—Fleet street—my father's house, and the church, and a good part of the Temple and the like." Seething Lane, where his own house was, remained just outside the area of destruction, but it burned down in another fire in 1673 when the Navy Office and adjacent houses were destroyed.

The Great Fire had wiped out more than four-fifths of the old walled city, including St. Paul's Cathedral, and extended just beyond the old city to the west. It had stopped short at the Tower on the east, Cripplegate on the north, and the Temple on the west. When Johnson first came to London in 1737 he lodged with a staymaker in Exeter Street, just beyond the westward limit of the fire, then, after a stay in Greenwich to work on his tragedy and a period back in his native Lichfield with his wife, he and his wife lodged well to the west of the fire area in Woodstock Street, near Hanover Square, an area developed by Lord Scarborough in George I's reign (hence Hanover Square), and then in Castle Street (now Eastcastle Street) also well west of the fire area. From 1748 to 1759 he lived in Gough Square, behind Fleet Street, almost on the western limit of the fire area and thus rebuilt after the fire. He spent the rest of his life in that area, never far from Fleet Street, at the western end of the rebuilt City. Thus the London that Johnson knew best and in which he delighted was not an old city in terms of the age of the buildings, but it was old in their siting and in the patterns of its streets and lanes.

The cities of London and Westminster were administratively separate, but by now the empty spaces between them had been filled in and they constituted a continuous built-up area, so that for Johnson "London" included both. The medieval ambiance of London, which had persisted well into the seventeenth century, was already diminishing with the growth of Palladian architecture in larger and more formal buildings even before the rebuilding after the fire replaced high-gabled, timbered houses with classically designed houses of brick or stone. Although Wren's plan for rebuilding the City was never put into effect in terms of its general design, he did rebuild all the destroyed City churches (including St. Paul's Cathedral) in neoclassical style, thus radically altering the appearance and feel of the City. Building continued apace in Johnson's lifetime, so that the London of his last years was different in many respects from the London he saw on his first arrival. One of the most significant changes was the result of the arching over of the Fleet Ditch. The rebuilding acts after the Great Fire had called for an ambitiously conceived Fleet Canal, which involved clearing the badly cluttered ditch (which by 1666 had become little better than a sewer); but this finally proved impracticable and in 1733 the ditch was arched over from Holborn Bridge to Fleet Bridge, and what had been intended to be wharves were converted into roads. In 1766 the lower reach was also covered in, and with the opening of Blackfriars Bridge in 1769 what had earlier been conceived as a navigable waterway running north up from the Thames finally emerged as a north-south roadway across the Thames. Blackfriars Bridge was now the third bridge over the Thames in London; Westminster Bridge had been opened in 1750, catering to the needs of the growing population in the West End and around Westminster. But when Johnson arrived in London in 1737 there was still only one bridge, the traditional London Bridge. The houses and other superstructures on that bridge were removed in 1757 and the bridge itself lasted until 1832.

Among the public buildings that arose during Johnson's residence in London were the Corn Exchange, the Mansion House and the Bank of England. Outside the City there were the Horse Guards in Whitehall and Somerset House in the Strand. But it was the expansion of house building that was really massive: a contemporary estimated that 42,000 houses were built in London between 1762 and 1779. The population of London (i.e., of the whole metropolitan area, including the City, Westminster and newly built-up suburbs) was probably nearly 700,000 in mid-century, though until the first official census of 1801 (which gave the population as 864,845) figures can only be estimates. In Johnson's day London itself was growing faster than its population, for increasing prosperity led the middle classes to be less satisfied with cramped dwelling houses and encouraged a move-ment westward to newer and larger houses. The development of squares

The London riverfront from Westminster to the Adelphi, the superb terrace of private houses designed by the brothers Adam. Painted by William Marlow c. 1771–2.

was a feature of the period, with their elegant and uniform frontages and pattern of subsidiary streets leading sometimes to main thoroughfares such as the Strand and Piccadilly. Red Lion Square and Bloomsbury Square had been developed by the end of the seventeenth century; in the eighteenth century aristocratic landowners developed residential areas on their property, and the results included Grosvenor Square, Cavendish Square (with its surrounding Wimpole Street, Harley Street and Welbeck Street) and Berkeley Square.

In spite of a lack of general planning, new developments were oriented towards a number of main thoroughfares, of which three ran more or less parallel to the Thames: the line from Fleet Street along the Strand to Whitehall, much redesigned and rebuilt by mid-century, especially by the clearing of the clutter around the Houses of Parliament in order to push through a broad new thoroughfare (Parliament Street) and improve the approaches to the new Westminster Bridge; the line from Lincoln's Inn Fields running along Great Queen Street across Drury Lane to come into the Strand near Charing Cross; the line along Holborn and High Holborn into what became Oxford Street which in turn ran into Tyburn Road, leading to the notorious gallows. (What is now Park Lane, connecting Tyburn with Hyde Park Corner, was then Tyburn Lane.) The ending of the Seven Years War in 1763 gave a great impetus to building. Portman Square was laid out to the west of Marylebone Lane in 1774, followed by

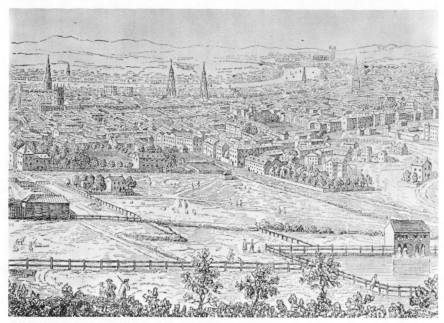

London across the fields from Clerkenwell. From a view by Canaletto, published in 1753.

Portland Place; Bedford Square was developed in the 1770s as part of the Duke of Bedford's plans for the development of his Bloomsbury estate; and further developments, including some of the finest examples of Georgian architecture, took place in the years just before and just after Johnson's death.

London still had its easily accessible rural hinterland, from which fresh vegetables, dairy produce and flowers were brought in daily; in these rural environs gentlemen had country seats and citizens had summer houses or took lodgings in the summer or simply went out for recreation on Sundays. And in London itself there were stables and cowsheds and pig-styes; cattle and deer grazed in St. James's Park and strollers in the park could buy milk straight from the cow. Peter Kalm, a Swede visiting London in 1748, described the market gardens near London, in the land around Chelsea and Fulham, the latter then being a village about four miles southwest of London, where people went on Sunday afternoons "to take the fresh air and to have the advantage of tasting the pleasures of a country life". But Kalm also complained of the "thick coal smoke" which obscured the otherwise "marvellous view on all sides" from the top of St. Paul's, and the fact is of course that in spite of its close connections with the countryside Johnson's London was a smoky and dirty city. It was a city of contrasts, of elegance and confusion, of high sensibility and appalling brutality, of spacious squares and narrow, filthy alleys where gin-soaked paupers lay

47

St. Marylebone

Southampton
House

Bloomsbury Sq.
(1665)

H

OXFORD STREET

HIGH ST.

Tyburn
Gibbet

TYBURN ROAD

St. Giles-in-
the-Fields

Linco
Inn
Field

DRURY LANE

Grosvenor Sq.
(1695)

Golden Sq.
(1700)

Covent
Garden

TYBURN LANE

Berkeley Sq.
(1700)

Leicester
House

EXETER ST.

Somer
Ho

Burlington House

STRAND

Sav

PICCADILLY

St. James's Sq.
(1665)

Mews

THAME

Knightsbridge

PALL MALL

Charing
Cross

Northumberland
House

RIVER

Palace of
St. James

St. James's Park

Privy
Stairs

N

Westminster
Hall

WESTMINSTER

Westminster
Abbey

Lambeth
House

Tothill
Fields

Lambeth
Stairs

to Chelsea

Horse
Ferry

0 yards   500
0 metres   500

Finsbury Fields

Charterhouse

Gray's
Inn

Red Lion Sq.
(1698)

BORN

St. Bartholomew

West
Smithfield

HOLBORN

Moorfields

CHANCERY LANE

Cripplegate

FETTER LANE

FLEET   STREET

Newgate

Aldersgate

Moorgate

Bishopsgate

The
Temple

Fleet
Prison

Ludgate

Temple
Stairs

St. Paul's
Cathedral
(1710)

St. Mary-le-Bow

CHEAPSIDE

CITY

CORNHILL

GRACECHURCH ST.

LEADENHALL ST.

Aldgate

Paris Garden

EAST   CHEAP

THAMES

TOWER STREET

BANKSIDE

STREET

The
Clink

London Bridge

Billingsgate

Custom
House

St. Mary Overy

SOUTHWARK

Tower of London

Marshalsea
Prison

King's Bench
Prison

BERMONDSEY

London
Early 18th century

49

about in squalor. London was, as Johnson wrote in 1741, "a city famous for wealth and commerce and plenty, and for every other kind of civility and politeness", but at the same time he conceded that it "abounds with such heaps of filth, as a savage would look on in amazement". He went on to specify: "That the present neglect of cleansing and paving the streets is such as ought not to be borne, that the passenger is everywhere either surprized or endangered by unexpected chasms, or offended or obstructed by mountains of filth, is well known to every one that has passed a single day in this great city; . . ." It was twenty-one years after this that the city undertook to provide street cleaning rather than leave each householder nominally responsible for cleaning the section in front of his door.

The dirtier and more dangerous manufactures were mostly carried on on the south side of the river: soap-making, tanning, the manufacture of vinegar and gunpowder, slaughter yards. Brewing was now a major industry: Samuel Whitbread set up as an independent brewer in 1750 and made a fortune out of beer, as, on a smaller scale, did Johnson's friend Henry Thrale. But it was as a commercial rather than an industrial city that London was pre-eminent; this was testified to by the vast number of ships crowding the Thames, which astonished foreign visitors. About 80 per cent of England's imports and nearly 74 per cent of her exports came in through or left from the port of London. The financial machinery necessary to carry on this huge amount of trade was centred on the Bank of England, but the East India Company and the South Seas Company were also important. Banking services for individuals were provided by many private bankers, most of them having their premises in or near Lombard Street, the financial centre of the City.

Coffee houses, which had first sprung up in the late seventeenth century, now played an important part in London life: some served purely social purposes, but many were associated with particular trades and professions and served as meeting places for those who practised them. Parks were important as places for strolling, relaxing and making assignations among all ranks of society. St. James's Park was the most popular; Kensington Gardens (originally laid out by William and Mary, whose favourite residence had been Kensington) was more socially exclusive, perhaps because it was really outside London. Hyde Park, the most extensive and in some respects the least artificial, was famous for its Ring, around which young bloods showed off their riding skills. Further west Kew Gardens was a favourite haunt of George III, who lived like a simple country gentleman at Richmond: it was the most exclusive of all. And all around London there were pleasure gardens, tea gardens, and similar places of resort and entertainment, some (like Marylebone Gardens) providing concerts and fireworks, some (like Sadler's Wells) providing acrobatic shows and pantomimes. The gardens at Bagnigge Wells (on the site of the present King's Cross Road) were a fashionable resort for parading and tea drinking as well as taking the

*"The place crowded with the gayest company . . . enlivened with mirth,
freedom, and good humour," wrote Lydia Melford of Vauxhall Gardens in
Smollett's* Humphry Clinker. *Vauxhall Gardens, from an engraving after
Rowlandson's watercolour. A rotund and inebriated Dr. Johnson is shown
seated in the supper box (bottom left), with Boswell, Oliver Goldsmith and
Mrs. Thrale, among others.*

waters. But the two most famous amusement gardens in Johnson's London
were Vauxhall (laid out in 1661) and Ranelagh (opened in 1742), the
former on the south bank of the Thames in the parish of Lambeth, and the
latter on the north bank of the Thames in Chelsea, in an area still verging
on open countryside though by now a fashionable district for the well-to-do
to build their houses. Both are vividly described in Smollett's *Humphry
Clinker* (Lydia Melford's letter from London to her friend Laetitia Willis).
"Imagine to yourself," Lydia wrote enthusiastically, ". . . a spacious garden,
part laid out in delightful walks, bounded with both hedges and trees, and
paved with gravel; part exhibiting a wonderful assemblage of the most
picturesque and striking objects, pavilions, lodges, groves, grottos, lawns,
temples, and cascades; porticos, colonnades, and rotundas; adorned with
pillars, statues, and paintings; the whole illuminated with an infinite
number of lamps, disposed in different figures of suns, stars, and constella-
tions; the place crowded with the gayest company, ranging through those
blissful shades, or supping in different lodges, on cold collations, enlivened
with mirth, freedom, and good humour, and animated by an excellent
band of music." Ranelagh, frequented by a less socially mixed variety of
visitors, "looks like the enchanted palace of a genio, adorned with the most
exquisite performances of painting, carving, and gilding, enlightened with

The execution of Lord Ferrers at Tyburn, May 5, 1760. "The day of execution is a holiday to the greatest part of the mob about town," wrote Fielding.

a thousand golden lamps, that emulate the noonday sun; crowded with the great, the rich, the gay, the happy, and the fair; glittering with cloth of gold and silver, lace, embroidery, and precious stones. While these exulting sons and daughters of felicity tread this round of pleasure, or regale in different parties, and separate lodges, with fine imperial tea and other delicious refreshments, their ears are entertained with the most ravishing delights of music, both instrumental and vocal." London also had its theatres; after the licensing act of 1737 only Drury Lane and Covent Garden were in strict legality entitled to present plays, but other theatres got around the law by advertising concerts in which a play was thrown in gratis.

There were also less savoury entertainments. Not only cock fighting and a brutal form of boxing (without gloves) were popular, but public hangings at Tyburn attracted huge crowds. It must not be forgotten that the back streets of Johnson's London proliferated with vice and crime and that one by-product of its crowded prosperity was a high proportion of human detritus, who took to all kinds of desperate activities, from picking pockets to highway robbery, and that all society could think of doing with them when they were caught was to lock them up in foul and pestilential prisons whence regularly large numbers of them—men, women and children— were sent out to be hanged, then the punishment for any crime described as a felony (and that could include the most trivial kind of theft).

The real connoisseur of eighteenth-century prisons is Tobias Smollett, who sends both his heroes and his villains to prison in all his novels except *Humphry Clinker*. Roderick Random is arrested for debt and spends some time in the Marshalsea. Peregrine Pickle is also arrested for debt and goes to the Fleet. Ferdinand Count Fathom, more deservedly, spends a considerable time in prison, both the King's Bench and the Marshalsea, in the latter of which, after having undergone a change of heart and a moral reformation, he meets and marries the unhappy Elinor whom he had earlier seduced and abandoned. That questing knight Sir Launcelot Greaves, bound on an errand of deliverance, visits "the Gate-house, Fleet, and Marshalsea" before coming to "the prison of the King's Bench, which is situated in St. George's Fields, about a mile from the end of Westminster Bridge, and appears like a neat little regular town, consisting of one street, surrounded by a very high wall, including an open piece of ground, which may be termed a garden, where the prisoners take the air and amuse themselves with a variety of diversions." Smollett proceeds to give a fascinating account of the self-sufficient prison community in what is virtually a small walled town, with its own "butchers' stands, chandlers' shops, a surgery, a tap-house well frequented, and a public kitchen. . . .".

Henry Fielding was active in opposing the indiscriminate hanging of the time. In the *Covent Garden Journal* of July 18, 1752, he wrote: "On Monday last eleven wretches were executed at Tyburn and the very next night one of the most impudent street-robberies was committed near St. James's Square, an instance of the little force which such examples have on the minds of the populace". He went on to deplore the fact that "the day of execution is a holiday to the greatest part of the mob about town" and concluded: "I wish some other punishments were invented, and that we may no longer proceed to string up hundreds of our fellow-creatures every year, a matter as shocking to all men of humanity, as it is entertaining to a dissolute rabble, who (I repeat again) instead of being terrified, are hardened and encouraged by the sight". Fielding also gave his view of hanging in the bitterly ironic account of the trial and execution of a horse thief in Book VIII, Chapter XI of *Tom Jones*.

The hanging itself was a fearful form of slow strangulation: the victim had the rope put round his neck while standing on a cart under the gallows: the cart then drove off, leaving the victim dangling: there was no drop, and the victim's friends would pull at his feet to hasten his death. This appalling scene was one of the most popular sights of London. "On the days when the prisons of this city are emptied into the grave," wrote Johnson in *The Rambler* for April 20, 1751, "let every spectator of the dreaded procession put the same question ['Who knows whether this man is less culpable than I?'] to his own heart. Few among those that crowd in thousands to the legal massacre, and look with carelessness, perhaps with triumph, on the uttermost excerbations of human misery, would then be able to return without horror and dejection." Yet after public hangings at Tyburn were abolished in 1783 (they were not abolished outside Newgate and elsewhere until 1868), Johnson protested that "the age is running mad after innovation" and insisted that "executions are intended to draw spectators. If they do not draw spectators, they don't answer their purpose". This was probably said in a fit of contrariness. Few writers were better aware than Dr. Johnson of the horrors of crime and poverty in his beloved city and of the extraordinary contrasts between elegance and squalor, kindly sentiment and callous brutality, which were so conspicuous in eighteenth-century London.

CHARLES DICKENS'S
LONDON

BETWEEN DR. JOHNSON's death in 1784 and the Dickens family settling in London in 1822, when young Charles was ten years old, London expanded steadily, eating up the green spaces between the built-up area and the surrounding villages. In 1801 its population was 864,000; thirty years later it was one-and-a-half million and by mid-century it was two-and-a-half million. It grew and it changed more rapidly during Dickens's lifetime (1812–1870) than in the immediately preceding decades, and Dickens took note of the changes and chronicled them in his novels. The London of the *Pickwick Papers* (1836–7) is a London more open, more cheerful and more easily come to terms with than the sinister and disturbing London of *Our Mutual Friend* (1864–5).

The Dickens family settled in a small, shabby-genteel house of four rooms, basement and garret in Bayham Street, Camden Town. It was one of a terrace of forty cheap brick houses built in 1812 as part of a continuous development of their land undertaken by the Camden family from 1790 onwards. (The first Lord Camden was also Viscount Bayham, after Bayham Abbey, the family's country seat, hence the name of this street.) Dickens remembered the Camden Town of his childhood when in Chapter VI of *Dombey and Son* he described the Toodles' home in Staggs's Gardens:

It was a little row of houses, with little squalid patches of ground before them, fenced off with old doors, barrel staves, scraps of tarpaulin, and dead bushes; with bottomless tin kettles and exhausted iron fenders, thrust into the gaps. Here the Staggs's Gardeners trained scarlet beans, kept fowls and rabbits, erected rotten summer houses (one was an old boat), dried clothes, and smoked pipes.

But Dickens was also thinking of the frantic railway developments of the 1840s which were to change so much of London. In this first view of Camden Town the change was only beginning:

The first shock of a great earthquake had, just at that period, rent the whole neighbourhood to its centre. Traces of its course were visible on every side. Houses were knocked down; streets broken through and stopped; deep pits and trenches dug in the ground; enormous heaps of earth and clay thrown up; buildings that were undermined and shaking, propped by great beams of wood. . . . Everywhere were bridges that led nowhere; thoroughfares that were wholly impassable; Babel towers of chimneys, wanting half their height; . . . carcases of ragged tenements, and fragments of unfinished walls and arches, and piles of scaffolding, and wildernesses of bricks, and giant forms of cranes, and tripods straddling above nothing. . . .

"The first shock of a great earthquake had . . . rent the neighbourhood to its centre," wrote Dickens in Dombey and Son. *Railway development in Camden Town, 1836 (from a series of lithographs by J. C. Bourne).*

In short, the yet unfinished and unopened railroad was in progress; and, from the very core of all this dire disaster, trailed smoothly away, upon its mighty course of civilisation and improvement.

A few years later, the whole street had vanished:

There was no such place as Staggs's Gardens. It had vanished from the earth. Where the old rotten summer houses once had stood, palaces now reared their heads, and granite columns of gigantic girth opened a new vista to the railway world beyond. The miserable waste ground, where the refuse-matter had been heaped of yore, was swallowed up and gone; and in its frowsy stead were tiers of warehouses, crammed with rich goods and costly merchandise. The old by-streets now swarmed with passengers and vehicles of every kind: the new streets that had stopped disheartened in the mud and waggon-ruts, formed towns within themselves, originating wholesome comforts and conveniences belonging to themselves, and never tried nor thought of until they sprung into existence.

(Chapter XV)

The railway now ran from Euston to Birmingham, and Mr. Toodle was an engine fireman, living in the railway company's own buildings.

Shortly after his family's settling in Bayham Street, young Dickens was

London
Early 19th century

The blacking factory at Hungerford Stairs, where Dickens worked as a boy.

sent to work in a blacking warehouse in a tumbledown old building by the river at Hungerford Stairs (Charing Cross Station now covers the site). And his ne'er-do-well father was sent to the Marshalsea Prison (in Southwark) for debt. Some months later a small legacy enabled Dickens senior to leave prison, and shortly afterwards Charles was freed from the blacking warehouse (but not before it had made a permanent and searing impression on him, as *David Copperfield* was to show). For the next two years he attended school at Wellington House Academy, Granby Street (off Hampstead Road and soon to be swallowed up by the development of Mornington Crescent, already begun): the family now lived in Johnson Street, a decayed street, long since vanished, between Camden Town and Somers Town.

Dickens left school early in 1827 and got a job as a solicitor's clerk with a firm that had its offices at Holborn Court and then in Raymond Buildings, Gray's Inn. Here he got to know the habits and practices of lawyers and the scenes of their activities: from the early *Pickwick Papers* to the late *Great Expectations* Dickens's novels bristle with scenes in law offices and recollections of the sights and characters he encountered during his brief spell as a solicitor's clerk. In 1829 he became a reporter at Doctor's Commons, where an antique complex of law courts operated, thus further extending his knowledge of the mustier aspects of the law. He then moved to parliamentary reporting, to emerge in 1833 as an accomplished writer of sketches of London life which were collected in 1836 as his first book, *Sketches by Boz*. From 1834 to 1837 he lived at Furnival's Inn (in Holborn, between Brook Street and Leather Lane). In 1837 he married, and moved to 48 Doughty Street, where he lived until 1839.

Doughty Street, which runs south from Mecklenburgh Square parallel to Gray's Inn Road, was part of an area developed in the eighteenth century by George Brownlow Doughty, his wife Elizabeth Tichbourne and their grandson Henry. Immediately to the northwest, in Coram's Fields, was the foundling hospital established in 1739 "for the maintenance and education of exposed and deserted young children" (it survived on that site until 1926). The hospital had an estate of fifty-six acres in this region of Bloomsbury: residential development on what had hitherto been pasture-land began in the last decade of the eighteenth century, and the names of the streets reflect the period—Guildford Place and Street after the powerful politician Lord North, who was also the second Earl of Guildford; Grenville Street after the foreign secretary Lord Grenville; Lansdowne Terrace after the first Marquis of Lansdowne, the unpopular but imaginative statesman who had conceded peace with the United States and thus ended the war; Mecklenburgh Square after Charlotte of Mecklenburgh, George III's queen; and Brunswick Square after Princess Caroline of Brunswick, whom the Prince Regent married under protest in 1795.

Dickens perambulated these streets as he perambulated so many parts of London. He was a great walker of London streets, noting the class flavour of each, the kinds of street life that went on, the way people lived and talked and carried on their affairs. This particular area retained unscathed its eighteenth-century elegance: it was in Brunswick Square that Isabella Knightley, elder sister of Jane Austen's *Emma*, lived, considering it "so very superior" to other parts of London. "I should be unwilling to live in any other part of the town;—there is hardly any other that I could be satisfied to have my children in:—but we are so remarkably airy!" But it lay between Holborn and Camden Town, and Dickens also observed attentively the more crowded and often decayed areas to the south and the region to the north where the building of the railway was causing such chaos.

Sketches by Boz first revealed Dickens's fascination with London. He noticed everything, and recorded what he noticed—the replacement of door knockers by bells in Eaton Square (part of the wealthy Grosvenor estates in what is now Mayfair, Belgravia and Pimlico, developed in the eighteenth century); Covent Garden Market at daybreak; sights observed on a walk from Covent Garden to St. Paul's Churchyard; hackney coach stands; Doctor's Commons (by St. Paul's); riverside scenes; the crowded squalor of Seven Dials. (Seven Dials was laid out at the end of the seven-teenth century by Thomas Neale, with seven streets radiating from a central

Seven Dials *by Gustav Doré. "A maze of streets, courts, lanes and alleys . . .
lost in the unwholesome vapour which hangs over the house-tops," wrote
Dickens.*

point just northwest of Covent Garden, but what Dickens called its "maze
of streets, courts, lanes and alleys . . . lost in the unwholesome vapour which
hangs over the house-tops, and renders the dirty perspective uncertain and
confined" had already become a notorious slum by the middle of the
eighteenth century.) These slum areas of London—Seven Dials, St. Giles
and the Saffron Hill district further east in Holborn were among the worst—
had come to public notice during the cholera epidemic of 1832, and facts
about the way people lived in them had been appearing annually since 1818
in the Reports of the Society for the Suppression of Mendicity. Dickens
was to set an important scene of *Oliver Twist* in Saffron Hill, and Tom-all-
Alone's in *Bleak House* is an even more vivid picture of the squalor and
poverty that existed in the rotting tenements of London's crowded slums.
It was the building later in the century of wide new streets—New Oxford
Street, Shaftesbury Avenue, Charing Cross Road and others—that largely
cleared these foetid areas.

With *Pickwick Papers* (1836–7) Dickens was embarked on his fantastically
successful career as a novelist. For the next twenty years, except for periods

abroad, he lived in London, and though he acquired Gad's Hill Place near Rochester in 1856 and spent much of his time there from 1858 he still had periods of residence in London in the last twelve years of his life. From 1839 to 1851 he lived at Devonshire Terrace (not the present Devonshire Terrace in Bayswater, which dates from 1855; this was a large house with a walled garden which stood at what is now the corner of Marylebone Road and Marylebone High Street: there is still a Devonshire Street off Marylebone High Street, commemorating Dorothy Cavendish, daughter of the fourth duke of Devonshire, who married the heir to the Harley estates in Marylebone in 1766). In 1851 he moved to Tavistock House, Tavistock Square (the house is now demolished), which was one of the seven squares developed at the end of the century by the Duke of Bedford when he extended northward his development of the Bedford estates.

Dickens did not love London as Dr. Johnson had loved it; yet if he was sometimes repelled by it, he was always fascinated by it. Interestingly enough, Dickens makes comparatively little use in his novels of scenes in those more elegant parts of London where he lived during the time of his prosperity and when he does they are presented as bleak and gloomy, as in his description of Mr. Dombey's house:

Mr. Dombey's house was a large one, on the shady side of a tall, dark, dreadfully genteel street in the region between Portland Place and Bryanstone Square. It was a corner house, with great wide areas containing cellars frowned upon by barred windows, and leered at by crooked-eyed doors leading to dustbins. It was a house of dismal state, with a circular back to it, containing a whole suit of drawing-rooms looking upon a gravelled yard, where two gaunt trees, with blackened trunks and branches, rattled rather than rustled, their leaves were so smoke-dried. The summer sun was never on the street, but in the morning about breakfast-time, when it came with the water-carts and the old-clothes-men, and the people with geraniums, and the umbrella-mender, and the man who trilled the little bell of the Dutch clock as he went along.

Dickens's sympathy is clearly with the old-clothes-men and the umbrella mender, and he would follow them home if he could. He is clearly more interested in the district in the City where Dombey and Son had their offices:

Though the offices of Dombey and Son were within the liberties of the City of London, and within hearing of Bow Bells, when their clashing voices were not drowned by the uproar in the streets, yet were there hints of adventurous and romantic story to be observed in some of the adjacent objects. Gog and Magog held their state within ten minutes' walk; the Royal Exchange was close at hand; the Bank of England, with its vaults of gold and silver "down among the dead men" underground, was their magnificent neighbour. Just round the corner

ISLINGTON

King's Cross Sta.
(1852)
Pancras
(1870)
(Northern Railway)

Sadler's Wells

Metropolitan Line (1836)

Brunswick
Sq.
Mecklenburg
Sq.

Russell
Sq.

Queen
Sq.
Gray's Inn

Charterhouse

Farringdon
St. Sta.

British
Museum
Bloomsbury
Sq.

Furnival's
Inn

Smithfield
Market

Liverpool St.
Sta. (1875)

HIGH HOLBORN   HOLBORN   High HOLBORN   HOLBORN

Lincoln's
Inn

Holborn Viaduct
Sta. (1874)

Courts
of Justice
FLEET   STREET

St. Paul's
Cathedral

CHEAPSIDE

Bank of England

CORNHILL

Fenchurch St.
Sta. (1841)

Covent
Garden

The
Temple

Mansion
House

Trinity
House

STRAND

Somerset
House

Blackfriars
Bridge

Cannon St.
Sta. (1866)

Charing Cross
Sta. (1864)

Waterloo
Bridge

BANKSIDE

Southwark
Bridge

London
Bridge
(1831)

Custom
Ho.

Tower of
London

EMBANKMENT

Waterloo
Sta. (1838)

WATERLOO ROAD

London Bridge
Sta. (1836)

Westminster
Bridge

Palace of
Westminster

Kings Bench
Prison

St. George

Horsemonger Lane
Prison

Lambeth
Palace

Bethlehem
Hospital

London

1870s

Lambeth
Bridge
(1862)

stood the rich East India House, teeming with suggestions of precious stuffs and stones, tigers, elephants, howdahs, hookahs, umbrellas, palm trees, palanquins, and gorgeous princes of brown complexion sitting on carpets, with their slippers very much turned up at the toes.

Dickens had a great sense of London contrasts: indeed, Chapter XXXIII of *Dombey and Son* is entitled "Contrasts" and sets the description of Mr. Carker's house "in the green and wooded country near Norwood" beside the "poor, small house, barely and sparsely furnished, but very clean" of John and Harriet Carker. The account of the latter shows Dickens's awareness of what happened when the suburbs pushed north into the fields:

The neighbourhood in which it stands has as little of the country to recommend it, as it has of the town. It is neither of the town nor country. The former, like the giant in his travelling boots, has made a stride and passed it, and has set his brick-and-mortar heel a long way in advance; but the intermediate space between the giant's feet, as yet, is only blighted country, and not town; and, here, among a few tall chimneys belching smoke all day and night, and among the brickfields and the lanes where turf is out, and where the fences tumble down, and where the dusty nettles grow, and where a scrap or two of hedge may yet be seen, and where the bird-catcher still comes occasionally, though he swears every time to come no more – this second home is to be found.

A comparable scene on the south side of the Thames is found in the first chapter of Book II of *Our Mutual Friend*:

The schools . . . were down in that district of the flat country tending to the Thames, where Kent and Surrey meet, and where the railways still bestride the market-gardens that will soon die under them. The schools were newly built, and there were so many like them all over the country, that one might have thought the whole were but one restless edifice with the locomotive gift of Aladdin's palace. They were in a neighbourhood which looked like a toy neighbourhood taken in blocks out of a box by a child of particularly incoherent mind, and set up anyhow: here, one side of a new street; there, a large solitary public house facing nowhere; here, another unfinished street already in ruins; there, a church; here, an immense new warehouse; there, a dilapidated old country villa; then, a medley of black ditch, sparkling cucumber-frame, rank field, richly cultivated kitchen-garden, brick viaduct, arch-spanned canal, and disorder of frowsiness and fog. As if the child had given the table a kick and gone to sleep.

The changing London of convulsive urban expansion fascinated and horrified Dickens. But it did not always horrify. The "collection of black lanes, ditches, and little gardens" in Walworth (also on the south side of the river) in the midst of which Wemmick's Aged Parent's house is set in *Great*

Expectations has its compensations. It was however the real slums, and the dark riverside scenes, that Dickens describes most memorably: Tom-all-Alone's and Saffron Hill and Jacob's Island and Folly Ditch (*Bleak House* and *Oliver Twist*) are seared into the reader's imagination, as is the opening river scene in *Our Mutual Friend*, perhaps Dickens's most obsessively London novel, and one in which the contrast between poverty and wealth, between old and new, between humanity and inhumanity, and between the filth of London and the wealth that can be made from it reaches remarkable heights of irony. Newness in this novel has no relation to progress or adventure: it is related to the manipulation of wealth for purposes of personal advantage without any social base or meaning or valid relationships. "Mr. and Mrs. Veneering were bran-new people in a bran-new house in a bran-new quarter of London." It is not long before that novelty is seen as something inimical to all human values.

It is only when we set Dickens's novels beside Henry Mayhew's *London Labour and London Poor*, first published in 1851, that we realize that Dickens understated the horrors of the London slums of his day, preferring to evoke an atmosphere by means of an almost surrealistic symbolism rather than to give the precise facts about filth and disease and desperate occupations. The *Report of the Sanitary Condition of the City of London* for the years 1848–9 gave details that Dickens dealt with very generally in Chapter XVI of *Bleak House*:

It is a black, dilapidated street, avoided by all decent people; where the crazy houses were seized upon, when their decay was far advanced, by some bold vagrants, who, after establishing their own possession, took to letting them out in lodgings. Now, these tumbling tenements contain, by night, a swarm of misery. As, on the ruined human wretch, vermin parasites appear, so, these ruined shelters have bred a crowd of foul existence that crawls in and out of gaps in walls and boards; and coils itself to sleep, in maggot numbers, where the rain drips in; and comes and goes, fetching and carrying fever, and sowing more evil in its every footprint than Lord Coodle, and Sir Thomas Doodle, and the Duke of Foodle, and all the fine gentlemen in office, down to Zoodle, shall set right in five hundred years – though born expressly to do it.

Mayhew's account of London sewer hunters, refuse collectors, river finders, mudlarks and "the London sewerage and scavengery" provides a fascinating commentary on scenes in *Our Mutual Friend* and elsewhere, while his interviews with prostitutes (whose number in London in mid–century he estimated at about eighty thousand), bawds, thieves, pickpockets, shoplifters, horse and dog stealers, highway robbers, housebreakers, mudlarks, sweeping boys, forgers, embezzlers, swindlers and an enormous variety of beggars and cheats, often with detailed accounts of how they came to be in the state in which he found them, shows how relatively delicately Dickens walked in *Oliver Twist*.

Underneath the Arches *by Doré, a first-hand view of "the London sewerage and scavengery"*.

Dickens's interest in prisons began with his father's incarceration in the Marshalsea, which he was later to make the home of William Dorrit. He knew also the other prisons in Southwark, Horsemonger Lane Gaol and the King's Bench, where Micawber was taken. He knew, too, the Fleet Prison, where Mr. Pickwick was confined. And most of all he knew and was fascinated by Newgate. "We shall never forget the mingled feelings of awe and respect with which we used to gaze on the exterior of Newgate in our schoolboy days," Dickens begins his two chapters on Newgate in *Sketches by Boz*. He used Newgate scenes in *Barnaby Rudge* and *A Tale of Two Cities*, put Fagin in the condemned cell there in *Oliver Twist*, and described Pip's horror at it in *Great Expectations*. There were still public executions in Dickens's day, outside Newgate and elsewhere, and Dickens himself witnessed two, in order to strengthen his hand in campaigning for their abolition, which finally happened in 1868.

Dickens's London was changing and various, as is its reflection in his novels. Dickens's views on London changed, too. Humphrey House symbolized the vast difference between the London of *Pickwick Papers* and the London of *Our Mutual Friend* by observing that "in *Pickwick* a bad smell was a bad smell; in *Our Mutual Friend* it is a problem". Yet even in those grimmer later novels where Dickens is concerned with apparently insoluble problems of human greed in metropolitan society there are still indications of the delight that, in spite of everything, he continued to take in the colour and multifariousness of London life.

VIRGINIA WOOLF'S
LONDON

VIRGINIA WOOLF ONCE wrote, but did not post, a letter to *The New Statesman* in which she proudly asserted that she was a highbrow and lived in Bloomsbury. "I ask nothing better than that all reviewers, for ever, and everywhere, should call me a highbrow," she concluded. "If they like to add Bloomsbury, W.C.1., that is the correct postal address, and my telephone number is in the Directory. But if your reviewer, or any other reviewer, dares hint that I live in South Kensington, I will sue him for libel." She was, of course, responding to what she called in her diary on March 16, 1935, "the bloomsbury baiters". If the Bloomsbury group were attacked as a group of highbrows living in Bloomsbury, she turned the attack back on the attackers: as far as she was concerned, she was proud to be a highbrow and respected lowbrows: but she detested middlebrows, "who do not live in Bloomsbury which is on high ground; nor in Chelsea, which is on low ground, they live perhaps in South Kensington, which is betwixt and between".

It is an odd cultural topography of London. Kensington boasted its great museums, the Imperial College of Science, one of London's principal concert halls, a notable public library, and other evidence of high culture. The original Kensington Manor can be traced back to the time of Edward the Confessor. William III took up his residence there and made it a brilliant place of resort. In Kensington Palace died William III and his consort Mary, Queen Anne and George II, and Queen Victoria was born there in 1819. Distinguished writers, from Addison to Thackeray, had lived there. Perhaps by specifying *South* Kensington Virginia Woolf wanted to differentiate the area around Brompton Road from those parts of Kensington to the north which had most of the cultural monuments and the historical association. But on the other hand, one of her charges against South Kensington was that it was both middlebrow and *rich*. She describes herself as "one who will stay in Bloomsbury until the Duke of Bedford, rightly concerned for the respectability of his squares, raises the rent so high that Bloomsbury is safe for middlebrows to live in. Then she will leave." Now South Kensington was not the richer part of Kensington: the rich houses were to the north and west. One is driven to conclude that Virginia Woolf resented the richness of North and West Kensington and the vulgarity of South Kensington and by putting "South" and "Kensington" together symbolically located the richness and the vulgarity in the same place. Or is it simply that she was born in Kensington, in Hyde Park Gate, and by specifying South Kensington she acquitted herself of impiety?

Virginia Woolf had a keen sense of the social and cultural atmosphere of different parts of London, though it was not always accurate and sometimes she invested a district with an atmosphere she needed at that point in her fiction rather than one which was sociologically precise. About Bloomsbury she had no doubts: as long as the Duke of Bedford kept the rents reasonably low, it was a highbrow district and therefore appropriate for her and her friends. We know that on the death of Leslie Stephen in 1904 his daughters Virginia and Vanessa and his sons Thoby and Adrian moved to 46 Gordon Square, Bloomsbury. When Vanessa married Clive Bell in 1907 they took over the Gordon Square house and Virginia and Adrian moved to 29 Fitzroy Square (Thoby had died in 1906). It is now a commonplace of twentieth-century English literary history that these two houses were the centres where the group met and conducted their now legendary conversations over whisky, buns and cocoa. At various other times various other members of the group lived nearby. Virginia lived at 38 Brunswick Square intermittently from November 1911 to October 1912 (by which time she was married to Leonard). For many years from 1915 the Woolfs lived at Hogarth House, Richmond, which housed the Hogarth Press founded in 1917. From 1924 until 1939 they lived at 52 Tavistock Square (the house was destroyed by bombing in October 1940). The press was moved to 37 Mecklenburgh Square in August 1939, and this became the Woolfs' London home, though they now spent most of their time in their house in Rodmell, Sussex. The Mecklenburgh Square house was severely damaged in an air raid in September 1940.

If the Bloomsbury Group was largely a matter of personal relationships rather than of precisely shared literary and artistic aims, the London that is specially associated with the group was also the product of personal relationships commemorated in the names of many of its squares and streets. In 1756 the second Duke of Grafton laid out the "new road from Paddington to Islington", long called simply the New Road (now the Marylebone and Euston Roads) to facilitate the movement of cattle to Smithfield market from the country. (You can see it plainly marked "New Road" in Collins's 1854 *Atlas of London*, the pioneering London street guide recently republished by Leicester University Press.) The Duke of Grafton's grandfather was Henry Fitzroy, illegitimate son of Charles II, and the Duke's father married the daughter of Lord Arlington (member of Charles II's "Cabal" ministry) who left her a country estate at Euston in Suffolk and the old manor of Tottenham Court, whose land extended from what is now Tottenham Court Road to Highgate. Much of Tottenham Court was demolished when the New Road was built, but what remained passed eventually to the second Duke's grandson, the first Baron Southampton, who developed the area around Fitzroy Square at the very end of the eighteenth century. The second Baron Southampton continued building northwards and by the 1840s was covering fields in Chalk Farm, north of Regent's Park. All this development of the Fitzroy estate went on parallel

"Kensington was a good address; Bloomsbury was not . . ." A view of the east side of Bedford Square in 1851, before the days when Virginia Woolf made it fashionably unfashionable to live in the area.

with the development of the adjacent Bedford estate, which had originated in land granted by Henry VIII to John Russell, later Earl of Bedford. The fourth Earl of Bedford developed Covent Garden in the first half of the seventeenth century; his grandson Lord William Russell married the daughter of the fourth Earl of Southampton who had inherited from her father the Manor of Bloomsbury with extensive lands between what is now (from west to east) Tottenham Court Road and Southampton Row and (from south to north) High Holborn and Euston Road. It was the Russells who developed Bloomsbury as a residential area in building on their land from the late seventeenth century until the middle of the nineteenth century. Bloomsbury Square was laid out as early as 1661. Bedford Square was laid out by the fourth Duke of Bedford in 1776. The Duke proceeded to pull down the old Russell mansion of Bedford House and develop northwards: Russell Square, Tavistock Square, Woburn Square, Gordon Square, were all built in the late eighteenth century and by the 1830s the Bedford estates were fully built over.

Just south of this area, more specifically between St. Giles High Street and Cambridge Circus, on land that had originally belonged to the medieval leper hospital of St. Giles, some of the worst slums of London grew up in the eighteenth century, but these were largely cleared, and the way from Bloomsbury to Holborn (described in Virginia Woolf's essay "Street Haunting") opened up, by the great nineteenth-century road developments—New Oxford Street (1845–7), Shaftesbury Avenue (1885–6),

London
Early 20th century

Charing Cross Road (1880s) and Kingsway (1901–5). Kingsway, linking Holborn and the Strand—a way also trodden in "Street Haunting"—and in the process clearing some terrible slums, was formally opened by King Edward VII in 1905, thus symbolizing the stabilization of Edwardian London in the very year when, a few streets to the northwest, Thoby Stephen started those Thursday evening conversation parties which were to provide the social basis for the Bloomsbury Group. But in spite of the clearing of the slums to the south, and in spite of the presence in the neighbourhood of such academic institutions as University College (in Gower Street) and Bedford College (in Bedford Square) and of the British Museum in Great Russell Street—or perhaps in some degree because of these—Bloomsbury was not considered a fashionable district, and even its respectability was called in question by some. Quentin Bell tells us that when the Stephen children planned their move to Gordon Square "their friends and relations [were] astonished and a little shocked. Kensington was a good address; Bloomsbury was not", and when Virginia and Adrian moved to Fitzroy Square, Virginia wrote to a friend: "Beatrice comes round, inarticulate with meaning, and begs me not to take the house because of the neighbourhood." She sought the advice of the police, who apparently reassured her.

Bloomsbury itself was still essentially Georgian. Though enormous changes had taken place in London between the last decade of Dickens's life and the first decade of the twentieth century, few of them were visible from where Virginia Stephen lived with her sister and brothers. They were not affected by the fact that the City had seen a residential exodus in the 1860s which reduced its population from 113,000 in 1861 to 76,000 in 1871. As Sir John Summerson has put it in his account of London building in the 1860s: "The old Stuart and Queen Anne mansions, long since deserted by their masters and made over to the managing clerks, were giving way to strictly business buildings, offices or warehouses. The breed of masters had gone to Bayswater or Kensington or perhaps to Hornsey or Clapham; now the breed of clerks was going to Camberwell or Peckham, Stoke Newington or Highbury."

In 1910 Roger Fry organized the first Post-Impressionist Exhibition at the Grafton Galleries. Fry was a member of the Bloomsbury Group, and the Group was deeply involved in the exhibition, which raised a howl of protest from conservative gallery visitors. The incident is central in the history of Bloomsbury—for it was in the years before Virginia Woolf produced her novels that the real germinating effect of Bloomsbury occurred—and it is therefore of interest to see how in this very year a distinguished social geographer described London's social topography. I quote from O. J. R. Howarth's account of London in the eleventh edition of the *Encyclopedia Britannica*:

In London north of the Thames, the salient distinction lies between West and East. From the western boundary of the City proper, an area covering the greater part of the city of Westminster, and extending into Chelsea, Kensington, Paddington and Marylebone, is exclusively associated with the higher-class life of London. Within the bounds of Westminster are the royal palaces, the government offices and many of the finest public buildings, and the wider area specified includes the majority of the residences of the wealthier classes, the most beautiful parks and the most fashionable places of recreation. "Mayfair", north of Piccadilly, and "Belgravia", south of Knightsbridge, are common though unofficial names for the richest residential districts. The "City" bears in all the great commercial buildings fringing its narrow streets all the marks of a centre of the world's exchanges. East of it there is an abrupt transition to a district commonly known as the "East End" as distinguished from the wealthy "West End", a district of mean streets, roughly coincident with the boroughs of Stepney and Poplar, Shoreditch and Bethnal Green, and primarily (though by no means exclusively) associated with the problems attaching to the life of the poor. On the Thames below London Bridge, London appears in the aspect of one of the world's great ports, with extensive docks and crowded shipping. North London is as a whole residential: Hackney, Islington and St. Pancras consist mainly of dwellings of artisans and the middle classes, while in Hampstead, St. Marylebone and Paddington are many terraces and squares of handsome houses. Throughout the better residential quarters of London the number of large blocks of flats has greatly increased in modern times. But even in the midst of the richest quarters, in Westminster and elsewhere, small but well-defined areas of the poorest dwellings occur.

The population of Greater London in 1901 was 6,581,402, compared to 4,766,661 in 1881 (the year before Virginia Woolf's birth) and 1,114,644 in 1801. But in 1801 the population of the City was 128,129, while by 1901, after a steady decrease throughout the nineteenth century, it had fallen to 26,923. Before the end of the nineteenth century London had already become a great railway centre, with thirteen terminal railway stations. An underground system had started in 1863, but it was the introduction of electric traction in the opening years of the twentieth century that enabled the "tube" to increase rapidly in extension and popularity especially between 1906 and 1910. The electrification of the suburban surface lines had to wait until after the First World War. Horse omnibuses had appeared on London streets as early as 1829 (between the Bank and Paddington), but from 1905 motor buses began to supplant them. Similarly, motor taxicabs began to replace horse cabs and by 1910 had overtaken the combined number of hansoms and four-wheelers. By the time we get to Mrs. Dalloway (1923), motor buses, taxis and motorcars had long been established features of the London scene, and figure prominently in the novel.

The Bayswater Omnibus *by G. W. Joy (1895), a familiar London scene harking back to the horse-bus days of Virginia Woolf's girlhood. Some thirty years later she would write in her diary, "One of these days I will write about London, and how it takes up the private life and carries it on, without any effort."*

There was poverty in Virginia Woolf's London, if not so horrifyingly squalid as in Dickens's time; the gap between rich and poor was enormous, and was visible on the streets. In her novels she recognizes the existence of poverty and gives us glimpses of it every now and again to support the structure of mood and feeling she is building up, but she does not explore it (as Gissing had done, for example, in *The Nether World*). The "battered old woman" singing outside Regent's Park tube station or the sentence "The mothers of Pimlico gave suck to their young" are offered in *Mrs. Dalloway* as fleeting symbolic pictures. In *The Years* more than in any other novel Virginia Woolf tries to build an awareness of poverty, especially of shabby-genteel poverty, into the structure of the work:

The shabby street on the south side of the river was very noisy. Now and again a voice detached itself from the general clamour. A woman shouted to her neighbour; a child cried. A man trundling a barrow opened his mouth and bawled up at the windows as he passed. There were bedsteads, grates, pokers and odd pieces of twisted iron on his barrow. But whether he was selling old iron or buying old iron it was impossible to say; the rhythm persisted; but the words were almost rubbed out.

This is from the section set in 1910. The shabby street on the south side of the river is called Hyams Place. There is, and was, no street of that name in London, south or north of the Thames. Its noise and its clamour are there to evoke a sense of poverty, and the rubbed out words of the man buying or selling old iron suggest the meaningless of repetitive street cries rather than the problems of those who utter them. It is the same with Virginia Woolf's use of the music of London streets, which she always found evocative and haunting. Indeed, she wrote an essay on "London Street Music" in 1905. Barrel organs she found particularly affecting. "It was January and dismal, but Mrs. Wagg stood on her doorstep, as if expecting something to happen. A barrel organ played like an obscene nightingale beneath wet leaves. Children ran across the road. Here and there one could see brown panelling inside the hall door." This is from *Jacob's Room* and the scene is Lamb's Conduit Street at the eastern edge of Bloomsbury. The barrel organ does not always suggest dreariness. Later in the same novel we find: "Bonamy sat with Clara in the sunny front room with the barrel organ piping sweetly outside; the water-cart going slowly along spraying the pavement; the carriages jingling, and all the silver and chintz, brown and blue rugs and cases filled with green boughs, striped with trembling yellow bars." The scene now is a "square behind Sloane Street where, on hot spring days, there are striped blinds over the front windows". The time is shortly before the outbreak of the First World War. Later we hear of a procession blocking traffic in Long Acre while "two barrel-organs played by the kerb". The most evocative of all Virginia Woolf's London barrel organs is the last of them, in the final, "present day" (1930s) section of *The Years*, when North Pargiter is visiting his Aunt Sara, in her shabby lodgings in Milton Street, "a dusky street, with old houses"—indeed, situated in one of the oldest parts of London, Cripplegate. Here the sense of dirt and shabbiness and genteel poverty is very strong:

He strolled to the window. The sun must be setting, for the brick of the house at the corner blushed a yellowish pink. One or two high windows were burnished gold. The girl was in the room, and she distracted him. Against the dull background of traffic noises, of wheels turning and brakes squealing, there rose near at hand the cry of a woman suddenly alarmed for her child; the monotonous cry of a man selling vegetables; and far away a barrel-organ was playing. It stopped; it began again . . .

The distant barrel organ here has the same function as the mandoline in Eliot's *The Waste Land*:

> O City city, I can sometimes hear
> Beside a public bar in Lower Thames Street,
> The pleasant whining of a mandoline . . .

The echo of Eliot must be deliberate, because a much stronger echo is found later in the same episode when Sara talks of her disillusion with the genteel life in this " 'polluted city, unbelieving city, city of dead fish and worn-out frying-pans'—thinking of a river's bank, when the tide's out, she explained".

The Milton Street scene in *The Years* represents the most sustained attempt in Virginia Woolf's novels to render the feeling of poverty, though it is not acute poverty. Even more than *The Waste Land* we can see, unusually for this writer, Dickens lying behind some of the description. I don't think it is coincidental that when North is approaching Milton Street he exclaims: "Where the dickens am I now?" Virginia Woolf continues:

Somebody had chalked a circle on the wall with a jagged line in it. He looked down the long vista. Door after door, window after window, repeated the same pattern. Everything was filled with a warm yellow haze. Barrows of fruit and flowers were drawn up at the curb.

He turns into Milton Street:

"What a dirty," he said, as he sat still in the car for a moment – here a woman crossed the street with a jug under her arms – "sordid," he added, "low-down street to live in." . . . He pressed the bell two or three times sharply. But no one answered. Then he gave the door a push; it was open. There was a curious smell in the hall; of vegetables cooking; and the oily brown paper made it dark. He went up the stairs of what had once been a gentleman's residence. The bannisters were carved, but they had been daubed over with some cheap yellow varnish.

This is not a typical Virginia Woolf scene. Far more typical is what she wrote in her diary on May 26, 1926:

London is enchanting. I step out upon a tawny coloured magic carpet, it seems, and get carried into beauty without raising a finger. The nights are amazing, with all the white porticos and broad silent avenues. And people pop in and out, lightly, divertingly like rabbits; and I look down Southampton Row, wet as a seal's back or red and yellow with sunshine, and watch the omnibuses going and coming and hear the old crazy organs. One of these days I will write about London, and how it takes up the private life and carries it on, without any effort.

She did write about London the following year, in the essay entitled "Street Haunting". (It first appeared in the *Yale Review* in 1927, so it could not have been written in 1930, the date Leonard Woolf gave in a note to the essay when it appeared in the posthumous collection *The Death of the Moth*.) She was living at 52 Tavistock Square at the time, and the essay evokes a winter ramble between Bloomsbury and the Embankment.

Though many of the most finely rendered London scenes in her novels are summer scenes, here she describes "rambling the streets of London" as "the greatest pleasure of town life in winter". The topography of the essay is not specific, but in general it takes us from "a London square, set about by offices and houses" (Tavistock Square apparently), down Woburn Place and Southampton Row to Holborn, emerging by "those narrow old houses between Holborn and Soho". At the same time there is a suggestion that she took a different route, down Tottenham Court Road and into Charing Cross Road, for she describes the second-hand bookshops in what must be Charing Cross Road. It is not important. She is going to the Strand to buy a pencil. Once in the Strand she looks down Lancaster Place by Somerset House and sees the river and Waterloo Bridge. (Elizabeth Dalloway had stood and looked here too, after she had had tea with Miss Kilman in the Army and Navy Stores.) She goes down to the river, then returns to the Strand and buys her pencil.

How beautiful a street is in winter! It is at once revealed and obscured. Here vaguely one can trace symmetrical straight avenues of doors and windows; here under the lamps are floating islands of pale light through which pass quickly bright men and women, who, for all their poverty and shabbiness, wear a certain look of unreality, an air of triumph, as if they have given life the slip . . .

How beautiful a London street is then, with its islands of light, and its long groves of darkness, and on one side of it perhaps some tree-sprinkled, grass-grown space where night is folding herself to sleep naturally and, as one passes the iron railing, one hears those little cracklings and stirrings of leaf and twig which seem to suppose the silence of fields all round them, an owl hooting, and far away the rattle of a train in the valley. But this is London, we are reminded; high among the bare trees are hung oblong frames of reddish light—windows; there are points of brilliance burning steadily like low stars—lamps; this empty ground, which holds the country in it and its peace, is only a London square, set about by offices and houses where at this hour fierce lights burn over maps, over documents, over desks where clerks sit turning with wetted forefinger the files of endless correspondences; or more suffusedly the firelight wavers and the lamp-light falls upon the privacy of some drawing-room, its easy chairs, its papers, its china, its inlaid table, and the figure of a woman accurately measuring out the precise number of spoons of tea which—She looks at the door as if she heard a ring downstairs and somebody asking, is she in?

The description moves in spite of itself into an embryo novel.

Peter Walsh in *Mrs. Dalloway*, walking from Bloomsbury to Westminster by a similar route, had noted a similar London scene, only a summer one:

Beauty anyhow. Not the crude beauty of the eye. It was not beauty pure and simple—Bedford Place leading into Russell Square. It was straightforwardness and emptiness of course; the symmetry of a corridor; but it was also windows lit up, a piano, a gramophone sounding; a sense of pleasure-making hidden, but now and again emerging when, through the uncurtained windows, the window left open, one saw parties sitting over tables, young people slowly circling, conversations between men and women, maids idly looking out (a strange comment theirs, when work was done), stockings drying on top ledges, a parrot, a few plants . . .

There are, of course, London scenes in the early novels, but it is not until *Jacob's Room* that we get what seems to me the characteristic flavour of Virginia Woolf on London:

At Mudie's corner in Oxford Street all the red and blue beads had run together on the string. The motor omnibuses were locked. Mr. Spalding going to the city looked at Mrs. Charles Budgeon bound for Shepherd's Bush. The proximity of the omnibuses gave the outside passengers an opportunity to stare into each other's faces. Yet few took advantage of it. . . . The omnibuses jerked on, and every single person felt relief at being a little nearer to his journey's end, though some cajoled themselves past the immediate engagement by promise of indulgence beyond—steak and kidney pudding, drink, or a game of dominoes in the smoky corner of a city restaurant. Oh yes, human life is very tolerable on the top of an omnibus in Holborn, when the policeman holds up his arms and the sun beats on your back, and if there is such a thing as a shell secreted by man to fit himself here we find it, on the banks of the Thames, where the great streets join and St. Paul's Cathedral, like the volute on the top of the snail shell, finishes it off.

Jacob watches the multitude from the steps of St. Paul's. "The streets belong to them; the shops; the churches; theirs the innumerable desks; the stretched office lights; the vans are theirs, and the railway slung high above the street." He passes an old blind woman singing in the street, as the Septimus Warren Smiths pass the singing old woman in *Mrs. Dalloway*. As the seasons change, London changes:

The lamps of London uphold the dark as upon the points of burning bayonets. The yellow canopy sinks and swells over the great four-poster. Passengers in the mail-coaches running into London in the eighteenth century looked through leafless branches and saw it flaring beneath them. The light burns behind yellow blinds and pink blinds, and above fanlights, and down in basement windows. The street market in Soho is fierce with light. Raw meat, china mugs, and silk stockings blaze in it. Raw voices wrap themselves round the flaring gas-jets . . .

Later, Jacob stands beneath the porch of the British Museum. "It was raining. Great Russell Street was glazed and shining—here yellow, here, outside the chemist's, red and pale blue. People scuttled close to the wall; carriages rattled down helter-skelter down the streets." We get a brief glimpse of "the woman in the mews behind Great Ormond Street who has come home drunk and cries all night long, 'Let me in! Let me in!' "—not for its own sake but as a counterpart to Jacob's steady reading of Plato. We move continually between Bloomsbury, Holborn and the Strand, with glances towards Piccadilly and Oxford Street and Trafalgar Square and Whitehall and south towards the river. The main direction of walking (as in "Street Haunting") is from Bloomsbury to Holborn, cleared by the great late-nineteenth-century road developments. "Jacob turned away. Two minutes later he opened the front door, and walked off in the direction of Holborn."

Towards the end of the book there is a scene, in the summer of 1914, which is a pre-war version, as it were, of a parallel scene in *Mrs. Dalloway* set in 1923. Here it is:

The omnibus stopped outside Charing Cross; and behind it were clogged omnibuses, vans, motor cars, for a procession with banners was passing down Whitehall, and elderly people were stiffly descending from between the paws of the slippery lions, . . .

The traffic stopped, and the sun, no longer sprayed out by the breeze, became almost too hot. But the procession passed; the banners glittered far away down Whitehall; the traffic was released; lurched on; spun to a smooth continuous uproar; swerving round the curve of Cockspur Street; and sweeping past Government offices and equestrian statues down Whitehall to the prickly spires, the tethered grey fleet of masonry, and the large white clock of Westminster.

Five clocks Big Ben intoned; Nelson received the salute. The wires of the Admiralty shivered with some far-away communication. A voice kept remarking that Prime Ministers and Viceroys spoke in the Reichstag; entered Lahore; said that the Emperor travelled; in Milan they rioted; said there were rumours in Vienna; said that the Ambassador at Constantinople had audience with the Sultan; the fleet was at Gibraltar . . .

And here is the parallel passage in *Mrs. Dalloway*:

Gliding across Piccadilly, the car turned down St. James's Street. Tall men, men of robust physique, well-dressed men with their tail-coats and their white slips and their hair raked back who, for reasons difficult to demonstrate, were standing in the bow window of Brooks's with their hands behind the tails of their coats, looking out, perceived instinctively that greatness was passing, and the pale light of the immortal presence fell upon them as it had fallen upon Clarissa Dalloway. At once they stood even straighter and removed their hands, and seemed ready to attend their Sovereign, if need be, to the cannon's mouth, as their ancestors had done before them. The white busts and the little tables in the background covered with copies of the *Tatler* and syphons of soda water seemed to approve; seemed to indicate the flowing corn and the manor house of England; and to return the frail hum of the motor wheels as the walls of a whispering gallery return a single voice expanded and made sonorous by the might of a whole cathedral. Shawled Moll Pratt with her flowers on the pavement wished the dear boy well (it was the Prince of Wales for certain) and would have tossed the price of a pot of beer—a bunch of roses—into St. James's Street out of sheer light heartedness and contempt of poverty had she not seen the constable's eye upon her, discouraging an old Irishwoman's loyalty. The sentries at St. James's saluted; Queen Alexandra's policeman approved.

A small crowd meanwhile had gathered at the gates of Buckingham Palace. Listlessly, yet confidently, poor people all of them, they waited; looked at the Palace itself with the flag flying; at Victoria, billowing on her mound, admired her shelves of running water, her geraniums; singled out from the motor cars in the Mall first this one, then that, bestowed emotion, vainly, upon commoners out for a drive; recalled their tribute to keep it unspent while this car passed and that; and all the time let rumour accumulate in their veins and thrill the nerves in their thighs at the thought of Royalty looking at them; the Queen bowing; the Prince saluting; at the thought of the heavenly life divinely bestowed upon Kings; of the equerries and deep curtsies; of the Queen's old doll's house; of Princess Mary married to an Englishman, and the Prince—ah! the Prince! who took wonderfully, they said, after old King Edward, but was ever so much slimmer. The Prince lived at St. James's; but he might come along in the morning to visit his mother.

The sense of rumour and royalty and government and history and populace all mixed up with the traffic and intermingling in the London air to create a part of its characteristic atmosphere is to be found in both these passages and represents a half-ironic, half genuinely felt attitude on the writer's part.

A Walking Tour with Mrs. Dalloway

DOROTHY BREWSTER has claimed *The Years* as the London novel, but though it is set in London throughout and has many descriptions of London scenes from 1880 to the 1930s it does not seem to me that the actual quality of the novel is significantly affected by its being set in London or that the descriptions of London (sometimes, as I have noted, of imaginary streets) reflect Virginia Woolf's deepest feelings about the city. For me *Mrs. Dalloway* is Virginia Woolf's London novel. Not only does it reveal her attitudes to London more continuously and sensitively than any other of her novels, but it is also a topographical London novel, in the same way (though on a smaller scale) as Joyce's *Ulysses* is a topographical Dublin novel. Every scene is specifically located in London and the main characters move about in London in a manner that is both precisely indicated and important to the novel's structure and meaning.

Mrs. Dalloway's London is not Bloomsbury. It stretches from Westminster, south of Victoria Street and near the Abbey, across St. James's Park northwards to Piccadilly and thence northwards up Bond Street to Brook Street: largely St. James's and Mayfair. But Bloomsbury is not ignored in the novel. Septimus and Rezia Warren Smith live there in lodgings (" 'These old Bloomsbury houses,' said Dr. Holmes, tapping the wall, 'are often full of very fine panelling, which the landlords have the folly to paper over' "), which are the scene of Septimus's suicide; and since near the end of the novel when Mrs. Dalloway hears of Septimus's death she feels a kind of identity with him, there is some sort of symbolic association between Westminster and Bloomsbury.

Mrs. Dalloway opens with Mrs. Dalloway leaving her house on a June morning in 1923 to buy flowers for the party she is giving that evening. We are not told exactly where her house is, but further on in the novel we follow Mr. Dalloway returning home from his lunch with Lady Bruton and learn that he enters Dean's Yard and approaches his door. (At the same time, inside the house, the sound of Big Ben is flooding Mrs. Dalloway's drawing room.) Dean's Yard is at the southwest corner of Westminster Abbey, so the Dalloways must live in its immediate neighbourhood. Mr. Dalloway is a Member of Parliament. At ten o'clock Mrs. Dalloway is waiting to cross Victoria Street (from the south side). We next see her entering St. James's Park, where she meets Hugh Whitbread, "coming along with his back against the Government buildings". (This suggests that she did not cross the centre of the park, going over the lake by the bridge, but went along the eastern end, parallel to Horse Guards Road. This is rather a long way round, since she is making for Piccadilly and Bond Street.) "Messages were passing from the Fleet to the Admiralty. Arlington Street and Piccadilly seemed to chafe the very air of the Park. . . ." She reaches the park gates, and stands a moment "looking at the omnibuses in Piccadilly". She walks eastward along Piccadilly towards Bond Street. (The park must be Green Park if she can see the omnibuses in Piccadilly.) She looks at Hatchard's shop window on the south side of Piccadilly beyond where Bond Street comes in on the north side, then turns back towards Bond Street, crosses, and walks up Bond Street to the flower shop. While she is in the flower shop, a car backfires outside, and "rumours were at once in circulation from the middle of Bond Street to Oxford Street". (At this point we catch a brief glimpse of Septimus and Rezia Warren Smith, who are also in Bond Street.) The car drives on towards Piccadilly and Mrs. Dalloway comes out of the flower shop with the flowers. We go back and follow the car, which turns down St. James's Street on its way to Buckingham Palace.

I have already quoted the passage describing how well-dressed men look down from the window of Brooks's (the old-established club in St. James's Street) as the royal car passes. Meanwhile, a crowd has gathered at Buckingham Palace: it includes Sarah Bletchley who lives in Pimlico (the area of London south of Belgravia, between Victoria Station and the river), which is used more than once in the novel as symbolic of working-class London, although the East End would have been more appropriate for this. An aeroplane overhead is heard by "all people in the Mall, in Green Park, in Piccadilly, in Regent Street, in Regent's Park"; it is seen by the Warren Smiths, who are now sitting in Regent's Park (they must have gone pretty smartly up New Bond Street and Harley Street). Maisie Johnson, up from Edinburgh two days before to take up a post at her uncle's in Leadenhall Street, is walking through the park and asks the Warren Smiths the way to Regent's Park tube station. Mrs. Dempster, "who saved crusts for the squirrels and often ate her lunch in Regent's Park", observes the Warren Smiths; she lives in Kentish Town, which is north of Regent's Park (the Warren Smiths, on the other hand, had approached the park from the south). Mrs. Dempster looks up at the aeroplane, which is simultaneously seen by Mr. Bentley as he rolls his strip of turf at Greenwich. The plane flies over Ludgate Circus, which is between Fleet Street and Ludgate Hill in the heart of the City, "while a seedy-looking nondescript man carrying a leather bag stood on the steps of St. Paul's Cathedral". People are still looking up at the plane when Mrs. Dalloway arrives home.

Relaxing at home, Mrs. Dalloway thinks of her dressmaker who has retired and lives in Ealing, an outer suburb of London. Peter Walsh visits Mrs. Dalloway, and we follow him after he leaves. We see him in Victoria Street as Big Ben strikes eleven-thirty. A group of uniformed boys march past him up Whitehall. He reaches Trafalgar Square, and follows an attractive young woman along Cockspur Street, up Haymarket, "on and on . . . across Piccadilly, and up Regent Street". He watches her cross Oxford Street and Great Portland Street to turn down "one of the little streets" where she enters a door and disappears. Peter Walsh now wonders where he should sit until it is time for his appointment with his solicitor in Lincon's Inn. He decides on Regent's Park.

We now turn to the Warren Smiths, who are still in Regent's Park. It is a quarter to twelve. Peter Walsh observes them in their distress and imagines that they are quarrelling: in fact, the mentally disturbed Septimus is being taken by his wife to see Sir William Bradshaw, a Harley Street specialist. Peter Walsh comes out of Regent's Park and hears an old woman singing opposite Regent's Park tube station. He then takes a taxi to his solicitor's office. The Warren Smiths also hear the woman singing, and Rezia pities her. We then see them in Portland Place. In a flashback we learn that Septimus as a young unmarried man before the war had lived "in a room off the Euston Road" and that he had attended Miss Isobel Pole's lectures on Shakespeare in the Waterloo Road (which is on the south side of the river).

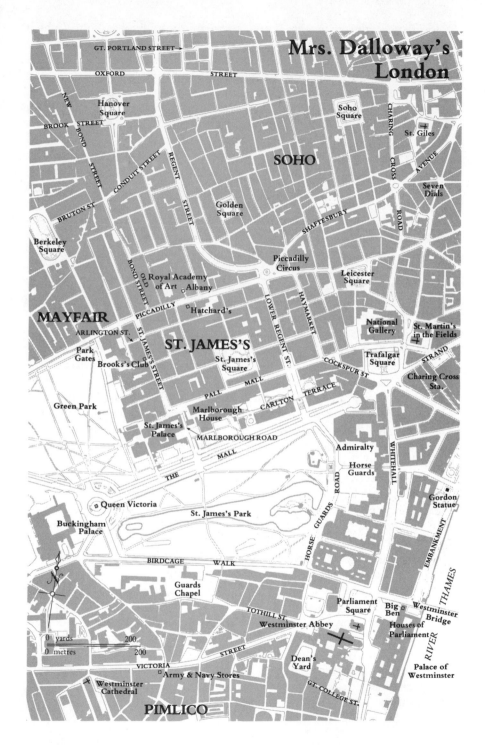

Mrs. Dalloway's London

GT. PORTLAND STREET →

OXFORD STREET

Hanover Square

Soho Square

NEW

BROOK STREET

BOND STREET

CHARING

St. Giles

CONDUIT STREET

REGENT STREET

SOHO

CROSS

AVENUE

Seven Dials

BRUTON ST.

Golden Square

SHAFTESBURY

ROAD

Berkeley Square

BOND STREET

Piccadilly Circus

Leicester Square

OLD

Royal Academy of Art

Albany

National Gallery

St. Martin's in the Fields

MAYFAIR

PICCADILLY

Hatchard's

HAYMARKET

LOWER REGENT ST.

ARLINGTON ST.

ST. JAMES'S

Park Gates

ST. JAMES'S STREET

Brooks's Club

St. James's Square

MALL

Trafalgar Square

STRAND

COCKSPUR ST.

Charing Cross Sta.

PALL

CARLTON TERRACE

Green Park

Marlborough House

St. James's Palace

MARLBOROUGH ROAD

MALL

Admiralty

WHITEHALL

Horse Guards

Queen Victoria

THE

St. James's Park

HORSE GUARDS ROAD

Gordon Statue

Buckingham Palace

EMBANKMENT

BIRDCAGE WALK

Guards Chapel

THAMES

Parliament Square

Big Ben

Westminster Bridge

TOTHILL ST.

Westminster Abbey

Houses of Parliament

RIVER

0 yards 200

0 metres 200

VICTORIA STREET

Army & Navy Stores

Dean's Yard

Palace of Westminster

Westminster Cathedral

GT. COLLEGE ST.

PIMLICO

We learn that his Italian wife Rezia has an aunt who lives in Soho (which had been known as a foreign quarter of London since the late seventeenth century), and that soon after their marriage five years earlier they had taken "admirable lodgings off the Tottenham Court Road".

We return to the present: it is twelve o'clock and the Warren Smiths are walking down Harley Street. Their appointment with Sir William Bradshaw is for twelve. After the unsatisfactory discussion with Sir William we see them walking down Harley Street again before we move to Hugh Whitbread in Oxford Street observing from the clock suspended above Messrs. Rigby and Lowndes that it is one-thirty. He is on his way to lunch with Lady Bruton in Brook Street, in Mayfair. (There is a Bruton Street quite near Brook Street: did Virginia Woolf think of Lady Bruton's name and then, perhaps subconsciously, give her an address not far from Bruton Street, or did she first think of Brook Street as a fashionable Mayfair address for Lady Bruton and then call her Lady Bruton from nearby Bruton Street?) Mr. Dalloway is also at Lady Bruton's for lunch. After lunch the two men walk to Conduit Street together; Conduit Street is, interestingly enough, a continuation of Bruton Street on the eastern side of New Bond Street. Mr. Dalloway walks across Green Park and enters Dean's Yard as Big Ben begins to strike three. In a minute he is at home.

At three-thirty Mrs. Dalloway's daughter Elizabeth and the governess Miss Kilman are walking to the Army and Navy Stores in Victoria Street. After they have had tea there, Elizabeth goes off on her own. Miss Kilman leaves the Army and Navy Stores, notices the tower of Westminster Cathedral (the nineteenth-century Roman Catholic cathedral in Ashley Place, behind Victoria Street) rising in front of her, and walks to Westminster Abbey, where she seeks religious comfort. Elizabeth takes a bus from Victoria Street, up Whitehall, along the Strand, and gets off at Chancery Lane. She walks east along Fleet Street and turns right along Middle Temple Lane: we see her "in the Temple" (the old Inns of Court, the Inner Temple and the Middle Temple) where she thinks "of ships, of business, of law, of administration", aware of the river nearby and of the thirteenth-century Temple Church (which survived the Great Fire of 1666 as one of the finest specimens of early Gothic architecture in England). She comes back into Fleet Street and walks "just a little way towards St. Paul's," i.e., eastward along Fleet Street towards Ludgate Hill. This was unfamiliar territory to a Dalloway: she felt like someone "exploring a strange house by night with a candle, on edge lest the owner should suddenly fling wide his bedroom door and ask her business, nor did she dare wander off into queer alleys, tempting bye-streets, . . . For no Dalloway came down the Strand daily; she was a prisoner, a stray, venturing, trusting". She turns back towards the Strand where she takes a bus back to Westminster.

The scene now changes to the Warren Smiths, at home in Bloomsbury.

The Strand in 1923, busy and bustling, exactly as Clarissa Dalloway might have found it.

Dr. Holmes comes to take Septimus away to an institution, and Septimus flings himself out of the window to his death. Peter Walsh sees the ambulance, summoned by Dr. Holmes, and hears its bell as it turns "down the next street" and crosses Tottenham Court Road. He speculates about the ambulance, and about life and death, as he passes "the pillar-box opposite the British Museum". He recalls going on a bus once with Mrs. Dalloway and thinks of what she said to him "sitting on the bus going up Shaftesbury Avenue". He continues to think of her as he reaches his hotel, which is not precisely located but which must be in Bloomsbury. Later we see him walking from his hotel to Mrs. Dalloway's party. He is enchanted by the London scenes he passes through this warm summer evening: I have already quoted his soliloquy at this point. He is walking from Mrs. Woolf's Bloomsbury south towards Mrs. Dalloway's Westminster. "He tripped through London, towards Westminster, observing", and we follow his

"So by Tube to the Temple; and there wandered in the desolate ruins of my old squares . . . all that completeness ravished and demolished." A view of Ludgate Hill during the Blitz.

observations. He comes at last to Clarissa Dalloway's street (is it perhaps Great College Street?). "But it was her street, this, Clarissa's; cabs were rushing round the corner, like water round the piers of a bridge, drawn together, it seemed to him, because they bore people going to her party, Clarissa's party." Sir William and Lady Bradshaw arrive late, explaining that Sir William had been telephoned just as they were starting out, "a very sad case". "A young man . . . had killed himself." Mrs. Dalloway feels she understands why the young man did it; she identifies herself with him against Sir William. As the clock strikes three A.M. she is still thinking about Septimus. The party goes on. Mrs. Dalloway's old friend Sally Seton tells her that she is "staying in Victoria Street, practically next door". We are still in the Dalloway's house in the last stages of the party, when the novel ends.

If one does not follow the topography of the novel one loses a great deal. Virginia Woolf's sense of London helps her to define the characters and her sense of the characters helps her to define London, to a greater degree than in any other of her novels. If we read *Mrs. Dalloway* in the light of all the references to London in the diary and the essays we see how much awareness of London's complex atmosphere has gone into the novel. Of course, Virginia Woolf was also interested in the London of the past—not only the recent past, as shown in the first parts of *The Years*, but also in medieval, Elizabethan and eighteenth-century London. *Orlando* bears witness to this, as do numerous references to London in earlier periods scattered throughout her essays. But the London that really haunted her imagination was her own London, where she was born and grew up and spent so much of her life, the London which, as her diary shows, she rediscovered with excitement every time she came back to it after an absence. Her last rediscovery was, however, a sad one. It was war-ravaged London she described shortly before her death, when she and her husband were briefly in the city from Rodmell:

We were in London on Monday. I went to London Bridge. I looked at the river; very misty; some tufts of smoke, perhaps from burning houses. There was another fire on Saturday. Then I saw a cliff of wall, eaten out, at one corner; a great corner all smashed; a Bank; the Monument erect; tried to get a bus; but such a block I dismounted; and the second bus advised me to walk. A complete jam of traffic; for streets were being blown up. So by Tube to the Temple; and there wandered in the desolate ruins of my old squares; gashed; dismantled; the old red bricks all white powder, something like a builder's yard. Grey dirt and broken windows. Sightseers; all that completeness ravished and demolished.

A sad picture, but it has its own grandeur. She might have painted an even sadder picture if she had lived to see what the developers have done to London.

BATH

IT WAS THE ROMANS who discovered the hot mineral springs at Bath and built there the elaborate bathing establishment of Aquae Sulis, with its great bath and three swimming baths, hot air bath, porticoed court-yards, temple of Sul Minerva (they associated the British goddess Sul with their own Minerva) and famous Gorgon sculpture. Modern excavation has revealed enough to enable us to form a picture of the whole elaborate establishment, which flourished from the first century A.D. until its destruction by the Saxons in the sixth century. The *Anglo-Saxon Chronicle* records that in A.D. 577 the Saxons fought with the Britons and took from them Gloucester, Cirencester and Bath. Medieval legends attributed the original founding of Bath to a British king, Bladud, in the ninth century B.C., and a statue of this mythical monarch was erected in the Pump Room in 1669. But there is no evidence of any pre-Roman exploitation of the hot springs.

In Anglo-Saxon times Bath was known as Akemanceaster and later Hat Bathum. King Edgar was crowned there in 973, as the *Anglo-Saxon Chronicle* records in verse. The city is mentioned in the Domesday Book in 1086. In medieval times it was noted for its great Benedictine monastery with its Abbey Church of St. Peter and St. Paul rebuilt in the fifteenth century as an especially fine example of late Perpendicular Gothic. The establishment of Bath as an episcopal see in the late eleventh century (jointly with Wells from the thirteenth century) meant that from then until the Reformation it was essentially a monastic and episcopal city. It was a royal borough, with charters granted by a succession of medieval kings, which among other things granted the city the right to hold a number of fairs in the summer which were flourishing centres of the cloth trade (we remember Chaucer's Wife of Bath was skilled in weaving cloth).

When John Leland wrote his famous *Itinerary* giving an account of his journeys in England between 1535 and 1543 he had this to say about Bath:

The cite of Bath is sette booth yn a fruteful and pleasant botom, the which is environid on every side with greate hilles, out of which cum many springes of pure water that be conveyid by dyverse ways to serve the cite. Insomuch that leade beyng made ther at hand many houses yn the toune have pipes of leade to convey water from place to place.

There be 4. gates yn the town by the names of est, west, north and south.

The toune waulle within the toune is of no great highth to theyes: but without it is *à fundamentis* of a reasonable highth, and it stondith almost alle. . . .

The visit of Anne of Denmark, James I's queen, to Bath in 1616 to benefit from its healing springs began the re-establishment of the city as a popular watering place, but it was not until Charles II and his Court visited Bath in 1663, in the vain hope of finding in its waters a cure for the sterility of his queen, Catherine of Braganza, that it began its steady rise to the position it achieved in the next century as a unique centre of fashion in the country. Pepys visited Bath in June 1668 and recorded his impressions:

Up at 4 a'clock by appointment called up to the Cross *Bath* [a triangular bath with a cross in the middle, the coolest of the baths, and so most used in summer) where we were carried after one another myself and wife and Betty Turner *Willet* and *WH*. And by and by though we designed to have done before company came much company came very fine ladies and the manner pretty enough only methinks it cannot be clean to go so many bodies together in to the same water. Good conversation among them that are acquainted here and stay together. Strange to see how hot the water is and in some places though this is the most temperate bath the springs so hot as the feet not to endure. But strange to see what women and men herein that live all the season in these waters that cannot but be parboiled and look like the creatures of the Bath. Carried back wrap in a sheet and in a chair home and there one after another thus carried (I staying above two hours in the water) home to bed sweating for an hour and by and by comes music to play to me extraordinary good as I ever heard at London almost anywhere.

Celia Fiennes visited Bath some twenty years later and left the classical account of its facilities in the late seventeenth century:

The ways to the bath are all difficult, the town lyes Low in a bottom and its steep ascents all wayes out of the town. The houses are indifferent, the streetes of a good size well pitched. There are several good houses built for Lodgings that are new and adorned, and good furniture, the baths in my opinion makes the town unpleasant, the aire so low, encompassed with high hills and woods. There is 5 baths the hot bath the most hot springs—its but small and built all round, which makes it the hotter—out of it runns the water into a bath called Le pours.
The third bath is called the Cross bath which is some thing bigger than the former and not so hot; the Cross in the middle has seates round it for the Gentlemen to sitt, and round the walls are Arches with seates for the Ladyes, all stone and the seate is stone and if you think the seate is too Low they raise it with a Coushon as they call it, another Stone, but indeed the water bears you up that the seate seemes as easy as a down Coushon. . . . You Generally sit up to the Neck in water, this Cross bath is much the Coolest and is used mostly in the heate of summer; there are Gallery's round the top that the Company that does not Bathe that day walkes in and lookes over the bath on their acquaintance and company— there are such a number of Guides to each bath of women to waite on the ladyes, and of men to waite on the Gentlemen, and they keepe their due distance. There

"Methinks it cannot be clean to go so many bodies together in to the same water," wrote Pepys. *Neither clean nor comfortable, if Rowlandson's* Comforts of Bath *is any indication!*

is a serjeant belonging to the baths that all the bathing tyme walkes in galleryes and takes notice order is observed and punishes the rude, and most people of fashion send to him when they begin to bathe, then he takes particular Care of them and Complements you every morning which deserves its reward at the end of the Season. . . . At the sides of the Arches are rings that you may hold on by and so walke a little way, but the springs bubble up so fast and so strong and are so hot up against the bottoms of ones feete, Especially in that they Call the Kitching in the bath, which is a great Cross with seates in the middle and many hot-springs riseth there. The Kings bath is very large, as large as the rest put togethr, in it is the hot pumpe that persons are pumpt at for Lameness or on their heads for palsyes. . . . The Ladyes goes into the bath with Garments made of a fine yellow canvas, which is stiff and made large with great sleeves like a parsons gown; the water fills it so that its borne off that your shape is not seen, it does not cling close as other linning, which lookes sadly in the poorer sort that go in their own linning. The Gentlemen have drawers and wastcoates of the same sort of canvas, this is the best lining for the bath water will change any other yellow. When you go out of the bath you go within a doore that leads to Steps which you ascend by degrees that are in the water, then the doore is shut which shutts down into the water a good way, so you are in a private place where you can still ascend several more steps and let your Canvess drop off by degrees into the water, which your women guides take off, and the meane tyme your maides flings a garment over your head, and the guides take the taile and so pulls it on you Just as you rise the steps, and your other garment drops off so you are wrapped up in the flannell and

*The Pump Room, "crowded like a Welsh fair" where "you see the highest
quality, and the lowest tradesfolk, jostling each other without ceremony".
Engraving by Rowlandson.*

your nightgown on the top, and your slippers and so you are set in Chaire which
is brought into the roome which are called slips, and there are Chimney's in them,
you may have fires. . . . The Chaires you go in are a low seat and with frames
round and over your head and all cover'd inside and out with red bayes and a
Curtaine drawn before of the same which makes it Close and warme; then a
Couple of men with staves takes and Carryes you to your lodging and sets you
at your bedside where you go to bed and lye and sweate some tyme as you please.
. . . The places for divertion about the bath is either the walkes in that they call
the Kings Mead which is a pleasant green meaddow, where are walkes round
and Cross it, no place for Coaches, and indeed there is little use of a Coach only to
bring and Carry the Company from the bath for the wayes are not proper for
Coaches.

Queen Anne visited Bath in 1702 and returned the following summer;
crowds of fashionable visitors swarmed into the city in her wake. It was now
that Richard Nash ("Beau Nash") began his career as the social dictator
of Bath. Oliver Goldsmith in his *Life of Richard Nash* (1762) gives a fascinating account of Bath in the years of Nash's reign, which covered the first
four decades of the eighteenth century although he stayed on with declining
influence until his death in comparative poverty at the age of eighty-seven
in 1761.

Goldsmith compared the state of Bath under the Master of Ceremonies
before Nash, one Captain Webster, with what it became under Nash:

Still however, the amusements of this place were neither elegant, nor conducted with delicacy. General society among people of rank or fortune was by no means established. The nobility still preserved a tincture of *Gothic* haughtiness, and refused to keep company with the gentry at any of the public entertainments of the place. Smoking in the rooms was permitted, gentlemen and ladies appeared in a disrespectful manner at public entertainments in aprons and boots. With an eagerness common to those whose pleasures come but seldom, they generally continued them too long, and thus they were rendered disgusting by too free an enjoyment. If the company liked each other they danced till morning, if any person lost at cards, he insisted on continuing the game till luck should turn. The lodgings for visitants were paltry, though expensive, the dining rooms and other chambers were floored with boards coloured brown with soot and small beer, to hide the dirt; the walls were covered with unpainted wainscot, the furniture corresponded with the meanness of the architecture; a few oak chairs, a small looking glass, with a fender and tongs, composed the magnificence of these temporary habitations. The city was in itself mean and contemptible, no elegant buildings, no open streets, no uniform squares. The Pump-house was without any director; the chairmen permitted no gentlemen or ladies to walk home by night without insulting them; and to add to all this, one of the greatest Physicians of his age conceived a design of ruining the city, by writing against the efficacy of the waters. It was from a resentment of some affronts he had received there, that he took this resolution; and accordingly published a pamphlet, by which he said *he would cast a toad into the spring.*

In this situation of things it was, that Mr. *Nash* first came into that city, and hearing the threat of this Physician, he humourously assured the people that if they would give him leave, he would charm away the poison of the Doctor's toad, as they usually charm the venom of the Tarantula, by music. He therefor was immediately empowered to set up the force of a band of music, against the poison of the Doctor's reptile; the company very sensibly encreased, *Nash* triumphed, and the sovereignty of the city was decreed to him by every rank of people.

We are now to behold this gentleman as arrived at a new dignity for which nature seemed to have formed him; we are to see him directing pleasures, which none had better learned to share; placed over rebellions and refractory subjects that were to be ruled only by the force of his address, and governing such as had been long accustomed to govern others. We see a kingdom beginning with him, and sending off *Tunbridge* as one of its colonies.

Goldsmith gives Nash's "Rules to be observed at Bath":

1. That a visit of ceremony at first coming, and another at going, are all that are expected or desired, by ladies of quality and fashion—except impertinents.
2. That ladies coming to the ball appoint a time for their footmen coming to wait on them home, to prevent disturbance and inconveniences to themselves and others.

3. That gentlemen of fashion never appearing in a morning before ladies in gowns and caps, shew breeding and respect.

4. That no person take it ill that any one goes to another's play, or breakfast, and not theirs:—except captious by nature.

5. That no gentleman give his ticket for the balls to any but gentlewomen.—N.B. Unless he has none of his acquaintance.

6. That gentlemen crowding before the ladies at the ball, shew ill manners; and that none do so for the future,—except such as respect nobody but themselves.

7. That no gentleman or lady takes it ill that another dances before them;—except such as have no pretence to dance at all.

8. That the elder ladies and children be content with a second bench at the ball, as being past or not come to perfection.

9. That the younger ladies take notice how many eyes observe them. N.B. This does not extend to *Have-at-alls*.

10. That all whisperers of lies and scandal be taken for their authors.

11. That all repeaters of such lies, and scandal be shunned by all company;—except such as have been guilty of the same crime.

N.B. Several men of no character, old women and young ones, of question'd reputation, are great authors of lies in these places, being of the sect of levellers.

Specific hours and orders of procedure were set for all social functions. Balls were to begin at six and end at eleven. Every ball had to open with a minuet "danced by two persons of the highest distinction present". Country dancing began at eight, "ladies of quality according to their rank standing up first". At nine there was an interval for rest, "the gentlemen to help their partners to tea". The proceedings ended precisely at eleven, and not even the most aristocratic of dancers would be allowed to continue longer.

Nash strictly forbade the wearing of white aprons by ladies, something that was common before his reign. "None but *Abigails* appeared in white aprons", he ruled. On one occasion he stripped a white apron off a duchess who appeared at a ball wearing one. He was violently opposed to duels. "Whenever . . . Nash heard of a challenge given, or accepted, he instantly had both parties arrested." This sheds a great deal of light on the duel scene in Sheridan's play *The Rivals*, which is set in Bath: although the play was first produced in 1775, after the end of Nash's reign, his rules still prevailed. "A sword seen in the streets of Bath would raise as great an alarm as a mad-dog," declares Captain Absolute at the beginning of Act V, Scene ii. Nash was also firmly opposed to the wearing of riding boots by gentlemen, in spite of the objection to this rule by country squires.

Goldsmith described the actual baths in detail:

The baths are five in number. On the south-west side of the abbey church is the King's Bath; which is an oblong square, the walls are full of niches, and at every corner are steps to descend into it; the bath is said to contain 427 tons and 50

Prior Park c. 1750. Designed by John Wood senior, the estate was the home of Ralph Allen, one of the great figures of eighteenth-century Bath.

gallons of water; and on its rising out of the ground on to the springs, it is sometimes too hot to be endured by those who bathe therin.

In the south-west part of the city are three other baths, viz—The Hot Bath, which is not much inferior in heat to the King's Bath, and contains 53 tons 2 hogsheads, and 11 gallons of water. The Cross Bath, which contains 52 tons 3 hogsheads and 11 gallons; and the Leper's Bath, which is not so much frequented as the rest.

The amusement of bathing [which was from six to nine in the morning] is immediately succeeded by a general assembly of people at the pump-house, some for pleasure, and some to drink the hot-waters. Three glasses at three different times, are the usual portion for every drinker; and the intervals between every glass are enlivened by the harmony of a small band of music, as well as by the conversation of the gay, the witty, or the forward.

From the pump-house the ladies, from time to time withdraw to a female coffee-house, and from thence return to their lodgings for breakfast. The gentlemen withdraw to their coffee-houses, to read the papers, or converse on the news of the day, with a freedom and ease, not to be found in the metropolis.

People of fashion make public breakfasts at the assembly-houses, to which they invite their acquaintances, and they sometimes order private concerts: or when so disposed, attend lectures upon the arts and sciences, which are frequently taught there in a pretty superficial manner, so as not to teize the understanding while they afford the imagination some amusement. The private concerts are performed in the ball-rooms, the tickets a crown each.

Concert breakfasts at the assembly-house, sometimes make a part of the morning's amusement here, the expenses of which are defrayed by a subscription among the men. Persons of rank and fortune, who can perform, are admitted into the orchestra, and find a pleasure in joining with the performers.

Thus we have the tedious morning fairly over. When noon approaches, and church (if any please to go there) is done, some of the company appear on the parade, and other public walks, where they continue to chat and amuse each other, 'till they have formed parties for the play, cards, or dancing for the evening. Others browse in bk. shops, take the air or exercise, some on horseback, some in coaches. Some walk the meadows round the town, winding along the side of the river Avon, and the neighbouring canal; while others are seen scaling some of the romantic precipices that over-hang the city. . . .

After dinner "the company meet a second time at the pump house. From this they retire to the walks, and from thence go to drink tea at the assembly-houses, and the rest of the evenings are concluded either with balls, plays or visits." The theatre was built in 1705, by subscription. "Every Tuesday and Friday evening is concluded with a public ball, the contributions to which are so numerous, that the price of the ticket is trifling. Thus *Bath* yields a continued rotation of diversions, and people of all ways of thinking, even from the libertine to the methodist, have it in their power to complete the day with employments suited to their inclinations."

Nash was largely responsible for changing the face of Bath. It was he who instigated the proper paving, lighting and cleaning of the streets and curbed the insolence of the "chairmen" by instituting severe penalties for any insulting or offensive behaviour. It was he who insisted on the importance of music among the city's entertainments, promoting a subscription for a band of six trained musicians to be paid one guinea a week. It was Nash who inspired Thomas Harrison to build the impressive Assembly Rooms close to the South Parade, where the varied evening entertainments took place. But it was the architectural genius of the two John Woods, father and son, that enabled Bath to achieve the visual splendour that Nash wished for it. John Wood senior, known as "Wood of Bath", settled in the city in 1727 and transformed it by his Palladian architecture. He designed the North and South Parades (several scenes in Sheridan's play *The Rivals* are set in the North Parade) and Queen Square and planned the Circus, which was finished by his son. He restored St. John's Hospital for the Duke of Chandos, for whom he also built Chandos Court. He also designed for his patron Ralph Allen the magnificent Palladian mansion of Prior Park outside the city. Ralph Allen was another of the great figures of eighteenth-century Bath. As deputy postmaster of the city he devised a postal service for the

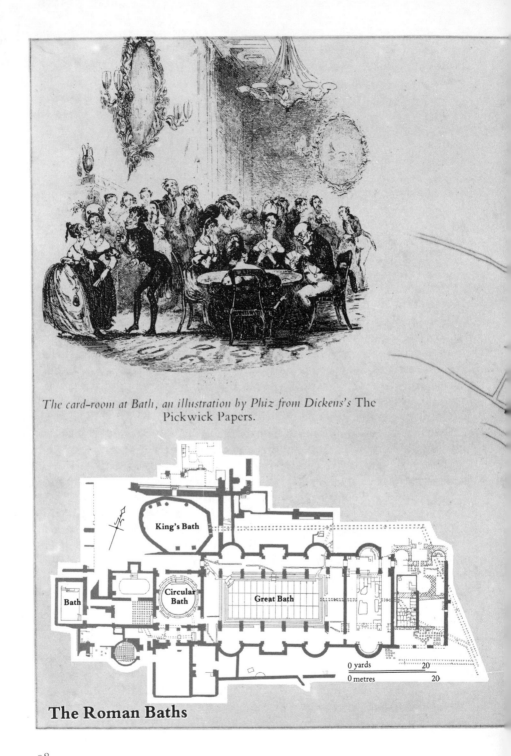

The card-room at Bath, an illustration by Phiz from Dickens's The Pickwick Papers.

The Roman Baths

King's Bath

Bath

Circular Bath

Great Bath

0 yards 20

0 metres 20

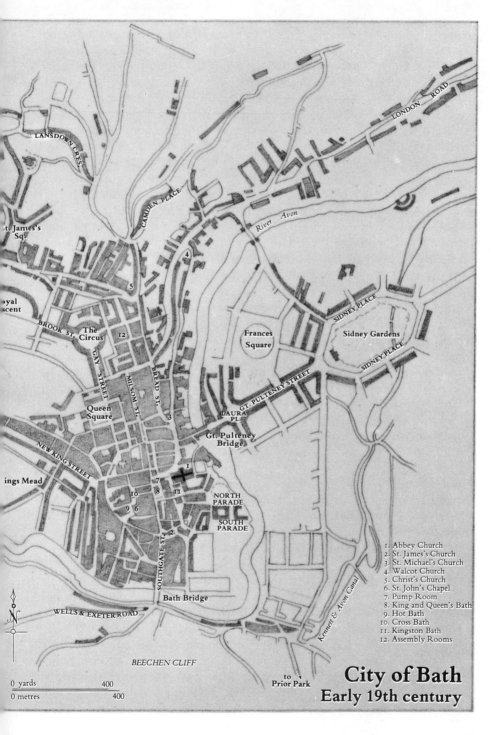

LANSDOWN CRES.

CAMDEN PLACE

River Avon

LONDON ROAD

SIDNEY PLACE

t. James's Sq.

Sidney Gardens

oyal scent

SIDNEY PLACE

4

5

Frances Square

BROOK ST.

The Circus

12

GAY STREET

MILSOM ST.

BREAD ST.

GT. PULTENEY STREET

Queen Square

3

LAURA PL.

Gt. Pulteney Bridge

NEW KING STREET

ings Mead

1

7

10

8

11

9 6

NORTH PARADE

SOUTH PARADE

SOUTHGATE ST.

2

1. Abbey Church
2. St. James's Church
3. St. Michael's Church
4. Walcot Church
5. Christ's Church
6. St. John's Chapel
7. Pump Room
8. King and Queen's Bath
9. Hot Bath
10. Cross Bath
11. Kingston Bath
12. Assembly Rooms

Bath Bridge

WELLS & EXETER ROAD

Kennett & Avon Canal

N

BEECHEN CLIFF

to Prior Park

City of Bath
Early 19th century

0 yards   400
0 metres   400

whole country which brought him a large fortune which he spent on patronizing the arts. (He is the model for Henry Fielding's Squire Allworthy in *Tom Jones*.) It was Allen who found ways of exploiting the rich stone quarries at Combe Down, near Bath and thus was responsible for the use of Bath freestone in the rebuilding and enlarging of the city, as well as in other cities. Beside Beau Nash, the two Woods and Ralph Allen as creators of eighteenth-century Bath, we should put Dr. William Oliver, who took up residence in Bath about 1725 and became its most distinguished physician. His *Practical Essay on the Use and Abuse of Warm Bathing in Gouty Cases* (1751) was one of several means by which he popularized Bath as a great health resort. A friend and colleague of Allen, Oliver was a philanthropist as well as a physician: he founded the Bath General Hospital (later the Royal Mineral Water Hospital) to enable the poor to make use of the healing waters of the Bath springs. He is remembered today by the Bath Oliver biscuit, which he invented.

Bath continued to develop architecturally after the age of Beau Nash. The splendid Royal Crescent was completed in 1775. The Assembly Rooms that were known as the "Upper Rooms" were the work of the younger Wood (they were largely destroyed in an air raid in 1942). It was the later decades of the eighteenth century, too, that saw the building of Camden Crescent, Lansdown Crescent, a new Pump Room and Milsom Street, which quickly developed into the new social centre of Bath. Lansdown Crescent, which dates from 1789–93, provides one of the most spectacular pieces of Bath townscape. John Betjeman has well described it: "Perched perilously high up on a south-facing hillside, the terraces wriggle along the contour, first convex, then concave, then convex again. The roadway, fenced off from the houses by elegant urn-topped railings, is built up over vaults, with a sheer drop on the other side down to trees and scrub."

But though the Bath townscape continued to acquire new glories in the latter part of the eighteenth century, there was a certain decline in what might be called its social tone after the golden age of Beau Nash. Under Nash, Bath was the capital of the English world of fashion, a distinction confirmed by two royal visits in 1734 and 1738. By the time that the city comes significantly into literature, with Smollett and Sheridan, it had become in many respects a city of middle-class hangers-on of the fashionable and aristocratic who followed them there and aped their manners and habits. In the late eighteenth and early nineteenth centuries it was gradually being transformed into what R. A. L. Smith called in his history of the city "the last refuge for half-pay officers and retired civil servants". Already in 1766, when Christopher Anstey published his lively satirical verses about social life in Bath entitled *The New Bath Guide*, there was a sense of a decline from a golden age, which Anstey reflects. The book consists largely of verse letters featuring Simkin Blunderhead, his sister Prudence, their

"Perched perilously high up on a south-facing hillside, the terraces wriggle along the contour, first concave, then convex, then concave again," wrote Betjeman, commenting on Lansdown Crescent and environs.

cousin Jenny and a maid Tabitha Runt. Jenny writes to "Lady Eliz. M-D-SS at—Castle, North" a description of the "View from the Parades at Bath, with some Account of the Dramatis Personae":

> Sweet are yon Hills, that crown this fertile Vale!
> Ye genial Springs! PIERIAN Waters; hail!
>
> Hail Woods and Lawns! Yes—oft I'll tread
>   Yon Pine-clad Mountains Side,
> Oft trace the gay enamel'd Mead,
>   Where AVON rolls his Pride.
>
> Sure, next to fair CASTALIA's Streams
>   And PINDUS' flow'ry Path,
> APOLLO most the Springs esteems
>   And verdant Meads of *Bath*.

Simkin Blunderhead gives a description of bathing:

> . . . Yet in searching about I had better Success
> For I got to a Place where the Ladies undress:
> Thinks I to myself, they are after some Fun,
> And I'll see what they're doing as sure as a Gun:
> So I peep'd at the Door, and I saw a great Mat
> That cover'd a Table, and got under that;
> And I laid myself down there, as snug and as still
> (As a Body may say) like a Thief in a Mill:
> And of all the fine Sights I have seen, my dear Mother,
> I never expect to behold such another:
> How the Ladies did giggle and set up their Clacks,
> All the while an old Woman was rubbing their Backs!
> Oh 'twas pretty to see them all put on their Flannels,
> And then take the Water like so many Spaniels.
> And tho' all the while it grew hotter and hotter
> They swam, just as if they were hunting an Otter;
> 'Twas a glorious sight to behold the fair Sex
> All wading with Gentlemen up to their Necks,
> And view them so prettily tumble and sprawl
> In a great smoaking Kettle as big as our Hall:
> And To-Day many Persons of Rank and Condition
> Were boil'd by Command of an able Physician: . . .

Blunderhead writes to his mother giving a rapturous description of the delights of the ball and the elegance and order produced by the régime of Beau Nash, whose death he laments:

> Yet here no Confusion, no Tumult is known,
> Fair Order and Beauty establish their Throne;
> For Order, and Beauty, and just Regulation,
> Support all the Works of this ample Creation.
> For This, in Compassion to Mortals below,
> The Gods, their peculiar favour to show,
> Sent HERMES to *Bath* in the shape of a BEAU:
> That Grandson of ATLAS came down from above
> To bless all the Regions of Pleasure and LOVE;
> To lead the fair nymph thro' the various MAZE,
> Bright Beauty to marshal, his Glory and Praise;
> To govern, improve, and adorn the gay Scene,
> By the Graces instructed, and *Cyprian* Queen: . . .
> Long reign'd the great NASH, this omnipotent Lord,
> Respected by Youth, and by Parents ador'd;

> For Him not enough at a Ball to preside,
> Th' unwary and beautiful Nymph would be guide;
> Oft tell her a Tale, how the credulous Maid
> By Man, by perfidious Man is betray'd;
> Taught Charity's Hand to relieve the Distrest,
> While Tears have his tender Compassion exprest:
> But alas! he is gone, and the City can tell
> How in Years and in Glory lamented he fell: . . .

Anstey laughs at the attempts of John Wesley and of the Countess of Huntingdon to evangelize the town, and he laughs most of all at the antics of the *nouveaux riches* and other upstarts aping the manners and ceremonies of the aristocratic. He describes the custom, introduced by Nash, of the ringing of bells to welcome each visitor:

> No City, dear Mother, this City excels
> For charming sweet sounds both of Fiddles and Bells.
> I thought, like a Fool, that they only would ring
> For a Wedding, or Judge or the Birth of a King,
> But I found 'twas for *Me*, that the good-natur'd people
> Rung so hard that I thought they would pull down the Steeple.
> So I took out my Purse, as I hate to be shabby,
> And paid all the Men when they came from the Abbey;
> Yet some think it strange they should make such a Riot
> In a Place where sick Folk would be glad to be quiet,
> But I hear 'tis the Bus'ness of this Corporation
> To welcome in all the *Great* Men of the Nation,
> For you know there is nothing diverts or employs
> The Minds of *Great* People like making a Noise:
> So with Bells they contrive all as much as they can
> To tell the arrival of any such Man.

This echoes precisely what Goldsmith had written:

Upon a stranger's arrival at *Bath* he is welcomed by a peal of the Abbey bells, and, in the next place, by the voice and music of the city waits. For these civilities the ringers have generally a present made them of half a guinea, and the waits of half a crown, or more, in proportion to the person's fortune, generosity or ostentation. . . . The greatest incommodity . . . is the disturbance the bells must give the sick.

The novelist Tobias Smollett was a frequent visitor to Bath in the middle of the century, and in 1752 wrote his *Essay on the External Use of Water, with particular Remarks on the Mineral Waters of Bath* (Smollett was trained as a doctor). But when he wrote his last novel, *The Expedition of Humphry Clinker*, published in 1771, he has the character in that novel who stands for himself complain that the city has sadly declined in the last thirty years. Matthew Bramble is writing from Bath to his friend Dr. Lewis:

You must know, I find nothing but disappointment at Bath, which is so altered, that I can scarcely believe it is the same place that I frequented about thirty years ago. Methinks I hear you say, "Altered it is, without all doubt; but then it is altered for the better; a truth which, perhaps you would own without hesitation, if you yourself was not altered for the worse." The reflection may, for aught I know, be just. The inconveniences which I overlooked in the heyday of health will naturally strike with exaggerated impression on the irritable nerves of an invalid, surprised by premature old age, and shattered with long suffering. But I believe you will not deny that this place, which Nature and Providence seem to have intended as a resource from distemper and disquiet, is become the very centre of racket and dissipation. Instead of that peace, tranquillity, and ease so necessary to those who labour under bad health, weak nerves, and irregular spirits, here we have nothing but noise, tumult, and hurry; with the fatigue and slavery of maintaining a ceremonial, more stiff, formal, and oppressive than the etiquette of a German elector. A national hospital it may be; but one would imagine that none but lunatics are admitted; and truly, I will give you leave to call me so, if I stay much longer at Bath. . . . I was impatient to see the boasted improvements in architecture, for which the upper parts of the town have been so much celebrated, and t'other day I made a circuit of all the new buildings. The square, though irregular, is, on the whole, pretty well laid out, spacious, open and airy; and, in my opinion, by far the most wholesome and agreeable situation in Bath, especially the upper side of it; but the avenues to it are mean, dirty, dangerous, and indirect. Its communication with the baths is through the yard of an inn, where the poor trembling valetudinarian is carried in a chair, betwixt the heels of a double row of horses, wincing under the curry-combs of grooms and postilions, over and above the hazard of being obstructed or overturned by the carriages which are continually making their exit or their entrance. I suppose after some chairmen have been maimed, and a few lives lost by those accidents, the corporation will think, in earnest, about providing a more safe and commodious passage. The Circus is a pretty bauble, contrived for show, and looks like Vespasian's amphitheatre turned outside in. If we consider it in point of magnificence, the great number of small doors belonging to the separate houses, the inconsiderable height of the different orders, the affected ornaments of the architrave, which are both childish and misplaced, and the areas projecting into the street, surrounded with iron rails, destroy a good part of its effect on the eye; and perhaps we shall find it still more defective, if we view it in the light of convenience. The figure of each separate dwelling-house being the segment of a circle, must spoil the symmetry of the rooms, by contracting them towards the street-windows, and leaving a larger sweep in the space behind. If, instead of the areas and iron rails, which seem to be of very little use, there had been a corridor with arcades all round, as in Covent-garden, the appearance of the whole would have been more magnificent and striking; those arcades would have afforded an agreeable covered walk, and sheltered the poor chairmen and their carriages from the rain, which is here almost perpetual. At present, the chairs stand soaking in the open street, from morning to night, till they become so many boxes of wet leather, for the benefit of the gouty and rheumatic, who are transported in them from place to place. Indeed this is a shocking inconvenience that extends over the whole city; and, I am persuaded, it produces infinite mischief to the delicate and infirm: even the close chairs, contrived for the sick, by standing in the open air, have their frieze linings impregnated, like so many sponges, with the moisture of the atmosphere, and those cases of cold vapour must give a charming check to the perspiration of a patient, piping hot from the bath, with all his pores wide open.

Bramble also comments on the social degeneration of the city:

Every upstart of fortune, harnessed in the trappings of the mode, presents himself at Bath, as in the very focus of observation. Clerks and factors from the East Indies, loaded with the spoil of plundered provinces; planters, negro-drivers, and hucksters, from our American plantations, enriched they know not how; agents, commissaries, and contractors, who have fattened, in two successive wars, on the blood of the nation; usurers, brokers, and jobbers of every kind; men of low birth, and no breeding, have found themselves suddenly translated into a state of affluence, unknown to former ages; and no wonder that their brains should be intoxicated with pride, vanity and presumption. Knowing no other criteron of greatness but the ostentation of wealth, they discharge their affluence, without taste or conduct, through every channel of the most absurd extravagance; and all of them hurry to Bath, because here, without any farther qualification, they can mingle with the princes and nobles of the land. Even the wives and daughters of low tradesmen, who, like shovel-nosed sharks, prey on the blubber of those uncouth whales of fortune, are infected with the same rage of displaying their importance; and the slightest indisposition serves them for a pretext to insist on being conveyed to Bath, where they may hobble country-dances and cotillons among lordlings, squires, counsellors and clergy. These delicate creatures from Bedfordbury, Butcher-row, Crutched-friars, and Botolph-lane, cannot breathe in the gross air of the lower town, or conform to the vulgar rules of a common lodging-house; the husband, therefore, must provide an entire house or elegant apartments in the new buildings. Such is the composition of what is called the fashionable company at Bath; where a very inconsiderable proportion of genteel people are lost in a mob of impudent plebeians, who have neither understanding nor judgment, nor the least idea of propriety and decorum; and seem to enjoy nothing so much as an opportunity of insulting their betters.

Lydia Melford, however, in the same novel, has a very different view of the city:

Bath is to me a new world—all is gaiety, good-humour, and diversion. The eye is continually entertained with the splendour of dress and equipage: and the ear with the sound of coaches, chaises, chairs, and other carriages. *The merry bells ring round* from morn till night. Then we are welcomed by the city waits in our own lodgings; we have music in the pump-room every morning, cotillons every forenoon in the rooms, balls twice a week, and concerts every other night, besides private assemblies and parties without number. As soon as we were settled in lodgings, we were visited by the master of ceremonies, a pretty little gentleman, so sweet, so fine, so civil, and polite, that in our country he might pass for the prince of Wales; then he talks so charmingly, both in verse and prose, that you would be delighted to hear him discourse; for you must know he is a great writer, and has got five tragedies ready for the stage. He did us the favour to dine with us by my uncle's invitation; and next day squired my aunt and me to every part of Bath, which, to be sure, is an earthly paradise. The Square, the Circus, and the Parades, put you in mind of the sumptuous palaces represented in prints and pictures: and the new buildings such as Prince's-row, Harlequin's-row, Bladud's-row, and twenty other rows, look like so many enchanted castles, raised on hanging terraces.

At eight in the morning we go in dishabille to the pump-room, which is crowded like a Welsh fair: and there you see the highest quality, and the lowest tradesfolk, jostling each other without ceremony—hail fellow! well met! The noise of the music playing in the gallery, the heat and flavour of such a crowd, and the hum and buzz of their conversation, gave me the headache and vertigo the first day; but afterwards, all these things became familiar, and even agreeable. Right under the pump-room windows is the king's bath; a huge cistern, where you see the patients up to their necks in hot water. The ladies wear jackets and petticoats of brown linen, with chip hats, in which they fix their handkerchiefs to wipe the sweat from their faces; but truly, whether it is owing to the steam that surrounds them, or the heat of the water, or the nature of the dress, or to all these causes together, they look so flushed and so frightful, that I always turn my eyes another way. . . .

The pumper, with his wife and servant, attend within a bar; and the glasses, of different sizes, stand ranged in order before them; so you have nothing to do but to point at that which you choose, and it is filled immediately, hot and sparkling from the pump. It is the only hot water I could ever drink, without being sick. Far from having that effect, it is rather agreeable to the taste, grateful to the stomach, and reviving to the spirits. You cannot imagine what wonderful cures it performs. . . .

Hard by the pump-room is a coffee house for the ladies; but my aunt says, young girls are not admitted, inasmuch as the conversation turns on politics, scandal, philosophy, and other subjects above our capacity; but we are allowed to accompany them to the booksellers' shops, which are charming places of re-sort, where we read novels, plays, pamphlets, and newspapers, for so small a subscription as a crown a quarter; and in these offices of intelligence (as my brother calls them) all the reports of the day, and all the private transactions of the bath, are first entered and discussed. From the bookseller's shop, we make a tour through the milliners and toymen; and commonly stop at Mr. Gill's, the pastry-cook, to take a jelly, a tart, or a small basin of vermicelli. There is, moreover, another place of entertainment on the other side of the water, opposite to the grove, to which the company cross over in a boat. It is called Spring Gardens; a sweet retreat, laid out in walks and ponds, and parterres of flowers; and there is a long room for breakfasting and dancing. . . .

After all, the great scenes of entertainment at Bath are the two public rooms, where the company meet alternately every evening. They are spacious, lofty, and, when lighted up, appear very striking. They are generally crowded with well-dressed people, who drink tea in separate parties, play at cards, walk, or sit and chat together, just as they are disposed. Twice a week there is a ball, the expense of which is defrayed by a voluntary subscription among the gentlemen; and every subscriber has three tickets.

Young Jerry Melford agrees with his sister Lydia against his uncle Matthew Bramble. He writes to a friend in Oxford:

I think those people are unreasonable who complain that Bath is a contracted circle, in which the same dull scenes perpetually revolve, without variation. I am, on the contrary, amazed to find so small a place so crowded with entertainment and variety. London itself can hardly exhibit one species of diversion to which we have not something analogous at Bath, over and above those singular ad-vantages that are peculiar to the place. Here, for example, a man has daily oppor-tunities of seeing the most remarkable characters of the community: he sees them in their natural attitudes and true colours; descended from their pedestals, and divested of their formal draperies, undisguised by art and affectation. Here we have ministers of state, judges, generals, bishops, projectors, philosophers, wits, poets, players, chemists, fiddlers, and buffoons. If he makes any considerable stay in the place, he is sure of meeting with some particular friend, whom he did not expect to see; and to me there is nothing more agreeable than such casual ren-counters. Another entertainment peculiar to Bath arises from the general mixture of all degrees assembled in our public rooms, without distinction of rank or fortune. This is what my uncle reprobates, as a monstrous jumble of hetero-geneous principles, a vile mob of noise and impertinence, without decency or subordination. But this chaos is to me a source of infinite amusement.

Fanny Burney's Evelina, heroine of the novel of that name published in 1778, could see no sign of decline, though she was disappointed in the Parades:

The charming city of Bath answered all my expectations. The Crescent, the prospect from it, and the elegant symmetry of the Circus, delighted me. The

Parades, I own rather disappointed me; one of them is scarce preferable to some of the best paved streets in London, and the other, though it affords a beautiful prospect of Prior Park and of the Avon, yet wanting something in *itself* of more striking elegance than a mere broad pavement, to satisfy the ideas I had formed of it.

Jane Austen knew Bath well for not only had she spent frequent holidays there but after her father's retirement in 1801 the family had lived there until his death in 1805. Two of her novels, *Northanger Abbey* (an early novel, but published posthumously with *Persuasion* in 1818) and her last one, *Persuasion*, are set in Bath. Both give a sense of a once fashionable watering place living on its past.

The first encounter of the heroine Catherine with the hero Henry Tilney in *Northanger Abbey* throws an ironical light on the social customs of Bath:

Every morning now brought its regular duties; — shops were to be visited; some new part of the town to be looked at; and the Pump-room to be attended, where they paraded up and down for an hour, looking at every body and speaking to no one. The wish of a numerous acquaintance in Bath was still uppermost with Mrs. Allen, and she repeated it after every fresh proof, which every morning brought, of her knowing nobody at all.

They made their appearance in the Lower Rooms; and here fortune was more favourable to our heroine. The master of ceremonies introduced her to a very gentlemanlike young man as a partner; — his name was Tilney. He seemed to be about four or five and twenty, was rather tall, had a pleasing countenance, a very intelligent and lively eye, and, if not quite handsome, was very near it. His address was good, and Catherine felt herself in high luck. There was little leisure for speaking while they danced; but when they were seated at tea, she found him as agreeable as she had already given him credit for being. He talked with fluency and spirit—and there was an archness and pleasantry in his manner which interested, though it was hardly understood by her. After chatting some time on such matters as naturally arose from the objects around them, he suddenly addressed her with—"I have hitherto been very remiss, madam, in the proper attentions of a partner here; I have not yet asked you how long you have been in Bath; whether you were ever here before; whether you have been at the Upper Rooms, the theatre, and the concert; and how you like the place altogether. I have been very negligent—but are you now at leisure to satisfy me in these particulars? If you are I will begin directly."

"You need not give yourself that trouble, sir."

"No trouble I assure you, madam." Then forming his features into a set smile, and affectedly softening his voice, he added, with a simpering air, "Have you been long in Bath, madam?"

"About a week, sir," replied Catherine, trying not to laugh.

"Really!" with affected astonishment.

'Why should you be surprized, sir?"

"Why indeed!" said he, in his natural tone—"but some emotion must appear to be raised by your reply, and surprize is more easily assumed, and not less reasonable than any other.—Now let us go on. Were you never here before, madam?"

"Never, sir."

"Indeed! Have you yet honoured the Upper Rooms?"

"Yes, sir. I was there last Monday."

"Have you been to the theatre?"

"Yes, sir, I was at the play on Tuesday."

"To the concert?"

"Yes, sir, on Wednesday."

"And are you altogether pleased with Bath?"

"Yes—I like it very well."

"Now I must give one smirk, and then we may be rational again."

When Henry Tilney temporarily disappears from Bath and Catherine looks for him in vain in the Pump Room and elsewhere, we get a sense of meaningless crowding reinforced, of course, by Catherine's own frustration:

As soon as divine service was over, the Thorpes and Allens eagerly joined each other; and after staying long enough in the Pump-room to discover that the crowd was insupportable, and that there was not a genteel face to be seen, which every body discovers every Sunday throughout the season, they hastened away to the Crescent, to breathe the fresh air of better company. Here Catherine and Isabella, arm in arm, again tasted the sweets of friendship in an unreserved conversation;—they talked much, and with much enjoyment; but again was Catherine disappointed in her hope of re-seeing her partner. He was no where to be met with; every search for him was equally unsuccessful, in morning lounges or evening assemblies; neither at the upper nor lower rooms, at dressed or undressed balls, was he perceivable; nor among the walkers, the horsemen, or the curricle-drivers of the morning.

Persuasion shows even more clearly how Bath had come to be a place of residence for gentlemen like Sir Walter Elliot, who had to retrench his expenses while claiming all the social privileges of a gentleman, and for retired naval and army officers. The foolishly snobbish Sir Walter and his equally foolish daughter Elizabeth liked Bath, but the younger daughter Anne, the heroine, who speaks for Jane Austen, did not. When Sir Walter had to quit his country seat for economic reasons, he chose to go to Bath as a genteel alternative. But Anne "disliked Bath, and did not think it agreed with her". When Anne arrives, her father and sister assure her how pleasant a place Bath is, but she compares it unfavourably in her mind to their former country house:

They had the pleasure of assuring her that Bath more than answered their expectations in every respect. Their house was undoubtedly the best in Camden-place; their drawing-rooms had many decided advantages over all the others which they had either seen or heard of; and the superiority was not less in the style of the fitting-up, or the taste of the furniture. Their acquaintance was exceedingly sought after. Every body was wanting to visit them. They had drawn back from many introductions, and still were perpetually having cards left by people of whom they knew nothing.

Here were funds of enjoyment! Could Anne wonder that her father and sister were happy? She might not wonder, but she must sigh that her father should feel no degradation in his change; should see nothing to regret in the duties and dignity of the resident land-holder; should find so much to be vain of in the littlenesses of a town; and she must sigh, and smile, and wonder too, as Elizabeth threw open the folding-doors, and walked with exultation from one drawing-room to the other, boasting of their space, at the possibility of that woman, who had been mistress of Kellynch Hall, finding extent to be proud of between two walls, perhaps thirty feet asunder.

In the novel, Bath is a place which brings out hypocrisy and pretentiousness in all the characters possessed of those vices, but it does also provide the occasion for the hero and heroine to get together after years of separation and misunderstanding. Although the social bustle of the city, its elegant buildings and seductive shopping streets are evoked with considerable zest in the novel, and in great detail, the underlying tone is one of irony.

By the time Charles Dickens brought Mr. Pickwick to Bath in Chapter 35 of the *Pickwick Papers* (1837) its social pretensions are a matter for pure mockery. Here is the Master of Ceremonies, Angelo Cyrus Bantam, Esquire, officially welcoming Mr. Pickwick:

"Welcome to Ba-ath, sir. This is indeed an acquisition. Most welcome to Ba-ath, sir. It is long—very long, Mr. Pickwick, since you drank the waters. It appears an age, Mr. Pickwick. Re-markable!"

Such were the expressions with which Angelo Cyrus Bantam, Esquire, M.C., took Mr. Pickwick's hand; retaining it in his, meantime, and shrugging up his shoulders with a constant succession of bows, as if he really could not make up his mind to the trial of letting it go again.

"It is a very long time since I drank the waters, certainly," replied Mr. Pickwick; "for to the best of my knowlege, I was never here before."

"Never in Ba-ath, Mr. Pickwick!" exclaimed the Grand Master, letting the hand fall in astonishment. "Never in Ba-ath! He! he! Mr. Pickwick, you are a

City of Bath
Present Day

wag. Not bad, not bad. Good, good. He! he! he! Re-markable!"

"To my shame, I must say that I am perfectly serious," rejoined Mr. Pickwick. "I really never was here before."

"Oh, I see," exclaimed the Grand Master, looking extremely pleased: "Yes, yes-good, good-better and better. You are the gentleman of whom we have heard. Yes: we know you, Mr. Pickwick; we know you."

"The reports of the trial in those confounded papers," thought Mr. Pickwick. "They have heard all about me."

"You are the gentleman residing on Clapham Green," resumed Bantam, "who lost the use of his limbs from imprudently taking cold after port wine; who could not be moved in consequence of acute suffering, and who had the water from the King's Bath bottled at one hundred and three degrees, and sent by waggon to his bed-room in town, where he bathed, sneezed, and same day recovered. Very re-markable!"

Mr. Pickwick acknowledged the compliment which the supposition implied, but had the self-denial to repudiate it, notwithstanding; and taking advantage of a moment's silence on the part of the M.C., begged to introduce his friends, Mr.

Tupman, Mr. Winkle, and Mr. Snodgrass. An introduction which overwhelmed the M.C. with delight and honour.

"Bantam," said Mr. Dowler, "Mr. Pickwick and his friends are strangers. They must put their names down. Where's the book?"

"The register of the distinguished visitors in Ba-ath will be at the Pump Room this morning at two o'clock," replied the M.C. "Will you guide our friends to that splendid building, and enable me to procure their autographs?"

"I will," rejoined Dowler. "This is a long call. It's time to go. I shall be here again in an hour. Come."

"This is a ball night," said the M.C., again taking Mr. Pickwick's hand as he rose to go. "The ball-nights in Ba-ath are moments snatched from Paradise; rendered bewitching by music, beauty, elegance, fashion, etiquette, and-and-above all, by the absence of tradespeople, who are quite inconsistent with Paradise; and who have an amalgamation of themselves at the Guildhall every fortnight, which is, to say the least, remarkable. Good bye, good bye!" and protesting all the way down stairs that he was most satisfied, and most delighted, and most overpowered, and most flattered, Angelo Cyrus Bantam, Esquire, M.C., stepped into a very elegant chariot that waited at the door, and rattled off.

That evening Mr. Pickwick and friends attend the Assembly Rooms:

At precisely twenty minutes before eight o'clock that night, Angelo Cyrus Bantam, Esq., the Master of the Ceremonies, emerged from his chariot at the door of the Assembly Rooms in the same wig, the same teeth, the same eye-glass, the same watch and seals, the same rings, the same shirt-pin, and the same cane. The only observable alterations in his appearance were, that he wore a brighter blue coat, with a white silk lining: black tights, black silk stockings, and pumps, and a white waistcoat, and was, if possible, just a thought more scented.

Thus attired, the Master of Ceremonies, in strict discharge of the important duties of his all-important office, planted himself in the rooms to receive the company.

Bath being full, the company and the sixpences for tea, poured in, in shoals. In the ball-room, the long card-room, the octagonal card-room, the staircases, and the passages, the hum of many voices, and the sound of many feet, were perfectly bewildering. Dresses rustled, feathers waved, lights shone, and jewels sparkled. There was the music—not of the quadrille band, for it had not yet commenced; but the music of soft tiny footsteps, with now and then a clear merry laugh—low and gentle, but very pleasant to hear in a female voice, whether in Bath or elsewhere. Brilliant eyes, lighted up with pleasurable expectation, gleamed from every side; and look where you would, some exquisite form glided gracefully through the throng, and was no sooner lost, than it was replaced by another as dainty and bewitching.

In the tea-room, and hovering round the card-tables, were a vast number of queer old ladies and decrepid old gentlemen, discussing all the small talk and scandal of the day, with a relish and gusto which sufficiently bespoke the intensity of the pleasure they derived from the occupation. Mingled with these groups, were three or four matchmaking mammas, appearing to be wholly absorbed by the conversation in which they were taking part, but failing not from time to time to cast an anxious sidelong glance upon their daughters, who, remembering the maternal injunction to make the best use of their youth, had already commenced incipient flirtations in the mislaying of scarves, putting on gloves, setting down cups, and so forth; slight matters apparently, but which may be turned to surprisingly good account by expert practitioners.

Lounging near the doors, and in remote corners, were various knots of silly young men, displaying various varieties of puppyism and stupidity; amusing all sensible people near them with their folly and conceit; and happily thinking themselves the objects of general admiration. A wise and merciful dispensation which no good man will quarrel with.

And lastly, seated on some of the back-benches, where they had already taken up their positions for the evening, were divers unmarried ladies past their grand climacteric, who, not dancing because there were no partners for them, and not playing cards lest they should be set down as irretrievably single, were in the favourable situation of being able to abuse everybody without reflecting on themselves. In short, they could abuse everybody, because everybody was there. It was a scene of gaiety, glitter, and show; of richly-dressed people, handsome mirrors, chalked floors, girandoles, and wax-candles; and in all parts of the scene, gliding from spot to spot in silent softness, bowing obsequiously to this party, nodding familiarly to that, and smiling complacently on all, was the sprucely attired person of Angelo Cyrus Bantam, Esquire, Master of the Ceremonies.

"Stop in the tea-room. Take your sixpenn'orth. They lay on hot water, and call it tea. Drink it," said Mr. Dowler, in a loud voice, directing Mr. Pickwick, who advanced at the head of the little party, with Mrs. Dowler on his arm. Into the tea-room Mr. Pickwick turned; and catching sight of him, Mr. Bantam corkscrewed his way through the crowd, and welcomed him with ecstasy.

"My dear sir, I am highly honoured. Ba-ath is favoured, Mrs. Dowler, you embellish the rooms. I congratulate you on your feathers. Re-markable!"

"Anybody here?" inquired Dowler, suspiciously.

"Anybody!" The *élite* of Ba-ath. Mr. Pickwick, do you see the lady in the gauze turban?"

"The fat old lady?" inquired Mr. Pickwick, innocently.

"Hush, my dear sir—nobody's fat or old in Ba-ath. That's the Dowager Lady Snuphanuph."

"Is it indeed?" said Mr. Pickwick.

"No less a person, I assure you," said the Master of Ceremonies. "Hush. Draw a little nearer, Mr. Pickwick. You see the splendidly dressed young man coming this way?"

"The one with the long hair, and the particularly small forehead?" inquired Mr. Pickwick.

"The same. The richest young man in Ba-ath at this moment. Young Lord Mutanhed."

But although Bath lost its splendour and exclusiveness as the metropolis of the world of fashion with the passing of the age of Beau Nash, its architectural splendours remained. It is still visually one of the great cities of Britain, its Palladian architecture of the mid-eighteenth century and its buildings in the freer style of Robert Adam in the last quarter of the century making it a rival of Edinburgh's New Town in neo-classical elegance. It is perhaps significant that when George Saintsbury retired from the Chair of Rhetoric and English Literature at Edinburgh in 1915 he chose to spend the years from then until his death in 1933 in Bath.

THE LAKE POETS

THE "LAKE SCHOOL" of poets was first so named in the *Edinburgh Review*, August 1817: they were Wordsworth, Coleridge and Southey. But though Southey lived at Keswick from 1803 until his death in 1843 and Coleridge lived in Keswick from 1800 to 1803, the real Lake Poet is Wordsworth, who was born at Cockermouth, Cumberland, in 1770. To a greater degree than any other major English poet, Wordsworth was a poet of *place*. The experiences out of which he created his finest poetry involved what he called "spots of time", each identified with a particular locality, and his poems are studded with precise topographical references. This was partly because the special view which he developed of man's relation to Nature arose out of his own experiences of natural objects, especially in the Lake District, but also because of his highly developed sense of locality with respect to experience in general. In his great autobiographical poem, *The Prelude*, we can trace vividly what might be called the topography of his life, and the same places are mentioned often in other poems.

Wordsworth's earliest years were spent by "the fairest of all rivers", the Derwent, which flows through Cockermouth on its way to the sea at Workington. He recalls in *The Prelude* how he was soothed by the sound of the Derwent "winding among grassy holms" making

> ceaseless music that composed my thoughts
> To more than infant softness, giving me
> Amid the fretful dwellings of mankind
> A foretaste, a dim earnest, of the calm
> That Nature breathes among the hills and groves.

He remembers, too, bathing in a mill stream that flowed into the Derwent:

> Oh, many a time have I, a five years' child,
> In a small mill-race severed from his stream,
> Made one long bathing of a summer's day;
> Basked in the sun, and plunged and basked again
> Alternate, all a summer's day, or scoured
> The sandy fields, leaping through flowery groves
> Of yellow ragwort; or when rock and hill,
> The woods, and distant Skiddaw's lofty height,
> Were bronzed with deepest radiance, stood alone
> Beneath the sky, . . .

Cockermouth, Wordsworth's birthplace, where the poet grew up "Fostered alike by beauty and by fear: | Much favoured in my birthplace . . ."

After attending an infant school at Penrith in 1776–7 he began attendance at Hawkshead Grammar School in 1779 (the year of his mother's death), lodging at Anne Tyson's cottage there.

> Fair seed-time had my soul, and I grew up
> Fostered alike by beauty and by fear:
> Much favoured in my birthplace, and no less
> In that belovèd Vale to which erelong
> We were transplanted—there were we let loose
> For sports of wider range. Ere I had told
> Ten birth-days, when among the mountain-slopes
> Frost, and the breath of frosty wind, had snapped
> The last autumnal crocus, 'twas my joy
> With store of springes o'er my shoulder hung
> To range the open heights where woodcocks run
> Among the smooth green turf. Through half the night
> Scudding away from snare to snare, I plied
> That anxious visitation;— moon and stars

> Were shining o'er my head. I was alone,
> And seemed to be a trouble to the peace
> That dwelt among them. Sometimes it befell
> In these night wanderings, that a strong desire
> O'erpowered my better reason, and the bird
> Which was the captive of another's toil
> Became my prey; and when the deed was done
> I head among the solitary hills
> Low breathings coming after me, and sounds
> Of undistinguishable motion, steps
> Almost as silent as the turf they trod.

The "belovèd Vale" was Esthwaite, which has Hawkshead at its northwest end. It was recollections of his childhood years here and his response to Nature during that period that so nourished Wordsorth's imagination in later years:

> Wisdom and Spirit of the Universe!
> Thou Soul that art the eternity of thought,
> That givest to forms and images a breath
> And everlasting motion, not in vain
> By day or star-light thus from my first dawn
> Of childhood didst thou intertwine for me
> The passions that build up our human soul;
> Not with the mean and vulgar works of man,
> But with high objects, with enduring things—
> With life and nature—purifying thus
> The elements of feeling and of thought,
> And sanctifying, by such discipline,
> Both pain and fear, until we recognise
> A grandeur in the beatings of the heart.
> Nor was this fellowship vouchsafed to me
> With stinted kindness. In November days,
> When vapours rolling down the valley made
> A lonely scene more lonesome, among woods,
> At noon and 'mid the calm of summer nights,
> When, by the margin of the trembling lake,
> Beneath the gloomy hills homeward I went
> In solitude, such intercourse was mine;
> Mine was it in the fields both day and night,
> And by the waters, all the summer long.

Particular occasions in this lakeland landscape were firmly etched in his memory, such as the famous winter skating scene on Esthwaite Water:

And, in the frosty season, when the sun
Was set, and visible for many a mile
The cottage windows blazed through twilight gloom,
I heeded not their summons: happy time
It was indeed for all of us—for me
It was a time of rapture! Clear and loud
The village clock tolled six,—I wheeled about,
Proud and exulting like an untired horse
That cares not for his home. All shod with steel,
We hissed along the polished ice in games
Confederate, imitative of the chase
And woodland pleasures,—the resounding horn,
The pack loud chiming, and the hunted hare.
So through the darkness and the cold we flew,
And not a voice was idle; with the din
Smitten, the precipices rang aloud;
The leafless trees and every icy crag
Tinkled like iron; while far distant hills
Into the tumult sent an alien sound
Of melancholy not unnoticed, while the stars
Eastward were sparkling clear, and in the west
The orange sky of evening died away.
Not seldom from the uproar I retired
Into a silent bay, or sportively
Glanced sideway, leaving the tumultuous throng,
To cut across the reflex of a star
That fled, and, flying still before me, gleamed
Upon the glassy plain; and oftentimes,
When we had given our bodies to the wind,
And all the shadowy banks on either side
Came sweeping through the darkness, spinning still
The rapid line of motion, then at once
Have I, reclining back upon my heels,
Stopped short; yet still the solitary cliffs
Wheeled by me—even as if the earth had rolled
With visible motion her diurnal round!
Behind me did they stretch in solemn train,
Feebler and feebler, and I stood and watched
Till all was tranquil as a dreamless sleep.

He remembers the impact on him of Nature when he was ten years old:

Yes, I remember when the changeful earth,
And twice five summers on my mind had stamped

A view of Saddleback and part of Skiddaw, pencil and watercolour drawing by John Constable (1806).

> The faces of the moving year, even then
> I held unconscious intercourse with beauty
> Old as creation, drinking in a pure
> Organic pleasure from the silver wreaths
> Of curling mist, or from the level plain
> Of waters coloured by impending clouds.

Wordsworth's father died in 1783 when he was still at school in Hawkshead, leaving his children in the guardianship of their uncles. In 1787 Wordsworth left his "dear native regions" (so addressed in a poem composed in 1786 "in anticipation of leaving school") to enter St. John's College, Cambridge: in the opening of Book III of *The Prelude* he describes his first sight of a scene so different from his native landscape:

> It was a dreary morning when the Chaise
> Roll'd over the flat Plains of Huntingdon
> And, through the open window, first I saw
> The long-back'd Chapel of King's College rear
> His pinnacles above the dusky groves.

He spent the long vacation of 1788 at Hawkshead, and in the autumn of that year paid his first visit to London. His feelings of excited happiness on returning to his "dear native regions" are vividly expressed in the opening of Book IV of *The Prelude*. It was during this summer vacation by mountain and lake, with "the Sea laughing at a distance", that his sense of dedication as a poet was born (*Prelude*, IV, 330–45). The long vacation of 1789 he spent with his sister Dorothy and his future wife Mary Hutchinson at Penrith, and in the following summer he went with his friend Robert Jones on a walking tour through France and Switzerland. He took his B.A. in 1791 and was in France again later that year. He then spent some time in London (*Prelude*, VII). And in 1793 he went on one of his many walking tours, this one taking him by way of Salisbury, Stonehenge, Bath, Bristol, Tintern Abbey (by Tintern Parva in Monmouthshire), Goodrich Castle, and Plas-yn-llan. In 1794 he was in the Lake District and Lancashire again, and it is interesting how clearly he later recalled exactly where he was when he heard of the death of Robespierre: he had been staying with his friends the Calverts at Windybrow under Skiddaw and

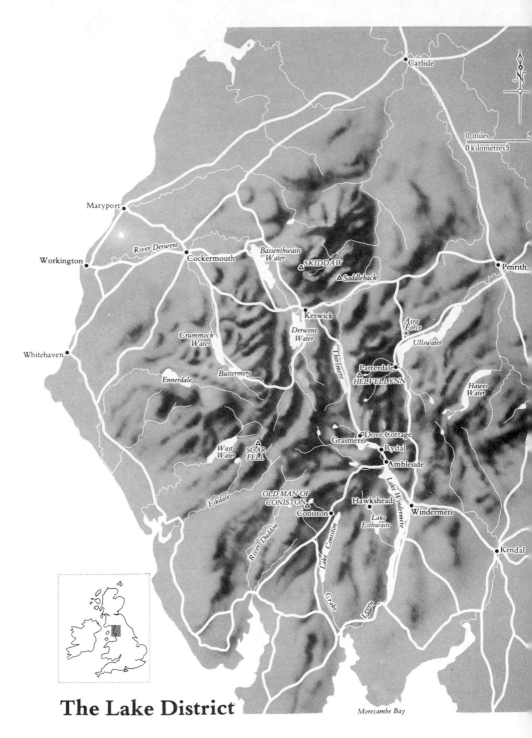

The Lake District

was now wandering through Lancashire and the Lake District. When he heard the news he was travelling by the shore of Morecambe Bay, where the rivers Crake and Leven enter in a common estuary:

> Over the smooth Sands
> Of Leven's ample Aestuary lay
> My journey, and beneath a genial sun;
> With distant prospects among gleams of sky
> And clouds, and intermingled mountain tops,
> In one inseparable glory clad, . . .

In October 1795 Wordsworth settled with his sister Dorothy at Racedown Farm, near Pilsdon, Dorset. He had met Coleridge briefly at Bristol, earlier that year, and in June 1797 Coleridge visited him at Racedown, thus beginning the great creative association between the two poets.

Coleridge was born at Ottery St. Mary, Devonshire, in 1772 and was educated at Christ's Hospital, London, and at Jesus College, Cambridge (he arrived in Cambridge just after Wordsworth left). In 1795 he was living in Bristol with Southey, with whom he had enthusiastically joined in the abortive scheme of Pantisocracy (a proposed idealistic community on the banks of the Susquehanna) and made the acquaintance of the Bristol bookseller Joseph Cottle who published his first volume of poems. In October 1795 he married Sarah Fricker and settled at Clevedon, Somerset, on the Bristol Channel. In 1797 he moved to a cottage at Nether Stowey, Somerset, where he was visited by Wordsworth and Dorothy, who in turn moved to Alfoxden, some three miles away, in order to be near Coleridge. It was while the two poets were living in this close association that the *Lyrical Ballads* were planned. Wordsworth, Dorothy and Coleridge tramped over the Somerset countryside, "three souls in one", discussing poetry and Nature. It was at Watchett, on the Bristol Channel, that Coleridge's "Ancient Mariner" first took shape. It was from nearby Porlock that the person came who interrupted his composition of "Kubla Khan".

Wordsworth, Dorothy and Coleridge went together to Germany after the publication of *Lyrical Ballads* in 1798. On their return in July 1799 Wordsworth, his brother John and Coleridge went on a walking tour in the Lake District before William and Dorothy settled at Dove Cottage, Town End, Grasmere, Wordsworth's home until 1808 when (having married in 1802) he moved to Allan Bank, Grasmere. In 1811 he moved to the Rectory, Grasmere. In 1813, having been appointed to the government sinecure position of Stamp-Distributor for Westmorland, he settled at Rydal Mount, between Grasmere and Ambleside, where he lived until his death in 1850.

During his nine-year stay at Dove Cottage, Wordsworth roamed over familiar scenes in the Lake District and recorded experiences that particu-

Grasmere from Loughrigh Fell, another of the sublime landscapes in which
Wordsworth's imagination was nurtured.

larly moved him, such as his sudden sight of daffodils in 1804 three miles
north of the village of Patterdale on the southwestern shore of Ullswater:

> I wandered lonely as a cloud
> That floats on high o'er vales and hills,
> When all at once I saw a crowd,
> A host, of golden daffodils;
> Beside the lake, beneath the trees,
> Fluttering and dancing in the breeze.

Daffodils still grow wild in the same place, in Gowbarrow Park near the
spectacular Aira Force waterfall.

Coleridge visited the Wordsworths at Dove Cottage in the spring of
1800 and, with his wife and son, stayed at the cottage throughout most of
July. In August Coleridge settled at Greta Hall, Keswick, thirteen miles
away. After his return to England from Malta in 1806, Coleridge paid a
long visit to Wordsworth at the farmhouse, Coleorton, Leicestershire,
which had been lent Wordsworth by Sir George Beaumont, and where

Aira Force waterfall, not far from where Wordsworth saw his "host of golden daffodils".

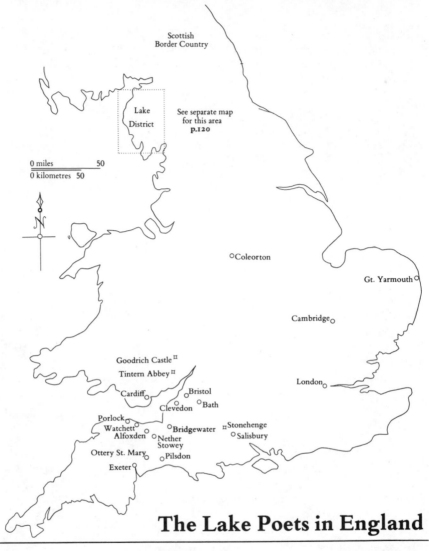

The Lake Poets in England

the Wordsworths were spending the winter of 1806–7. Sara Hutchinson, Wordsworth's sister-in-law, was also there, and Coleridge fell deeply in love with her. Coleridge was with the Wordsworths and Sara Hutchinson again in Grasmere in 1808–10 before returning to London. It was then that the estrangement between the two poets began, lasting until 1812. Coleridge was now living in London: in 1816 he took up residence with Dr. James Gillman at Highgate in North London, and spent the rest of his life there in Gillman's care.

It is Wordsworth who is thus the true Lake Poet, but though he had his home in the Lake District for nearly all of his life he made several important trips to other parts of the country, as well as abroad, which are reflected in his poetry. The most important of these were tours in Scotland in 1803, 1814 and 1831. He made a final tour in Scotland in 1833. Each of these tours produced topographical poems: *Memorials of a Tour in Scotland, 1803* included seventeen such poems, among them "At the Grave of Burns" (in Dumfrics), "To a Highland Girl, at Inversnaid, upon Loch Lomond", "The Solitary Reaper" (place not specified, but in the Argyllshire highlands), "Sonnet in the Pass of Killicranky", and "Yarrow Unvisited". The poems in *Memorials of a Tour in Scotland, 1814* include "The Brownie's Cell" ("suggested by a beautiful ruin upon one of the islands of Loch Lomond") and "Yarrow Visited". The 1831 tour produced the twenty-six poems of "Yarrow Re-visited and Other Poems". He visited Scott at Abbotsford, just before the novelist left for Italy on a last journey in a vain pursuit of health, and addressed two poems to him. The 1833 tour produced forty-eight poems, addressed to particular rivers, towns, mountains, castles, and historical characters associated with particular places. But the most famous series of topographical poems written by Wordsworth was *The River Duddon, a Series of Sonnets*, thirty-four sonnets composed between 1806 and 1820, of which the last is the best known. This poem is significant as showing the mature Wordsworth introducing the dimension of time in counterpoint with the dimension of space in the service of a deeper moral understanding:

> I Thought of Thee, my partner and my guide,
> As being past away.—Vain sympathies!
> For, backward, Duddon! as I cast my eyes,
> I see what was, and is, and will abide;
> Still glides the Stream, and shall for ever glide;
> The Form remains, the Function never dies;
> While we, the brave, the mighty, and the wise,
> We Men, who in our morn of youth defied
> The elements, must vanish;—be it so!
> Enough, if something from our hands have power
> To live, and act, and serve the future hour;
> And if, as toward the silent tomb we go,
> Through love, through hope, and faith's transcendent dower,
> We feel that we are greater than we know.

THE ROMANTIC POETS
ABROAD

THERE WERE FOUR centres of interest for the Romantic poets when they turned their attention towards the Continent. The first was France in the early years of the French Revolution,

> France standing on the top of golden hours
> And human nature seeming born again,

as Wordsworth put it in *The Prelude*. It was a time when, as Wordsworth expressed it in another passage of the same work,

> Bliss was it in that dawn to be alive,
> But to be young was very Heaven!

The second was Switzerland, known as the land of liberty and of romantic mountain scenery. The third was Italy, which had held a fascination for English poets from the time of Chaucer but which had a special appeal for the second generation of the Romantics. The fourth was Greece in the period of her fight for freedom from the Turkish yoke, when philhellenism was rife in England and Byron was moved to leave Italy to give his personal assistance to Greece, where he died.

In 1790, when he was twenty, in the Long Vacation before his final year at Cambridge, Wordsworth, with Robert Jones, "a youthful friend, he too a mountaineer", set out for the Alps:

> Lightly equipped, and but a few brief looks
> Cast on the white cliffs of our native shore
> From the receding vessel's deck, we chanced
> To land at Calais on the very eve
> Of that great federal day; and there we saw
> In a mean city, and among a few,
> How bright a face is worn when joy of one
> Is joy for tens of millions.

This was Wordsworth's first contact with the French Revolution. He and Jones pursued their way south, noting scenes of enthusiasm as they went:

> On the public roads,
> And once, three days successively, through paths
> By which our toilsome journey was abridged,

"Along the Simplon's steep and rugged road" — The Prelude.

> Among sequestered villages we walked
> And found benevolence and blessedness
> Spread like a fragrance everywhere, . . .

They passed under

> The vine-clad hills and slopes of Burgundy,
> Upon the bosom of the gentle Saone

and sailed down the Rhone

> Clustered together with a merry crowd
> Of those emancipated, a blithe host
> Of travellers, chiefly delegates returning
> From the great spousals newly solemnized
> At their chief city, in the sight of Heaven.

They then visited "the Convent of Chartreuse", where they were taken aback to find that a body of soldiers had arrived "commissioned to expel /The blameless inmates".

They proceeded on their way "at military speed", and crossed into Italy by the Simplon Pass. It was here that Wordsworth had the experience memorably recorded in *The Prelude*:

When from the Vallais we had turned, and clomb
Along the Simplon's steep and rugged road,
Following a band of muleteers, we reached
A halting-place, where all together took
Their noon-tide meal. Hastily rose our guide,
Leaving us at the board; awhile we lingered,
Then paced the beaten downward way that led
Right to a rough stream's edge, and there broke off;
The only track now visible was one
That from the torrent's further brink held forth
Conspicuous invitation to ascend
A lofty mountain. After brief delay
Crossing the unbridged stream, that road we took,
And clomb with eagerness, till anxious fears
Intruded, for we failed to overtake
Our comrades gone before. By fortunate chance,
While every moment added doubt to doubt,
A peasant met us, from whose mouth we learned
That to the spot which had perplexed us first
We must descend, and there should find the road,
Which in the stony channel of the stream
Lay a few steps, and then along its banks;
And, that our future course, all plain to sight,
Was downwards, with the current of that stream.
Loth to believe what we so grieved to hear,
For still we had hopes that pointed to the clouds,
We questioned him again, and yet again;
But every word that from the peasant's lips
Came in reply, translated by our feelings,
Ended in this,—*that we had crossed the Alps*.

They came down to Lake Maggiore then went on to Lake Como, where they had two "golden days" before setting off for home again. Though he admired the beauty of the two lakes, Wordsworth had no serious interest in Italy at this time. In 1837, as an elderly man of sixty-seven, he went with Henry Crabbe Robinson through France and Italy to Rome, and in a group of sonnets and other poems entitled *Memorials of a Tour in Italy*, recorded the expected "musings" and raptures before historic sites. ("Is this, ye Gods, the Capitolian Hill?") But it was his youthful excitement about France and the French Revolution and his response to the grandeur of the Swiss Alps that produced his most memorable travel poetry.

He was in France again from late 1791 to the end of 1792—Paris, then Orleans, then Blois (where he made friends with Michel Beaupuy and fell in love with Marie Anne Vallon, generally known as Annette). He does not overtly mention Annette in Book IX of *The Prelude* where he recounts his residence in France that year, but he describes enthusiastically his friend Beaupuy and their walks and talks together along the banks of the Loire, "innocent yet of civil slaughter". As the months went by he saw with dismay the degeneration of Revolution into Terror, when "domestic carnage filled the whole year" and "enormities" were perpetrated in the name of Liberty. In the struggle for power between the Jacobins and the Girondins he sympathized with the latter (who eventually lost) and was about to offer himself as their leader when he was recalled to England in December 1792.

Wordsworth made other journeys abroad, to Germany with Coleridge in 1798–9, with his wife, and sister Dorothy through Switzerland to the Italian Lakes and home through Paris in 1820, with Coleridge up the Rhine in 1828, as well as the visit to Rome with Crabbe Robinson in 1837 already referred to, but none of these provided any genuine poetic excitement.

Though John Keats had been fascinated by the art, mythology and spirit of ancient Greece ever since he read George Chapman's translation of Homer (which produced the famous sonnet on the subject) just before his twenty-first birthday in October 1816, and had that enthusiasm further developed by his visit to the Elgin Marbles with the painter Benjamin Haydon the following year (which also produced a notable sonnet), his Greece was essentially a Greece of the imagination, inspired by those events and by his early reading in John Lemprière's *Classical Dictionary*. He never visited Greece. He did visit Italy, in the vain hope that the climate would cure his tuberculosis, and spent his last months in Rome, in rooms still preserved in the Piazza di Spagna beside the Spanish Steps, leading what he called "a posthumous existence". The *Maria Crowther*, with Keats and the painter Joseph Severn on board, entered the Bay of Naples on October 21, 1820, after a three weeks' journey from England. After they had been kept in the bay in quarantine for ten days, the passengers were allowed to land on Keats's twenty-fifth birthday, October 31. It was chilly and rainy in Naples, and for most of the eight days he spent there Keats was depressed. They made a slow and roundabout journey to Rome, arriving at the city on November 15. He died there on February 23, 1821. The devoted Severn was with him and recorded his last moments.

Lord Byron's relationship with Italy was of a very different kind: he was the true Romantic exile, "the wandering outlaw of his own dark mind", like his own Childe Harold. In April 1816, Byron, who was born in January 1788, left England for ever, a social outcast because of the scandal associated with his separation from his wife and rumours about his relationship with his half-sister. He lived abroad until his death in Missolonghi, Greece, in April 1824. He had travelled before his final departure. Between July 1809 and July 1811 he travelled in Portugal, Spain, Greece and the

Levant. He used his experiences abroad in the first two cantos of *Childe Harold's Pilgrimage*, published in 1812, Childe Harold follows Byron's route, he is a projection of the poet, portrayed as a sensitive, disillusioned, generous-minded character, prone to rhapsodize over history and to exhort degenerate nations to recover their lost glory. He is also the disenchanted libertine ("For he who Sin's long labyrinth had run"), racked by "disappointed passion", who has been alone and unloved in the midst of the wildest revelry—the quintessential Romantic hero, in fact. Harold sails to Lisbon:

> What beauties doth Lisboa first unfold!
> Her image floating on that noble tide, . . .

But there is squalor and filth there too: "the dingy denizens are reared in dirt". He goes on to Spain:

> Oh, lovely Spain! renowned, romantic Land!

He bids the Spaniards awake and recover their former chivalric glory:

> Awake, ye Sons of Spain! awake! advance!
> Lo! Chivalry, your ancient Goddess, cries, . . .

He visits (and apostrophizes) "proud Seville" and "fair Cadiz" before sailing "through Calpe's [Gibraltar's] straits" and past "Calypso's isles" to the Balkans and Greece. He penetrates "ev'n to the centre of Illyria's vales", then

> He passed bleak Pindus, Acherusia's lake,
> And left the primal city of the land,
> And onwards did his further journey take
> To greet Albania's Chief, whose dread command
> Is lawless law.

He apostrophizes "Monastic Zitza" and celebrates the fierce Albanian warriors in language that, quite unintentionally, verges on the comic:

> Tambourgi! Tambourgi! thy 'larum afar
> Gives hope to the valiant, and promise of war;
> All the Sons of the mountains arise at the note,
> Chimariot, Illyrian, and dark Suliote!

> Oh! who is more brave than a dark Suliote,
> In his snowy camese and his shaggy capote?

> To the wolf and the vulture he leaves his wild flock
> And descends to the plain like the stream from the rock.

He then proceeds to

> Fair Greece! sad relic of departed Worth!
> Immortal, though no more; though fallen, great!

His account of Greece is general and rhetorical, full of apostrophes to the country's past and regret for its present. He refers to Thermopylae, Thebes, Athens, Delphi, but in a context of generalized excitement and self-conscious attitudinizing:

> Greece is no lightsome land of social mirth:
> But he whom Sadness sootheth may abide,
> And scarce regret the region of his birth,
> When wandering slow by Delphi's sacred side,
> Or gazing o'er the plains where Greek and Persian died.

These travels also inspired a series of melodramatic verse tales, *The Giaour* (1813), *The Bride of Abydos, a Turkish Tale* (1813), *The Corsair* and *Lara* (1814).

Byron left England for good on April 16, 1816, with the melodramatic young Dr. Polidori as his personal physician and a train of servants. He and Polidori travelled in a specially commissioned large travelling carriage "copied from the celebrated one of Napoleon taken at Genappe" through Bruges to Ghent and on to Antwerp, then Brussels, from which they went on horseback to the battlefield of Waterloo. The journey is described in Canto III of *Childe Harold,* published later the same year:

> And Harold stands upon this place of skulls,
> The grave of France, the deadly Waterloo!

From Brussels they moved on to the Rhineland:

> The crested crag of Drachenfels
> Frowns o'er the wide and winding Rhine, . . .

They went through Cologne, Bonn, Coblenz, Ehrenbreitstein (no longer in existence, the former town now being incorporated in Coblenz), then bade "Adieu to thee, fair Rhine!" and crossed the frontier into Switzerland, the "home of freedom". There Byron first visited the battlefield of Morat where in 1476 the Swiss had gained their decisive victory over Charles the Bold of Burgundy and then, on May 26, reached the shores of Lake Geneva

ENGLAND

London

Calais Bruges Antwerp
Ghent Cologne
Douai Bonn GERMANY
Brussels Coblenz

Paris
Orleans Châlons-
Blois sur-Marne

FRANCE SWITZERLAND For these areas see
inset maps

Lyons

Chartreuse

ALPS ITALY

PORTUGAL SPAIN

Lisbon Rome

Seville

Cadiz
Gibraltar

Calypso's Isles

Mediterranean Se

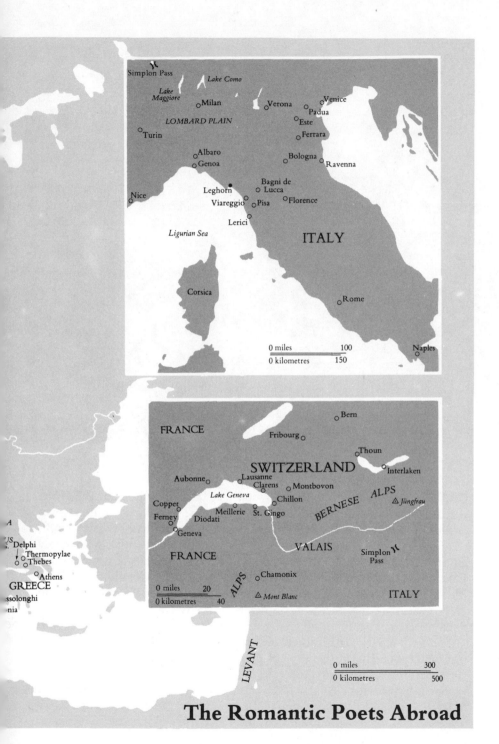

The Romantic Poets Abroad

Villa Diodati, on the shores of Lake Geneva, where Byron encountered Shelley, Mary Godwin and Jane Clairmont.

("lake Leman woos me with its crystal face"). They put up at the Hôtel d'Angleterre in the Genevan suburb of Sécheron: Byron put himself down in the hotel register as aged a hundred years. He was actually twenty-eight, but felt old and disillusioned, though this feeling was in part a deliberately cultivated piece of self-dramatization. On May 27 Byron was rowed across Lake Geneva to Diodati, and on stepping ashore found himself confronting Shelley, with Mary Godwin (who was to become Shelley's wife in December, after the suicide of his deserted first wife) and Jane Clairmont, who preferred to call herself Claire Clairmont; she had fallen in love with Byron in London, had insisted on being seduced by him, and was now pursuing him again in the hope of becoming his permanent mistress.

Shelley and Mary, with Claire, had left England in May and hastened on through France to Geneva. They were already installed at the Hôtel d'Angleterre in Sécheron when Byron and his retinue arrived, and exactly why the groups did not meet until the encounter at Diodati is obscure.

Anyway, they now made up for it by breakfasting and dining with each other regularly.

At the end of May, Shelley and his household moved from the Hôtel d'Angleterre to a cottage on the other side of the Lake, not far from the Villa Diodati, known as Campagne Chapusis or Mont Allègre. Two weeks later Byron and his retinue moved to Diodati, and on June 23 the two poets set out in a boat they shared to circumnavigate Lake Geneva. They sailed to the village of Meillerie, where they entered the landscape of Rousseau's *La Nouvelle Heloïse*, and both poets enthused about the book and its author. When they resumed their sailing they were overtaken by a hurricane. Byron later described what happened in a letter to his publisher, John Murray:

We were five in the boat—a servant, two boatmen, and ourselves. The sail was mismanaged, and the boat was filling fast. He [Shelley] can't swim. I stripped off my coat—made him strip off his, and take hold of an oar, telling him that I thought (being myself an expert swimmer) I could save him, if he would not struggle when I took hold of him—unless we got smashed upon the rocks, which were high and sharp, with an awkward surf on them at that minute. We were then about a hundred yards from shore, and the boat in peril. He answered me with the greatest coolness, that "he had no notion of being saved, and that I would have enough to do to save myself, and begged not to trouble me." Luckily, the boat righted, and, baling, we got round a point into St. Gingo, where the inhabitants came down and embraced the boatmen on their escape, the Wind having been high enough to tear up some huge trees from the Alps above us, as we saw next day.

The following day they travelled as far as the source of the Rhône. The weather turned dismal and rainy, with thunder in the mountains. They visited the Castle of Chillon, which inspired Byron to write his narrative poem *The Prisoner of Chillon*, which he completed within a few days. They went on to Clarens, "sweet Clarens, birthplace of deep love", again with its associations with Rousseau, and then proceeded to Lausanne, where Byron gathered acacia leaves on the terrace from which Gibbon, having just completed his *Decline and Fall of the Roman Empire*, looked across at Mont Blanc: Shelley, however, made no such gesture, "fearing to outrage the greater and more sacred name of Rousseau". On June 30 they returned to Mont Allègre.

Byron paid several visits to Madame de Staël (whom he had known in London) at Coppet, and listened patiently to her holding forth. Early in August, Matthew Gregory Lewis ("Monk" Lewis, from his authorship of the best-selling Gothic novel *The Monk*) arrived, and Byron introduced him to Shelley. On August 14 Byron and Lewis made a pilgrimage to Voltaire's house at Ferney. Shelley and his household left for England at the end of August, taking a mass of Byron's manuscripts to give to Murray. Shelley also took Claire Clairmont back with him: she was pregnant by Byron, having succeeded in persuading him briefly to renew their intimacy. But Byron resented her advances, and though he was happy she was going to have a child, he did not want her company any more.

Soon after Shelley's departure, Byron's friends John Cam Hobhouse and Scrope Davies arrived: the three of them, with the excitable Dr. Polidori, made an expedition to Chamonix. Then Davies left; Byron dismissed Polidori, having had enough of his melodramatic moods, and Byron and Hobhouse took a thirteen-day tour through the Bernese Alps. Byron kept a journal of this tour for his sister Augusta. They started out on September 17 and got back on the 29th. He visited Clarens again, then "crossed the mountains to Montbovon on horseback, admired the view from the summit of Mont Davant", "saw the bridge of La Roche, passed the boundaries, out of Vaud and into Bern Canton; French exchanged for bad German; the district famous for Cheese, liberty, property, and no taxes". On September 21 he entered "the plain of Thoun" with its "high rocks, wooded to the top". "Lake of Thoun; extensive plain with a girdle of Alps. Walked down to the Château de Schadam . . . Thoun a very pretty town. The whole day's journey Alpine and proud." They left Thoun (Thun) by boat and landed at Neuhasse. Then Interlaken, and to the foot of the Jungfrau. "Glaciers; torrents; one of these torrents *nine hundred feet* in height of visible descent. Lodged at the Curate's. Set out to see the valley; heard an Avalanche fall, like thunder; saw Glacier—enormous. Storm came on, thunder, lightning, hail; all in perfection, and beautiful."

When they came out of the mountains they went "from Thoun to Bern, good roads, villages, industry, property, and all sorts of tokens of insipid civilisation". From Berne they went to Fribourg, then, on the evening of the 29th, "reached Aubonne . . . which commands by far the fairest view of the Lake of Geneva; twilight; the Moon on the Lake; a grove on the height, and of very noble trees". He was now within a few hours of Diodati, and here he concluded his journal.

On October 6, 1816, Byron and Hobhouse left Diodati for Italy, crossing the Alps by the Simplon Pass and descending into the Lombard plain. They proceeded to Milan, where Byron met Henri Beyle (not yet the famous novelist Stendhal) and a number of Italian writers, as well as his old friends Lord and Lady Jersey. Polidori was there, his usual melodramatic self, and he, Byron and Hobhouse became involved in a ridiculous scene at La Scala opera house. Milan, like all Lombardy, was at this time under Austrian dominion, and Polidori quarrelled with an Austrian officer whose grenadier's shako was obscuring his view of the stage. Byron himself eventually sorted out the resulting fracas. Polidori had to leave the city.

Byron was in Milan for about a month, and in spite of his occasional repining about his greying hair ("Would you not think I was sixty instead

"I stood in Venice, on the Bridge of Sighs;/A palace and a prison on each hand . . ."—Canto IV, Childe Harold. *Engraving after a painting by J. M.W. Turner.*

of not quite nine and twenty?" he wrote to Augusta) and other signs of age, he seems to have enjoyed himself there. From Verona, where he went in the first week of November, he wrote to Thomas Moore:

Among many things at Milan, one pleased me particularly, viz. the correspondence (in the prettiest love-letters in the world) of Lucretia Borgia with Cardinal Bembo, . . . and a lock of her hair, and some Spanish verses of hers,—the lock is very fair and beautiful. I took one single hair of it as a relic, and wished sorely to get a copy of one or two of the letters; but it is prohibited: *that* I don't mind; but it was impracticable; and so I only got some of them by heart. They are kept in the Ambrosian Library, which I often visited to look them over—to the scandal of the librarian, who wanted to enlighten me with sundry valuable MSS., classical, philosophical, and pious. But I stick to the Pope's daughter, and wish myself a cardinal.

At Verona he admired the amphitheatre ("beats even Greece") and expressed scepticism about Juliet's tomb (though he brought away a few pieces of granite). On November 11 he arrived in Venice, described in the opening of Canto IV of *Childe Harold*:

> I stood in Venice, on the Bridge of Sighs;
> A palace and a prison on each hand:
> I saw from out the wave her structures rise

As from the stroke of the enchanter's wand:
A thousand years their cloudy wings expand
Around me, and a dying Glory smiles
O'er the far times, when many a subject land
Look'd to the winged Lion's marble piles,
Where Venice sate in state, throned on her hundred isles!

In Venice Tasso's echoes are no more,
And silent rows the songless gondolier;
Her palaces are crumbling to the shore,
And music meets not always now the ear:
Those days are gone—but Beauty still is here.
States fall, arts fade—but Nature doth not die,
Nor yet forget how Venice once was dear,
The pleasant place of all festivity,
The revel of the earth, the masque of Italy!

In Venice "the *besoin d'amour* came back upon my heart" and he found himself a mistress in the shape of the wife of his landlord, a draper whose house and shop were in the Frezzeria. She was twenty-two year old Marianna Segati. "She is by far the prettiest woman I have seen here," he wrote to Thomas Moore on December 24, "and the most lovable I have met anywhere—as well as one of the most singular." He threw himself into the spirit of Venice at carnival time, and reported to his correspondents in England, with a mixture of triumph and self-mockery, his many adventures. He reported to Moore on January 28 a remarkable incident: Marianna's brother's wife made advances to him, was discovered in the act by Marianna who physically attacked her sister-in-law, and subsequently threw a fainting fit of some virtuosity: while Byron was trying to revive her, her husband walked in, "and finds me with his wife fainting upon the sofa, and all the apparatus of confusion, dishevelled hair, hats, handkerchiefs, salts, smelling bottles—and the lady pale as ashes, without sense or motion." But "jealousy is not the order of the day in Venice, and daggers are out of fashion". The husband, though nettled, accepted the situation. "It is very well known that almost all married women have a lover; but it is usual to keep up the forms, as in other nations."

Eventually the pleasures of Venice at carnival time began to pall, and by the time the abstinence and sacred music of Lent succeeded the carnival atmosphere, Byron was feeling weary and nostalgic. He wrote his finest lyric, "So we'll go no more a roving". He had an attack of fever, which left him feeling he needed a change from Venice. He toyed with the idea of returning to England, but in fact set off on further Italian adventures in mid-April. He went, with his usual retinue of servants, in his enormous travelling carriage by way of Ferrara, Padua, Bologna and Florence to

Rome, where he arrived on April 29. He stayed in Rome until May 28, genuinely moved by its antiquities. He wrote of Rome in Canto IV of *Childe Harold*:

> Oh Rome! my country! city of the soul!
> The orphans of the heart must turn to thee,
> Lone mother of dead empires! and control
> In their shut breasts their petty misery.
> What are our woes and sufferance? Come and see
> The cypress, hear the owl, and plod your way
> O'er steps of broken thrones and temples, Ye!
> Whose agonies are evils of a day—
> A world is at our feet as fragile as our clay.
>
> The Niobe of nations! there she stands,
> Childless and crownless, in her voiceless woe;
> An empty urn within her wither'd hands,
> Whose holy dust was scatter'd long ago;
> The Scipios' tomb contains no ashes now;
> The very sepulchres lie tenantless
> Of their heroic dwellers: dost thou flow,
> Old Tiber! through a marble wilderness?
> Rise, with thy yellow waves, and mantle her distress.
>
> The Goth, the Christian, Time, War, Flood, and Fire,
> Have dealt upon the seven-hill'd city's pride;
> She saw her glories star by star expire,
> And up the steep barbarian monarchs ride,
> Where the car climb'd the Capitol; far and wide
> Temple and tower went down, nor left a site:
> Chaos of ruins! who shall trace the void,
> O'er the dim fragments cast a lunar light,
> And say, "here was, or is," where all is doubly night?

On returning to Venice he stayed only briefly at his former lodgings before moving to a *villegiatura* beside the Brenta, where he installed Marianna. While riding in the neighbouring countryside in the summer of 1817, he encountered a lively and forward girl from the Venetian slums, Margarita Cogni, known as La Fornorina, married to a baker whom she despised. She was a passionate, domineering and self-assertive character, who became Byron's mistress in the literal sense by taking over the running of his household as well as ousting Marianna. "After a precious piece of work," he reported to Murray in August 1819, after it was all over, "she fixed herself in my house, really and truly without my consent, but, owing to my indolence, and not being able to keep my countenance; for if I began in a rage, she always finished by making me laugh with some Venetian pantaloonery or other; and the Gipsy knew this well enough, as well as her other powers of persuasion, and exerted them with the usual tact and success of all She-things; high and low, they are all alike for that.''

On November 13, 1817, Byron left his *villegiatura* to return to Venice, staying during the autumn and winter at his old lodgings in the Frezzeria while his friend Hobhouse took lodgings opposite. They often rowed out together to the Lido in the afternoon, and rode on the beach in the damp melancholy Venetian winter. Early in 1818 Byron established himself with great magnificence in the large and gloomy Palazzo Mocenigo, on the Grand Canal, and settled down to a long residence in Venice and a life of studied debauchery with fluctuating mistresses, mostly from the poorer classes, Italian footmen and large numbers of Venetian parasites. He made friends with the British Consul and his wife, Mr. and Mrs. Hoppner, and rode daily along the Lido with Mr. Hoppner, as he had previously done with Hobhouse.

In March 1818 Shelley left England with Mary (now his wife), Claire, and Claire's daughter by Byron, Allegra. From Calais they took the most direct route to Switzerland, via Douai, Châlons-sur-Marne and Lyons. They reached Milan on April 4, and there Allegra was handed over to a Swiss nursemaid who brought her to join her father's household at the Palazzo Mocenigo. Byron was happy to receive his daughter, but not his daughter's mother. Though the first reports of Allegra at the Palazzo Mocenigo were that "they dress her in little trousers trimmed with lace and treat her like a little princess", Shelley and Claire were later disturbed by reports from Allegra's nursemaid that she was surrounded by Venetian servants and hangers-on of dubious morals. Claire determined that she must see Allegra. She and Shelley had left Milan for Pisa on May 1 and in June moved into a house in Bagni di Lucca. In August, Shelley escorted Claire to Venice so that she could see her daughter. They visited the Hoppners, and Mrs. Hoppner (who had taken an interest in Allegra's welfare) sent for the little girl and she was reunited with her mother. Byron was willing to give back Allegra to Claire if she wanted her, but remained unwilling to see Claire. In fact in October Allegra was put in the charge of Mrs. Hoppner.

Meanwhile, Byron had suggested to the Shelleys that they should occupy a villa he had rented from the Hoppners near Este among the Euganean Hills, so there the Shelleys went and there their second child Clara died of dysentery on September 24. They paid several visits to Byron in Venice. Byron himself was becoming dissatisfied with his bohemian life and became, as Shelley reported, "heartily and deeply discontented with himself". His extraordinary household, with its menagerie (including a fox, a wolf, and dogs, birds and monkeys), the motley collection of servants and parasites and the going and coming of mistresses, gave rise to all sorts of scandalous stories about him. He was putting on weight, and his curly hair was growing grey. He felt himself already middle-aged. His poetic genius, however, soared to new heights: it was now that he began writing his masterpiece, *Don Juan*, the first canto of which he sent back to London with Lord Lauderdale in November 1818. Early in 1819 he finally succeeded in expelling La Fornarina, in spite of her violent objections and her threats of suicide. Byron continued having affairs with other girls, one of whom, a young unmarried Venetian called Angelina, wished to marry him and on learning that he was already married (though separated) calmly suggested that his wife could be poisoned. Byron's unconventional morality did not go that far, and he was shocked.

In April 1819 Byron, still in Venice, met the last of his mistresses, Teresa Guiccioli, young wife of a sixty-year old landowner and papal count. She fell for him even more passionately than he fell for her, and a long liaison resulted. The tradition of the *cavaliere servente*, the acknowledged lover of a married woman, was long established in Venice, but certain rules were expected to be obeyed. Byron and Teresa made their own rules. When Teresa and her husband left Venice early in the summer of 1819, Byron followed, going via Padua, Ferrara and Bologna to Ravenna, whither Teresa summoned him from the family palazzo. Teresa was ill, and Byron's regular visits (with her husband's approval) speeded her recovery. After two months in Ravenna, when his relationship with Teresa grew steadily closer, he followed the Guicciolis to Bologna on August 11. When a few days later the Guicciolis left for a short visit to the country, Byron became so disconsolate that he sent for Allegra to cheer him up. When the Guicciolis returned to Bologna, Count Guiccioli moved to his estates near the town while Byron remained in Bologna in charge of Teresa. To the astonishment of the Austrian police spies, who were watching their movements as both the Guiccioli family and Byron himself were known to be in sympathy with Italian liberal patriotic sentiment, he took her to Venice and installed her at La Mira, his house on the Brenta. Count Guiccioli responded by asking Byron for a loan of a thousand pounds, which Byron refused. In November the count arrived and demanded his wife back, and Byron persuaded her to return to Ravenna with her husband, promising her that he would eventually rejoin her there. In Ravenna Teresa became ill again, and her father Count Ruggiero Gamba obtained Count Guiccioli's permission to send for Byron, who duly arrived at the Palazzo Guiccioli to be welcomed by both Teresa's father and her husband. For over a year he lived there, settling into a dull routine life as Teresa's tacitly recognized lover. (He actually rented a set of rooms in the palazzo, to the financial benefit of Count Guiccioli.) He continued working on *Don Juan*.

In February 1821 Count Gamba and his brother were expelled from Ravenna for their political activities by the authorities of the Papal States (which included Ravenna). Teresa went with them to Florence, but Byron remained at Ravenna in the Palazzo Guiccioli until the end of October. Meanwhile, Shelley had left Este and had been visiting Florence, Rome and Naples, where he stayed until the spring of 1819. His "Stanzas written in dejection near Naples" express the contrast between the warm sun, clear sky, dancing waves, blue isles, and snowy mountains on the one hand and his own dejection on the other. In Rome he was moved by the antiquities and disenchanted by the political and social scene in the modern city. He and Mary climbed Vesuvius on mules and visited Pompeii. In October the Shelleys took an apartment in Florence for six months, at the Palazzo Marino in the Via Valfonda. It was there, on November 12, that Percy Florence Shelley was born. The following spring the Shelleys moved to Pisa. In August, Shelley visited Byron at the Palazzo Guiccioli. Claire's daughter Allegra was now being educated in a nearby convent (where she had been sent on her fifth birthday, January 12, 1822) and Shelley visited her there and reported her undisciplined and vain. Byron he found "much improved in every respect—in genius, in temper, in moral issues, in health, in happiness", and the two poets sat up through the night talking. The Hoppners tried to persuade Byron to drop Shelley by writing him of his depraved behaviour: Byron showed the letter to Shelley, who was shocked and shaken at the lies the letter contained. He returned to Pisa and Mary to write a refutation which he sent to Byron and asked him to send it to the Hoppners, but it seems doubtful if Byron did pass the letter on.

Shelley persuaded Byron that he and Teresa should join them in Pisa, together with Teresa's father and brother. Byron arrived in Pisa early in November and established himself at the Palazzo Lanfranchi. It was at Pisa that Byron met Shelley's friend Edward John Trelawney, whose reminiscences of the two poets later caused so much controversy. The way of life at the Palazzo Lanfranchi aroused the suspicions of the police (who were watching Byron and the Gambas anyway) and in April 1822 the Gambas were told to leave the city. Byron rented a villa for them on Monte Nero near Leghorn, but he himself stayed on at Pisa. In the same month little Allegra died, and soon afterwards the Shelleys moved from Pisa to Lerici on the Gulf of Spezia. In June, Byron and Teresa moved to Leghorn, to a modern villa on Monte Nero, where they were joined by the Gambas. Meanwhile Shelley, living at the Casa Magni at Lerici, was spending much of his time with his friend Edward Williams sailing in his boat the *Ariel*. He was visited by Leigh Hunt and his family, whom he installed (at his own expense) on the ground floor of the Palazzo Lanfranchi in Pisa. At the end of June the authorities caught up with Byron and the Gambas, and they were expelled from Monte Nero. The Gambas went to Genoa, and Byron and Teresa returned to the Palazzo Lanfranchi.

Shelley and Williams were with Leigh Hunt in Pisa at the beginning of June 1822. On the morning of June 8 Shelley and Williams shopped at

Palazzo Lanfranchi in Pisa.

Leghorn and at one o'clock they set off in the *Ariel* for Lerici. A sudden storm removed the boat from the sight of observers, and when soon afterwards visibility improved the boat had vanished. Ten days later the bodies of Shelley and Williams were washed ashore, and on August 14 their two bodies, which had been temporarily buried in the sand, were disinterred and cremated on the beach near Viareggio. Byron was present, and watched the burning of Shelley's body in fascinated horror.

Byron was left to look after Shelley's improvident dependent Leigh Hunt, but the two did not get on (Mrs. Hunt especially offended Byron). Teresa was still with him, but she was now a mild habit rather than a passion. In September 1822 they all left the Palazzo Lanfranchi for the Casa Negroto in the village of Albaro on a hilltop overlooking Genoa. There Byron gloomed, and thought of Shelley's death. He cheered up at the arrival of Lord and Lady Blessington at Genoa, and flirted with Lady Blessington. But he now planned to relieve his sense of gloom and emptiness by going to Greece and assisting personally in the Greek struggle against the Turks. He left Italy and Teresa for a melodramatic adventure in which he only partly believed but to which he was impelled both by his own emotional needs and the pressures of Greek propagandists and of philhellenists in England. He set out from Leghorn in July 1823, lived from August to December in Cephalonia, and reached Missolonghi in January where he died of fever on April 19, 1824.

So of the three great Romantic poets of the second generation, two, Keats and Shelley, died in Italy and the third died in Greece. The first generation, Wordsworth and Coleridge, grew old and died in their beloved England.

THE BRONTË COUNTRY

PROBABLY NO NOVEL is so saturated in the atmosphere of a particular kind of countryside as Emily Brontë's *Wuthering Heights*, set in the moors of the West Riding of Yorkshire with which the author was so familiar. Heathcliff, the central male figure of the book, described by the heroine Catherine (who nevertheless feels a sense of identification with him) as an "unreclaimed creature, without refinement, without cultivation; an arid wilderness of furze and whinstone", is, like Catherine herself, in some ways symbolic of the rough vitality of a landscape which had changed little with the centuries and seemed to speak for some elemental force at the heart of nature. J. B. Harley, writing as a geographer on "England *c.* 1850" (*Wuthering Heights* first appeared in 1847), refers to the very limited progress that had been made in the enclosure movement in the moors of the West Riding and to the fact that the first Ordnance Survey maps for northern England show that "the upper end of cultivation was ragged, with many single enclosures detached, here and there, from the body of the improved land". The contrast between the great mass of unimproved common in its pristine natural state and improved pockets of enclosed land was thus vividly present to the eye, and parallels the contrast between the soft gentility of Thrushcross Grange (modelled on Ponden Hall) inhabited by the weak if civilized Lintons and the rough vitality of Wuthering Heights (possibly modelled on the now ruined High or Top Withens) and the symbolically named Heathcliff.

It was in April 1820 that Patrick Brontë brought his wife and six young children to the parsonage of the moorland village of Haworth where he had recently been appointed perpetual curate. Haworth, four miles south-west of Keighley, Yorkshire, was and is surrounded by moors—Haworth Moor, Keighley Moor, Wadsworth Moor, Cullingworth Moor, Thornton Moor. It is situated on a steep slope, at the top of which were the church, the churchyard and—the last and highest house in the village—the parsonage. Haworth Parsonage was described by Mrs. Gaskell (Charlotte Brontë's friend and biographer) as "an oblong stone house, facing down the hill on which the village stands, and with the front door right opposite to the western door of the church, distant about a hundred yards. Of this space twenty yards or so in depth are occupied by a grassy garden, which is scarcely wider than the house. The grave-yard goes round house and garden, on all sides but one. The house consists of four rooms on each floor, and is two stories high." Only the kitchen on the ground floor and the servant's bedroom upstairs did not overlook the churchyard: these were at the back of the house and faced the moors, where sheep might be found grazing right up to the house.

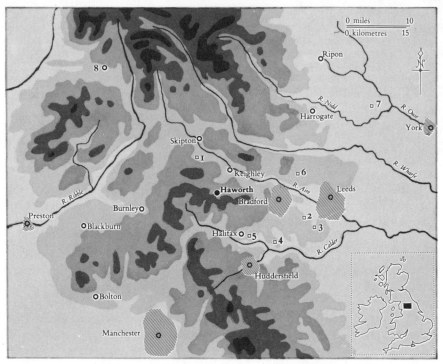

Key to Map numbers

Brontë Country

1. Stonegappe, "Gateshead Hall" of *Jane Eyre*

2. Oakwell Hall, "Fieldhead" of *Shirley*

3. The Rydings, "Thornfield Hall" of *Jane Eyre*

4. Roe Head, Charlotte at School

5. Lawhill, Emily taught at School

6. Upperwood House, Charlotte as governess

7. Thorpe Green, Anne and Branwell stayed

8. Cowan Bridge, "Lowood School" of *Jane Eyre*

Mrs. Brontë died at Haworth in September 1821, leaving the children to the care of her sister Elizabeth Branwell, who came up from Penzance to look after the Brontë household where she spent the rest of her life. The two elder children, Maria and Elizabeth, died in childhood. The others—Charlotte, born in 1816; Branwell, born in 1817; Emily, born in 1818; and Anne, born in 1820—formed their own closely integrated little society in their isolation from the rest of the world, feeding their imagination on Bunyan, Scott, Byron, Shakespeare, Ossian, and a variety of magazines including what Charlotte later called "the mad Methodist magazines" subscribed to by their aunt, "full of miracles and apparitions and pre-ternatural warnings, ominous dreams and frenzied imaginations". They walked the moors at all seasons of the year and in all weathers and, Emily

Haworth church and parsonage, an engraving from Mrs. Gaskell's Life of Charlotte Brontë *(1857). "I lingered round them, under that benign sky, watched the moths fluttering among the heath and hare-bells; listened to the soft wind breathing through the grass; and wondered how any one could ever imagine unquiet slumbers for the sleepers in that unquiet earth." —Lockwood, from the final passage of* Wuthering Heights.

especially, got to know and love their changing moods and aspects. And, starting from tales made up for the wooden soldiers Mr. Brontë had brought back to Branwell in 1826 on his return from a visit to Leeds, they steadily built up an extraordinary series of interconnected stories, novels, histories and plays involving imaginary characters in imagined countries. Thus their reading, their intimacy with the lonely moors, the stories of great preachers and great sinners they acquired from the Methodist magazines and from local tradition as retailed by the Brontës' faithful domestic servant, Tabitha Ackroyd, all helped to nurture that special kind of imagination which turned the three girls into novelists and Branwell into a brilliant, frustrated, reckless and finally doomed and drunken rake.

In 1824–5 the Brontë girls were boarders at the Clergy Daughters' School at Cowan Bridge (in Lancashire, two miles southeast of Kirkby Lonsdale), recently founded by the evangelical clergyman William Carus Wilson. Charlotte attributed the death of Maria from tuberculosis in May 1825 and of Elizabeth from typhus the following June to conditions at the school, of which she painted a harsh picture as Lowood in *Jane Eyre* (1847). In 1831–2 Charlotte was at school in Roehead, between Leeds and Huddersfield, where she later taught, as did Emily, very briefly, and Anne. In

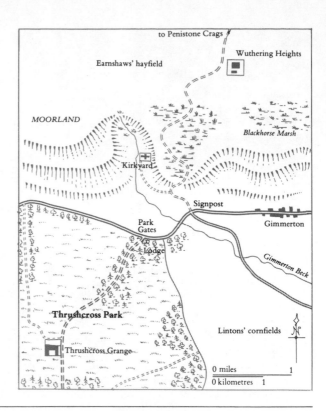

The following labels appear on the map:

to Penistone Crags

Earnshaws' hayfield

Wuthering Heights

MOORLAND

Blackhorse Marsh

Kirkyard

Signpost

Gimmerton

Park Gates

Lodge

Gimmerton Beck

Thrushcross Park

Lintons' cornfields

Thrushcross Grange

0 miles 1

0 kilometres 1

Wuthering Heights— Fiction . . .

1836 Emily taught for six months at a school in Halifax, while from 1838 Charlotte and Anne tried to make a living as governesses—Anne's unhappy experiences in this capacity are fictionalized in her novel *Agnes Grey*, published with *Wuthering Heights* in 1847. In 1842 Charlotte and Emily studied at the Pensionat Héger at Brussels, where Charlotte later taught and where her experiences inspired her novels *The Professor* (published posthumously in 1857) and *Villette* (1853). Her *Jane Eyre* (1847) is the classic governess novel of the nineteenth century, in which all the frustrations as well as the secret wishes of her life were given expression.

Emily, the most individual genius of the three sisters, died of tuberculosis in 1848; Branwell had died the previous year and Anne died in 1849. The only Brontë of her generation to reach her thirties was Charlotte, who died in 1855 shortly after marrying her father's curate A. B. Nicholls. Patrick Brontë long survived all his gifted children.

The Brontë story has become one of the great literary legends of Britain and is permanently associated with Haworth and the Yorkshire moors. Emily's *Wuthering Heights* is the quintessential novel of the moors. Its seasons, its different kinds of weather, are closely bound up with the whole pattern of the strange story. In the very first paragraph of the novel the principal narrator, Mr. Lockwood, who has just agreed to lease Thrush-

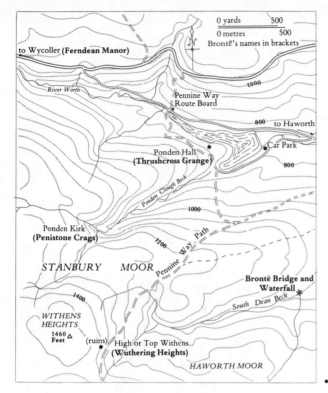

0 yards   500

0 metres   500

Brontë's names in brackets

to Wycoller **(Ferndean Manor)**

River Worth

1000

Pennine Way
Route Board

800   to Haworth

Car Park

Ponden Hall
(Thrushcross Grange)

800

Ponden Clough Beck

1000

Ponden Kirk
(Penistone Crags)

1200

Pennine Way Path

STANBURY   MOOR

Pennine Way

**Brontë Bridge and
Waterfall**

South Dean Beck

1400

*WITHENS
HEIGHTS*

1460
Feet

(ruins)   High or Top Withens
(Wuthering Heights)

HAWORTH MOOR

. . . and Fact

cross Grange from Heathcliff, says: "This is certainly a beautiful country! In all England, I do not believe that I could have fixed on a situation so completely removed from the stir of society. A perfect misanthropist's heaven—and Mr. Heathcliff and I are such a suitable pair to divide the desolation between us." The paradox of the combination of beauty and desolation, of love of natural scenery and misanthropy, is only one of the many paradoxes that run through the novel and are bound up with its setting.

Lockwood has leased Thrushcross Grange; Heathcliff lives in Wuthering Heights: in a variety of brilliantly contrived flashbacks the earlier history of these two places and their inhabitants, and the relation between them, is slowly unravelled. On describing his first visit to Heathcliff, Lockwood tells of the significance of the name of his dwelling:

Wuthering Heights is the name of Mr. Heathcliff's dwelling. "Wuthering" being a significant provincial adjective, descriptive of the atmospheric tumult to which its station is exposed in stormy weather. Pure, bracing ventilation they must have up there, at all times, indeed: one may guess the power of the north wind, blowing over the edge, by the excessive slant of a few stunted firs at the end of the house, and by a range of gaunt thorns all stretching their limbs one way, as if craving alms

of the sun. Happily, the architect had foresight to build it strong: the narrow windows are deeply set in the wall, and the corners defended with large jutting stones.

The difference between Thrushcross Grange and Wuthering Heights is both geographical and psychological: it also goes beyond both to reach a strange symbolic level. It is about three miles from the farmhouse of Wuthering Heights to the gates of Thrushcross Park and two miles from the gates to the house of Thrushcross Grange, with its garden in front, its plantations of trees bordering its surrounding parkland, and its general air of protected seclusion as opposed to the open and exposed position of Wuthering Heights. Lockwood makes the journey from Wuthering Heights (having spent the night there) to Thrushcross Grange on a bitter cold winter morning with snow lying on the moors:

I declined joining their breakfast, and, at the first gleam of dawn, took an opportunity of escaping into the free air, now clear and still, and cold as impalpable ice.

My landlord hallooed for me to stop, ere I reached the bottom of the garden, and offered to accompany me across the moor. It was well he did, for the whole hill-back was one billowy, white ocean, the swells and falls not indicating corresponding rises and depressions in the ground: many pits, at least, were filled to a level; and entire ranges of mounds, the refuse of the quarries, blotted from the chart which my yesterday's walk left pictured in my mind.

I had remarked on one side of the road, at intervals of six or seven yards, a line of upright stones, continued through the whole length of the barren: these were erected, and daubed with lime, on purpose to serve as guides in the dark, and also, when a fall, like the present, confounded the deep swamps on either hand with the firmer path: but, excepting a dirty dot pointing up here and there, all traces of their existence had vanished; and my companion found it necessary to warn me frequently to steer to the right or left, when I imagined I was following, correctly, the windings of the road.

We exchanged little conversation, and he halted at the entrance of Thrushcross park, saying, I could make no error there. Our adieux were limited to a hasty bow, and then I pushed forward, trusting to my own resources, for the porter's lodge is untenanted as yet.

The distance from the gate to the Grange is two miles: I believe I managed to make it four, what with losing myself among the trees, and sinking up to the neck in snow, a predicament which only those who have experienced it can appreciate. At any rate, whatever were my wanderings, the clock chimed twelve as I entered the house, and that gave exactly an hour for every mile of the usual way from Wuthering Heights.

OPPOSITE: *The ruin of Top Withens farm, supposed site of Wuthering Heights.* "*Pure, bracing ventilation they must have up there, at all times . . . .: one may guess the power of the north wind . . . by the excessive slant of a few stunted firs at the end of the house.*"

Ponden Hall, on which Thrushcross Grange was modelled. Its protected seclusion is the antithesis of the exposed position of Top Withens. "Ah, it was beautiful—a splendid place carpeted with crimson and crimson-covered chairs and tables . . ."

The difference between the Earnshaws of Wuthering Heights and the Lintons of Thrushcross Grange (this is part of the story of what happened there before Lockwood arrives, which he slowly unravels) is made strikingly clear in Heathcliff's description of how he and Catherine Earnshaw first saw Thrushcross Grange on one of their escapades across the moors:

We crept through a broken hedge, groped our way up to the path, and planted ourselves on a flower-pot under the drawing-room window. The light came from thence; they had not put up the shutters, and the curtains were only half closed. Both of us were able to look in by standing on the basement, and clinging to the ledge, and we saw—ah! it was beautiful—a splendid place carpeted with crimson, and crimson-covered chairs and tables, and a pure white ceiling bordered by gold, a shower of glass-drops hanging in silver chains from the centre, and shimmering with little soft tapers. Old Mr. and Mrs. Linton were not there. Edgar and his sister had it entirely to themselves; shouldn't they have been happy? We should have thought ourselves in heaven! And now, guess what your good children were doing? Isabella—I believe she is eleven, a year younger than Cathy —lay screaming at the farther end of the room, shrieking as if witches were running red hot needles into her. Edgar stood on the hearth weeping silently, and in the middle of the table sat a little dog shaking its paw and yelping, which, from their mutual accusations, we understood they had nearly pulled in two between them. The idiots! That was their pleasure! To quarrel who should hold a heap of warm hair, and each begin to cry because both, after struggling to get it, refused to take it. We laughed outright at the petted things, we did despise them! When would you catch me wishing to have what Catherine wanted? or find us by ourselves, seeking entertainment in yelling, and sobbing, and rolling on the ground, divided by the whole room? I'd not exchange, for a thousand lives, my condition here, for Edgar Linton's at Thrushcross Grange . . .

The difference between Wuthering Heights and Thrushcross Grange, so central in the novel, is not simply a difference between storm and calm. Wuthering Heights can have its own kind of calm, and Thrushcross Grange its own kind of storm. But the storm of the Grange is psychological; the calm of the Heights is a temporary phase in the changing pattern of weather:

That Friday made the last of our fine days, for a month. In the evening, the weather broke; the wind shifted from south to northeast, and brought rain first, and then sleet and snow.
On the morrow one could hardly imagine that there had been three weeks of summer: the primroses and crocuses were hidden under wintry drifts; the larks were silent, the young leaves of the early trees smitten and blackened. And dreary, and chill, and dismal that morrow did creep over!

Catherine, languishing in Thrushcross Grange after her ill-fated marriage to Edgar Linton, listens to the ringing of the bells of Gimmerton kirk or chapel, which stands between Thrushcross Park and Wuthering Heights:

Gimmerton chapel bells were still ringing; and the full, mellow flow of the beck in the valley came soothingly on the ear. It was a sweet substitute for the yet absent murmur of the summer foliage, which drowned that music about the Grange when the trees were in leaf. At Wuthering Heights it always sounded on quiet days, following a great thaw or a season of steady rain; and of Wuthering Heights, Catherine was thinking as she listened—that is, if she thought, or listened, at all—but she had the vague, distant look I mentioned before, which expressed no recognition of material things by ear or eye.

The chapel, once much used but now abandoned, is described by Lockwood when he tells of a dream he had:

We came to the chapel. I have passed it really in my walks, twice or thrice; it lies in a hollow, between two hills—an elevated hollow, near a swamp, whose peaty moisture is said to answer all the purposes of embalming on the few corpses deposited there. The roof has been kept whole hitherto, but, as the clergyman's stipend is only twenty pounds per annum, and a house with two rooms, threatening speedily to determine into one, no clergyman will undertake the duties of pastor, especially as it is currently reported that his flock would rather let him starve than increase the living by one penny from their own pockets.

The chapel, associated with the dark and passionate utterances of obsessed Methodist preachers, loses its significance as the novel progresses: it is the natural scene outside that matters. Catherine is not buried inside, but on a green slope in the churchyard:

The place of Catherine's interment, to the surprise of the villagers, was neither in the chapel, under the carved monument of the Lintons, nor yet by the tombs of her own relations, outside. It was dug on a green slope, in a corner of the kirkyard, where the wall is so low that heath and bilberry plants have climbed over it from the moor, and peat mould almost buries it. Her husband lies in the same spot, now; and they have each a simple headstone above, and a plain grey block at their feet, to mark the graves.

Before Catherine's death we are given several powerful scenes showing the psychological relation between her and the two houses of the novel. In her delirium at Thrushcross Grange she imagines that she can see Wuthering Heights, her old home where she had grown up with Heathcliff, even though the houses were in fact miles apart and not mutually visible:

"Look!" she cried eagerly, "that's my room, with the candle in it, and the trees swaying before it; and the other candle is in Joseph's garret. Joseph sits up late, doesn't he? He's waiting till I come home that he may lock the gate. Well, he'll wait a while yet. It's a rough journey, and a sad heart to travel it; and we must pass by Gimmerton Kirk, to go that journey! We'd braved its ghosts often together, and dared each other to stand among the graves and ask them to come. But Heathcliff, if I dare you now, will you venture? If you do, I'll keep you. I'll not lie there by myself, they may bury me twelve feet deep, and throw the church down over me, but I won't rest till you are with me. I never will!"

Young Cathy, daughter of Catherine Earnshaw and Edgar Linton, yearns from her home in Thrushcross Grange to cross the moors towards Wuthering Heights:

Till she reached the age of thirteen, she had not once been beyond the range of the park by herself. Mr. Linton would take her with him a mile or so outside, on rare occasions; but he trusted her to no one else. Gimmerton was an unsubstantial name in her ears; the chapel, the only building she had approached or entered, except her own home. Wuthering Heights and Mr. Heathcliff did not exist for her; she was a perfect recluse, and, apparently, perfectly contented. Sometimes, indeed, while surveying the country from her nursery window, she would observe—

"Ellen, how long will it be before I can walk to the top of those hills? I wonder what lies on the other side—is it the sea?"

"No, Miss Cathy," I would answer, "it is hills again just like these."

"And what are those golden rocks like, when you stand under them?" she once asked.

The abrupt descent of Penistone Crags particularly attracted her notice, especially when the setting sun shone on it and the topmost heights, and the whole extent of landscape besides lay in shadow.

I explained that they were bare masses of stone, with hardly enough earth in their clefts to nourish a stunted tree.

"And why are they bright so long after it is evening here?" she pursued.

"Because they are a great deal higher up than we are," replied I; "you could not climb them, they are too high and steep. In winter the frost is always there before it comes to us; and, deep into summer, I have found snow under that black hollow on the north-east side!"

"Oh, you have been on them!" she cried, gleefully. "Then I can go too, when I am a woman. Has papa been, Ellen?"

"Papa would tell you, Miss," I answered hastily, "that they are not worth the trouble of visiting. The moors, where you ramble with him, are much nicer; and Thrushcross park is the finest place in the world."

"But I know the park, and I don't know those," she murmured to herself. "And I should delight to look round me from the brow of that tallest point—my little pony, Minny, shall take me some time."

The summer comes; the moors put on their summer dress, and Cathy is enchanted with them:

The summer shone in full prime; and she took such a taste for this solitary rambling that she often contrived to remain out from breakfast till tea; and then the evenings were spent in recounting her fanciful tales. I did not fear her breaking bounds, because the gates were generally locked, and I thought she would scarcely venture forth alone, if they had stood wide open.

Cathy is trapped into marrying Heathcliff's effeminate son by Isabella Linton (part of Heathcliff's elaborate plot to take revenge on the Linton family for taking his fellow spirit, Catherine Earnshaw, away from him), and the change of the novel's mood as this ill-boding marriage is fore-shadowed is indicated by a change in the weather on the moors:

On an afternoon in October, or the beginning of November—a fresh watery afternoon, when the turf and paths were rustling with moist, withered leaves, and the cold, blue sky was half hidden by clouds, dark grey streamers, rapidly mounting from the west, and boding abundant rain—I requested my young lady to forego her ramble because I was certain of showers. She refused; and I unwillingly donned a cloak, and took my umbrella to accompany her on a stroll to the bottom of the park: a formal walk which she generally affected if low-spirited—and that she invariably was when Mr. Edgar had been worse than ordinary; a thing never known from his confession, but guessed both by her and me from his increased silence, and the melancholy of his countenance.

She went sadly on: there was no running or bounding now, though the chill wind might well have tempted her to a race. And often, from the side of my eye, I could detect her raising a hand, and brushing something off her cheek.

I gazed round for a means of diverting her thoughts. On one side of the road rose a high, rough bank, where hazels and stunted oaks, with their roots half exposed, held uncertain tenure: the soil was too loose for the latter; and strong winds had blown some nearly horizontal. In summer, Miss Catherine delighted to climb along these trunks, and sit in the branches, swinging twenty feet above the ground; and I, pleased with her agility, and her light, childish heart, still considered it proper to scold every time I caught her at such an elevation, but so that she knew there was no necessity for descending. From dinner to tea she would lie in her breeze-rocked cradle, doing nothing except singing old songs—my nursery lore—to herself, or watching the birds, joint tenants, feed and entice their young ones to fly, or nestling with closed lids, half thinking, half dreaming, happier than words can express.

"Look, Miss!" I exclaimed, pointing to a nook under the roots of one twisted tree. "Winter is not here yet. There's a little flower, up yonder, the last bud from the multitude of blue-bells that clouded those turf steps in July with a lilac mist. Will you clamber up, and pluck it to show to papa?"

Cathy stared a long time at the lonely blossom trembling in its earthy shelter, and replied, at length—

"No, I'll not touch it—but it looks melancholy, does it not, Ellen?"

One of the most memorable passages indicating the symbolic part played by the weather and atmosphere of the moors in the novel is when young Cathy (who fancies herself in love with the feeble young Linton) tells her old nurse Ellen how she and Linton differed in their view of the best kind of day to be spent in the open. It is a difference between movement and repose, two opposing ideals of bliss:

"One time, however, we were near quarrelling. He said the pleasantest manner of spending a hot July day was lying from morning till evening on a bank of heath in the middle of the moors, with the bees humming dreamily about among the bloom, and the larks singing high over head, and the blue sky and bright sun shining steadily and cloudlessly. That was his most perfect idea of heaven's happiness. Mine was rocking in a rustling green tree, with a west wind blowing, and bright, white clouds flitting rapidly above; and not only larks, but throstles, and blackbirds, and linnets, and cukoos pouring out music on every side, and the moors seen at a distance, broken into cool dusky dells; but close by, great swells of long grass undulating in waves to the breeze; and woods and sounding water, and the whole world awake and wild with joy. He wanted all to lie in an ecstasy of peace; I wanted all to sparkle, and dance in a glorious jubilee.

"I said his heaven would be only half alive, and he said mine would be drunk; I said I should fall asleep in his, and he said he could not breathe in mine, and began to grow very snappish. . . ."

At the end of the novel, Lockwood walks past the now quite decayed Gimmerton church, and the clashing contradictions of the novel are resolved in a mood of peace in nature.

My walk home was lengthened by a diversion in the direction of the Kirk. When beneath its walls, I perceived decay had made progress, even in seven months: many a window showed black gaps deprived of glass; and slates jutted off, here and there, beyond the right line of the roof, to be gradually worked off in coming autumn storms.

I sought, and soon discovered, the three head-stones on the slope next to the moor—the middle one, grey, and half buried in heath—Edgar Linton's only harmonized by the turf, and moss creeping up its foot—Heathcliff's still bare.

I lingered round them, under that benign sky, watched the moths fluttering among the heath and hare-bells; listened to the soft wind breathing through the grass; and wondered how any one could ever imagine unquiet slumbers for the sleepers in that quiet earth.

Whether this mood of peace is an adequate resolution of the contradictions and paradoxes which flash throughout the novel is a matter on which critics differ. But certainly *Wuthering Heights* ends, as it begins, with the moors at their most paradisial.

THOMAS HARDY'S WESSEX

HARDY IS THE MOST regional of English novelists, setting most of his novels and stories in those areas of southern and southwestern England which he called by the Old English name of Wessex. In general, it can be said that Lower Wessex was Devon, Mid Wessex was Wiltshire, North Wessex was Berkshire, Outer Wessex was Somerset, South Wessex was Dorset, and Upper Wessex was Hampshire. Dorset, or South Wessex, was for Hardy in the centre of the picture. He was born there on June 2, 1840 in the little village of Higher Bockhampton, a few miles east of Dorchester (which Hardy called Casterbridge in his novels) in a house built in 1801 by his grandfather who, like his father, was a stone-mason. Much of the atmosphere of the village of his birth and the surrounding area can be found in *Under the Greenwood Tree* (1872). In the nearby church at Stinsford (which Hardy calls Mellstock) Hardy's father and grandfather had been prominent members of the church choir which, as Hardy describes in this novel with affectionate humour, provided both the singing and the instrumental playing in the church gallery. The Dewys' house in *Under the Greenwood Tree* is the Hardy house at Higher Bockhampton. Here is Hardy's description of it:

It was a small low cottage with a thatched pyramidal roof, and having dormer windows breaking up into the eaves, a single chimney standing in the very midst. The window-shutters were not yet closed, and the fire and candle-light within radiated forth upon the bushes of variegated box and thick laurestinus growing in a throng outside, and upon the bare boughs of several codlin-trees hanging about in various distorted shapes, the result of early training as espaliers, combined with careless climbing into their boughs in later years. The walls of the dwelling were for the most part covered with creepers, though these were rather beaten back from the doorway—a feature which was worn and scratched by much passing in and out, giving it by day the appearance of an old keyhole. Light streamed through the cracks and joints of a wooden shed at the end of the cottage, a sight which nourished a fancy that the purpose of the erection must be rather to veil bright attractions than to shelter unsightly necessaries. The noise of a beetle and wedges and the splintering of wood was periodically heard from this direction; and at the other end of the house a steady regular munching and the occasional scurr of a rope betokened a stable, and horses feeding within it.

Hardy first went to school at Lower Bockhampton. His father for a time did repairs on the nearby Kingston Maurward estate north of Dorchester, and bought a small farm to the southeast called Talbothays, on the other

"It was a small low cottage with a thatched pyramidal roof . . ." Hardy's birthplace in Higher Bockhampton.

side of the Frome valley on the road east of the village of West Stafford. After Hardy's parents died, his brother Henry built a house there and called it Talbothays, but long before this Hardy must have been familiar with the whole area of what he calls in his map of Wessex the Valley of the Great Dairies, the Frome valley, which figures so prominently in *Tess of the D'Urbervilles* (1891). In that novel he actually gives the name of Talbothays to the farm where Tess worked and where Angel Clare found her and fell in love with her. "The oozing fatness and warm ferments of the Var Vale" (*Tess*, Chapter XXIV) is a reference to the fertility of the Frome valley and its dairy farms: Hardy also sometimes called the River Frome the Froom.

Tess is realized in the most specific geographical detail. In Chapter I Parson Tringham tells Jack Durbeyfield that rows and rows of his ancestors lie in the vaults at Kingsbere-sub-Greenhill. Kingsbere-sub-Greenhill is Bere Regis, some five miles east of Dorchester. Durbeyfield is walking home from Shaston (Shaftesbury) to the village of Marlott (Marnhull) "in the adjoining Vale of Blakemore or Blackmoor". In Hardy's novels Blackmoor Vale covers a wider area than it does in fact, extending over all the undulating pastoral and wooded country that extends north from the chalk hills which include Babb Down, High Stoy, Nettlecombe-Tout and Bulbarrow Hill. Running just north of Blackmoor Vale is what Hardy calls the Vale of the Little Dairies.

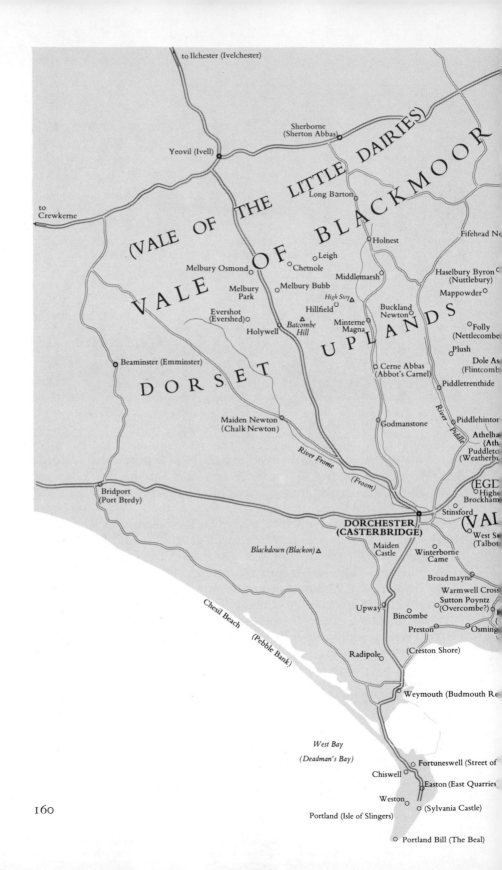

to Ilchester (Ivelchester)

Sherborne
(Sherton Abbas)

Yeovil (Ivell)

Long Barton

to
Crewkerne

(VALE OF THE LITTLE DAIRIES)

VALE OF BLACKMOOR

Holnest

Fifehead N

Leigh

Melbury Osmond   Chetnole

Middlemarsh

Haselbury Byron
(Nuttlebury)

Melbury Bubb

Melbury
Park

High Stoy

Mappowder

Hillfield

Evershot
(Evershed)

Batcombe
Hill

Buckland
Newton

Folly
(Nettlecombe

Holywell

Minterne
Magna

Plush

DORSET UPLANDS

Beaminster (Emminster)

Cerne Abbas
(Abbot's Carnel)

Dole As
(Flintcomb

Piddletrenthide

River Piddle

Maiden Newton
(Chalk Newton)

Godmanstone

Piddlehintor

Athelha
(Ath

River Frome

Puddleto
(Weatherbu

(Froom)

(EGD

Bridport
(Port Bredy)

Highe
Brockham

Stinsford

DORCHESTER
(CASTERBRIDGE)

(VA

West S
(Talbot

Maiden
Castle

Blackdown (Blackon)

Winterborne
Came

Broadmayne

Warmwell Cross

Sutton Poyntz
(Overcombe?)

Upway

Bincombe

Preston

Osming

Radipole

(Creston Shore)

Chesil Beach

(Pebble Bank)

Weymouth (Budmouth R

West Bay

(Deadman's Bay)

Fortuneswell (Street of

Chiswell

Easton (East Quarries

Weston

(Sylvania Castle)

Portland (Isle of Slingers)

Portland Bill (The Beal)

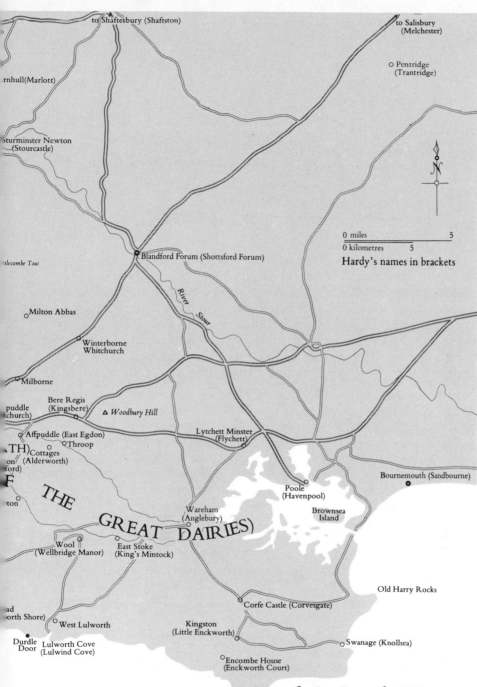

to Shaftesbury (Shaftston)

to Salisbury
(Melchester)

rnhull(Marlott)

○ Pentridge
(Trantridge)

Sturminster Newton
(Stourcastle)

N

0 miles   5
0 kilometres   5

Hardy's names in brackets

tlecombe Tout

○Blandford Forum (Shottsford Forum)

River Stour

Milton Abbas
○

Winterborne
Whitchurch

○Milborne

Bere Regis
(Kingsbere)
puddle
church)

△ Woodbury Hill

Lytchett Minster
(Flychett)

○Affpuddle (East Egdon)
TH)
on/
ford)
Cottages
(Alderworth)
○Throop

Bournemouth (Sandbourne)

F

ton
○

THE
GREAT DAIRIES)

Poole
(Havenpool)

Wareham
(Anglebury)

Brownsea
Island

Wool
(Wellbridge Manor)

East Stoke
(King's Mintock)

Old Harry Rocks

ad
orth Shore)

○West Lulworth

Corfe Castle (Corvesgate)

Durdle
Door
Lulworth Cove
(Lulwind Cove)

Kingston
(Little Enckworth)

Swanage (Knollsea)

Encombe House
(Enckworth Court)

St. Aldhelm's Head

Hardy's South Wessex

When Tess goes to the D'Urbervilles she takes the van that travels east from Shaston (Shaftesbury) and passes near Trantridge (Pentridge), where the D'Urbervilles live. "Tess's route on this memorable morning lay amid the north-eastern undulations of the Vale in which she had been born, and in which her life had unfolded. The Vale of Blackmoor was to her the world, and its inhabitants the races thereof."

When Tess leaves home for the second time, after the death of her baby, she goes through Stourcastle (Sturminster Newton), Puddletown (which is the setting of *Far from the Madding Crowd*, and stands for Weatherbury), westward by Kingsbere (Bere Regis, where "her useless ancestors lay entombed"), then south to the Valley of the Great Dairies in the Frome valley. It is there, at Talbothays Dairy, that she gets a job and her recovery takes place.

Seeking work again after Angel Clare has left her, Tess proceeds eastward through Chalk Newton (Maiden Newton) to the "starve-acre" farm of Flintcombe Ash (Dole Ash). When she decides to visit Angel's parents at Emminster (Beaminster) Vicarage she goes from Flintcombe Ash by way of Evershed (Evershot), where she stops for breakfast. It is on her way back from this fruitless visit that she is astonished to find Alec D'Urberville preaching in a barn at Evershed. Tess goes on her way back to Flintcombe Ash and is overtaken by Alec at Cross-in-Hand, "of all spots on the

Hardy's Wessex

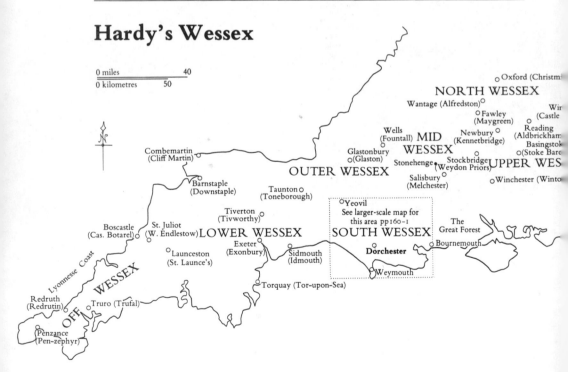

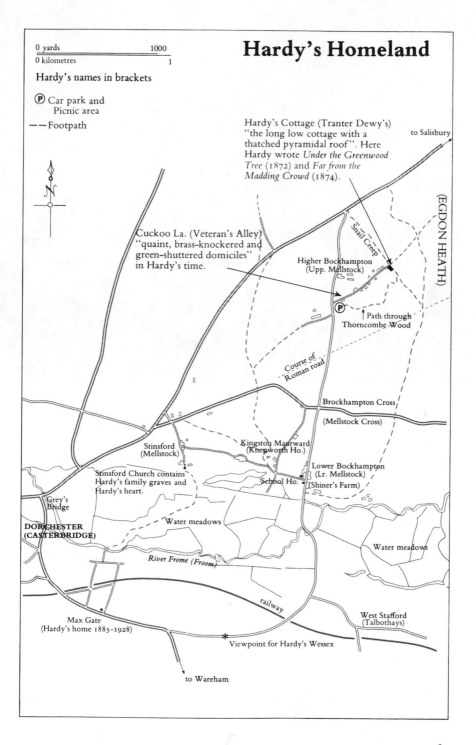

0 yards 1000

0 kilometres 1

Hardy's Homeland

Hardy's names in brackets

(P) Car park and
  Picnic area

——Footpath

N

Hardy's Cottage (Tranter Dewy's)
"the long low cottage with a
thatched pyramidal roof". Here
Hardy wrote *Under the Greenwood
Tree* (1872) and *Far from the
Madding Crowd* (1874).

to Salisbury

(EGDON HEATH)

Cuckoo La. (Veteran's Alley)
"quaint, brass-knockered and
green-shuttered domiciles"
in Hardy's time.

Snail Creep

Higher Bockhampton
(Upp. Mellstock)

(P)

↑ Path through
Thorncombe Wood

Course of
Roman road

Brockhampton Cross

(Mellstock Cross)

Kingston Maurward
(Knapwoth Ho.)

Stinsford
(Mellstock)

Lower Bockhampton
(Lr. Mellstock)

School Ho. (Shiner's Farm)

Stinsford Church contains
Hardy's family graves and
Hardy's heart.

Grey's
Bridge

DORCHESTER
(CASTERBRIDGE)

Water meadows

Water meadows

River Frome (Froom)

railway

West Stafford
(Talbothays)

Max Gate
(Hardy's home 1885-1928)

*

Viewpoint for Hardy's Wessex

to Wareham

A view of the bridge over the River Frome at Wool, Dorset, with the splendid seventeenth-century manor house which was the residence of the D'Urbervilles.

bleached and desolate upland . . . the most forlorn": it is a stone pillar on the road that runs over Batcombe Hill to Holywell and Evershot. Eventually, when she learns that her mother is dying, Tess returns to her native village of Marlott, where the family is evicted from their cottage. The carter sets down the family and their chattels by the church wall at Kingsbere their ancestral home, and it is there that Alec finds Tess and renews his plea that she should come and live with him.

When Angel Clare finds Tess, she is living with Alec at Sandbourne (Bournemouth), and it is at The Herons in Sandbourne that Tess, realizing that Alec had lied to her about Angel's attitude and had thus doubly betrayed her, murders him. On their last sad journey together Angel and Tess move northwards from Sandbourne to Melchester (Salisbury). From there they go to Stonehenge, where Tess is at last apprehended by the police. It is at Wintoncester (Winchester), "that fine old city, aforetime capital of Wessex", that the last act takes place. Clare and Tess's sister look down from West Hill over the city and see the black flag go up on the prison tower to announce that "Justice was done, and the President of the Immortals . . . had ended his sport with Tess".

A view of the River Stour as seen from the gardens of "Riverside", the house where Hardy wrote The Return of the Native.

The Return of the Native (1878) uses landscape in a more concentrated and symbolic way than *Tess*. It is dominated by Egdon Heath. As Hardy describes it, the heath runs eastward for about fourteen miles from Lower Bockhampton to the region north of Wareham (Hardy's Anglebury) and Poole Harbour (Hardy's Havenpool). "Under the general name of 'Egdon Heath'," Hardy wrote in his 1895 Preface to the novel, "which has been given to the sombre scene of the story, are unified or typified heaths of various real names, to the number of at least a dozen; these being virtually one in character and aspect, though their original unity, or partial unity, is now somewhat disguised by intrusive slips and slices brought under the plough with varying degrees of success, or planted to woodland." He added in a Postscript in 1912 that "though the action of the narrative is supposed to proceed in the central and most secluded part of the heaths united into one whole, as above described, certain topographical features resembling those delineated really lie on the margin of the waste, several miles to the westward of the centre." Bloom's End, where Mrs. Yeobright lived, is presented as a valley running southwards parallel to the Tincleton road (Tincleton is Hardy's Stickleford), while Clym and

Eustacia after their marriage lived "in their little house at Alderworth, beyond East Egdon", and this must be Affpuddle, "in the green valley of the River Puddle, which is bordered by heath". Budmouth, where Eustacia was born and after which she hankered, is Weymouth.

Dorchester, Hardy's Casterbridge, is the scene of most of the action of *The Mayor of Casterbridge*, although the novel opens near "the large village of Weydon-Priors, in Upper Wessex", which must be Stockbridge in Hampshire. This is where Henchard sells his wife to the sailor, before the start of his new life in Casterbridge. Dorchester is still full of reminiscences of this and other Hardy novels. The King's Arms in the High Street, "the chief hotel in Casterbridge", is where Susan Henchard sees her husband through the window, presiding over a dinner as the Mayor of Casterbridge. The hotel is mentioned many times in the novel: it is also here that, in *Far from the Madding Crowd* (1874), Farmer Boldwood carried Bathsheba after she had fainted outside the Corn Exchange (next to the hotel) on hearing that Sergeant Troy was supposed to be drowned. In spite of changes since Hardy's day, the reader of the Wessex novels can have little difficulty in identifying many of the Dorchester scenes described by Hardy, especially if he equips himself with M. R. Skilling's helpful pamphlet (with map) issued in 1975 by the Thomas Hardy Society Ltd. (The Society also publishes a series of tour pamphlets on individual novels, under the general editorship of Kenneth Carter.) The Three Mariners Inn, where Susan Henchard and her daughter stay, is now the British Legion Club, just a little further east along the High Street from the King's Arms. The Ring at Casterbridge, where Susan and Michael have their secret meeting, is Maumbury Ring at the southwest corner of the city.

Hardy, of course, knew Dorchester intimately. He went to school there from 1849 to 1856, walking from Higher Bockhampton, and in 1856 he was articled to John Hicks, a Dorchester architect and church-restorer. He moved to London in 1862 to further his architectural studies, but was back in Dorchester working for Hicks from 1867 to 1870. In February 1870 he returned to Higher Bockhampton, and shortly afterwards visited St. Juliot in Cornwall to make plans for the rebuilding of a church there. He stayed at the rectory, and fell in love with and eventually married the rector's sister-in-law, Emma Lavinia Gifford. Later he looked back with nostalgia to the excursions in Cornwall taken in Emma's company, using the old romantic Arthurian name "Lyonesse" for the Cornish coast: that name became permanently associated with memories of his wife. Hardy did some work on church restoration in Weymouth before moving again to London in 1870, to work on church restoration. He was in Cornwall once more in 1871, but returned to London in 1872. He was in Cornwall again visiting Emma in August 1872, staying this time at her father's house at Kirland, near Bodmin. He and Emma married at St. Peter's, Paddington (her family disapproving of the match) in September 1874. They took

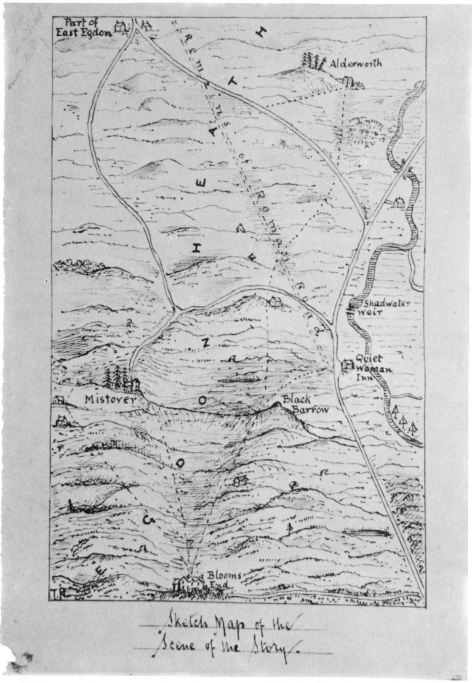

Hardy's map for The Return of the Native.

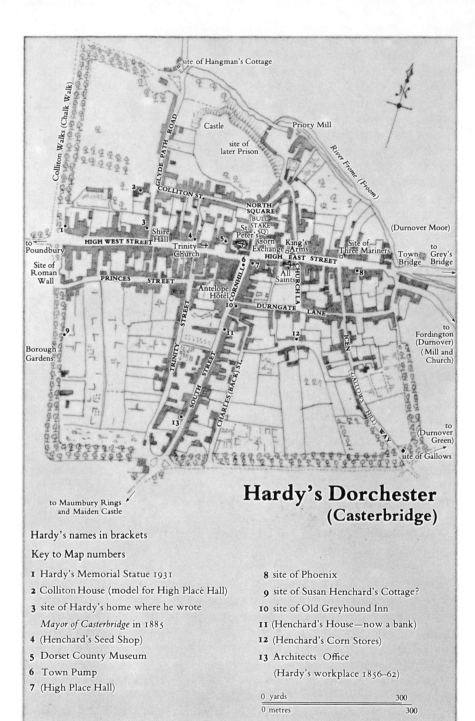

Hardy's Dorchester
(Casterbridge)

Hardy's names in brackets

Key to Map numbers

1 Hardy's Memorial Statue 1931

2 Colliton House (model for High Place Hall)

3 site of Hardy's home where he wrote
   Mayor of Casterbridge in 1885

4 (Henchard's Seed Shop)

5 Dorset County Museum

6 Town Pump

7 (High Place Hall)

8 site of Phoenix

9 site of Susan Henchard's Cottage?

10 site of Old Greyhound Inn

11 (Henchard's House—now a bank)

12 (Henchard's Corn Stores)

13 Architects Office
   (Hardy's workplace 1856–62)

0 yards		300
0 metres		300

rooms in Surbiton before moving to lodgings in Yeovil in March 1876. The following June they moved to a house called Riverside just outside Sturminster Newton, overlooking the River Stour in the Vale of Blackmoor, where Hardy, already established as a novelist, wrote *The Return of the Native* and the couple spent their happiest days.

The Hardys returned to London in 1878, Hardy apparently believing that a professional novelist had to live in the capital, but in May 1881 they decided to look for a house in Dorset. Eventually, in 1885, their house in Wareham Road, Dorchester, was completed and they moved into it in June. They called it Max Gate, because nearby there had once stood the house of a toll-keeper called Mack and Hardy wished to preserve this association. He lived here till his death in 1928.

Some of the most important scenes in Hardy's last novel, *Jude the Obscure* (1896), are set in "Christminster", which is clearly Oxford. Jude originally lived at Fawley (Hardy's Marygreen) a small village south of Wantage, Berkshire, with his great-aunt Drusilla Fawley. Christminster is identifiable as Oxford (which Hardy had often visited) by its streets and buildings. Christ Church is "Cardinal College"; Balliol is "Biblioll College"; St. Aldate's Street is "Cardinal Street"; The Sheldonian Theatre is the "Wren or circular theatre"; New College is "Oldgate College".

All Hardy's Wessex novels gain what might be called an emotional rhythm from their setting, and none more so than *Tess*, where we see more vividly than elsewhere in Hardy historical as well as topographical factors at work. Hardy was very much aware of changes in country living caused by the agricultural depression of the 1870s and, more generally, by the intrusion of the modern world into traditional ways of life and work. In *The Mayor of Casterbridge* the conflict between Henchard and Farfrae is partly the conflict between a way of life based on instinct and tradition and one based on modern technology as well as between one rooted in local customs and superstitions and one developed by a man "far frae" home who makes his own way by intelligent planning. In *Tess* the degeneration of the D'Urbervilles into the humble Durbeyfields and the assumption of the old D'Urberville name by a family of modern imposters, are part of the historical process that the novel never allows us to forget. And Tess herself, with her startling view that the world we live in is a blighted planet, "was expressing in her own native phrases—assisted a little by her Sixth Standard training—feelings which might almost have been called those of the age— the ache of modernism".

In *Tess* Nature sometimes appears to be doing her best to make amends for the wrongs wrought by man:

But this encompassment of her own characterization, based on shreds of convention, peopled by phantoms and voices antipathetic to her, was a sorry and mistaken creation of Tess's fancy—a cloud of moral hobgoblins by which she was terrified without reason. It was they that were out of harmony with the actual world, not she. Walking among the sleeping birds in the hedges, watching the skipping rabbits on a moonlit warren, or standing under a pheasant-laden bough, she looked upon herself as a figure of Guilt intruding into the haunts of Innocence. But all the while she was making a distinction where there was no difference. Feeling herself in antagonism, she was quite in accord. She had been made to break an accepted social law, but no law known to the environment in which she fancied herself such an anomaly.

Working in the fields, it is women rather than men who become one with Nature:

But those of the other sex were the most interesting of this company of binders, by reason of the charm which is acquired by woman when she becomes part and parcel of outdoor nature, and is not merely an object set down therein as at ordinary times. A fieldman is a personality afield; a field-woman is a portion of the field; she has somehow lost her own margin, imbibed the essence of her surrounding, and assimilated herself with it.

In the section of the novel called "The Rally" Hardy specifically associates Tess's recovery from gloom to content with the special kind of agricultural landscape in which she now finds herself:

The bird's-eye perspective before her was not so luxuriantly beautiful, perhaps, as that other one which she knew so well; yet it was more cheering. It lacked the intensely blue atmosphere of the rival vale, and its heavy soils and scents; the new air was clear, bracing, ethereal. The river itself, which nourished the grass and cows of these renowned dairies, flowed not like the streams in Blackmoor. Those were slow, silent, often turbid; flowing over beds of mud into which the in-cautious wader might sink and vanish unawares. The Froom waters were clear as the pure River of Life shown to the Evangelist, rapid as the shadow of a cloud, with pebbly shallows that prattled to the sky all day long. There the water-flower was the lily; the crow-foot here.

Either the change in the quality of the air from heavy to light, or the sense of being amid new scenes where there were no invidious eyes upon her, sent up her spirits wonderfully. Her hopes mingled with the sunshine in an ideal photosphere which surrounded her as she bounded along against the soft south wind. She heard a pleasant voice in every breeze, and in every bird's note seemed to lurk a joy.

Her face had latterly changed with changing states of mind, continually fluctuating between beauty and ordinariness, according as the thoughts were gay or grave. One day she was pink and flawless; another pale and tragical. When she was pink she was feeling less than when pale; her more perfect beauty accorded with less elevated mood; her more intense mood with her less per-fect beauty. It was her best face physically that was now set against the south wind.

The irresistible, universal, automatic tendency to find sweet pleasure some-where, which pervades all life, from the meanest to the highest, had at length mastered Tess. Being even now only a young woman of twenty, one who mentally and sentimentally had not finished growing, it was impossible that any event should have left upon her an impression that was not in time capable of transmutation.

And thus her spirits, and her thankfulness, and her hopes, rose higher and higher. She tried several ballads, but found them inadequate; till, recollecting the psalter that her eyes had so often wandered over of a Sunday morning before she had eaten of the tree of knowledge, she chanted: 'O ye Sun and Moon ... O ye Stars ... ye Green Things upon the Earth ... ye Fowls of the Air ... Beasts and Cattle ... Children of Men ... bless ye the Lord, praise Him and magnify Him for ever!'

This is the prelude to her falling in love with Angel Clare, just as the "starve-acre" Flintcomb-Ash farm, where she goes after her desertion by Clare, is set in a landscape that corresponds to her new mood and situation:

Here the air was dry and cold, and the long cartroads were blown white and dusty within a few hours after rain. There were few trees, or none, those that would have grown in the hedges being mercilessly plashed down with the quick-set by the tenant-farmers, the natural enemies of tree, bush and brake. In the middle distance ahead of her she could see the summits of Bulbarrow and of Nettlecombe Tout, and they seemed friendly. They had a low and unassuming aspect from this upland, though as approached on the other side from Blackmoor in her childhood they were as lofty bastions against the sky. Southerly, at many miles distance, and over the hills and ridges coastward, she could discern a surface like polished steel: it was the English Channel at a point far out towards France.

Before her, in a slight depression, were the remains of a village. She had, in fact, reached Flintcomb-Ash, the place of Marian's sojourn. There seemed to be no help for it; hither she was doomed to come. The stubborn soil around her showed plainly enough that the kind of labour in demand here was of the roughest kind; but it was time to rest from searching, and she resolved to stay, particularly as it began to rain.

Tess presents a vision of human destiny through a rendering of a single fate in a given society dependent on Nature. It is not Wordsworth's Nature, for it has baleful as well as beneficent aspects. It is a Nature which, indifferent to human laws, can work with man or against him, as circumstances determine. And man has in the course of history developed techniques and rituals that help him to cope with Nature. But no technique and no ritual can insure against disaster, and it is his sense of this ineluctable fact—that Nature is basically and essentially indifferent to man, who has to make such terms with it as he can—that, in spite of scenes of natural beauty and harmony, provides Hardy's essentially tragic view of life.

THE BLACKENING
OF ENGLAND

THE FIRST PHASE of what became known as the Industrial Revolution changed the face of England between 1760 and 1830: open land was enclosed by hedges or fences; small villages grew into crowded towns; tall factory chimneys came to dominate parts of the landscape. Although the distinctive features of these changes did not become clearly evident on a large scale until the nineteenth century, the technical achievement which underlay them was the product of the eighteenth century, which made the successful effort to unlock the secrets of Nature and dominate natural forces that hitherto had dominated man. The consequences were not only a changed landscape but also a rapid growth in population and a shift in its balance. At the beginning of the eighteenth century it was the southern part of the country that supported the largest number of people: Middlesex, Surrey, Kent, Gloucestershire, Somerset, Wiltshire and Devonshire together represented about one-third of the population of England, and the largest towns after London were Norwich and Bristol. By the end of the century the North had established itself as the region of vigorous industrial growth and new ideas and inventions so that, as Asa Briggs has put it, "a nineteenth-century conflict between North and South was as much a leading theme of English as of American history". Mrs. Gaskell's novel, *North and South*, published in 1855, is only one, if the most explicit, of many literary works reflecting this division. It was in the North as well as in the West Midlands that the changes effected by the Industrial Revolution were first strikingly manifested: these changes included increasing specialization of work and mobility of labour; people born in the country crowding into cities to earn their living no longer as traditional groups working in long-recognized relationships with each other but as units in a factory labour force; and enormous improvements in transport (of both goods and people) and means of communication. And these changes in turn produced others which affected all aspects of peoples' lives and stirred the emotions of artists and writers.

In spite of industrial advances, agriculture continued to occupy a majority of the population right through the eighteenth century, though its forms changed. The enclosure movement, which had been developing since the Middle Ages, now went ahead at an increasing pace and much more systematically: literally thousands of Acts of Parliament authorizing enclosure of particular areas were passed in the last forty years of the century. This increased the amount of cultivated land and the use of what had hitherto been waste, facilitated new systems of drainage, made possible experiment with new methods of cultivation, new crops and new kinds of

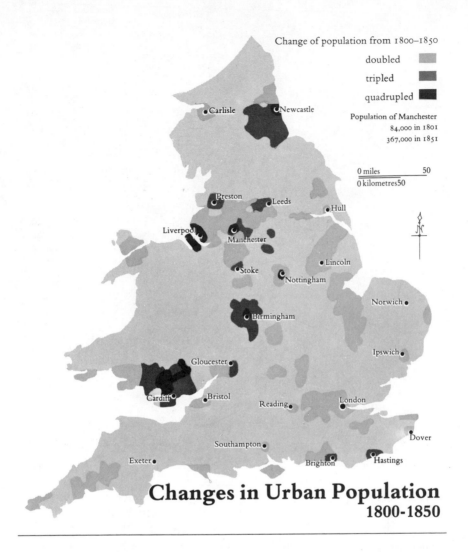

Change of population from 1800–1850

doubled

tripled

quadrupled

Population of Manchester
84,000 in 1801
367,000 in 1851

0 miles   50
0 kilometres 50

- Carlisle
- Newcastle
- Preston
- Leeds
- Hull
- Liverpool
- Manchester
- Stoke
- Lincoln
- Nottingham
- Birmingham
- Norwich
- Ipswich
- Gloucester
- Cardiff
- Bristol
- Reading
- London
- Dover
- Southampton
- Exeter
- Brighton
- Hastings

Changes in Urban Population
1800-1850

agricultural machinery, and so greatly increased production. But it also dispossessed cottagers who had cultivated a few strips of land in hitherto open fields and ousted even humbler marginal characters who had traditionally managed to exist on the fringes of the old village society, driving them to vagrancy or to unskilled labour in towns. It was the large tenant farmer, interested in agricultural improvement, who now dominated the agricultural scene, and though the progressive reorganization of units of administration on the land in favour of such a farmer with capital helped to produce the disappearance of both yeoman and cottager, it nevertheless provided the produce to feed a fast-growing and increasingly urbanized population.

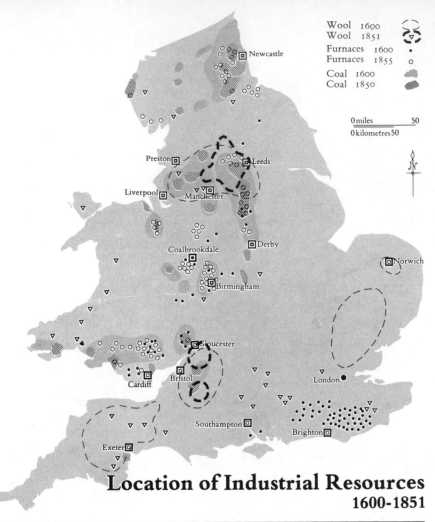

Wool 1600
Wool 1851
Furnaces 1600 •
Furnaces 1855 ○
Coal 1600
Coal 1850

0 miles   50
0 kilometres 50

Newcastle

Preston   Leeds
Liverpool   Manchester

Coalbrookdale   Derby
  Norwich
Birmingham

Gloucester

Cardiff   Bristol   London

Southampton
Brighton

Exeter

Location of Industrial Resources
1600-1851

In its early stages the Industrial Revolution depended on a traditional source of power—water. It was water power that enabled cotton mills to lead the change from cottage work to factory work. Various inventions helped to speed up the manufacture of textiles, to change the traditional method of carding, spinning and bleaching wool and to rationalize the production of linen and cotton, the latter providing the cheap calicoes that some economists have seen as the basis of the first stage of the Industrial Revolution as well as for the first time providing cheap cotton underwear for working people. Requiring water power, the textile industry grew up on hill tops and on valley bottoms beside fast-running streams. Steam power began to replace water power towards the end of the century, and this produced a significant change in the siting of textile mills, which no longer required to be beside streams. They tended to be sited in areas where coal was readily available, and where coal was not easily got, pressure to improve its transport led to the growth first of canals and then of railways.

Coalbrookdale on the River Severn, where Abraham Darby set up his ironworks. "Scene of superfluous grace, and wasted bloom, /O, violated COLEBROOK*!" wrote Anna Seward.*

A similar change took place in the production of iron, which traditionally had been a rural industry situated in the vicinity of wood and water. In the Sussex weald, the Forest of Dean, and by the fast high streams of Yorkshire, Derbyshire, Shropshire and Wales, iron ore was smelted in blast furnaces with lime and charcoal, the bellows often worked by water power. A shortage in the supply of timber for charcoal hastened the change from charcoal to coke. The pioneer here was Abraham Darby of Bristol, who took over an old ironworks in the Shropshire valley of Coalbrookdale on the River Severn early in the eighteenth century: the application of steam power in the last two decades of the century produced further significant changes. At this stage, however, as F. D. Klingender has pointed out, the change in the landscape produced by the great new iron works, "with their smouldering lime kilns and coke ovens, blazing furnaces and noisy forges", was not yet regarded as a woeful blackening but rather as producing examples of the romantic and the sublime. It is true that Anna Seward, the

"Swan of Lichfield", wrote in 1785 of the violation of natural beauty by the ironworks at Coalbrookdale:

> Scene of superfluous grace, and wasted bloom,
> O, violated COLEBROOK! in an hour,
> To beauty unpropitious and to song,
> The Genius of thy shades, by Plutus brib'd
> Amid thy grassy lanes, thy woodwild glens,
> Thy knolls and bubbling wells, thy rocks, and streams,
> Slumbers!—whole tribes fuliginous invade
> The soft, romantic, consecrated scenes; . . .
>
>   —Now we view
> Their fresh, their fragrant, and their silent reign
> Usurpt by Cyclops;—hear, in mingled tones,
> Shout their throng'd barge, their pond'rous engines clang
> Through thy coy dales; while red the countless fires,
> With umber'd flames, bicker on all thy hills,
> Dark'ning the Summer's sun with columns large
> Of thick, sulphureous smoke, which spread, like palls,
> That screen the dead, upon thy sylvan robe
> Of thy aspiring rocks; pollute thy gales,
> And stain thy glassy waters.

Yet there is a reluctant admiration here, seen perhaps more clearly in lines which turn to other industrial areas:

> Grim WOLVERHAMPTON lights her smouldering fires,
> And SHEFFIELD, smoke-involv'd; dim where she stands
> Circled by lofty mountains, which condense
> Her dark and spiral wreaths to drizzling rains,
> Frequent and sullied; as the neighbouring hills
> Ope their deep veins, and feed her cavern'd flames;
> While, to her dusky sister, Ketley yields,
> From her long-desolate, and livid breast,
> The ponderous metal.

The first true factory in England was John and Thomas Lombe's silk mill built at Derby in 1718–22: it was five or six storeys high, employed thirty-five men and used water power from the River Derwent. But silk was not nearly as important as cotton, wool and iron, and it was when steam power reached these industries that the blackening of England became visible. Matthew Boulton (partner of James Watt in invention and enterprise) opened his great factory in 1765 in Soho, near Birmingham, where he soon began the manufacture of steam engines, and this was the beginning of a rush of further inventions and new factories. "The people in London, Manchester and Birmingham are *steam mill mad*," Boulton wrote to Watt in 1781: the two of them supplied steam engines to the Coalbrookdale Company, to Josiah Wedgwood's pottery factory at Etruria in North Staffordshire, and to Richard Arkwright for one of his great spinning factories in Derbyshire.

It was the enormous inventiveness of the eighteenth century that propelled the Industrial Revolution and until the effects of steam power in blackening the face of much of the country became visible, men of letters were more likely to praise that inventiveness and write admiringly of ingenious machines and techniques than to deplore the destruction of the landscape or the loss of traditional ways of life. John Dyer, in his poem *The Fleece* (1757), describes with unqualified admiration the textile mills

> Where tumbling waters turn enormous wheels
> And hammers, rising and descending, learn
> To imitate the industry of man.

He wanted such "houses of labour" multiplied throughout the country:

> O when, through every province, shall be raised
> Houses of labour, seats of kind constraint,
> For those, who now delight in fruitless sports,
> More than in cheerful works of virtuous trade,
> Which honest wealth would yield, and portion due
> Of public welfare. . . .

He describes the wonder and joy with which visitors view

> The sprightly scene, where many a busy hand,
> Where spoles, cards, wheels, and looms, with motion quick,
> And ever-murmuring sound, the unwonted sense
> Wrap in surprise.

And he is encouraged rather than worried by

> The increasing walls of busy Manchester,
> Sheffield, and Birmingham, whose reddening fields
> Rise and enlarge their suburbs.

In subsequent decades these places looked less idyllic to observers. Even in the age of water power the rapid growth of child labour in textile mills disturbed some people: in 1789 more than two-thirds of the 1,150 workers in Arkwright's three mills in Derbyshire were children. (In fact the coming of steam reduced the proportion of children at work: in M'Connel and Kennedy's textile factory in Manchester in 1816 only 3 per cent of the 1,020 employees were under ten, though nearly half were eighteen or younger: the problem of young people in factories was to last a long time.)

The development of steam power is closely connected with the development of the iron and steel industry. The movement from charcoal to coke for smelting changed the location of the iron industry in Britain: by the mid-eighteenth century the most important area was the West Midlands and by 1800 there were important centres of iron production in South Wales and the West Midlands (Shropshire and Staffordshire, and South Yorkshire). The invention of new ways of applying steam power to furnaces, forges and mills also encouraged the growth of the iron industry in Scotland, and J. B. Neilson's invention of the "hot blast" technique in iron manufacture in 1830 made West Central Scotland (where the Carron Iron Company had been working since 1760) an important centre of pig iron and steel by the mid-nineteenth century. It was the application of steam power to the production of iron and steel that brought about the easy availability of wrought iron which was a condition for the development of the railways. It was also this application that was the prime factor in blackening much of the face of England, notably the Black Country of the West Midlands.

Before railways came canals, which have been called "the eighteenth century's first attempt to cope with transport problems created by growing towns and expanding industry". The third Duke of Bridgewater was the pioneer here: it was he who commissioned James Brindley to build the first great summit-level canal in England, the Bridgewater Canal, opened in 1761, linking his mines at Worsley to Manchester: it was later extended westward to Liverpool. What has been called "canal mania" reached its peak in the early 1790s, when Parliament authorized a total of fifty-three canal and navigation bills. Canals significantly altered the English landscape: aqueducts, cuttings, embankments, tunnels, locks and bridges added to the variety, and often to the attractiveness of both the rural and the urban scene, and in one case, Stourport, Worcestershire, canals actually created a town, with its distinctive and pleasing canal architecture flanking the waterways. The canals were dirty and grimy enough in industrial districts, but in pastoral areas, in W. G. Hoskins's approving words, "the canals flowed clear and sparkling in the sunshine, something new in the landscape with their towpaths, lock-keepers' cottages, stables for canal horses, their *Navigation* or *Canal* inns where they met a main road, and their long and narrow gaily painted boats".

But the canals soon proved inadequate for the industrial needs of the country, and the canal age had barely consolidated itself when it was overtaken by the railway age, which altered the landscape much more drastic-

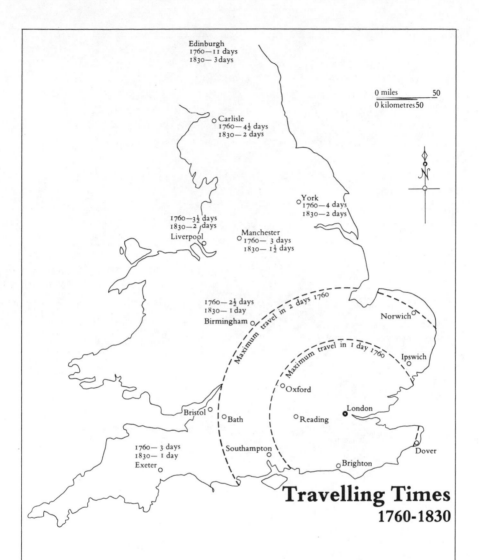

Edinburgh
1760—11 days
1830— 3 days

Carlisle
1760—4½ days
1830— 2 days

0 miles   50
0 kilometres 50

York
1760—4 days
1830—2 days

1760—3½ days
1830—2 days
Liverpool

Manchester
1760— 3 days
1830— 1½ days

1760—2½ days
1830— 1 day
Birmingham

Maximum travel in 2 days 1760

Norwich

Maximum travel in 1 day 1760

Ipswich

Oxford

Bristol
Bath

Reading

London

1760— 3 days
1830— 1 day
Exeter

Southampton

Brighton

Dover

Travelling Times
1760-1830

"It must be very agreeable to her to be settled within so easy a distance of her own family and friends."

"An easy distance do you call it? It is nearly fifty miles."

"And what is fifty miles of good road? Little more than half a day's journey. Yes, I call it a *very* easy distance."

—from Chapter 32, *Pride and Prejudice* by Jane Austen (1813)

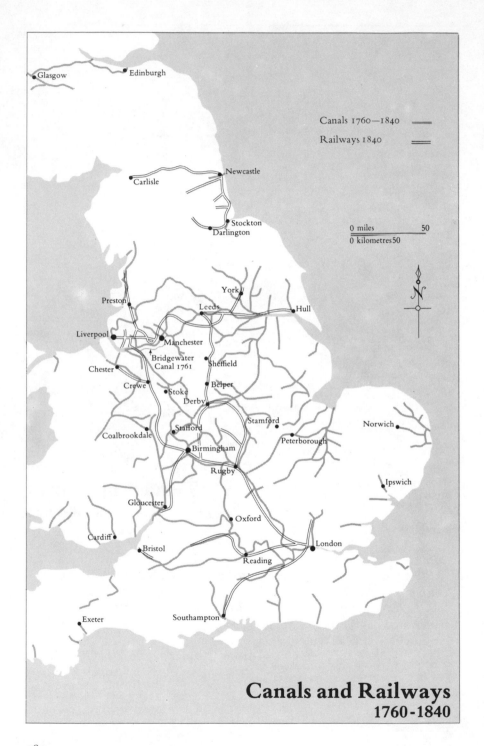

Canals 1760—1840

Railways 1840

0 miles 50

0 kilometres 50

Glasgow

Edinburgh

Newcastle

Carlisle

Stockton

Darlington

York

Preston

Leeds

Hull

Liverpool

Manchester

Bridgewater
Canal 1761

Sheffield

Chester

Crewe

Stoke

Belper

Derby

Coalbrookdale

Stafford

Stamford

Norwich

Birmingham

Peterborough

Rugby

Ipswich

Gloucester

Oxford

Cardiff

Bristol

London

Reading

Exeter

Southampton

Canals and Railways
1760-1840

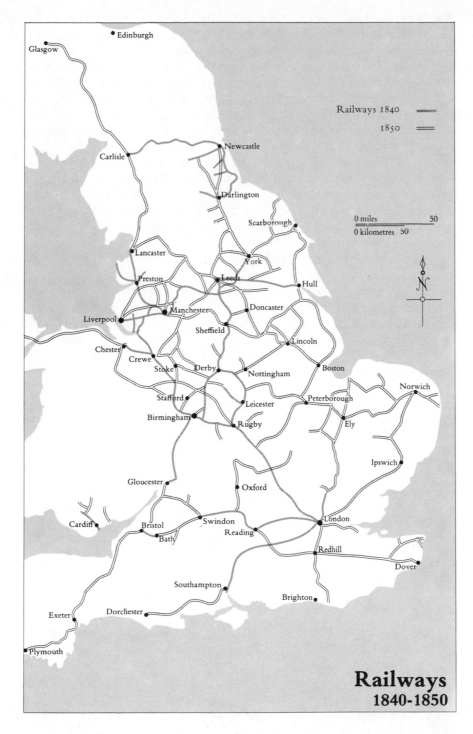

Railways 1840 ⎯
1850 ⎯⎯

0 miles   50
0 kilometres 50

N

Edinburgh
Glasgow
Carlisle
Newcastle
Darlington
Scarborough
Lancaster
York
Preston
Leeds
Hull
Liverpool
Manchester
Doncaster
Sheffield
Chester
Lincoln
Crewe
Stoke
Derby
Nottingham
Boston
Stafford
Leicester
Peterborough
Norwich
Birmingham
Rugby
Ely
Ipswich
Gloucester
Oxford
Cardiff
Bristol
Swindon
London
Bath
Reading
Redhill
Dover
Southampton
Brighton
Exeter
Dorchester
Plymouth

Railways
1840-1850

ally. The canal age more or less coincided with the first phase of the Industrial Revolution, 1760–1830, and by the time it was drawing to a close great changes in the economic life of the nation had been effected. The transport of bulky and heavy goods was immeasurably improved, with significant effects on (among other things) local styles of building, which no longer had to depend on local materials. (This effect became even more marked in the railway age, when a depressing uniformity of building styles often replaced interesting local traditional styles.) Some old market towns (Stamford, for example) declined, while new industrial towns developed. The town of Belper, small and poor in 1770, was by 1811 the second largest town in Derbyshire. Sheffield, Birmingham, Liverpool, Manchester, were among the towns that grew rapidly. There was considerable redistribution both of activities and of the balance of population. The canals also produced two classes of people, at opposite ends of the social scale, without whom the development of the railways would have been impossible—civil engineers and navvies (from "navigators", the canal labourers).

The Stockton–Darlington railway opened in 1825, the Liverpool–Manchester line in 1830. As Samuel Lilley has argued, the technical innovations which made steam locomotion possible and then kept improving it came when economic conditions required them. Nobody knew quite what he was doing when the railways began to be built in Britain, but the pace of railway construction expanded as financial enthusiasm backed up industrial pressures, until by 1850 six thousand miles of railway had been laid and both townscape and landscape permanently altered. The expansion was not planned in any organized way; it was done, in Lilley's phrase, in a

"sleep-walking manner", and its social effects were not foreseen. We have already noted, in the account of Dickens's London, the effects in London of railway construction and Dickens's response to it. There were similar upheavals in other cities and in open country, but none found a Dickens to describe them. Francis Klingender, in his classic book *Art and the Industrial Revolution* (edited and revised by Arthur Elton in 1968) has described the enormous impact on the English landscape of the coming of the railway and shown by reproductions of some splendid pictures of railways under construction both the visual glories and horrors of the process.

In the same way as, ironically, railways began to replace canals just when canals had reached their peak, so they replaced roads after decades of steady improvement in roads and coaches had enormously increased the efficiency of travel by coach. Roads had been deteriorating ever since the Romans left until the turnpike movement of the eighteenth century and new techniques of road-building resulted in roads capable of taking "flying coaches". The era of the flying coach—about 1815 to 1835—was the high point in romantic transport in England: busy yet picturesque coaching inns, splendid horses, heroic and idiosyncratic coach drivers—these are documented in the early Dickens, who was fascinated by the coaching age. When Dickens was young, every small boy wanted to be a flying coach driver when he grew up, just as in a later age he wanted to be an engine driver. The place of the coaching inn, the coach and road travel in *The Pickwick Papers* (1836–7), described with such relish and enjoyment, is in sharp contrast to the nightmare impressions of rail travel we find in *Dombey and Son* (1847–8) and *Hard Times* (1854).

Leeds, as seen from Holbeck Junction, 1868.

North country mails at the Peacock, Islington, in the era of the flying coach.

There was another field in which a splendid new development was over-taken at the height of its glory by a yet newer one, and this was long-distance shipping. The development of new and more efficient design of the sailing ship reached its peak in the "clippers" of the mid-nineteenth century. For some time the clippers successfully fought off the challenge of the steamship, for they had more cargo space than the latter, which needed much space for carrying coal. It was not until the 1880s that the steamship began to overtake the clipper on long sea routes, largely as the result of the opening of the Suez Canal in 1869, which gave easy access to the coaling stations now established worldwide. So the sailing ship dominated the imagination of writers longer than the coach did. The steamship comes effectively into literature with Kipling's admiration of the typical Scottish marine engineer, expressed in his poem "MacAndrew's Hymn". The romance of the steamer is largely the romance of technology and reflects a state of mind which first emerges in the eighteenth century; or it is the romance not of speed and efficiency, but of Masefield's

> Dirty British coaster with a salt-caked smoke stack
> Butting through the Channel in the mad March days.

Yet Masefield's primary allegiance was to the sailing ship, as is seen in his long narrative poem *Dauber* and in "Sea Fever":

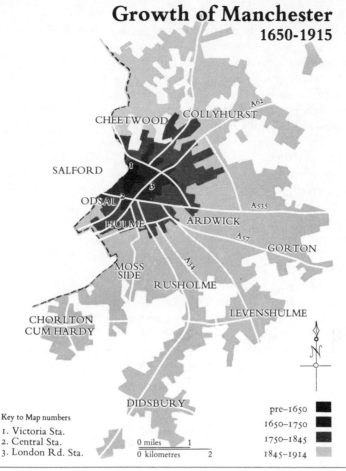

Growth of Manchester
1650-1915

COLLYHURST

CHEETWOOD

SALFORD

ODSAL

HULME

ARDWICK

GORTON

MOSS
SIDE

RUSHOLME

CHORLTON
CUM HARDY

LEVENSHULME

DIDSBURY

Key to Map numbers
1. Victoria Sta.
2. Central Sta.
3. London Rd. Sta.

0 miles 1
0 kilometres 2

pre–1650
1650–1750
1750–1845
1845–1914

I must down to the seas again, to the lonely sea and the sky,
And all I ask is a tall ship and a star to steer her by,
And the wheel's kick and the wind's song and the white sail's shaking,
And a grey mist on the sea's face and a grey dawn breaking.

This takes us a long way from city slums, but it is city slums that are an important feature of the new townscape brought about by the developments discussed above. Sheffield was already "smoke-involv'd" when Anna Seward described it in 1785. But Preston in 1795 was still, as John Aikin described it, "a handsome well-built town, with broad regular streets, and many good houses. The Earl of Derby has a large modern mansion in it. The place is rendered gay by assemblies and other places of amusement, suited to the genteel style of the inhabitants." Cotton spinning was introduced into the town in 1777, when its population was roughly 6,000, but that did not immediately transform it. It was in the very last years of the eighteenth century and the early years of the nineteenth that Preston was

185

rapidly transformed into a crowded and smoky workshop and it remained like that throughout the nineteenth century and later. By the beginning of the nineteenth century its population had risen to about 17,000. By the end of the century it was over 100,000. It was the steam-powered textile factories of Lancashire that caused this kind of growth; besides Preston, the Lancashire towns of Manchester, Bury, Oldham and Chorley had early steam-powered factories. Oldham grew from a village to a crowded town of 12,000 in a few years. Manchester grew fastest of all, as the centre of cotton manufacture, "a branch of commerce," wrote Aikin in 1795 (in his *Description of the country from thirty to forty miles around Manchester*) "the rapid and prodigious increase of which is, perhaps, absolutely unparalleled in the annals of trading nations". Comparing the census figures for 1801 (the first official census) with those of 1851 we find that Manchester–Salford had grown from 84,000 to 367,000; Liverpool had grown from 78,000 to 376,000 (thus overtaking Manchester); Birmingham had grown from 74,000 to 233,000; Leeds had grown from 53,000 to 172,000; and Sheffield had grown from 31,000 to 135,000 (figures to the nearest thousand in each case). Such rapid growth was the direct product of industrialization and involved the crowding of workers into poorly built back-to-back small terraced houses. And this meant slums.

The slums were born in the canal age, when houses for workers were built on low ground because that was where the canals lay and because it was easier and cheaper to build on flat ground than on the higher ground which had previously been chosen. The difficulty of draining this flat ground produced terrible sanitary problems: the word "slum" is said to come from an old provincial dialect word, "slump", meaning "wet mire". In the 1780s and 1790s the industrialists who used running water for their power as a rule housed their workers in houses of some dignity and comfort, but the outbreak of war in 1793 and the subsequent rise in the price of materials and of wages in the building trades, together with a rise in the price of land resulting from the growing scarcity of building land, brought a permanent decline in the standard of working-class houses, a decline both in the quality of the materials used and in workmanship. There were terrible slums in London from a much earlier period than this, as the chapters on London make clear, but the Northern and West Midland slums produced by the Industrial Revolution in its heyday have a character all their own. And they aroused a special kind of emotion among writers who observed them.

Dickens wrote *The Pickwick Papers* in 1836–7 and *The Old Curiosity Shop* in 1840–1. Both novels contain a description of a Black Country urban scene, and although only four years separate them the descriptions are very different. This was not only because in 1840 Dickens was a more sensitive observer of human misery, but also because by now he had developed a horror of mob violence which, like so many members of the middle class at this time, he erroneously associated with the Chartist movement.

Here is Dickens on Birmingham in *Pickwick*:

It was quite dark when Mr. Pickwick roused himself sufficiently to look out of the window. The straggling cottages by the road-side, the dingy hue of every object visible, the murky atmosphere, the paths of cinders and brick-dust, the deep-red glow of furnace fires in the distance, the volumes of dense smoke issuing heavily forth from high toppling chimneys, blackening and obscuring everything around; the glare of distant lights, the ponderous waggons which toiled along the road, laden with clashing rods of iron, or piled with heavy goods—all betokened their rapid approach to the great working town of Birmingham.

As they rattled through the narrow thoroughfares leading to the heart of the turmoil, the sights and sounds of earnest occupation struck more forcibly on the senses. The streets were thronged with working-people. The hum of labour resounded from every house, lights gleamed from the long casement windows in the attic stories, and the whirl of wheels and noise of machinery shook the trembling walls. The fires, whose lurid sullen light had been visible for miles, blazed fiercely up, in the great works and factories of the town. The din of hammers, the rushing of steam, and the dead heavy clanking of engines, was the harsh music which arose from every quarter.

And here are Little Nell and her grandfather:

Advancing more and more into the shadow of this mournful place, its dark depressing influence stole upon their spirits, and filled them with a dismal gloom. On every side, and far as the eye could see into the heavy distance, tall chimneys, crowding on each other, and presenting that endless repetition of the same dull, ugly form which is the horror of oppressive dreams, poured out their plague of smoke, obscured the light, and made foul the melancholy air. On mounds of ashes by the wayside, sheltered only by a few rough boards, or rotten pent-house roofs, strange engines spun and writhed like tortured creatures; clanking their iron chains, shrieking in their rapid whirl from time to time as though in torment unendurable, and making the ground tremble with their agonies. Dismantled houses here and there appeared, tottering to the earth, propped up by fragments of others that had fallen down, unroofed, windowless, blackened, desolate, but yet inhabited. Men, women, children, wan in their looks and ragged in attire, tended the engines, fed their tributary fire, begged upon the road, or scowled half-naked from the doorless houses. Then, came more of the wrathful monsters, whose like they almost seemed to be in their wildness and their untamed air, screeching and turning round and round again; and still, before, behind, and to the right and left, was the same interminable perspective of brick towers, never ceasing in their black vomit, blasting all things living or inanimate, shutting out the face of day, and closing in on all these horrors with a dense dark cloud.

But, night-time in this dreadful spot!—night, when the smoke was changed to fire; when every chimney spirted up its flame; and places, that had been dark vaults all day, now shone red-hot, with figures moving to and fro within their blazing jaws and calling to one another with hoarse cries—night, when the noise of every strange machine was aggravated by the darkness; when the people near them looked wilder and more savage; when bands of unemployed labourers paraded the roads, or clustered by torch-light round their leaders, who told them, in stern language, of their wrongs, and urged them on to frightful cries and threats; when maddened men, armed with sword and fire-brand, spurning the tears and prayers of women who would restrain them, rushed forth on errands of terror and destruction, to work no ruin half so surely as their own—night, when carts came rumbling by, filled with rude coffins (for contagious disease and death had been busy with the living crops); when orphans cried, and distracted women shrieked and followed in their wake—night, when some called for bread, and some for drink to drown their cares, and some with tears, and some with staggering feet, and some with bloodshot eyes, went brooding home—night, which, unlike the night that Heaven sends on earth, brought with it no peace, nor quiet, nor signs of blessed sleep—who shall tell the terrors of the night to the young wandering child!

The hysterical description of the mob was chosen to be illustrated by Hablot Brown, who showed the vanguard of a motley collection of distraught men armed with knives and guns and scythes and brandishing flaming torches; one carries a banner bearing a skull and crossbones; all are advancing on the industrial town which shows its tall chimneys in the background, clearly bent on its destruction. Like Dickens's prose, the illustration shows an apprehensive sense of the gap between rich and poor, between the affluent and the desperate, between those for whom industrialization meant affluence or at least a steady rise in the standard of living and those whom it brutalized or rejected or drove to despair. For this was the paradox which the Industrial Revolution brought about in nineteenth-century Britain and which haunted the imagination of so many Victorian writers: poverty in the midst of plenty, the country growing richer and more prosperous while segments of its population lived in squalor and hopelessness.

Some observers attributed this paradox to the workings of a *laisser-faire* economy, which was based on the assumption that every individual pursuing his own economic interests automatically contributes to the good of society as a whole. Thomas Carlyle attacked this view in 1843:

It is not to die, or even to die of hunger, that makes a man wretched; many men have died; all men must die,—the last exit of us all is in a Fire-Chariot of Pain. But it is to live miserable we know not why; to work sore and yet gain nothing; to be heart-worn, weary, yet isolated, unrelated, girt-in with a cold universal Laissez-faire: it is to die slowly all our life long, imprisoned in a deaf, dead, Infinite injustice, as in the accursed iron belly of a Phalaris' Bull. This is and remains forever intolerable to all men whom God has made. . . . The times, if we will consider them, are really unexampled.

Carlyle looked back to the ordered, hierarchical society of the Middle Ages as an antidote for the chaotic *laisser-faire* society which produced such misery as well as such wealth. Benjamin Disraeli, equally aware of the great paradox of poverty in the midst of plenty and the gap between rich and poor, looked to a restoration of responsible paternalism among the upper classes and of the mutual duties and responsibilities of all classes. Others looked to what we would now call more left-wing solutions. Friedrich Engels, Karl Marx's colleague and collaborator, produced his classic work, *The Condition of the Working Class in England*, in 1845. In the description of Manchester included in Chapter III Engels notes that the middle- and working-class districts of the city were quite distinct (thus marking a difference between the Victorian era and the earlier era of water-powered industry, when industrialists lived by their factories):

A view of the River Irk from Blackfriars Bridge in Manchester. "It is a narrow, coal-black, stinking river full of filth and rubbish," wrote Engels.

Engels' Manchester
Mid-19th century

He who visits Manchester simply on business or for pleasure need never see the slums, mainly because the working-class districts and the middle-class districts are quite distinct. This division is due partly to deliberate policy and partly to instinctive and tacit agreement between the two social groups. In those areas where the two social groups happen to come into contact with each other the middle classes sanctimoniously ignore the existence of their less fortunate neighbours.

Engels goes on to give a description of the working-class districts of Manchester. Here is part of his description of "the crazy layout of the whole district near the River Irk" (figures in parentheses refer to the map opposite):

There is a very sharp drop of some 15 to 30 feet down to the south bank of the Irk at this point. As many as three rows of houses have generally been squeezed on to this precipitous slope. The lowest row of houses stands directly on the bank of the river while the front walls of the highest row stand on the crest of the ridge in Long Millgate (1). Moreover, factory buildings are also to be found on the banks of the river. In short the layout of the upper part of Long Millgate at the top of the rise is just as disorderly and congested as the lower part of the street. To the right and left a number of covered passages from Long Millgate give access to several courts. On reaching them one meets with a degree of dirt and revolting filth the like of which is not to be found elsewhere. The worst courts are those leading down to the Irk (2), which contain unquestionably the most dreadful dwellings I have ever seen. In one of these courts, just at the entrance where the covered passage ends, there is a privy without a door. This privy is so dirty that the inhabitants of the court can only enter or leave the court if they are prepared to wade through puddles of stale urine and excrement. Anyone who wishes to confirm this description should go to the first court on the bank of the Irk above Ducie Bridge (3). Several tanneries are situated on the bank of the river and they fill the neighbourhood with the stench of animal putrefaction. The only way of getting to the courts below Ducie Bridge is by going down flights of narrow dirty steps and one can only reach the houses by treading over heaps of dirt and filth. The first court below Ducie Bridge is called Allen's Court (4). At the time of cholera [1832] this court was in such a disgraceful state that the sanitary inspectors [of the local Board of Health] evacuated the inhabitants. The court was then swept and fumigated with chlorine. In his pamphlet Dr. Kay gives a horrifying description of conditions in this court at that time. Since Kay wrote this pamphlet, this court appears to have been at any rate partly demolished and rebuilt. If one looks down the river from Ducie Bridge one does at least see several ruined walls and high piles of rubble, side by side with some recently built houses. The view from this bridge, which is mercifully concealed by a high parapet from all but the tallest mortals, is quite characteristic of the whole district. At the bottom the Irk flows, or rather, stagnates. It is a narrow, coal-black, stinking river full of filth and rubbish which it deposits on the more low-lying right bank. In dry weather this bank presents the spectacle of a series of the most revolting blackish-green puddles of slime from the depths of which bubbles of miasmatic gases constantly rise and create a stench which is unbearable even to those standing on the bridge forty or fifty feet above the level of the water. Moreover, the flow of the river is continually interrupted by numerous high weirs, behind which large quantities of slime and refuse collect and putrefy. Above Ducie Bridge there are some tall tannery buildings (5), and further up there are dye-works (6), bone mills, and gasworks. All the filth, both liquid and solid, discharged by these works finds its way into the River Irk, which also receives the contents of the adjacent sewers and privies. The nature of the filth deposited by this river may well be imagined. If one looks at the heaps of garbage below Ducie Bridge one can gauge the extent to which accumulated dirt, filth, and decay permeate the courts on the steep left bank of the river. The houses are packed very closely together and since the bank of the river is very steep it is possible to see a part of every house. All of them have been blackened by soot, all of them are crumbling with age and all have broken window panes and window frames. In the background there are old factory buildings which look like barracks. On the oposite, low-lying bank of the river, one sees a long row of houses and factories. The second house is a roofless ruin, filled with refuse, and the third is built in such a low situation that the ground floor is uninhabitable and has neither doors nor windows. In the background one sees the paupers' cemetery (7), and the stations of the railways (8) to Liverpool and Leeds. Behind these buildings is situated the workhouse (9), Manchester's "Poor Law Bastille". The workhouse is built on a hill and from behind its high walls and battlements seems to threaten the whole adjacent working-class quarter like a fortress.

In the same year, 1845, that Engels wrote his account, Disraeli published his novel *Sybil*, with the significant sub-title *The Two Nations*.

"Well, society may be in its infancy," said Egremont, slightly smiling; "but, say what you like, our queen reigns over the greatest nation that ever existed."

"Which nation?" asked the younger stranger, "for she reigns over two."

The stranger paused; Egremont was silent, but looked inquiringly.

"Yes," resumed the younger stranger after a moment's interval. "Two nations; between whom there is no intercourse and no-sympathy; who are as ignorant of each other's habits, thoughts, and feelings as if they were dwellers in different zones, or inhabitants of different planets; who are formed by a different breeding, are fed by a different food, are ordered by different manners, and are not governed by the same laws."

"You speak of—" said Egremont, hesitatingly.

"THE RICH AND THE POOR."

Disraeli's contempt for the utilitarianism, the lack of imagination, the self-seeking politicking and the other factors which in his view had produced the two nations (and what came to be known as "the condition of England question") did not mean that he lacked admiration for the commercial and industrial progress represented by the great new industrial towns. He admired the vision and energy that had gone to produce them, though he deplored the littleness of those who directed affairs in his own time. His account of Manchester in his novel *Coningsby* (1844) is eloquent with admiration:

What Art was to the ancient world, science is to the modern: the distinctive faculty. In the minds of men the useful has succeeded to the beautiful. Instead of the city of the Violet Crown, a Lancashire village has expanded into a mighty region of factories and warehouses. Yet, rightly understood, Manchester is as great a human exploit as Athens.

The inhabitants, indeed, are not so impressed with their idiosyncrasy as the countrymen of Pericles and Phidias. They do not fully comprehend the position which they occupy. It is the philosopher alone who can conceive the grandeur of Manchester, and the immensity of its future. There are yet great truths to tell, if we had either the courage to announce or the temper to receive them.

Yet the paradox remained: the grandeur and the squalor coexisted, the product, it seemed, of the same forces. It was in the 1840s that English novelists turned from traditional scenes to confront the realities of urban life in an industrial society. By this time awareness that the traditional patterns of English life, symbolized by the country town in which socially responsible landowners, farmers and tradespeople cohered in an organic community (as in Jane Austen's *Emma*: Jane Austen, though her life and work spanned the late eighteenth and early nineteenth centuries, was essentially a writer of preindustrial provincial England), were seen to have broken down, at least in the big industrial cities, and the problem was what to do about it. Suggested solutions came both from the right and from the left but more often the novelist faced the situation with mounting frustration (as in Dickens's later novels) and a sense that only some ethical and psychological improvement in human behaviour could provide a solution. Mrs. Gaskell's *Mary Barton*, subtitled *A Tale of Manchester Life*, was published in 1848. It gives a vivid picture of the distress caused by industrial depression in the 1840s and of the desperation to which men of high ideals could be driven. Mrs. Gaskell paints an unsympathetic picture of employers' attitude to workers, and the implication is that a change of heart among employers might help to provide a solution. In *North and South* (1854–5) not only does she emphasize the differences which had developed between the industrial north and the rural south, but she makes a remarkable effort to understand from the inside both the aims and the motives of workers who organize and strike and those of the industrialists who employ them. Her portrait of Mr. Thornton, one of the tough, self-made "new men" of industry, combines criticism with admiration. She allows both him and his workers to learn from experience. Such learning, the implication is, can mitigate the rigours of the class struggle though it cannot do away with the struggle altogether.

That the Industrial Revolution enabled Englishmen to feed and clothe generations of an expanding population who would otherwise have remained hungry and backward seems beyond dispute. That the price of progress was in some respects high is also generally accepted. In spite of the blackening of large areas, in spite of smoke and slag-heaps and slums, there was a conspicuous overall rise in the standard of living as the consequences of the Industrial Revolution manifested themselves. Men of letters for the most part were more conscious of the losses than of the gains, although the most eloquent of all defenders of industrialism as unqualified progress was Lord Macaulay, whose famous review of Robert Southey's *Colloquies* in 1830 is one of the great professions of faith in the progress resulting from *laisser-faire* capitalism and individualism. But the poets and novelists tended to be more sceptical. As early as 1814 Wordsworth, in *The Excursion*, deplored the round-the-clock shift labour of the new factories. Night falls, and the stars appear—

> Then, in full many a region, once like this
> The assured domain of calm simplicity
> And pensive quiet, an unnatural light
> Prepared for never-resting Labour's eyes
> Breaks from a many-windowed fabric huge;
> And at the appointed hour a bell is heard,
> Of harsher import than the curfew-knoll
> That spake the Norman Conqueror's stern behest—
> A local summons to unceasing toil.
> Disgorged are now the ministers of day;
> And, as they issue from the illumined pile,
> A fresh band meets them, at the crowded door—
> And in the courts—and where the rumbling stream,
> That turns the multitude of dizzy wheels,
> Glares, like a troubled spirit, in its bed
> Among the rocks below. Men, maidens, youths
> Mother and little children, boys and girls,
> Enter, and each the wonted task resumes
> Within this temple, where is offered up
> To Gain, the master-idol of the realm,
> Perpetual sacrifice.

This was still in the age of water power, and the objection is moral rather than social or aesthetic. Wordsworth's objections were aesthetic as well as moral when in 1844 he combated a proposal to build a railway from Kendal to the shores of Lake Windermere:

> Proud were ye, Mountains, when, in times of old,
> Your patriot sons, to stem invasive war,
> Intrenched your brows; ye gloried in each scar:
> Now, for your shame, a Power, the Thirst of Gold,
> That rules o'er Britain like a baneful star,
> Wills that your peace, your beauty, shall be sold,
> And clear way made for her triumphal car
> Through the beloved retreats your arms enfold.
>
> Heard YE that Whistle? As her long-linked Train
> Swept onwards, did the vision cross your view?
> Yes, ye were startled;—and, in balance true,
> Weighing the mischief with the promised gain,
> Mountain, and Vales, and Floods, I call on you
> To share the passion of a just disdain.

Time has long since mellowed the railways, in the Lake District as elsewhere, into an acceptable feature of the landscape: indeed, the closing of many miles of railway in the age of the motorcar and the aeroplane has led to Wordsworthian complaints from lovers of the countryside. But some aspects of the blackening of England have not mellowed with time and in many areas the mid-nineteenth-century industrial landscape is still visible, not only in the big cities but also in what W. G. Hoskins has called "the miles of torn and poisoned countryside" between them—"the mountains of waste from mining and other industries; the sheets of sullen water, known as 'flashes', which had their origin in subsidence of the surface as a result of mining below; the disused pit-shafts; the derelict and stagnant canals. The train journey between Leeds and Sheffield shows one this nineteenth-century landscape to perfection."

Later Victorian "prophets" such as John Ruskin and William Morris preached a revival of old handicrafts ousted by industrial mass production and combined in various intriguing ways a neo-medievalism with a utopian socialism in their search for a remedy for the ills of an industrialized society. Later still Arnold Bennet wrote of the pottery towns of Staffordshire and D. H. Lawrence, in *Women in Love*, of a mining area in Nottinghamshire and the moral and psychological problems presented by factory bosses and their relation to the workers and by the middle-class ethic generally. But the trauma produced by industrialization was at its greatest in the first half of the nineteenth century, particularly in the 1840s. It was then that blackened England could be seen in its most comfortless aspects.

SCOTLAND IN LITERATURE

THE KINGDOM OF SCOTLAND was born about 843, when the Scot Kenneth MacAlpin, who ruled the kingdom of Dalriada in the west of Scotland, acquired the throne of the Picts and united Dalriada and Pictland (which comprised much of northern Scotland) under his own rule. The MacAlpin kings expanded eastward and southward to the Lowlands, which had been controlled by Angles from Northumbria since the seventh century. Late in the tenth century they captured Edinburgh, and by 1034, under King Duncan, Scotland's boundaries were pretty much what they are today, with the Scottish–English border running from the Solway on the west to the Tweed on the east.

Scotland was and is geographically divided by what is known as the Highland line, a great geological fault running from southwest to northeast in a roughly diagonal line across the country. The range of hills that mark this fault is punctuated by individual mountains over three thousand feet, Ben Ledi, Ben Vorlich (both part of the scenery of the opening of Scott's narrative poem *The Lady of the Lake*) and Ben Lomond, which rises from the eastern side of the loch of the same name, with its famous bonny banks. Communications between Highlands and Lowlands were for centuries a real problem for those who were trying to govern Scotland as a single unified country. This can be seen at once if you look down from the castle rock at Stirling, which commands the bridge over the Forth which for centuries was the most effective way of getting from the Lowlands to the Highlands. It is no accident that the decisive battle of Scottish history was fought below Stirling Castle, at Bannockburn in 1314, for possession of this vital fortress. The Scottish victory over the English King Edward II and his army at Bannockburn effectively frustrated the English Crown's long continued attempts to establish English overlordship in Scotland and was remembered by later generations of Scots as a great national triumph. John Barbour's fourteenth-century narrative poem *The Bruce* is an account of the exploits of Robert Bruce, the victor of Bannockburn: its praise of freedom ("A! fredome is a noble thing!") and its account of the battle are two of its high points. Four centuries later Robert Burns wrote, to a traditional air, his "Scots wha hae" as Bruce's address to his troops before Bannockburn.

North of the Highland line at its eastern end there are low-lying parts, including substantial parts of Aberdeenshire and Morayshire, and these parts, notably Aberdeen, produced individual contributions to Scottish culture. And the Lowlands were far from being all flat: there are Lowland hills too, the Lammermuirs (scene of those parts of R. L. Stevenson's *Weir of*

Hermiston that are not set in Edinburgh), the Moorfoots, and the picturesque and rugged Border country including Tweeddale and Ettrick Forest and such famous rivers as the Ettrick and the Yarrow, which figure prominently in the famous Border Ballads and haunted the imagination of Wordsworth among others. Scott, though born in Edinburgh, was essentially a man of the Borders, where his ancestors had lived and where he spent much of his childhood. As a young man he made annual "raids" into Liddesdale exploring the countryside, thrilling to ruined towers and collecting much of the material he was to use in his ballad collection, *Minstrelsy of the Scottish Border*. For centuries the Borders had a culture of their own: the way of life of the Border leaders consisted largely of making and resisting forays into and from England. Their fortified "peels", whose ruins so delighted Scott, testify to the life of raiding, cattle lifting and constant attack and defence that is reflected in the Border Ballads. The battle of Otterburn, remembered in more than one ballad, was the result of a Scottish raid into the English side of the Border in 1385.

Edinburgh gradually emerged as Scotland's capital in the fifteenth century. Dunfermline, Linlithgow and Stirling were also royal residences and important centres in medieval Lowland Scotland. Edinburgh began as a fortress on a hill, and is first referred to in the poem *Y Gododdin* by the sixth-century Welsh poet Aneirin as Dineidin, "fortress of the hill-slope", the Welsh equivalent of the Scots Gaelic Dunedin. The Gaelic word *dun* (fortress, castle) translates into Old English *burh*: hence when the Northumbrians occupied much of the Lowlands Dunedin became Edinburgh, a name which stuck.

The trouble with having Edinburgh as a capital was its accessibility to English invaders. Anyone who crosses the Border today at Carter Bar and proceeds north by Jedburgh through Lauderdale to Soutra Hill and then looks down on Edinburgh will be able to see at once how invaders were able to march on the city, so much nearer the Scottish–English Border than the distant English capital. When the Scots marched into England they rarely got very far south. When James IV marched south against England in 1513 in support of his French ally he boasted that he would soon reach York, but in fact he and his army were destroyed at Flodden, just south of the Border. This defeat, where Scotland lost her king and the flower of her nobility, long stayed in the Scottish imagination as the greatest national disaster the country had ever experienced, and an old lament for Flodden, "The Flowers o' the forest are a' wede awa' ", was rewritten twice by Scottish literary ladies in the eighteenth century. It is known today as a moving pipe tune, played on memorial occasions. The battle itself is vividly described in Scott's *Marmion*.

On two occasions Jacobite armies from Scotland, supporting the exiled Stewart line against the reigning Hanoverians, penetrated some distance into England, but in neither case with any ultimate success. The first

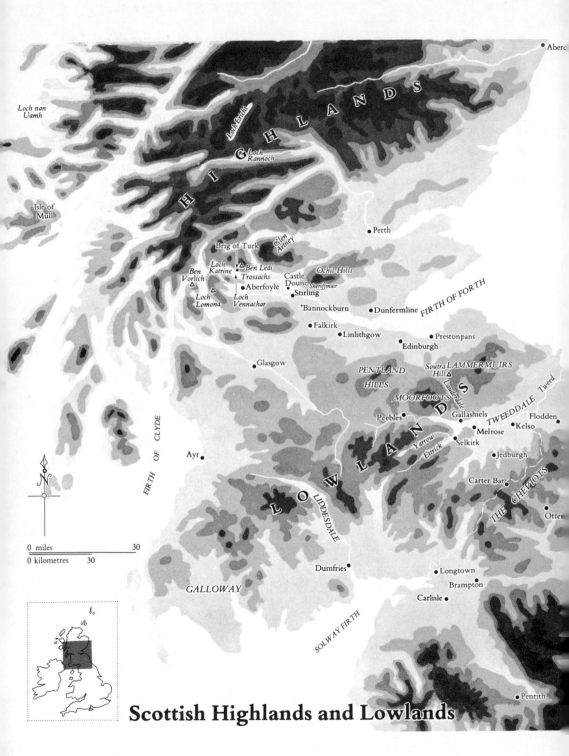

Loch nan
Uamh

Isle of
Mull

Loch Ericht

Loch
Rannoch

HIGHLANDS

Aberd

• Perth

Brig of Turk   Glen
Artney

Loch   △ Ben Ledi
Katrine

Ben   ↑ Trossachs
Vorlich △   • Aberfoyle

Loch △
Lomond   Loch
Vennachar

Castle
Doune   Ochil Hills

Sheriffmuir
• Stirling

†Bannockburn

• Dunfermline   FIRTH OF FORTH

• Falkirk

• Linlithgow

• Glasgow

PENTLAND
HILLS

Soutra
Hill △ LAMMERMUIRS

MOORFOOTS

Edinburgh   • Prestonpans
•   • Linlithgow
         Pentland

Lauderdale

Tweed

Peebles   Gallashiels   TWEEDDALE   • Flodden
•   •   • Kelso
                    Yarrow   Melrose

Ayr •   Ettrick • Selkirk

                              • Jedburgh

FIRTH OF CLYDE

L O W L A N D S

LIDDESDALE

Carter Bar

THE CHEVIOTS

• Otter

N

0 miles   30
0 kilometres   30

GALLOWAY

Dumfries •

SOLWAY FIRTH

• Longtown
• Brampton
Carlisle •

• Penrith

Scottish Highlands and Lowlands

occasion was in the Jacobite rising of 1715, where a mixed Jacobite force of men from Northumberland, Scottish Borderers and Highlanders marched south from the Borders through Longtown, Brampton, Penrith, Appleby, Kendal and Lancaster to Preston, where they were decisively defeated at almost exactly the same time as the undecisive battle of Sheriffmuir was being fought at the foot of the Ochil Hills in southern Perthshire by Jacobite forces under the Earl of Mar against government forces commanded by the second Duke of Argyll. Sheriffmuir was a strange battle, for Mar's Highlanders routed Argyll's right wing at the same time as the cavalry on Argyll's left wing drove back the Highland foot opposite them. There are several versions of an old song recording that in this battle both sides ran away:

> There's some say that we won,
> And some say that they won,
> And some say that nane won at a' man;
> But one thing I'm sure,
> That at Sheriffmuir
> A battle there was which I saw, man.
> And we ran, and they ran,
> And they ran, and we ran,
> And we ran, and they ran awa' man.

The more serious of the two Jacobite penetrations into England from Scotland was that of 1745, when Bonnie Prince Charlie led his largely Highland army as far south as Derby after his victory over the government forces of Sir John Cope at Prestonpans in September. But Charlie and his army had to turn back after reaching Derby to avoid virtually certain defeat by a large English army. They retreated to Scotland, and won the battle of Falkirk against a government army before retreating ever further north, to be finally and utterly defeated at Culloden, Inverness-shire, in April 1746. The adventures of the fugitive Prince Charlie, hunted throughout the Highlands and Islands by government forces, until he was finally taken off by a French ship at Loch nan Uamh and brought to exile in France (and later in Italy), is a story that took hold of the imagination of many Scotsmen. Indeed, it was only after the final defeat of the Jacobite movement at Culloden that the lost cause took on a romantic glow that was to attract poets and novelists. Folk songs and imitation folk songs about Bonnie Prince Charlie range from "Charlie he's my darling" (of which Burns produced a version) to Lady Nairne's "Will ye no come back again?", still popular as a song to a parting guest, although in fact Bonnie Prince Charlie never came back. But the writer who did most to show both the appeal and the anachronistic nonsense of the Jacobite movement was Sir Walter Scott, whose first novel *Waverley* gives a vivid and remarkably

The battle of Culloden, 1746.

accurate account of the beginnings of the 1745 rising, the battle of Preston-pans, and the march to Derby. The earlier parts of the novel, which bring Captain Waverley to visit Baron Bradwardine at Tully-Veolan, uses scenery from the Trossachs (which Scott had made popular earlier in *The Lady of the Lake*) and other parts of the Perthshire Highlands as well as reminiscences of houses in and near Edinburgh. "There is no particular mansion described under the name of Tully-Veolan," Scott wrote in a footnote, "but the peculiarities of the description occur in various old Scottish Seats. The House of Warrender upon Bruntsfield Links [on Edinburgh's south side], and that of Old Ravelston . . . have contributed several hints to the description in the text. The House of Dean, near Edinburgh, has also some points of resemblance in the text. The author has, however, been informed, that the House of Grandtully [on the south bank of the Tay, in Perthshire] resembles that of the Baron of Bradwardine still more than any of the above." The romantic scene by the waterfall in

Chapter 22, where Flora MacIvor sings to Waverley, is based on a Trossachs memory. The waterfall, Scott tells us, "is taken from that of Ledeard, at the farm so called on the northern side of Ledeard, and near the head of the Lake, four or five miles from Aberfoyle". (Scott was to use this scenery again in *Rob Roy*.) Scott also brings Waverley to the Castle of Doune, which was garrisoned by the Jacobites during the 1745 rising. "It holds a commanding station on the banks of the river Teith," Scott tells us in a note, "and has been one of the largest castles in Scotland." It was from Castle Doune that the wife of "the bonny Earl o' Moray" looked in vain for her husband's return after his murder in 1592:

> O lang will his ladie look
>   Owre the Castle Doune,
> Ere she see the Earl o Moray
>   Come soundan throu the toun.

With *The Lady of the Lake* (1810) Scott did for the Trossachs what Wordsworth did for the Lake District. "The whole country rang with the praises of the poet," wrote young Robert Cadell, then a trainee publisher in Edinburgh, "—crowds set off to the scenery of Loch Katrine, till then com-

The Trossachs, where "mountains, that like giants, stand/To sentinel enchanted land".

paratively unknown; and as the book came out just before the season for excursions, every house and inn in that neighbourhood was crammed with a constant succession of visitors. It is a well ascertained fact that from the date of the publication of *The Lady of the Lake* the post-horse duty in Scotland rose in an extraordinary degree, and indeed it continued to do so regularly for a number of years, the author's succeeding works keeping up the enthusiasm for our scenery which he had thus originally created." Here is part of Scott's opening description of the stag hunt in the Trossachs:

> The stag at eve had drunk his fill,
> Where danced the moon on Monan's rill,
> And deep his midnight lair had made
> In lone Glenartney's hazel shade;
> But, when the sun his beacon red
> Had kindled on Benvoirlich's head,
> The deep-mouth'd bloodhound's heavy bay
> Resounded up the rocky way,
> And faint, from farther distance borne,
> Were heard the clanging hoof and horn.
>
> 'Twere long to tell what steeds gave o'er,
> As swept the hunt through Cambus-more;
> What reins were tighten'd in despair,
> When rose Benledi's ridge in air;
> Who flagg'd upon Bochastle's heath,
> Who shunn'd to stem the flooded Teith,—
> For twice that day, from shore to shore,
> The gallant stag swam stoutly o'er.
> Few were the stragglers, following far,
> That reach'd the lake of Vennachar;
> And when the Brigg of Turk was won,
> The headmost horseman rode alone. . . .
>
> And now, to issue from the glen,
> No pathway meets the wanderer's ken,
> Unless he climb, with footing nice,
> A far projecting precipice.
> The broom's tough roots his ladder made,
> The hazel saplings lent their aid;
> And thus an airy point he won,
> Where, gleaming with the setting sun,
> One burnish'd sheet of living gold,
> Loch Katrine lay beneath him roll'd,
> In all her length far winding lay,
> With promontory, creek, and bay,

And islands that, empurpled bright,
Floated amid the livlier light,
And mountains, that like giants stand,
To sentinel enchanted land.
High on the south, huge Benvenue
Down on the lake in masses threw
Crags, knolls, and mounds, confusedly hurl'd,
The fragments of an earlier world;
A wildering forest feather'd o'er
His ruin'd sides and summit hoar
While on the north, through middle air,
Ben-an heaved high his forehead bare.

Kidnapped: *A Topographical Novel*

SCOTT WAS A topographical as well as an historical novelist; Robert Louis Stevenson's *Kidnapped* is even more a topographical novel than Scott's *Waverley*. Stevenson takes his hero from a Border village to Cramond (where the River Almond comes into the Firth of Forth just northwest of Edinburgh), to the Hawes Inn at South Queensferry (which still exists) and then, having been kidnapped at South Queensferry and put on board the brig *Covenant* of Dysart (in Fife) by sea up the east coast of Scotland, through the stormy Pentland Firth, then south through the Western Isles:

On the day when the fog fell and we ran down Alan's boat, we had been running through the Little Minch. At dawn after that battle, we lay becalmed to the east [*sic*] of the Isle of Canna or between that and Isle Eriska in the chain of the Long Island. Now to get from there to Linnhe Loch, the straight course was through the narrows of the Sound of Mull. But the captain had no chart; he was afraid to trust his brig so deep among the islands; and the wind serving well, he preferred to go by-west of Tiree and come up under the southern coast of the great Isle of Mull.

The ship is wrecked on a reef, and the hero, David Balfour, spends four days alone on the little Isle of Erraid before discovering that when the tide was out he could walk on to the shore of Mull. From Mull he crosses by ferry to Lochaline on the mainland and in the mouth of Loch Aline sees "an emigrant ship bound for the American colonies" from which comes "a great sound of mourning". He crosses Morven into Ardgour, where he finds a fisherman to take him across to Loch Linnhe and set him ashore in the wood of Lettermore (Leitir Mhor on the modern Ordnance Survey map) in the Appin country of Alan Breck, whom he is seeking. It is here that he unwittingly becomes involved in the murder of Colin Roy Campbell of Glenure, and from now on he is a hunted man.

PENTLAND FIRTH

WESTERN ISLES

LITTLE MINCH

Isle of
Skye

Isle of
Eriskay

Isle of
Canna

Pass of Corrieyairick

BEN
ALDER

Loch Ericht

Ardgour
Morven   Ballachulish
Lochaline   Lettermore
                (Leitir Mhor)

Loch Rannoch

Tiree

Isle of Mull

Isle of Erraid

Braes of
Balquidder

Strathyre

Loch
Lomond

Alloa   Dysart
Stirling   Clackmannan
            Culross   FIRTH OF FORTH
South Queensferry
            Cramond
                  Edinburgh

N

0 miles   50
0 kilometres   50

Stevenson's *Kidnapped*

Balfour finds Alan Breck between Leitir Mhor and Ballachulish, and the novel now becomes the story of their joint flight from the redcoats. They move northeast and cover some of the route that the fugitive Prince Charlie had covered five years before (the time of the novel is 1751), the Pass of Corrieyairick and then south to Ben Alder, where they visit Cluny's "cage" as Charles had done. They cross Loch Ericht by night and proceed "down its eastern shore to another hiding-place near the head of Loch Rannoch". They cross Loch Rannoch and move south to the Braes of Balquidder. After a night at Strathyre they push on southward and eventually reach Allan Water and follow it down; "and coming to the edge of the hills saw the whole Carse of Stirling underfoot, as flat as a pancake, with the town and castle on a hill in the midst of it, and the moon shining on the Links of Forth". They move eastwards "under the high line of the Ochil mountains; and by Alloa and Clackmannan and Culross, all of which we avoided; and about ten in the morning, mighty hungry and tired, came to the little clachan of Limekilns" on the north side of the Firth of Forth. A sympathetic girl is persuaded to ferry them across the Forth secretly at night. Once in Queensferry, David can call on the friendly solicitor Mr. Rankeillor and claim his inheritance at "the British Linen Company's bank".

Of course, the story of David Balfour's search for his inheritance is a mere device, used to start and finish the plot. Essentially *Kidnapped* is a topographical novel about Scotland in 1751, a picture of Scotland after the "Forty-Five".

Throughout his life as a writer Stevenson was much concerned with what he called in an essay "fitness in events and places", in virtue of which a given locality becomes associated with an appropriate invented action:

The effects of night, of any flowing water, of lighted cities, of the peep of day, of ships, of the open ocean, calls up in the mind an army of anonymous desires and pleasures. Something, we feel, should happen, we know not what, yet we proceed in quest of it. . . . Some places speak distinctly. Certain dank gardens cry aloud for murder; certain old houses demand to be haunted; certain coasts are set apart for shipwreck. . . . I have lived both at the Hawes and Burford in a perpetual flutter, on the heels, as it seemed, of some adventure that should justify the place; but though the feeling had me to bed at night and called me again at morning in one unbroken round of pleasure and suspense, nothing befell me in either worth remark. The man or the hour had not yet come; but some day, I think, a boat shall put off from the Queen's Ferry, fraught with a dear cargo, and some frosty night a horseman, on a tragic errand, rattle with his whip upon the green shutters of the inn at Burford.

He wrote this before he wrote *Kidnapped*, where a boat did indeed "put off from the Queen's Ferry, fraught with a dear cargo".

In *Kidnapped* he also made use of his three weeks' stay in the little island of

Erraid, off Mull, as a young man, and he used the same memories to provide the vivid setting for his short story "The Merry Men". In his story "The Pavilion on the Links" he made dramatic use of the atmosphere of the Scottish east coast. In the masterpiece which he left unfinished at his death, *Weir of Hermiston*, he makes effective use of the difference in atmosphere between late eighteenth-century Edinburgh and the Pentland Hills to the south, relating it to different rhythms of life, different psychological patterns and the conflict between generations.

Edinburgh

THE EDINBURGH that David Balfour saw was still essentially the old medieval city, built on the ridge that runs from the Castle to the Palace of Holyroodhouse. The old High Street ran eastward along this ridge as far as the Nether Bow, where the Netherbow Port marked the eastern entrance through the wall erected in 1513 after the defeat at Flodden. East of that lay the Canongate and the sloping road to Holyrood. The herringbone pattern, with narrow "wynds" and "closes" going off from the wide main street, remained the basic shape of the city for centuries. Parallel to the High Street to the south was the Cowgate, with the wide Grassmarket at its western end. The city could not expand to the north, until the North Loch that lay where Princes Street Gardens now are was drained and its valley bridged, and this did not happen until the second half of the eighteenth century. Shortly before this there had been some expansion southward, but in the age of the Scottish Enlightenment the town council was more interested in planning an elegant New Town to the north, after it had been made accessible by draining and bridging.

The late eighteenth-century New Town stood for order and elegance, while the Old Town stood for picturesqueness, violence, and unsanitary habits (such as the nightly pitching of refuse out of the windows, with the cry of "Gardyloo" to warn passers-by to take evasive action). The Old Town was distinguished for its tall "lands", multi-storeyed dwelling houses divided into flats, for, with expansion limited by geographical factors, there was nowhere to go but up. The fifteenth-century Edinburgh so colourfully abused by the Middle Scots poet William Dunbar was essentially the same Edinburgh as the city so boisterously described by Robert Fergusson (1750–1744), who died aged twenty-four in the public Bedlam of the city and, while living long enough to see the beginning of the elegantly planned New Town, lived and worked and drank and sang in the Old. Dunbar and Fergusson were essentially Edinburgh poets, the latter particularly.

Edinburgh of the late fifteenth and early sixteenth centuries comes vividly into literature in the poetry of William Dunbar. He portrays the bustling,

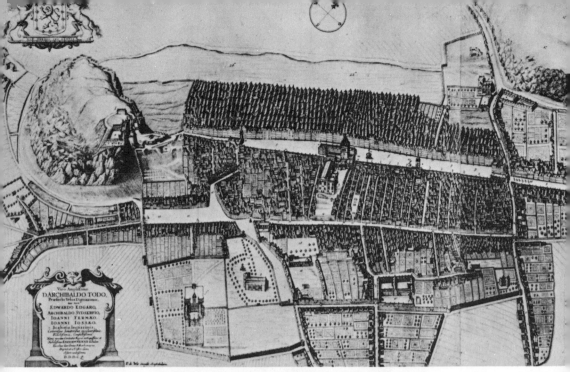

Detail of James Gordon's bird's-eye view of Edinburgh, 1647.

noisy, smelly city with its broad High Street running along the ridge from the Castle on the west towards Holyrood in the east, flanked by narrow closes and wynds. He reproaches Edinburgh merchants for their dirty habits, their quarrelling, and their lack of concern for the good name of the city:

> Quhy will ye, merchantis of renoun,
> Lat Edinburgh, your nobill toun,
> For laik of reformatioun
> The commone proffeitt tyine and fame?[1]
>   Think ye not schame,
> That onie uther regioun
> Sall with dishonour hurt your name!
>
> May nane pas throw your principall gaittis
> For stink of haddockis and of scattis,
> For cryis of carlingis[2] and debaittis,
> For fensum flyttingis[3] of defame:
>   Think ye not schame,
> Befoir strangeris of all estaittis
> That sic[4] dishonour hurt your name!

1. lose the common profit and fame.
2. carling: contemptuous term for a woman.

3. fensum flyttingis: filthy quarrels.
4. sic: such.

The Edinburgh painted by Robert Fergusson nearly three hundred years later is still essentially the same city, for Fergusson concentrated on the noise and colour and drinking and violence of the Old Town. His poems "The King's Birthday in Edinburgh", "Caller Oysters", "Hallow Fair", "The Rising of the Session", "The Sitting of the Session", and, most of all, "Auld Reikie", evoke the Edinburgh of 1770 with liveliness and humour. "Auld Reikie" takes us through the city from dawn to dusk and from weekdays to Sunday. Here is a night scene, after the pubs have closed:

> Frae joyous Tavern, reeling drunk,
> Wi' fiery Phizz, and Ein half sunk,
> Behad the Bruiser, Fae to a'
> That in the reek o' Gardies fa'[5]:
> Close by his Side, a feckless Race
> O' Macaronies[6] shew their Face,
> And think they're free frae Skaith[7] or Harm,
> While Pith befriends their Leaders Arm:
> Yet fearfu' aften o' their Maught,
> They quatt the Glory o' the Faught
> To this same Warrior wha led
> Thae Heroes to bright Honour's Bed:
> And aft the hack o' Honour shines
> In Bruiser's Face wi' broken Lines:
> Of them and Tales he tells anon,
> Whan Ramble and whan Fighting's done;
> And, like Hectorian, ne'er impairs
> The Brag and Glory o' his Sairs[8].
>
> Whan Feet in dirty Gutters plash,
> And Fock to wale their Fitstaps fash[9];
> At night the Macaroni drunk,
> In Pools or Gutters aftimes sunk:
> Hegh! what a Fright he now appears,
> Whan he his Corpse dejected rears!
> Look at that Head, and think if there
> The Pomet[10] slaister'd up his Hair!
> The Cheeks observe, where now cou'd shine
> The sancing Glories o' Carmine?
> Ah, Legs! in vain the Silk-worm there
> Display'd to View her eidant[11] Care;
> For Stink, instead of Perfumes, grow,
> And clarty[12] Odours fragrant flow.

5. who come within reach of his arms.
6. Macaronies: dandies.
7. Skaith: scathe, damage.
8. Sairs: bruises.
9. folk take trouble to choose their footsteps.
10. Pomet: pomatum.
11. eidant: busy.
12. clarty: dirty.

"Auld Reekie"—Edinburgh looking west from the Crags to the Castle. (Photograph by Edwin Smith)

Burns, who was born and brought up in Ayrshire and ended his life in Dumfries, made his first visit to Edinburgh (staying in a close in the Old Town) in the autumn of 1776, where he was fêted by the "literati" of the Scottish Enlightenment and given bad advice about the kind of poetry he ought to write. The social and cultural tensions built up between the brilliant and proud peasant poet and the genteel leaders of Edinburgh thought are reflected in the architectural differences between the Old Town and the New. The Edinburgh of David Hume, William Robertson, Henry Mackenzie and others of the "literati" was in spirit, if not always in fact, the Edinburgh of James Craig's 1767 plan of the New Town, with its symmetrically planned streets and squares and its sense of embodying a vision of civic enlightenment.

Edinburgh remained a city of contrasts. Scott's elder brothers and sisters (none of whom survived infancy) were born in the Old Town, but shortly before he was born his parents moved out of it to George Square, part of what might be called the first New Town, built in a vernacular classical style as distinct from the more formal international classical style of the New Town to the north. But Scott was very much aware of the Old Town and its romantic appeal—"mine own romantic town" he called Edinburgh in *Marmion*. Stevenson, who was born in the New Town, wrote much about Edinburgh and the contrasts—social and economic as well as architectural—between the Old Town and the New. He also knew and loved (as Scott did, too) the countryside around Edinburgh, the lion bulk of Arthur's Seat rising in the very midst of the city, Blackford Hill to the south and behind it the Braid Hills and the Pentlands, where he particularly loved to walk. By the beginning of the nineteenth century Edinburgh was still "Auld Reekie" ("Old Smokey", because housewives in Fife could tell when it was approaching dinner time across the Forth in Edinburgh by the pall of smoke that rose over the city when cooking commenced) but it was also the "Athens of the North".

In his *Edinburgh: Picturesque Notes* (1878) Stevenson gave the fullest account given by any Scottish man of letters of the appeal of the city and its environs to the literary imagination. Here is part of his description of a Pentland scene:

Kirk Yetton forms the north-eastern angle of the range; thence, the Pentlands trend off to south and west. From the summit you look over a great expanse of champaign sloping to the sea and behold a large variety of distant hills. There are the hills of Fife, the hills of Peebles, the Lammermoors and the Ochils, more or less mountainous in outline, more or less blue with distance. Of the Pentlands themselves, you see a field of wild heathery peaks with a pond gleaming in the midst; and to that side the view is as desolate as if you were looking into Galloway or Applecross. To turn to the other, is like a piece of travel. Far out in the lowlands Edinburgh shows herself, making a great smoke on clear days and spreading her suburbs about her for miles; the Castle rises darkly in the midst; and close by, Arthur's Seat makes a bold figure in the landscape. All around, cultivated fields, and woods, and smoking villages, and white country roads, diversify the uneven surface of the land. Trains crawl slowly abroad upon the railway lines; little ships are tacking in the Firth; the shadow of a mountainous cloud, as large as a parish, travels before the wind; the wind itself ruffles the wood and standing corn, and sends pulses of varying colour across the landscape. So you sit, like Jupiter upon Olympus, and look down from afar upon men's life. The city is as silent as a city of the dead: from all its humming thoroughfares, not a voice, not a footfall, reaches you upon the hill. The sea surf, the cries of ploughmen, the streams and the mill-wheels, the birds and the wind, keep up an animated concert through the plain; from farm to farm, dogs and crowing cocks contend together in defiance; and yet from this Olympian station, except for the whispering rumour of a train, the world has fallen into a dead silence and the business of town and country grown voiceless in your ears. A crying hill-bird, the bleat of a sheep, a wind singing in the dry grass, seem not so much to interrupt, as to accompany, the stillness; but to the spiritual ear, the whole scene makes a music at once human and rural, and discourses pleasant reflections on the destiny of man. The spiry, habitable city, ships, the divided fields, and browsing herds, and the straight highways, tell visibly of man's active and comfortable ways; and you may be never so laggard and never so unimpressionable, but there is something in the view that spirits up your blood and puts you in the vein for cheerful labour.

Edinburgh expanded steadily, to take in the towns and villages to the north and to build up to the foot of the Pentland Hills in the south, so that it now lies between the Pentlands and the Firth of Forth, with a great variety both of architecture and scenery within walking distance. To the south, the large park known as the Meadows was laid out in the eighteenth century (Burns's father worked on it as a gardener) and south of the Meadows as well as to the north of the New Town Victorian Edinburgh arose, solid freestone terrace houses and rows of flats. As one goes further south towards Blackford Hill the houses get larger, the streets more sedate and tree-lined: this is the Edinburgh of Victorian gentility. But the New Town remained the great professional area of Edinburgh, inhabited by advocates and prosperous solicitors and other kinds of successful professional men.

Each area of the city has its own flavour: Princes Street, the international shopping centre, with its confused architecture redeemed by its marvellous open vista to the north, over which the Castle presides; narrow Rose Street, behind Princes Street, with its remarkable assortment of pubs; George Street flanked by Charlotte Square on the west and St. Andrew Square on the east (not quite how the original planners conceived it), each street and each square with its own social flavour; Heriot Row, where Stevenson grew up, parallel to Queen Street to the north, divided from it by Queen Street Gardens across which the young Stevenson, lying ill and wakeful in bed at night, would see the lights of Queen Street windows and wonder whether other little boys were similarly ill and wakeful. Then there is Telfer's spectacular Dean Bridge of 1832 spanning the Water of Leith, with the picturesque old Dean Village to the west and to the east the socially varied quarter of Stockbridge. On the other side of the city, south of the Meadows, there is the rigid respectability of the Marchmont and Warrender areas and the gradual merging of the city into the country further south and west.

This variety of scene and atmosphere dates from the building of the New Town in the latter half of the eighteenth century and the early years of the nineteenth. What modern "planners" have done in the last decade, with horrors such as the St. James' Centre and the virtual destruction of George Square, is another matter. But though damage has been wrought, much of the Old Town has been imaginatively refurbished and the New Town has been proudly preserved. It is the area between the High Street and the Meadows that has suffered most. But a civic consciousness has been aroused with respect to these areas too, and the prospect for the city looks brighter now. It continues to attract writers and television cameras, and remains one of the most beautiful cities of Europe.

Most of all, Edinburgh still has its poets, working in the tradition of Dunbar and Fergusson. Norman McCaig writes of Edinburgh in English, but with a strong Scots accent. Here are the first two stanzas of his poem "Double Life":

This wind from Fife has cruel fingers, scooping
The heat from streets with salty finger-tips
Crusted with frost; and all Midlothian,
Stubborn against what heeled the sides of ships
Off from the Isle of May, stiffens its drooping
Branches to the south. Each man
And woman put their winter masks on, set
In a stony flinch, and only children can
Light with a scream an autumn fire that says
With the quick crackle of its smoky blaze,
'Summer's to burn and it's October yet.'

My Water of Leith runs through a double city;
My city is threaded by a complex stream.
A matter for regret. If these cold stones
Could be stones only, and this watery gleam
Within the chasms of tenements and the pretty
Boskage of Dean could echo the groans
Of cart-wheeled bridges with only water's voice,
October would be just October. The bones
Of rattling winter would still lie underground,
Summer be less than ghost, I be unbound
From all the choking folderols of choice.

Sydney Goodsir Smith and Robert Garioch write of Edinburgh in "Lallans" or Scots. Here is the opening of Goodsir Smith's Edinburgh poem, "Kynd Kittock's Land" (Kynd Kittock is a character in Dunbar's poetry):

This rortie[13] wretched city
Sair come down frae its auld hiechts
—The hauf[14] o't smug, complacent,
Lost til all pride of race or spirit,
The tither[15] wild and rouch[16] as ever
In its secret hairt
But lost alsweill[17], the smeddum[18] tane,
The man o' independent mind has cap in hand the day
—Sits on its craggy spine
And drees[19] the wind and rain
That nourished all its genius
—Weary wi centuries
This empty capital snorts like a great beast

13. rortie: splendid, jolly.   15. tither: the other.   17. alsweill: also.
14. hauf: half.   16. rouch: rough.   18. smeddum: gumption.   19. drees: endures.

Caged in its sleep, dreaming of freedom
But with nae belief,
Indulging an auld ritual
Whase meaning's been forgot owre lang,
A mere habit of words—when the drink's in—
And signifying naething.

But the quintessential modern poet of Edinburgh is Robert Garioch. His "Edinburgh Sonnets" brilliantly evoke the modern city, and in one of them he makes moving contact with Edinburgh's past and with his predecessor Robert Fergusson. He is describing a civic ceremony at Fergusson's grave in the Canongate Churchyard in October 1962, remembering how when Robert Burns visited Edinburgh in 1786 he went to Fergusson's unmarked grave where he knelt down and paid tribute to the man he called his "elder brother in the Muse":

Canogait kirkyaird in the failing year
is auld and grey, the wee roseirs [20] are bare,
five gulls leam [21] white agen the dirty air:
why are they here? There's naething for them here.

Why are we here oursels? We gaither near
the grave. Fergusons mainly, quite a fair
turn-out, respectfu, ill at ease, we stare
at daith—there's an address—I canna hear.

Aweill, we staund bareheidit in the haar [22],
murnin a man that gaed back til the pool
twa hunner-year afore our time. The glaur [23]

that haps his banes glowres [24] back. Strang present dool [25]
ruggs at my hairt; Lichtlie [26] this gin ye daur [27]:
here Robert Burns knelt and kissed the mool [28].

20. roseirs: rose-trees.
21. leam: glow.
22. haar: mist.

23. glaur: mud.
24. glowres: stares.
25. dool: woe.

26. Lichtlie: scorn.
27. gin ye daur: if you dare.
28. mool: mould.

THE DUBLIN OF YEATS AND JOYCE

After Parnell

DUBLIN AT THE BEGINNING of this century was the capital city of an Ireland that had been part of the United Kingdom since the Union of Great Britain and Ireland in 1801. Its population as recorded in the census of 1901 (three years before the famous Dublin June 16, 1904 that Joyce recorded in *Ulysses*) was 290,638. In this year Yeats was thirty-six, J. M. Synge was thirty, Joyce was nineteen and Sean O'Casey was twenty-one. All these writers were born in Dublin, and although none lived there continuously throughout his life and Joyce lived nearly all his adult life in self-imposed exile on the Continent, the social, intellectual and political atmosphere of the city deeply influenced them as it influenced other Irish-born writers who though not born in the city were at different times active in it. The main fact about Dublin at this time was that it was the centre of the Anglo-Irish ascendancy, visibly represented by the vice-regal demesne and lodge in Phoenix Park, home of the British-appointed lord-lieutenant who carried on the executive government of Ireland from Dublin Castle with the help of a chief secretary and a privy council (all equally British-appointed), and at the same time it was the natural home of a great variety of Irish national aspirations both political and cultural.

The English connection with Ireland began with the Anglo-Norman invasions of the twelfth century, after which the Anglo-Norman settlement of Dublin marked the first permanent foothold in the country of what was to become for centuries the dominant power in it, so often resented and resisted and at the same time assimilated into and modifying native patterns of national consciousness. Dublin had previously been attacked by the Danes with whom the Irish struggled at intervals from the ninth to the twelfth centuries, but their influence did not permanently affect the cultural patterns of the city the way the English influence did. The Anglo-Irish produced their own culture heroes, and Yeats (himself a member of the Protestant Anglo-Irish ascendancy, at least by descent) later made them into something of a cult. For him the heroes of Ireland were: Swift, born in Dublin in 1667 and as Dean of St. Patrick's from 1713 to 1745 a passionate fighter for the interests of the Irish people; Edmund Burke, born in Dublin about 1729; Sheridan, born in Dublin in 1751; Bishop Berkeley, born near Kilkenny in 1685 but at one time Fellow of Trinity College, Dublin, with many connections with the city; Henry Grattan, born in Dublin in 1756, the great Irish nationalist writer and speaker who founded the first, short-lived independent Irish Parliament in Dublin in 1782 and fought bitterly against the Union with Great Britain; the romantic revolutionary

The Campanile, Trinity College.

Irish nationalist Robert Emmet, born in Dublin in 1778; and Charles Stewart Parnell, who was born in Avondale, County Wicklow, in 1846 but whose influence on Irish nationalist opinion in Dublin (he was given the freedom of the city in 1881) was enormous and whose death in October 1891 marked a turning point in the history of Irish sensibility and was seen both by Yeats and Joyce as the crucial event in the Ireland of their time.

Yeats tended to idealize eighteenth-century Dublin, with its elegant Georgian architecture and what he considered its Anglo-Irish intellectual tradition. And he idealized the Anglo-Irish Protestant tradition of Irish patriotism, as in his famous speech in the debate on divorce in the Irish Senate in February 1925. He is complaining that the Irish government has legislated to make divorce illegal even for Protestants in the Irish Free State:

I think it is tragic that within three years of this country gaining its independence we should be discussing a measure which a minority of this nation considers to be grossly oppressive. I am proud to consider myself a typical man of that minority. We against whom you have done this thing are no petty people. We are the people of Burke; we are the people of Grattan; we are the people of Swift, the people of Emmet, the people of Parnell. We have created the most of the modern literature of this country. We have created the best of its political intelligence. . . .

Five and a half years later he wrote to Joseph Hone (who, together with

M. M. Rossi, had just written a book on Bishop Berkeley, for which Yeats had provided an introduction): "I want Protestant Ireland to base some vital part of its culture upon Burke, Swift and Berkeley." The second section of his poem "Blood and the Moon" (published in *The Winding Stair* in 1933) is largely a celebration of Yeats's Anglo-Irish heroes of the eighteenth century—Goldsmith, Swift ("the Dean"), Berkeley and Burke:

> I declare this tower is my symbol; I declare
> This winding, gyring, spiring treadmill of a stair is my
>   ancestral stair;
> That Goldsmith and the Dean, Berkeley and Burke
>   have travelled there.

Joyce, on the other hand, had no claim to represent the Protestant Anglo-Irish minority in Dublin. His people were genuine Catholic Irish. He did not idealize eighteenth-century Dublin, but described vividly those parts of it that were decayed or shabby-genteel by his time. And he rebelled against the Dublin and indeed the Ireland of his time with a fierceness that only an embittered native son could manifest. His book of stories about life and character in Dublin, *Dubliners* (1914), was written to exhibit what he called, in a letter to the publisher Grant Richards, "the centre of the paralysis" of Irish life. Yeats, too, rebelled against much in Dublin life: as a descendant of that Protestant-Irish line that he so much admired, he despised the philistine Roman Catholic shopkeepers of the city:

> What need you, being come to sense,
> But fumble in a greasy till
> And add the halfpence to the pence
> And prayer to shivering prayer, until
> You have dried the marrow from the bone?

He continued to attack "the obscure spite of our old Paudeen in his shop" until the courageous but reckless and doomed Eastern Rising of 1916 showed that even the shops and the countinghouses of Dublin could produce their heroes:

> All changed, changed utterly:
> A terrible beauty is born.

Though it retained traces of its eighteenth-century elegance (as in the unspoilt Merrion Square, where Yeats lived in later life, and Gandon's fine Custom House of 1781–91) and had some fine wide streets, such as Sackville Street (which became O'Connell Street in 1924), Dublin was in the early years of this century also a city of poverty, slums and near-starvation. In

"All changed, changed utterly . . ."—Dublin in the aftermath of the Easter Rising, 1916.

1900 the Superintendent Medical Officer of Health for Dublin stated categorically that the city exceeded all other towns in the United Kingdom in the number of families in one house. He also said that he did not think that there was a more underfed population than the poor of Dublin. The 1911 census revealed some improvement on the figures shown by the census of 1901, but there were still 21,000 tenements containing accommodation of only one room, nearly a third of which were occupied by more than four people. This side of Dublin is not shown by Yeats, who was born in "Georgeville", a six-roomed semidetached house in the Dublin suburb of Sandymount, or for that matter by Joyce, even though his shiftless Micawber-like father kept moving down the social scale as he and his family flitted from one shabby-genteel house to another, shabbier and less genteel. This is the Dublin of Sean O'Casey's childhood, so vividly described in the first volume of his autobiography, *I Knock at the Door* (1939). If we compare this book with Yeats's autobiographical writing and with Joyce's *Dubliners* and *A Portrait of the Artist as a Young Man*, we shall begin to understand some of the different social, political and religious currents that swirled around early twentieth-century Dublin and lie behind the meticulously charted presentation of the city in *Ulysses*.

217

The death of Parnell, who was both a Protestant and the great Irish nationalist of his day, brought together many disparate elements in Dublin in a union of passion and grief, while at the same time splitting Catholics between those who approved the Church's attack on (and, some said, destruction of) Parnell because of his association with Mrs. O'Shea and those to whom his Irish patriotism was all that mattered. The Christmas dinner scene in *A Portrait of the Artist as a Young Man*, with the great quarrel between the anticlerical Parnellites and the loyal Roman Catholic, evokes this with great intensity. O'Casey, in the chapter entitled "A Coffin Comes to Ireland" in *Pictures in the Hallway* (1942), gives an account of Dublin's reaction to Parnell's death from a somewhat different, but not dissimilar, point of view. No Irish writer who lived through that period in and following October 1891 ever forgot what Parnell's death meant to Dublin and the country: it haunted the imagination of every one of them. And it marked the end of an era in Irish nationalist activity. In what Yeats called "the first lull in politics" after Parnell's death he saw the opportunity to replace the temporarily failed political activity of Irish nationalists by a literary revival that would restore Irish dignity and excellence in a way that was for him even more necessary than the way of political independence. Book II of his autobiographical work *The Trembling of the Veil* (1922) is entitled "Ireland after Parnell", and contains an account of the almost feverish activity that went on in search of an Irish cultural identity. He talked of Douglas Hyde, the great Irish Protestant Gaelic scholar and the influence of his translations from the Gaelic into "the beautiful English of Connaught, which is Gaelic in idiom and Tudor in vocabulary"; of Standish O'Grady, whose unfinished *History of Ireland* began with the heroes of ancient Irish tradition, Fion and Oisin and Cuchullan, and so made them available to the modern Irish poetic imagination; of George Russell (A.E.) and the strange weekly meetings in his Dublin house:

The one house where nobody thought or talked politics was a house in Ely Place, where a number of young men lived together, and, for want of a better name, were called Theosophists. Beside the resident members, other members dropped in and out during the day, and the reading-room was a place of much discussion about philosophy and about the arts. The house had been taken in the name of an engineer to the Board of Works, a black-bearded young man, with a passion for Manichean philosophy, and all accepted him as host; and sometimes the conversation, especially when I was there, became too ghostly for the nerves of his young and delicate wife, and he would be made angry. I remember young men struggling, with inexact terminology and insufficient learning, for some new religious conception, on which they could base their lives, and some few strange or able men. . . .

At the top of the house, and at the time I remember best in the same room with the young Scotchman, lived Mr. George Russell (A.E.), and the house and the

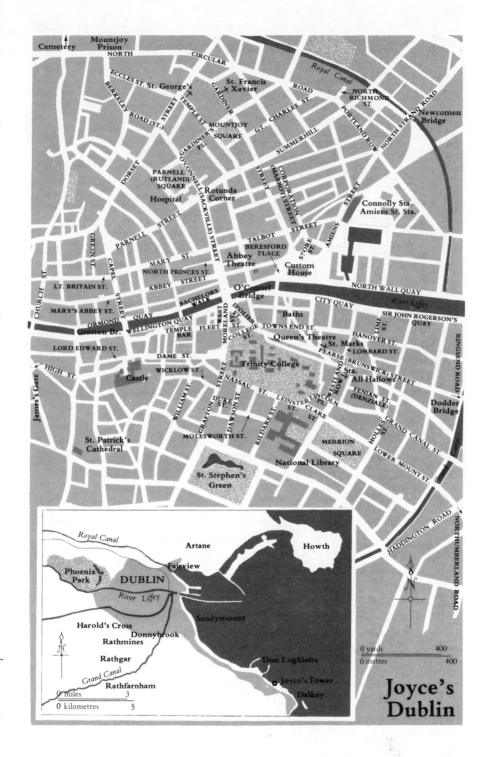

Joyce's
Dublin

society were divided into his adherents and those of the engineer; and I heard of some quarrelling between the factions. The rivalry was subconscious. Neither had willingly opposed the other in any matter of importance. The engineer had all the financial responsibility, and George Russell was, in the eyes of the community, saint and genius. Had either seen that the question at issue was the leadership of mystical thought in Dublin, he would, I think, have given way, but the dispute seemed trivial. At the weekly meetings, anything might be discussed; no chairman called a speaker to order; an atheistic workman could denounce religion, or a pious Catholic confound theosophy with atheism; and the engineer, precise and practical, disapproved. He had an object. He wished to make converts for a definite form of belief, and here an enemy, if a better speaker, might make all the converts. He wished to confine discussion to members of the society, and had proposed in committee, I was told, a resolution on the subject; while Russell, who had refused to join my National Literary Society, because the party of Harp and Pepperpot had set limits to discussion, resisted, and at last defeated him. In a couple of years some new dispute arose; he resigned, and founded a society which drew doctrine and method from America or London; and Russell became, as he is today, the one masterful influence among young Dublin men and women who love religious speculation, but have no historical faith.

The Irish literary revival was well away, and although Yeats himself divided his time between Dublin, London and the west of Ireland (he not only visited Sligo, where in childhood he had stayed with his maternal grandparents, but also stayed with Lady Gregory at Coole Park and absorbed her enthusiasm for a vernacular Irish literature as well as for the ordered elegance of life in a Great House), Dublin remained its centre. Here the great debates went on, here the Abbey Theatre was opened by Yeats and Lady Gregory in 1904 (the original building burned down in 1951 and was replaced by a new one in 1966), to put on plays by Synge and Yeats and Lady Gregory and Sean O'Casey and introduce such Irish actors and actresses as Sara Allgood, Maire O'Neil and Barry Fitzgerald. Here the great battle between the poets and the philistines was waged; with violent protests by some members of the audience at what was considered the degradation of Irish character in Yeats's play *The Countess Cathleen* and Synge's *Playboy of the Western World,* the production of the latter in 1907 producing disturbances in the theatre and rioting outside, thereby infuriating Yeats, who now declared that there could be no true appreciation of the arts in "this blind bitter land". But the Abbey Theatre continued, and among the dramatists of its later years were Lennox Robinson, Padraic Colum, T. C. Murray, Paul Vincent Carroll and Denis Johnston. Between the burning down of the original Abbey Theatre and the opening of the new one in July 1966 the company used the Queen's Theatre in Pearse (formerly Brunswick) Street, which has now given way to an office block.

The old Abbey Theatre, 1947.

As for the physical atmosphere of Dublin in the earlier part of this century, it is all in *Ulysses*. There have been many changes in Dublin since June 1904, but the Dublin through which Leopold Bloom wandered on that day remained substantially unchanged through the age of Yeats and Joyce, which can roughly be said to have lasted from the death of Parnell to the outbreak of the Second World War, 1871–1940. The establishment of the Irish Free State in 1922 brought some changes in names and monuments, but the more significant changes took place in later decades.

The Wanderings of Ulysses

Joyce's *Ulysses* is probably the most conscientiously topographical novel ever written. In it Joyce re-creates, with almost fanatical care, the Dublin of June 16, 1904, drawing not only on his own lively memory of the city where he was born, grew up and spent his youth until his insistent feeling that to be an artist meant to be an exile drove him abroad, but also on newspapers, Thom's *Dublin Directory* of 1904, and a mass of detailed information requested from and supplied by his Aunt Josephine in Dublin (typical example, on a postcard written from Trieste on January 5, 1920: "Another thing I wanted to know is whether there are trees (and of what kind) behind the Star of the Sea church in Sandymount visible from the shore and also whether there are steps leading down at the side of it from Leahy's terrace").

The Ulysses of the title is Leopold Bloom, and Bloom's wanderings through Dublin weave the main pattern of the novel. But the other principal character is Stephen Dedalus, on whom the book concentrates in the first three episodes, Bloom himself not entering until the fourth episode. Bloom's and Stephen's paths cross in Dublin several times until they finally meet in the maternity hospital in the fourteenth episode, after which Bloom adopts a paternal role towards Stephen, protects him during his adventure in the brothel, and takes him home with him to 7 Eccles Street.

Joyce himself did not use in the actual novel the Homeric titles which critics now consistently employ to denote the different episodes of *Ulysses*; but the titles are Joyce's, and he used them frequently in correspondence and in conversations with friends. We shall therefore employ them here, together with the sequential number of each episode, for purposes of identification, since *Ulysses* has no numbered chapters.

The opening episode, "Telemachus", is set in the Martello tower in Sandycove where Stephen Dedalus is living with Buck Mulligan.[1] This is not in Dublin proper, for Sandycove is a suburb southeast of the city, in what is now Dún Laoghlaire. In the second episode ("Nestor") we see Stephen teaching at the school where he is employed, but which he decides to leave this very day. The school is not named, but Joyce clearly based it on Clifton School, Dalkey, where he himself taught briefly as a young man. Clifton School was in Dalkey Avenue, Dalkey (another suburb southeast of Dublin), very near the Martello tower. In the third episode ("Proteus") we see Stephen walking alone on the shore at Sandymount (a few miles further up the coast, northwest, from Sandycove). "Am I walking into Eternity along Sandymount strand?" He sees two women coming "down the steps from Leahy's terrace prudently". At the end of this episode we see him sitting on a rock with his back to the sea: his face is turned over his shoulder, "rere regardant", and he sees "a threemaster, her sails brailed up on the crosstrees, homing, upstream, silently moving, a silent ship'. In the sixteenth episode ("Eumaeus") we meet able seaman W. B. Murphy who has come ashore from that very ship, which we now learn is "the three-master *Rosevean* from Bridgewater with bricks". The time of the first three episodes, which constitute a sort of prelude to the novel proper, is 8.00 to 11.00 A.M.

With the fourth episode ("Calypso")—which is also the start of the second and by far the largest of the three parts into which the novel is divided—we

1. Like Stephen and Buck Mulligan, Joyce and Oliver Gogarty took up temporary residence in the tower for a few months in 1904. The building now houses the James Joyce Tower Museum.

return to eight o'clock in the morning, but now we are in Dublin proper, at 7 Eccles Street, home of Mr. and Mrs. Leopold Bloom. From this shabby-genteel, brick, three-storey terraced house in north Dublin, Bloom sallies forth to buy a kidney for his breakfast at Dlugacz the butcher in Dorset Street. "He crossed to the bright side" (the southwest side) of Eccles Street, walks the short distance to Dorset Street, which runs at right angles to Eccles Street, and turns right into Dorset Street. He notices the sun nearing the steeple of St. George's church on the other side of Dorset Street on Temple Street. He passes Larry O'Rourke, licensed grocer (74 Dorset Street, at the corner of Eccles Street) and greets him as he turns the corner. Going along Dorset Street he passes St. Joseph's National School and comes to Dlugacz's window. (It is interesting that Dlugacz, the Hungarian-Jewish pork butcher on Dorset Street, is an invention of Joyce's, unlike nearly all the other shopkeepers mentioned in *Ulysses*. A Jewish pork butcher who keeps Zionist leaflets on his counter is a complete absurdity sociologically and psychologically: Joyce had his own reasons for introducing this strange figure.) As he waits to buy the kidney he stands by the maid from next door. "Woods his name is." (Thom's *Directory* gives R. Woods, 8 Eccles Street.) Bloom returns to his house at no. 7.

At the opening of the fifth episode ("The Lotus Eaters") we see Bloom, at 10.00 A.M., walking along Sir John Rogerson's Quay on his rather casual way to Westland Row Post Office and then to the public baths in Leinster Street. (7 Eccles Street has no bath, and only an outside lavatory.) When we first see him he is walking east towards Lime Street. He passes Windmill Lane, passes "Leask's the linseed crusher's" (14–15 Sir John Rogerson's Quay), "the postal telegraph office" (18 Sir John Rogerson's Quay), the sailors' home (no. 19), and turns south down Lime Street. He then turns right along Hanover Street to Townsend Street, which he crosses in order to proceed south along Lombard Street. He passes "Nichols' the undertaker's" (26 Lombard Street) and goes into Westland Row, where he halts "before the window of the Belfast and Oriental Tea Company" (6 Westland Row). He crosses the street to the Westland Row Post Office (nos. 49–50) where he collects the letter from his clandestine correspondent Martha Clifford. He comes out of the post office, turns right, goes along Westland Row past the Grosvenor Hotel (no. 5) and strolls towards Brunswick Street (now Pearse Street). He then turns right into Cumberland Street and halts "in the lee of the station wall" (i.e., Westland Row Station, now Pearse Station) so that he can read Martha's letter in privacy. He reads the letter, goes under the railway arch where he tears up the envelope, hears an incoming train clanking above his head, and goes to the back door of nearby All Hallows Church, which he enters. He emerges on to Westland Row again and walks south. He turns right along Lincoln Place where he calls at Sweny's (F. W. Sweny, dispensing chemist, 1 Lincoln Place) to get a lotion made up for his wife and buy a cake of soap. (That cake of soap has a saga of its own throughout the novel; it plays a symbolic part when it twinkles in the sky in the "Circe" episode, and is used at last by Bloom to wash his hands when he returns home with Stephen at the end of his exhausting day.) On emerging from Sweny's he meets Bantam Lyons, who asks if he can borrow Bloom's newspaper and interprets Bloom's reply that he was going to throw it away anyway as a cryptic hint to back the horse Throwaway in that day's Ascot Gold Cup, with fateful consequences. (Throwaway, a complete outsider, really did win the Gold Cup at Ascot on Thursday, June 16, 1904, as reported in that day's Dublin *Evening Telegraph*.) He then proceeds along Lincoln Place to the baths at Leinster Street, and the episode ends with him in his bath.

At the beginning of the sixth episode ("Hades") we see Bloom and others (including Stephen's father) in a cab on the way to Glasnevin Cemetery for Paddy Dignam's funeral. The time is eleven o'clock. The cab is coming from the Sandymount area, for Martin Cunningham tells his companions that their route will be "Irishtown, Ringsend, Brunswick street". (Brunswick Street, it will be remembered, is now Pearse Street.) We first see the cab on Tritonville Road, which connects Sandymount with Irishtown. It proceeds along Irishtown Road, turns left across Dodder Bridge to go along Ringsend Road. It crosses the Grand Canal, where it stops for a moment and Bloom puts his head out of the window to report where they are, then proceeds along Great Brunswick Street. They pass the Ancient Concert Rooms at no. 42, St. Mark's Church at no. 40, the Queen's Theatre at no. 209, Plasto's at no. 1, where Bloom had bought his hat, and "Sir Philip Crampton's memorial fountain" at the corner of College Street. They catch a glimpse of Blazes Boylan, who has an assignation with Bloom's wife Molly later in the day. They pass the statue of Smith O'Brien, by Farrell ("Farrell's statue"), at the corner of Westmoreland Street and D'Olier Street, then cross O'Connell Bridge to pass the statue of Daniel O'Connell ("They passed under the hugecloaked Liberator's form") at the entrance to Sackville Street, which is now O'Connell Street. They go up Sackville Street, past Nelson's pillar to the Rotunda Corner. On the way they pass the "temperance hotel" (which was at 56 Sackville Street), "Falconer's railway guide" (i.e., the publishers of that work, at no. 53), the "civil service college" (at no. 51), Gill's the bookseller's (at no. 50), the "catholic club" (at no. 42), and the foundation for "the industrious blind" (no. 41). Past the Rotunda, the carriage "climbed more slowly the hill of Rutland square" (now Parnell Square). They turn into Berkeley Street (Berkeley Road) and go past the top of Eccles Street ("My house down there," thinks Bloom), past the "ward for incurables" and "Our Lady's Hospice for the Dying" (34–8 Eccles Street), by the North Circular Road to turn into Phibsborough Road. The cab proceeds along Phibsborough Road, crosses the Royal Canal and bears left into Finglas Road and the cemetery.

A turn-of-the-century view of Sackville St. looking across O'Connell Bridge toward "the hugecloaked Liberator's form" of Daniel O'Connell.

The seventh episode ("Aeolus") opens with an outdoor scene "before Nelson's pillar", which was halfway up Sackville Street. It is noon. We hear the noise of the tramcars and see the mail vans in North Prince's Street (which runs at right angles to Sackville Street, parallel to and north of Middle Abbey Street). We then move into the offices of the *Evening Telegraph*, which were at 4–8 North Prince's Street and in fact extended from North Prince's Street to Middle Abbey Street. The bulk of the episode takes place inside the newspaper office, where both Stephen and Bloom come on different errands, but Bloom leaves the office for a short while. "I'm just running round to Bachelor's walk, Mr. Bloom said, about this ad of Keyes's. . . . They tell me he's round there in Dillon's. . . . Back in no time." Dillon's Auction Rooms were at 25 Bachelor's Walk, a few minutes walk away. Bloom returns to the *Evening Telegraph* office where he meets with a less cordial reception from Myles Crawford, the editor, than he had before. But this episode is largely Stephen's: he is in the office all the time, talking to his friends.

At the beginning of the eighth episode ("Lestrygonians") we see Bloom, at one o'clock, walking south down Sackville Street from the *Evening*

Telegraph office. He is handed a "throwaway" announcing the arrival of the American evangelist Dr. John Alexander Dowie, which he crumples into a paper ball and later throws into the Liffey as he is crossing it: the journey downstream of this "crumpled throwaway" is to be charted at intervals later in the novel. As he passes the corner of Sackville Street and Bachelor's Walk he looks right, along Bachelor's Walk "from Butler's monument house corner" (music sellers, 34 Bachelor's Walk), and sees "Dedalus' daughter [i.e., Stephen's sister] there still outside Dillon's auctionrooms". He crosses O'Connell Bridge, buys two Banbury cakes from an "old applewoman" to feed the seagulls, crosses Westmoreland Street and notes "Rover Cycleshop" (at 23 Westmoreland Street), meets Mrs. Breen outside Harrison's restaurant (no. 29), passes the offices of the *Irish Times* (no. 31), crosses Fleet Street, continues along Westmoreland Street past "Bolton's Westmoreland house" (restaurant, nos. 35–6), passes the "huge high door of this Irish house of parliament" (now the Bank of Ireland), goes on past "Trinity's surly front" into Grafton Street, where he notices John Howard Parnell (brother of the dead Irish political leader Charles Stewart Parnell) passing the window of Walter Sexton's (jewellers, 118 Grafton Street). "He crossed at Nassau street corner and stood before the window of Yeates and Son" (opticians, 2 Grafton Street). "He passed, dallying, the windows of Brown Thomas, silk mercers" (15–17 Grafton Street) and turns left into Duke Street. He thinks of lunching at the Burton (18 Duke Street), but finds the atmosphere nauseating, so he leaves it and turns back towards Grafton Street. As he passes Davy Byrne's pub at 21 Duke Street he decides to have a snack there and goes in for a cheese sandwich and a glass of burgundy. Refreshed, he leaves the pub reflecting on "who distilled first?" and decides to go to the national library to look up a back number of the *Kilkenny People* in connection with the advertisement he is trying to persuade Alexander Keyes to take in the *Telegraph* (Bloom's job is canvassing advertisements for newspapers). He passes "the window of William Miller, plumber" (17 Duke Street) and turns into Dawson Street "at Gray's confectioner's window" (13 Dawson Street). He helps a "blind stripling" across the road in Dawson Street opposite Molesworth Street (the young man is on his way to tune the piano at the Ormond Hotel, as we learn later). Bloom himself goes along Molesworth Street, looking in at the post office at no. 4 to buy "a postal order two shillings half a crown" as a "little present" to send to Martha Clifford. He finally arrives at the National Library in Kildare Street, near which he catches a glimpse of Blazes Boylan who he knows is on his way to visit Molly. He does not wish to encounter Boylan and pretends to be looking anxiously for something in his pockets. In the process he finds the bar of soap he had bought earlier at Sweny's stuck in his hip pocket. He enters the library gate and finds safety there.

The ninth episode ("Scylla and Charybdis") presents no topographical problems. It takes place entirely inside the National Library, and concentrates on Stephen's display of his theory about Shakespeare before the librarian and others. It begins at about two o'clock in the afternoon. As Stephen and Mulligan leave the library "a man passed out between them, bowing, greeting"—this is Bloom. The scene ends with Stephen emerging into the afternoon quiet of Kildare Street.

The tenth episode ("Wandering Rocks") moves in what at first sight may appear a bewildering fashion from place to place in Dublin and from one group of people to another. It is now approaching three o'clock in the afternoon. Joyce's aim is to present different people simultaneously moving about in different parts of the city, and in order to achieve the effect of simultaneity (for language cannot, except in an isolated pun, describe several quite separate things at the same time) he occasionally introduces a sentence or two from an account of one group in one place into his account of a quite different group in a different place. It is only when we come to the account of the other group later on in the episode that we discover what the puzzling intrusion in the preceding description had been about. (Joyce intended that the reader should read *Ulysses* often enough to be able to carry the whole book in his mind at once, and thus be able to see the multiple allusions, cross-references, and iteration of themes most of which cannot be recognized at first reading.)

The longest section of this episode is the opening account of Father Conmee's journey. Father Conmee, Rector of Clongowes Wood College, is on his way to the orphanage at Artane (in northeast Dublin) to arrange for the admission there of a son of the recently deceased Paddy Dignam. ("What was that boy's name again? Dignam, yes.") Father Conmee's watch registers five to three as he descends the presbytery steps by St. Francis Xavier's Church in Gardiner Street. He crosses to Mountjoy Square, greets Mrs. Sheehy, then stops three small schoolboys from nearby Belvedere College and sends them to post a letter in "the red pillar box at the corner of Fitzgibbon street". He walks along Mountjoy Square East, then turns right along Great Charles Street, turns the corner into the North Circular Road, and walks southeast along Portland Row to North Strand Road. There he turns right and walks northeast along North Strand Road to Newcomen Bridge (across the Royal Canal), where he boards a tramcar. He alights "at the Howth road stop", but does not go up Howth Road: instead, he goes up Malahide Road which leads to Artane and the orphanage. The picture of Father Conmee's "thicksocked ankles" "tickled by the stubble of Clongowes field", which follows, is to be understood as a scene in his mind: he is not actually at Clongowes at this time: it is some fourteen miles to the southwest.

We then move to Corny Kelleher the undertaker finishing his accounts. (He works at "H. J. O'Neill's funeral establishment" at Newcomen Bridge, which Father Conmee had passed on his way to board the tramcar.) We get a fleeting glimpse of "a generous white arm from a window in

Eccles Street" (Mrs. Bloom) flinging down a coin to a beggar. The beggar, we soon learn, is a "onelegged sailor" whom we see jerking himself up Eccles Street singing "For England home and beauty". We then move to Katey and Boody Dedalus in the Dedalus family home, which is un-identified but might be imagined as 7 St. Peter's Terrace, Cabra, where Joyce's father, brother and sisters were in fact living in June 1904: it is the quintessence of shabbiness. We next get a brief glimpse of the "crumpled throwaway" floating down the Liffey. Then we see Blazes Boylan buying fruit (to present to Mrs. Bloom) at Thornton's, 63 Grafton Street. After that we see Stephen talking with Almidano Artifoni outside Trinity Col-lege. (Artifoni is based on Father Charles Ghessi, Joyce's Italian lecturer at University College, Dublin: Joyce took the name from the director of the Berlitz school in Trieste.) We then move to Boylan's office (unidentified) where we see his secretary Miss Dunne answering the phone. This scene is important as it gives us the date of *Ulysses*: Miss Dunne clicks on her type-writer "16 June 1904".

The next shake of the kaleidoscope brings Ned Lambert showing "the historic council chamber of saint Mary's abbey" to the Reverend Hugh C. Love. The historic site is on the little street called Mary's Abbey which is a continuation of Abbey Street on the west side of Capel Street. Then we see Lenehan, M'Coy and friends strolling around the centre of Dublin. They are just south of the Liffey, in the neighbourhood of Temple Bar. Lenehan and M'Coy see Bloom scanning "books on the hawker's cart" near the metal bridge (west of O'Connell Bridge), then they "walk along Welling-ton quay by the river wall". Shortly afterwards we turn directly to Bloom scanning books: he buys *Sweets of Sin*. The next scene shows us Dilly Dedalus and her father meeting by Dillon's auction rooms in Bachelor's Walk. Then Tom Kernan, tea merchant, walks by James's Gate along James's Street south of Victoria Quay. He passes Shackleton's offices (millers) at 35 James Street, then "halted and preened himself before the sloping mirror of Peter Kennedy, hairdresser" (no. 48). He turns north "down the slope of Watling street" and approaches Island Street. He just misses the vice-regal cavalcade trotting along Pembroke Quay (now Wolfe Tone Quay) on the other side of the Liffey.

We turn to Stephen Dedalus watching through a jeweller's window a lapidary polishing a gem. He goes down Bedford Row and looks at the window of Clohissey's the bookseller's at nos. 10–11. He meets his sister Dilly, and feels guilt. We then move to Stephen's father Simon Dedalus and Father Cowley, who meet outside Reddy and Daughters (antiques, 19 Ormond Quay). The next scene begins with Martin Cunningham coming "out of the Castleyard gate". He goes by cab towards Lord Edward Street. Councillor Nannetti comes down the steps of City Hall. Cunningham and John Wyse Nolan go down Parliament Street. They see the vice-regal procession pass. We then turn to Buck Mulligan and Haines at "a small table near the window" of a tea shop, D.B.C. (Dublin Bakery Company, 33 Dame Street). We get another glimpse of the "crumpled throwaway" sailing "eastward by flanks of ships and trawlers, amid an archipelago of corks, beyond new Wapping street past Benson's ferry, and by the threemasted schooner Rosevean from Bridgewater with bricks". Almidano Artifoni walks past Holles Street. The mad Cashel Farrell walks in Merrion Square and strides on to Clare Street, where he passes "Mr. Bloom's dental windows" (nothing to do with Leopold Bloom, but M. Bloom, dentist, 2 Clare Street). Young Master Dignam, having bought a pound and a half of "porksteaks he had been sent for" at Mangan's the butchers (1 William Street) dawdles along Wicklow Street, Grafton Street and Nassau Street, thinking of his dead father. (He is going to take a tram back to Sandymount. But why was he sent to such a distant butcher's?)

This episode ends with an account of the procession from the vice-regal lodge in Phoenix Park, which passes in its progress the various characters in different parts of Dublin previously mentioned, welding them into a kind of unity and testifying to their simultaneous presence in the city. "William Humble, Earl of Dudley, and Lady Dudley, accompanied by lieutenant-colonel Hesseltine" drive out with their entourage "by the lower gate of Phoenix Park" along the quays on the north side of the Liffey. As they go along Ormond Quay the two barmaids of the Ormond Hotel (who are to play a significant part in the next episode) watch through the bar window and admire. The procession passes Simon Dedalus, and Hugh C. Love, crosses the river by Grattan Bridge where Lenehan and M'Coy are "taking leave of each other", passes Gerty MacDowell (heroine of the thirteenth episode) and John Wyse Nolan, goes "past Micky Anderson's all times ticking watches" (30 Parliament Street) and "Henry and James's wax smartsuited freshcheeked models" (1–3 Parliament Street). Tom Rochford and Nosey Flynn watch the approach of the cavalcade "over against Dame gate". Mulligan and Haines "gaze down on the viceregal equipage" from the window of the D.B.C. Dilly Dedalus sees the procession from Fownes Street as it goes along Dame Street. It passes John Henry Menton and Mrs. Breen and Blazes Boylan and Cashel Farrell and Master Patrick Dignam and the blind stripling as it makes its way by Nassau Street, Leinster Street, Merrion Square North, Lower Mount Street, Northumberland Road and Lansdowne Road towards the suburb of Haddington where the lord-lieutenant of Ireland is to open a charity bazaar. (The lord-lieutenant was indeed the Earl of Dudley, as Joyce says, but his name was William Humble Ward, not William Humble. He was lord-lieutenant of Ireland from 1902 to 1905.)

The eleventh episode ("Sirens"), after the introduction in which all the themes that are to appear in the episode make a brief appearance in a kind of anticipatory overture (there are many references to music in the pages that follow), opens at four o'clock in the afternoon with the two barmaids,

Miss Douce and Miss Kennedy, watching the vice-regal procession from the Ormond bar as it goes along Ormond Quay. Bloom's progress towards the Ormond Hotel is introduced briefly at scattered intervals into the account of what is going on in the bar. Simon Dedalus enters the bar. Then Lenehan enters. We hear at intervals the jingling of Blazes Boylan's jaunting-car as he approaches the hotel, and at last he too enters the bar. We get a glimpse of Bloom buying two sheets of writing paper in order to write to Martha Clifford. Bloom catches a glimpse of Boylan in his jaunting-car. Then Bloom enters the Ormond Hotel, finds Ritchie Goulding there, and the two decide to have a belated lunch in the hotel's dining room. Boylan leaves the bar (he is off to Eccles Street and Molly). Simon Dedalus, Ben Dollard and Father Cowley gather round the hotel piano. Father Cowley sings. Bloom and Goulding never encounter Simon Dedalus and his companions, but they hear the piano and the singing from the dining room and later, when Bloom is writing his letter to Martha, he hears Simon Dedalus singing the love song from the opera *Martha*. We hear Boylan jingling on his way to Eccles Street—he goes past the Rotunda, he is in Rutland Square, he jingles "by Dlugacz' porkshop" in Dorset Street. More music floats through to Bloom. The blind piano tuner taps his way back to the hotel to retrieve the tuning fork he had left. Bloom leaves the hotel, walks along Ormond Quay, passes "Lionel Marks's antique saleshop window" (16 Ormond Quay) and is still looking at a painting in Marks's window when the piano tuner enters the Ormond Hotel.

The twelfth episode ("Cyclops") is set in Barney Kiernan's pub, Little Britain Street, at 5.00 P.M. When Bloom, assaulted by the Citizen, leaves the pub in a hurry and escapes by boarding a tram, the mock-heroic description of his ascension shows him ascending "to the glory of the brightness at an angle of forty-five degrees over Donohoe's in Little Green Street like a shot off a shovel". Green Street is round the corner from Little Britain Street (running at right angles to it, parallel to Capel Street) and Donohoe's (grocer) was at nos. 4–5.

The thirteenth episode ("Nausikaa") finds Bloom, together with Gerty MacDowell and her friends, on the beach at Sandymount—the same beach where Stephen had walked at eleven o'clock that morning. It is now eight o'clock in the evening.

The fourteenth episode ("Oxen of the Sun") is set in the National Maternity Hospital, Holles Street (at the corner of Lower Mount Street). Stephen is drinking here with his medical student friends, and Bloom arrives to inquire after Mrs. Purefoy, who is having a baby. When Stephen and his drunken friends stream out of the hospital "with punctual Bloom at heels", they make for "Burkes of Denzille and Holles" (Denzille Street is now Fenian Street), and after drinking there (Bloom, who goes along only because he feels protective towards Stephen, takes only a "ginger cordial") the cry is "Change here for Bawdyhouse" and Stephen and his medical friends stream out again. What happens after this is not made clear until well into the fifteenth episode ("Circe"). Stephen and his friends go to Westland Row Station (now Pearse Station), where there is a mix-up. Bloom keeps Stephen in sight. ("What am I following him for? Still, he's the best of the lot.") Later Bloom reflects on "the very unpleasant scene at Westland Row terminus when it was perfectly evident that the other two, Mulligan, that is, and that English tourist friend of his [Haines], who eventually euchred their third companion, were patently trying, as if the whole bally station belonged to them, to give Stephen the slip in the confusion". Stephen apparently takes the train from Westland Row Station to Amiens Street Station (now Connolly Street Station) and Bloom follows, catching up with Stephen in Mabbot Street (now Corporation Street: this whole area has been much changed through slum clearance). "The Mabbot street entrance of nighttown" is part of the brothel district of Dublin north of the Custom House, much of it in the angle between Mabbot Street and Talbot Street. Protectively following the drunken Stephen, Bloom drops in at Olhausen's the pork butchers (72 Talbot Street) to buy something for the next morning's breakfast. He has already passed Gillen's, the hairdresser, at 64 Talbot Street and Antonio Rabaiotti, ice-cream merchant, at no. 65. He follows Stephen into Bella Cohen's brothel (81 Mabbot Street). In the whole of this scene Bloom's fatigue and Stephen's drunkenness produce in them a series of phantasmagoria which confuse what is going on around them in the brothel with their own deepest feelings of desire and guilt. Bloom as always is there to protect Stephen. When Stephen finally leaves, Bloom follows him. Stephen offends a couple of passing soldiers (who are walking with Cissy Caffrey, of the "Nausikaa" episode) and one of the soldiers knocks him out. Corny Kelleher, who turns up providentially (taking friends on a tour of Dublin's red-light district for purposes about which he is evasive), sorts it out with the police, who happen to be passing. Bloom, feeling increasingly protective towards the incapacitated Stephen, looks down on him as he lies in the Mabbot Street gutter and as he looks he sees his own son Rudy in his coffin ("with glass shoes and a little bronze helmet"), "a fairy boy of eleven", a fantastic image of Rudy as he would have been if he had not died in infancy.

In the sixteenth episode ("Eumaeus") Bloom takes charge of Stephen. It is now one o'clock in the morning. Having raised him from the gutter and got him looking more or less respectable, Bloom goes with Stephen along Beaver Lane (no longer in existence) to the corner of Montgomery Street "where they made tracks to the left from thence debouching into Amiens Street round by the corner of Dan Bergin's" (a pub at 46 Amiens Street). Bloom is looking for a cab, but though he sees one outside the North Star Hotel (26–30 Amiens Street) he is unable to hail it. So they proceed towards Amiens Street Station (now Connolly Station) and then go on to Store Street, where they pass the back door of the morgue. They pass the "warehouses of Beresford Place". They pass the back of the Custom House and go under the railway bridge. After a fairly lengthy stop at a cabman's shelter, where they converse with a sailor, Bloom suggests that Stephen come home with him to Eccles Street. They cross Beresford Place on their way to Gardiner Street.

In the seventeenth episode ("Ithaca") we are first told the precise route by which Bloom and Stephen walk to Eccles Street: "from Beresford place they followed in the order named Lower and Middle Gardiner street and Mountjoy square, west: then, at reduced pace, each beating left, Gardiner's place by inadvertence as far as the farther corner of Temple street, north: then at reduced pace with interruptions of halt, bearing right, Temple street, north, as far as Hardwick place. Approaching, disparate, at relaxed walking pace they crossed both the circus before George's church diametrically, the chord in any circle being less than the arc which it subtends." And so to 7 Eccles Street. It is two o'clock in the morning. Stephen declines "promptly, inexplicably, with amicability, gratefully" Bloom's offer of hospitality for the night, and leaves. Bloom goes to bed. "He rests. He has travelled." The final episode ("Penelope") consists of Molly's soliloquy in bed at 7 Eccles Street.

Other Testimony

WE GET EVOCATIONS of Dublin and its atmosphere in other of Joyce's books, though nowhere else is the city evoked with the vividness and particularity of *Ulysses*. *Dubliners* is more concerned with people than with place, but some of the stories present aspects of the city, especially those shabby-genteel streets that the young Joyce had known so well. The opening of "Araby" shows us such a street:

North Richmond Street, being blind, was a quiet street except at the hour when the Christian Brothers' School set the boys free. An uninhabited house of two stories stood at the blind end, detached from its neighbours in a square ground. The other houses of the street, conscious of decent lives within them, gazed with brown imperturbable faces. . . .

When the short days of winter came, dusk fell before we had well eaten our dinners. When we met in the street the houses had grown sombre. The space of sky above us was the colour of ever-changing violet and towards it the lamps of the street lifted their feeble lanterns. The cold air stung us and we played till our bodies glowed. Our shouts echoed in the silent street. The career of our play brought us through the dark muddy lanes behind the houses, where we ran the gauntlet of the rough tribes from the cottages, to the back doors of the dark dripping gardens where odours arose from the ashpits, to the dark odorous stables where a coachman smoothed and combed the horse or shook music from the buckled harness. When we returned to the street, light from the kitchen windows had filled the areas. If my uncle was seen turning the corner, we hid in the shadow until we had seen him safely housed.

In *A Portrait of the Artist as a Young Man* we see Stephen Dedalus prowling around the less savoury quarters of Dublin:

The swift December dusk had come tumbling clownishly after its dull day and as he stared through the dull square of the window of the schoolroom he felt his belly crave for its food. He hoped there would be stew for dinner, turnips and carrots and bruised potatoes and fat mutton pieces to be ladled out in thick peppered flourfattened sauce. Stuff it into you, his belly counselled him.

It would be a gloomy secret night. After early nightfall the yellow lamps would light up, here and there, the squalid quarter of the brothels. He would follow a devious course up and down the streets, circling always nearer and nearer in a tremor of fear and joy, until his feet led him suddenly round a dark corner. The whores would be just coming out of their houses making ready for the night, yawning lazily after their sleep and settling the hairpins in their clusters of hair.

But the *Portrait* also shows us another Dublin, a Dublin that suggests Stephen's (and so Joyce's) association of language with both geography and history. Stephen has "turned seaward from the road at Dollymount" and looks back at Dublin:

—A day of dappled seaborne clouds.—

The phrase and the day and the scene harmonised in a chord. Words. Was it their colours? He allowed them to glow and fade, hue after hue: sunrise gold, the russet and green of apple orchards, azure of waves, the greyfringed fleece of clouds. No, it was not their colours: it was the poise and balance of the period itself. Did he then love the rhythmic rise and fall of words better than their associations of legend and colour? Or was it that, being as weak of sight as he was shy of mind, he drew less pleasure from the reflection of the glowing sensible world through the prism of a language many coloured and richly storied than from the contemplation in a lucid supple periodic prose?

He passed from the trembling bridge on to firm land again. At that instant, as it seemed to him, the air was chilled; and looking askance towards the water he saw a flying squall darkening and crisping suddenly the tide. A faint click at his heart, a faint throb in his throat told him once more of how his flesh dreaded the cold infra-human odour of the sea: yet he did not strike across the downs on his left but held straight on along the spine of rocks that pointed against the river's mouth.

A veiled sunlight lit up faintly the grey sheet of water where the river was embayed. In the distance along the course of the slowflowing Liffey slender masts flecked the sky and, more distant still, the dim fabric of the city lay prone in haze. Like a scene on some vague arras, old as man's weariness, the image of the seventh city of Christendom was visible to him across the timeless air, no older nor more weary nor less patient of subjection than in the days of the thingmote.

Disheartened, he raised his eyes towards the slowdrifting clouds, dappled and seaborne. They were voyaging across the deserts of the sky, a host of nomads on the march, voyaging high over Ireland, westward bound. The Europe they had come from lay out there beyond the Irish Sea, Europe of strange tongues and valleyed and woodbegirt and citadelled and of entrenched and marshalled races. He heard a confused music within him as of memories and names which he was conscious of but could not capture even for an instant; then the music seemed to recede, to recede, to recede: and from each receding trail of nebulous music there fell always one long-drawn calling note, piercing like a star the dusk of silence. Again! Again! Again! A voice from beyond the world was calling.

The age of Joyce and Yeats and O'Casey could be called Dublin's heroic age in literature. It was also the age of Oliver St. John Gogarty (model for Buck Mulligan in Joyce's *Ulysses*), whose autobiography *As I Was Going down Sackville Street* is set in what is still essentially Joyce's Dublin (Sackville Street is now O'Connell Street). Later generations of Irish writers have less to say about the atmosphere of the city. Brendan Behan, who was born in Dublin in 1923 and died there in 1964, served three years in an English borstal as a teenager for his IRA activities and then six years in a Dublin prison. His first play, *The Quare Fellow*, depicts life in an Irish prison, while his autobiography, *Borstal Boy*, tells the story of his early life. His drunken roisterings in Dublin in his last years were frequently reported in the popular press and remain a Dublin legend, but they resulted in no memorable evocations of the city. Modern Dublin does not seem to attract the passionate chronicling that it did in its heroic age. For most people, certainly for most readers, Dublin is still the city through which Leopold Bloom walked on June 16, 1904, and on the anniversary of that day, "Bloomsday", innumerable lovers of Joyce are to be found retracing Bloom's footsteps from Eccles Street through the city and back again. Indeed, it is hardly an exaggeration to say that *Ulysses* stamped on Dublin a character that makes it unique among cities.

ATLAS AND GAZETTEER

This self-contained Atlas and Gazetteer Section presents biographical information on 236 leading literary figures active in the British Isles during the past 900 years. The majority of writers included were obvious candidates for selection. The more minor figures were included at the discretion of the authors in full recognition that, as with all such compilations, many marginal inclusions—as well as omissions—are open to debate. Living writers have been excluded.

All information is plotted on the region-by-region sequence of maps in the Atlas so that the life details of leading authors and the literary associations of about 475 towns and villages can be seen at a glance. Access to the maps is provided by a series of gazetteers organized as follows:

GENERAL GAZETTEER: *p. 262* This lists all names in alphabetical order, indicates birth and death dates, and gives information about places in the British Isles where authors were born, lived (short visits are generally ignored), died, were buried or are commemorated (activities outside the British Isles are not included). Map references against each place outside London direct readers to the appropriate map and grid reference in the Atlas (e.g., 23.C3 means that the reader should consult Atlas Map 23 and then locate C3 on the grid of the map). Brief references are also given to London dates (where applicable); for precise street information on London, readers should consult the separate London Gazetteer. Cross-references to all other gazetteers are also included.

LONDON GAZETTEER: *p. 271* Authors associated in some way with London are listed in alphabetical order, with dates, events and street addresses where known. The locations are keyed numerically to the London Atlas Maps (24–25).

WESTMINSTER ABBEY, ST. PAUL'S CATHEDRAL AND INNS OF COURT: *p. 278* This is a supplementary listing of writers who are buried or commemorated in Westminster Abbey and St. Paul's Cathedral, and of those who were members of the Inns of Court.

SCHOOLS GAZETTEER: *p. 279* A supplementary listing of public schools where two or more authors were educated, including map and grid references to the Atlas.

GEOGRAPHICAL INDEX: *p. 280* This lists all the places plotted in the Atlas, along with their Atlas Map and grid references.

Special maps in the Atlas Section

LONDON: *Atlas Maps 24 and 25* The numbers here correspond to the numbered sequence of entries in the London Gazetteer. To "decode" a particular plotting, simply consult the appropriate reference numbered in the London Gazetteer.

EDINBURGH AND DUBLIN: *Atlas Maps 15 and 16* Separate street guides for Edinburgh and Dublin, organized and keyed numerically in the same way as the London Atlas Map, have been included on these Atlas Maps. Cross-references in the General Gazetteer to these cities should be followed up here.

OXFORD AND CAMBRIDGE: *Atlas Maps 18 and 19* In addition to the street maps provided for these cities, there is an alphabetical listing of the colleges of each university indicating the authors who were resident there and their dates.

How to use the Gazetteers

If information is sought on a particular author, refer first to the General Gazetteer, which provides access to the Atlas Maps and all supplementary gazetteers.

If information is sought on a particular location, refer first to the Geographical Index. This directs readers to the appropriate Atlas Map, from which a locality's literary associations can be seen at a glance.

KEY TO COUNTIES AND REGIONS

England
1 Avon
2 Bedfordshire
3 Berkshire
4 Buckinghamshire
5 Cambridgeshire
6 Cheshire
7 Cleveland
8 Cornwall
9 Cumbria
10 Derbyshire
11 Devon
12 Dorset
13 Durham
14 East Sussex
15 Essex
16 Gloucestershire
17 Gt. Manchester
18 Hampshire
19 Hereford and Worcester
20 Hertfordshire
21 Humberside
22 Kent
23 Lancashire
24 Leicestershire
25 Lincoln

26 London
27 Merseyside
28 Norfolk
29 Northampton
30 Northumberland
31 North Yorkshire
32 Nottinghamshire
33 Oxfordshire
34 Shropshire
35 Somerset
36 South Yorkshire
37 Staffordshire
38 Suffolk
39 Surrey
40 Tyne and Wear
41 Warwickshire
42 West Midlands
43 West Sussex
44 West Yorkshire
45 Wiltshire

Ireland
46 Carlow
47 Cavan
48 Clare
49 Cork
50 Donegal

51 Dublin
52 Galway
53 Kerry
54 Kildare
55 Kilkenny
56 Laois
57 Leitrim
58 Limerick
59 Longford
60 Louth
61 Mayo
62 Meath
63 Monaghan
64 Offaly
65 Roscommon
66 Sligo
67 Tipperary
68 Waterford
69 Westmeath
70 Wexford
71 Wicklow

Northern Ireland
72 Antrim
73 Armagh
74 Down
75 Fermanagh

76 Londonderry
77 Tyrone

Scotland
78 Borders
79 Central
80 Dumfries and Galloway
81 Fife
82 Grampian
83 Highland
84 Lothian
85 Orkney Islands
86 Shetland Islands
87 Strathclyde
88 Tayside
89 Western Islands

Wales
90 Clwyd
91 Dyfed
92 Gwent
93 Gwynedd
94 Mid Glamorgan
95 Powys
96 South Glamorgan
97 West Glamorgan

Key map to Atlas section

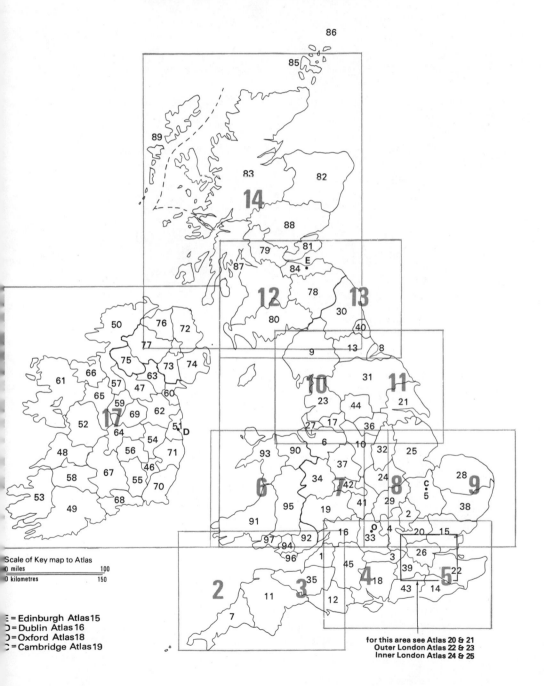

Scale of Key map to Atlas

| 0 miles | 100 |
| 0 kilometres | 150 |

E = Edinburgh Atlas 15
D = Dublin Atlas 16
O = Oxford Atlas 18
C = Cambridge Atlas 19

for this area see Atlas 20 & 21
Outer London Atlas 22 & 23
Inner London Atlas 24 & 25

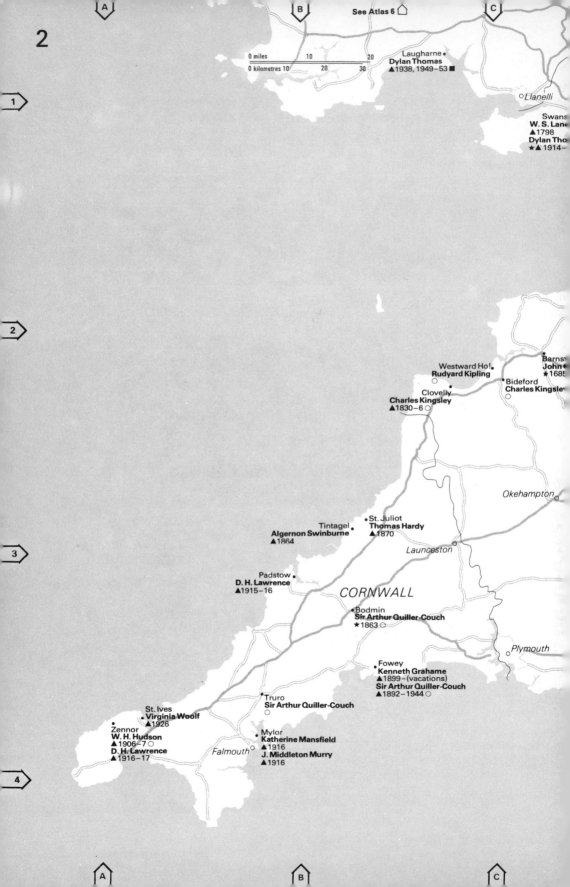

2

0 miles   10   20
0 kilometres 10   20   30

Laugharne •
Dylan Thomas
▲1938, 1949–53 ■

○ Llanelli

1

Swans
W. S. Lan
▲1798
Dylan Tho
★▲1914–

2

Westward Ho! ○
Rudyard Kipling

Barnst
John •
★168£

Bideford •
Charles Kingsle

Clovelly •
Charles Kingsley
▲1830–6 ○

○ Okehampton

• St. Juliot
Thomas Hardy
▲1870

Tintagel •
Algernon Swinburne
▲1864

Launceston ○

3

Padstow •
D. H. Lawrence
▲1915–16

CORNWALL

• Bodmin
Sir Arthur Quiller-Couch
★1863 ○

○ Plymouth

Fowey •
Kenneth Grahame
▲1899 –(vacations)
Sir Arthur Quiller-Couch
▲1892–1944 ○

St. Ives •
Virginia Woolf
▲1926

• Truro
Sir Arthur Quiller-Couch

• Zennor
W. H. Hudson
▲1906–7 ○
D. H. Lawrence
▲1916–17

Falmouth ○

• Mylor
Katherine Mansfield
▲1916
J. Middleton Murry
▲1916

4

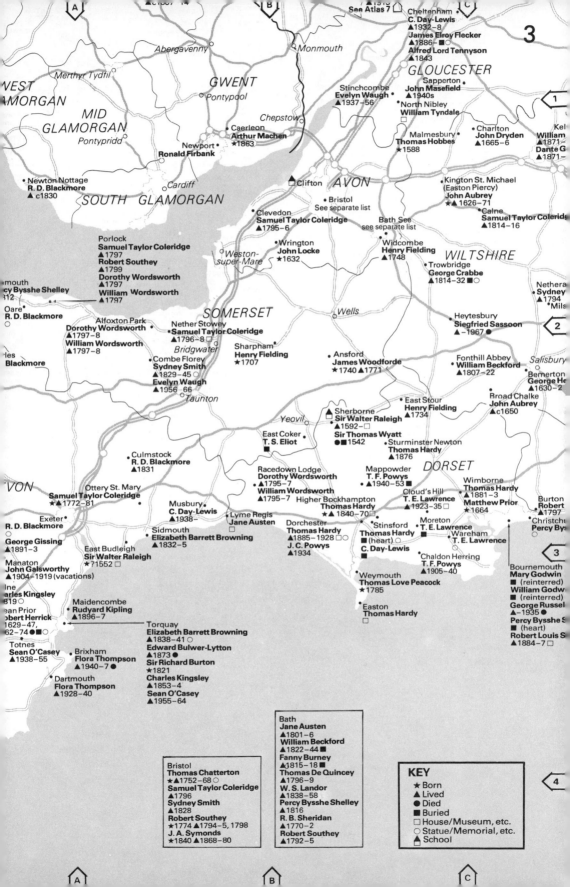

Abergavenny
Monmouth

Cheltenham
C. Day-Lewis
▲1932–8
James Elroy Flecker
▲1886–■
Alfred Lord Tennyson
▲1843

GLOUCESTER

Merthyr Tydfil

GWENT

Sapperton
John Masefield
▲1940s

Stinchcombe
Evelyn Waugh
▲1937–56

North Nibley
William Tyndale
□

WEST MORGAN

MID GLAMORGAN
Pontypool

Pontypridd

Chepstow

Caerleon
Arthur Machen
★1863

Newport
Ronald Firbank

Cardiff

Malmesbury
Thomas Hobbes
▲1588

Charlton
John Dryden
▲1665–6

Kel
William
▲1871–
Dante G
▲1871–

• Newton Nottage
R. D. Blackmore
▲ c1830

SOUTH GLAMORGAN

Clifton ▲

AVON

Kington St. Michael
(Easton Piercy)
John Aubrey
★▲1626–71

Calne
Samuel Taylor Coleridge
▲1814–16

Clevedon
Samuel Taylor Coleridge
▲1795–6

Bristol
See separate list

Bath See
see separate list

WILTSHIRE

Porlock
Samuel Taylor Coleridge
▲1797
Robert Southey
▲1799
Dorothy Wordsworth
▲1797
William Wordsworth
▲1797

Weston-super-Mare

Wrington
John Locke
★1632

Widcombe
Henry Fielding
▲1748

Trowbridge
George Crabbe
▲1814–32 ■○

mouth
cy Bysshe Shelley
312

SOMERSET

Wells

Nethera
• **Sydney**
▲1794
• **Mils**

Oare
R. D. Blackmore
○

Alfoxton Park
Dorothy Wordsworth
▲1797–8
William Wordsworth
▲1797–8

Nether Stowey
• **Samuel Taylor Coleridge**
▲1796–8 □ ○

Bridgwater

Sharpham
Henry Fielding
★1707

Heytesbury
Siegfried Sassoon
▲ –1967 ●

les
Blackmore

Combe Florey
Sydney Smith
▲1829–45 ○
Evelyn Waugh
▲1956–66

Taunton

Ansford
James Woodforde
★1740 ▲1771

Fonthill Abbey
William Beckford
▲1807–22

Salisbury

Bemerton
George He
▲1630–2

Sherborne ▲
Sir Walter Raleigh
▲1592–□

East Stour
Henry Fielding
▲1734

Broad Chalke
John Aubrey
▲c1650

Yeovil

East Coker
T. S. Eliot
■

Sir Thomas Wyatt
● ■ 1542

Sturminster Newton
Thomas Hardy
▲1876

DORSET

Culmstock
R. D. Blackmore
▲1831

Racedown Lodge
Dorothy Wordsworth
• ▲1795–7
William Wordsworth
▲1795–7

Mappowder
T. F. Powys
• ▲1940–53 ■

Wimborne
Thomas Hardy

VON

Ottery St. Mary
Samuel Taylor Coleridge
★▲1772–81

Musbury
C. Day-Lewis
▲1938–

Higher Bockhampton
Thomas Hardy
★▲1840–70■

Cloud's Hill
T. E. Lawrence
▲1923–35 □

Matthew Prior
▲1664

Burton
Robert
▲1797

Exeter
R. D. Blackmore

Sidmouth
Elizabeth Barrett Browning
▲1832–5

Lyme Regis
Jane Austen

Dorchester
Thomas Hardy
▲1885–1928 □○
J. C. Powys
▲1934

Stinsford
Thomas Hardy
■ (heart) ○
C. Day-Lewis
■

Moreton
T. E. Lawrence
■
Wareham
T. E. Lawrence

Christchu
Percy Bys

George Gissing
▲1891–3

East Budleigh
Sir Walter Raleigh
★?1552 □

Chaldon Herring
T. F. Powys
▲1905–40

Manaton
John Galsworthy
▲1904–1919 (vacations)

Bournemouth
Mary Godwin
■ (reinterred)
William Godw
■ (reinterred)
George Russel
▲–1935 ■
Percy Bysshe S
■ (heart)
Robert Louis S
▲1884–7 ■

ine
arles Kingsley
1819

an Prior
obert Herrick
1629–47,
62–74 ■○

Weymouth
Thomas Love Peacock
★1785

Maidencombe
• **Rudyard Kipling**
▲1896–7

Easton
Thomas Hardy
□

Totnes
Sean O'Casey
▲1938–55

Brixham
Flora Thompson
▲1940–7 ●

Torquay
Elizabeth Barrett Browning
▲1838–41 ○
Edward Bulwer-Lytton
▲1873 ●
Sir Richard Burton
★1821
Charles Kingsley
▲1853–4
Sean O'Casey
▲1955–64

• Dartmouth
Flora Thompson
▲1928–40

Bath
Jane Austen
▲1801–6
William Beckford
▲1822–44 ■
Fanny Burney
▲1815–18 ■
Thomas De Quincey
▲1796–9
W. S. Landor
▲1838–58
Percy Bysshe Shelley
▲1816
R. B. Sheridan
▲1770–2
Robert Southey
▲1792–5

Bristol
Thomas Chatterton
★▲1752–68 ○
Samuel Taylor Coleridge
▲1796
Sydney Smith
▲1828
Robert Southey
★1774 ▲1794–5, 1798
J. A. Symonds
★1840 ▲1868–80

KEY
★ Born
▲ Lived
● Died
■ Buried
□ House/Museum, etc.
○ Statue/Memorial, etc.
▲ School

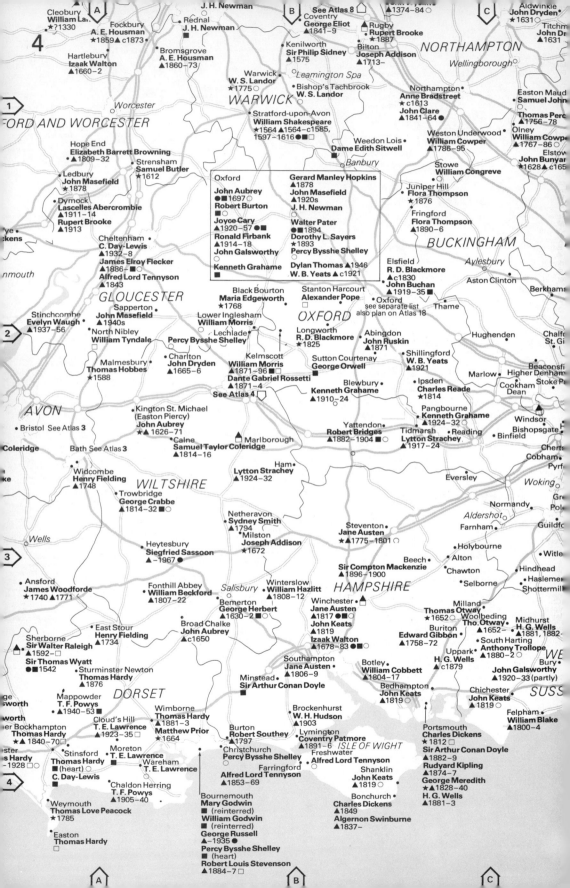

4

Cleobury
William La...
★?1330

Fockbury
A. E. Housman
★1859▲c1873

Hartlebury
Izaak Walton
▲1660–2

Rednal
J. H. Newman

Bromsgrove
A. E. Housman
▲1860–73

J. H. Newman

A

B

Coventry
George Eliot
▲1841–9

Kenilworth
Sir Philip Sidney
▲1575

Warwick
W. S. Landor
★1775

Bishop's Tachbrook
W. S. Landor

Stratford-upon-Avon
William Shakespeare
★1564▲1564–c1585,
1597–1616●■□

Leamington Spa

WARWICK

See Atlas 8
▲1374–84

Rugby
Rupert Brooke
★1887

Bilton
Joseph Addison
▲1713–

NORTHAMPTON

Wellingborough

Northampton
Anne Bradstreet
★c1613
John Clare
▲1841–64●

C

Aldwinkle
John Dryden
★1631

Titchm...
John Dr...
▲1631

Easton Maud...
Samuel John...

Thomas Perc...
▲1756–78

Olney
William Cowper
▲1767–86○

Elstow
John Bunyan
★1628▲c165...

Weedon Lois
Dame Edith Sitwell
■

Weston Underwood
William Cowper
▲1786–95

1

FORD AND WORCESTER

Worcester

Hope End
Elizabeth Barrett Browning
●1809–32

Strensham
Samuel Butler
★1612

Ledbury
John Masefield
★1878

Dymock
Lascelles Abercrombie
▲1911–14
Rupert Brooke
▲1913

Cheltenham
C. Day-Lewis
▲1932–8
James Elroy Flecker
★1886–■
Alfred Lord Tennyson
▲1843

GLOUCESTER

Sapperton
John Masefield
▲1940s

North Nibley
William Tyndale

Charlton
John Dryden
▲1665–6

Malmesbury
Thomas Hobbes
★1588

AVON

Bristol See Atlas 3

Bath See Atlas 3

Coleridge

Stinchcombe
Evelyn Waugh
▲1937–56

Black Bourton
Maria Edgeworth
★1768

Lower Inglesham
William Morris

Lechlade

Kelmscott
William Morris
▲1871–96●
Dante Gabriel Rossetti
▲1871–4
See Atlas 4 □

Kington St. Michael
(Easton Piercy)
John Aubrey
★▲1626–71

Calne
Samuel Taylor Coleridge
▲1814–16

Marlborough

Stanton Harcourt
Alexander Pope

OXFORD

Longworth
R. D. Blackmore
★1825

Sutton Courtenay
George Orwell

Blewbury
Kenneth Grahame
▲1910–24

Stowe
William Congreve

Juniper Hill
Flora Thompson
★1876

Fringford
Flora Thompson
▲1890–6

BUCKINGHAM

Aylesbury

Elsfield
R. D. Blackmore
★c1830
John Buchan
▲1919–35■

Oxford
see separate list
also on plan on Atlas 18

Abingdon
John Ruskin
▲1871

Shillingford
W. B. Yeats
▲1921

Ipsden
Charles Reade
★1814

Pangbourne
Kenneth Grahame
▲1924–32

Tidmarsh
Lytton Strachey
▲1917–24

Reading

Aston Clinton

Berkhams...

Thame

Hughenden

Marlow

Higher Denham
Cookham
Dean

Beaconsfield
Stoke Po...

Windsor
Bishopsgate
Binfield

Cherts...
Cobham...
Pyrf...

(box)
Oxford
John Aubrey
●■1697○
Robert Burton
■
Joyce Cary
▲1920–57●
Ronald Firbank
▲1914–18
John Galsworthy

Kenneth Grahame
■

Gerard Manley Hopkins
▲1878
John Masefield
▲1920s
J. H. Newman

Walter Pater
●■1894
Dorothy L. Sayers
★1893
Percy Bysshe Shelley

Dylan Thomas ▲1946
W. B. Yeats ★c1921

2

Yattendon
Robert Bridges
▲1882–1904■○

Chalfo...
St. Gi...

Beaconsfield

WILTSHIRE

Widcombe
Henry Fielding
▲1748

Trowbridge
George Crabbe
▲1814–32■○

Netheravon
Sydney Smith
★1794

Milston
Joseph Addison
★1672

Ham
Lytton Strachey
▲1924–32

Marlborough

Eversley

Normandy

Aldershot

Woking

Gre...
Pol...

3

Wells

Heytesbury
Siegfried Sassoon
▲–1967●

Ansford
James Woodforde
★1740▲1771

Fonthill Abbey
William Beckford
▲1807–22

Salisbury

Winterslow
William Hazlitt
▲1808–12

HAMPSHIRE

Steventon
Jane Austen
★▲1775–1801○

Farnham

Holybourne

Beech

Alton

Chawton

Selborne

Holybourne

Hindhead

Haslemer...

Shottermil...

Witle...

Sir Compton Mackenzie
▲1896–1900

Guildf...

Sherborne
Sir Walter Raleigh
▲1592–□
Sir Thomas Wyatt
●■1542

East Stour
Henry Fielding
★1734

Sturminster Newton
Thomas Hardy
▲1876

Mappowder
T. F. Powys
▲1940–53■

...worth
...worth
er Bockhampton
Thomas Hardy
★▲1840–70■

...ster
...s Hardy
...1928□○

Stinsford
Thomas Hardy
(heart)
C. Day-Lewis

Moreton
T. E. Lawrence
Wareham
T. E. Lawrence

Cloud's Hill
T. E. Lawrence
▲1923–35■

Chaldon Herring
T. F. Powys
▲1905–40

DORSET

Sherborne

Broad Chalke
John Aubrey
▲c1650

Bemerton
George Herbert
▲1630–2■○

Wimborne
Thomas Hardy
▲1881–3
Matthew Prior
▲1664

Burton
Robert Southey
▲1797

Christchurch
Percy Bysshe Shelley

Weymouth
Thomas Love Peacock
★1785

Easton
Thomas Hardy

Bournemouth
Mary Godwin
(reinterred)
William Godwin
(reinterred)
George Russell
▲–1935●
Percy Bysshe Shelley
(heart)
Robert Louis Stevenson
▲1884–7□

Winchester
Jane Austen
▲1817●■
John Keats
▲1819
Izaak Walton
▲1678–83●■

Southampton
Jane Austen
▲1806–9

Minstead
Sir Arthur Conan Doyle
■

Brockenhurst
W. H. Hudson
▲1903

Lymington
Coventry Patmore
▲1891–6●

Farringford
Alfred Lord Tennyson
▲1853–69

ISLE OF WIGHT

Freshwater
Alfred Lord Tennyson

Shanklin
John Keats
▲1819○

Bonchurch
Charles Dickens
▲1849
Algernon Swinburne
▲1837–

Botley
William Cobbett
▲1804–17

Bedhampton
John Keats
▲1819

Buriton
Edward Gibbon
▲1758–72

Uppark
H. G. Wells
▲c1879

Milland
Thomas Otway
★1652○

Woolbeding
Tho. Otway

South Harting
Anthony Trollope
▲1880–2○

Midhurst
H. G. Wells
▲1881, 1882–...

Chichester
John Keats
▲1819○

Felpham
William Blake
▲1800–4

Portsmouth
Charles Dickens
★1812□
Sir Arthur Conan Doyle
▲1882–9
Rudyard Kipling
▲1874–7
George Meredith
★▲1828–40
H. G. Wells
▲1881–3

WE...

Bury
John Galsworthy
▲1920–33 (partly)

SUSS...

Windsor
Bishopsgate

4

A

B

C

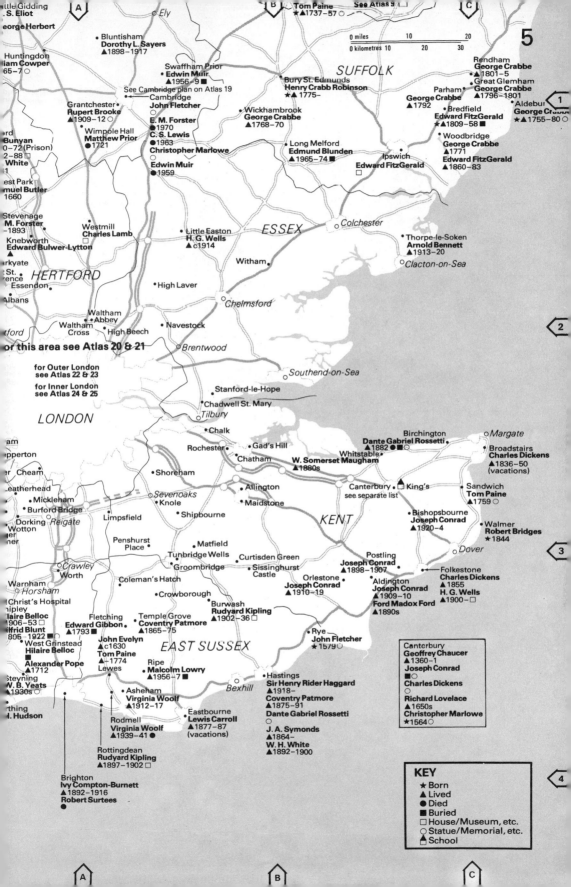

Little Gidding
.S. Eliot

eorge Herbert

Huntingdon
iam Cowper
65–7 ○

Ely

• Bluntisham
Dorothy L. Sayers
▲1898–1917

Swaffham Prior
Edwin Muir
▲1956–9 ■

See Cambridge plan on Atlas 19
Cambridge

Grantchester
Rupert Brooke
▲1909–12 ○

Wimpole Hall
Matthew Prior
● 1721

John Fletcher

E. M. Forster
● 1970
C. S. Lewis
● 1963
Christopher Marlowe
●

Edwin Muir
● 1959

ord
Bunyan
0–72 (Prison)
2–88 □
1
White
1

est Park
muel Butler
1660

Stevenage
M. Forster
–1893
Knebworth
Edward Bulwer-Lytton
▲

HERTFORD

arkyate
: St.
rence
Essendon ○
Albans

Westmill
Charles Lamb
•

• Little Easton
H. G. Wells
▲ c1914

Witham •

• High Laver

Tom Paine
★▲1737–57 ○

See Atlas 9

SUFFOLK

• Bury St. Edmunds
Henry Crabb Robinson
★▲ 1775–

• Wickhambrook
George Crabbe
▲1768–70

• Long Melford
Edmund Blunden
▲1965–74 ■

ESSEX

Colchester ○

• Thorpe-le-Soken
Arnold Bennett
▲1913–20

Clacton-on-Sea

Rendham
George Crabbe
▲1801–5
Great Glemham
George Crabbe
▲1796–1801

Parham
George Crabbe
▲1792

• Bredfield
Edward FitzGerald
★▲1809–58 ■

• Woodbridge
George Crabbe
▲1771
Edward FitzGerald
▲1860–83

Ipswich
Edward FitzGerald
□

Aldebur
George Crabb
★▲1755–80 ○

0 miles   10   20
0 kilometres 10   20   30

Chelmsford

Waltham
• Abbey
Waltham
Cross
• High Beech

• Navestock

○ *Brentwood*

Southend-on-Sea

or this area see Atlas 20 & 21

for Outer London
see Atlas 22 & 23

for Inner London
see Atlas 24 & 25

LONDON

Stanford-le-Hope •

• Chadwell St. Mary
Tilbury

• Chalk

Rochester •

Chatham •

• Gad's Hill

Birchington
Dante Gabriel Rossetti
▲1882 ● ■

Whitstable ○
W. Somerset Maugham
▲1880s

○ *Margate*

Broadstairs
Charles Dickens
▲1836–50
(vacations)

am
pperton

er Cheam

eatherhead

• Mickleham

• Burford Bridge
Dorking
Wotton
er

Reigate

• Shoreham

Sevenoaks
• Knole

• Allington

• Shipbourne

Maidstone •

Canterbury
see separate list

KENT

□ King's ▲

• Sandwich
Tom Paine
▲1759 ○

Bishopsbourne
Joseph Conrad
▲1920–4

• Walmer
Robert Bridges
★1844

Crawley
• Worth

Warnham ○
Christ's Hospital
ipley
laire Belloc
906–53 ■
ifrid Blunt
805 – 1922 ●

Horsham

Limpsfield •

Penshurst
Place •

• Matfield
Tunbridge Wells •
• Groombridge

Curtisden Green •

• Sissinghurst
Castle

Postling
Joseph Conrad
▲1898–1907

Orlestone
Joseph Conrad
▲1910–19

Aldington
Joseph Conrad
▲1909–10
Ford Madox Ford
1890s

• *Dover*

Folkestone
Charles Dickens
▲1855
H. G. Wells
▲1900 – □

Fletching
Edward Gibbon
▲1793 ■

• West Grinstead
Hilaire Belloc
●
Alexander Pope
▲1712

Steyning
W. B. Yeats
1930s

rthing
. Hudson

Coleman's Hatch •

• Crowborough

Temple Grove
Coventry Patmore
▲1865–75

John Evelyn
▲c1630
Tom Paine
▲–1774
Lewes

• Ripe
Malcolm Lowry
▲1956–7 ■

Asheham
Virginia Woolf
▲1912–17

Rodmell
Virginia Woolf
▲1939–41 ●

Rottingdean
Rudyard Kipling
▲1897–1902 □

Brighton
Ivy Compton-Burnett
▲1892–1916
Robert Surtees
●

Burwash
Rudyard Kipling
▲1902–36 □

Rye
John Fletcher
★1579 ○

• Hastings
Sir Henry Rider Haggard
▲1918–
Coventry Patmore
▲1875–91
Dante Gabriel Rossetti
○

Eastbourne
Lewis Carroll
▲1877–87
(vacations)

Bexhill

EAST SUSSEX

J. A. Symonds
▲1864–
W. H. White
▲1892–1900

KEY
★ Born
▲ Lived
● Died
■ Buried
□ House/Museum, etc.
○ Statue/Memorial, etc.
▲ School

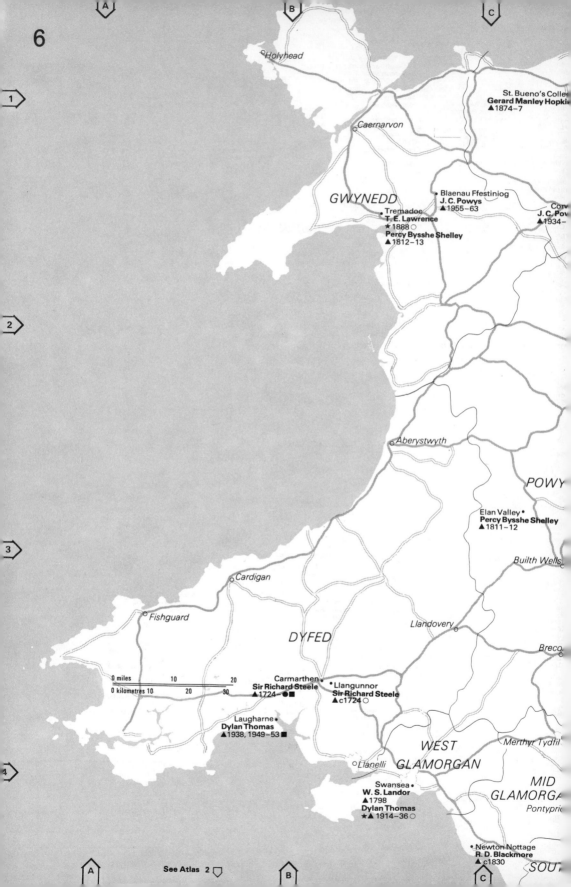

A

B

C

1

○Holyhead

St. Bueno's Colle
Gerard Manley Hopkir
▲1874-7

○Caernarvon

GWYNEDD

• Blaenau Ffestiniog
J. C. Powys
▲1955-63

Cor
J. C. Pov
▲1934-

• Tremadoc
T. E. Lawrence
★ 1888 ○
Percy Bysshe Shelley
▲1812-13

2

○Aberystwyth

POWY

Elan Valley •
Percy Bysshe Shelley
▲1811-12

3

Builth Wells

○Cardigan

○Fishguard

DYFED

Llandovery ○

Breco

0 miles   10   20
0 kilometres 10   20   30

Carmarthen •
Sir Richard Steele
▲1724-●■

• Llangunnor
Sir Richard Steele
▲c1724○

Laugharne •
Dylan Thomas
▲1938, 1949-53 ■

WEST

Merthyr Tydfil

○Llanelli

GLAMORGAN

MID
GLAMORGA

4

Swansea •
W. S. Landor
▲1798
Dylan Thomas
★▲ 1914-36 ○

Pontypri

• Newton Nottage
R. D. Blackmore
▲ c1830

SOU

A

See Atlas 2 ▽

B

C

Map: Literary Britain — West Midlands and surrounding counties

Grid references: A B C at top; 7, 1, 2, 3, 4 along right edge; A B C at bottom

Top area:

Liverpool
Matthew Arnold ● 1888
A. H. Clough ★ 1819 ▲ 1836
Sir James Frazer ▲ 1907–22
John Masefield ▲ 1891–4
Lytton Strachey ▲ 1897–9

Birkenhead

MERSEYSIDE

Ashton-upon-Mersey •
Lascelles Abercrombie ★ 1881

See Atlas 10

Rotherham
Sheffield

Daresbury
Lewis Carroll ★ 1832 ▲ 1832–43 □

Knutsford
Mrs Elizabeth Gaskell ▲ 1811–32 ■ □

Macclesfield

CHESHIRE

Renishaw
Dame Edith Sitwell ▲ 1877–8

Mount St.
Gerard Ma
★ 1877–8

Chesterfield

DERBY

Chester

ntasaph
rancis Thompson
893–7

CLWYD

Crewe

Ault Hucknall
Thomas Hobbes •
▲ –1679 ■

Mansf

Middleton-by-Wirksworth
D. H. Lawrence •
▲ 1918–19

NOTT

Wrexham

Llantysilio
Robert Browning •

Stoke-on-Trent
Arnold Bennett ★ ● 1867–89 ■

Newstead Abbey
Lord Byron ▲ 1808–16 □

Eastwood
D. H. Lawrence ★ 1885 ▲ 1887– 1902 □

Hucknall
Lord Byr

Llangollen
Robert Browning ▲ 1886

ge Borrow •

Shirley
J. C. Powys ★ 1872
T. F. Powys ★ 1875

Nottingham
Lord Byron ▲ 1798

Oswestry
Wilfred Owen •
▲ 1893–7

Wem
William Hazlitt •
★ c1786

Shallowford
Izaak Walton ▲ □

STAFFORD

Uttoxeter
Samuel Johnson •

Derby
Maria Edgeworth ▲ 1775–81 •

Preston Brockhurst
William Wycherley ★ 1640

Stafford
R. B. Sheridan •

Burton-upon-Trent

Grace Dieu
Francis Beaumont ★ 1584

Loughborough

Izaak Walton ★ 1593 ○

Coleorton Hall
Francis Beaumont •

Shrewsbury
George Farquhar ▲ 1705
Sir Philip Sidney ○

SHROPSHIRE

Stretton Hall •
William Congreve ▲ 1689

Lichfield
Joseph Addison ▲ 1683–98
James Boswell ▲ 1735–7
Samuel Johnson ★ 1709 ○

Edial
Samuel Johnson •

Dorothy Wordsworth ▲ 1806–7
William Wordsworth ▲ 1806–7

Leicester

Market Bosworth •
Samuel Johnson ▲ 1731–

lshpool

ntgomery
orge Herbert
593

Bridgnorth
Thomas Percy ★ 1729

Stourbridge
Samuel Johnson ▲ 1726–7

WEST MIDLANDS

Birmingham
Samuel Johnson ▲ c1734
Louis MacNeice ▲ 1930–5
J. H. Newman

Lindley
Robert Burton ★ 1577

Nuneaton •
George Eliot ★ 1819 ▲ 1820–41 □

Lutte
John
137–

Cleobury Mortimer
William Langland ★? 1330

Fockbury
A. E. Housman ★ 1859 ▲ c1873

Rednal •
J. H. Newman ■

Coventry
George Eliot ▲ 1841–9

Rugby
Rupert Bro ★ 1887

Ludlow •
Samuel Butler ▲ 1661–2
A. E. Housman ■ ○

Hartlebury
Izaak Walton ▲ 1660–2

Bromsgrove
A. E. Housman ▲ 1860–73

Kenilworth
Sir Philip Sidney ▲ 1575

Bilton
Joseph Addis ▲ 1713–

Leominster

Warwick
W. S. Landor ★ 1775

Bishop's Tachbrook
W. S. Landor •

Leamington Spa

HEREFORD AND WORCESTER

Kington

Worcester

WARWICK

Credenhill
Thomas Traherne ▲ 1661–7

Hope End •
Elizabeth Barrett Browning ▲ 1809–32

Stratford-upon-Avon
William Shakespeare ★ 1564 ▲ 1564–c1585, 1597–1616 ● ■ □

Weedon Lois
Dame Edith Sitwell ■

Hereford
Thomas Traherne ★ ? 1638

Strensham •
Samuel Butler ★ 1612

Banbury

Ledbury
John Masefield ★ 1878

Dymock
Lascelles Abercrombie ▲ 1911–14
Rupert Brooke ▲ 1913

Ross-on-Wye
Charles Dickens •

lanthony
S. Landor
1807–14

Oxford box:

Oxford
John Aubrey ● ■ 1697
Robert Burton ■
Joyce Cary ▲ 1920–57 ● ■
Ronald Firbank ▲ 1914–18
John Galsworthy

Gerard Manley Hopkins ▲ 1878
John Masefield ▲ 1920s
J. H. Newman
Walter Pater ● ■ 1894
Dorothy L. Sayers ★ 1893
Percy Bysshe Shelley
Dylan Thomas ▲ 1946
W. B. Yeats ▲ c1921

Kenneth Grahame ■

Cheltenham
C. Day-Lewis ▲ 1932–8
James Elroy Flecker ★ 1886– ■
Alfred Lord Tennyson ▲ 1843

Black Bourton
Maria Edgeworth ★ 1768

Stanton Harcourt
Alexander Pope ▲

Elsfie
R. D.
▲ c18
John
▲ 19

Oxford
see separate
also plan on A1

GLOUCESTER

OXFORD

Abergavenny

Monmouth

Stinchcombe
Evelyn Waugh ▲ 1937–56

Sapperton
John Masefield ▲ 1940s

North Nibley •
William Tyndale ★

Lechlad
Percy Bysshe Shelle •

GWENT

Pontypool

Chepstow

Caerleon
Arthur Machen ★ 1863

Malmesbury
Thomas Hobbes ★ 1588

Charlton •
John Dryden ▲ 1665–6

Key box:

KEY
★ Born
▲ Lived
● Died
■ Buried
□ House/Museum, etc.
○ Statue/Memorial, etc.
▲ School

Newport •
Ronald Firbank ★

Cardiff

AMORGAN

Clifton ▲

AVON

See Atlas 3 □

Clevedon

Bristol See Atlas 3

Kington St. Michael
(Easton Piercy)
John Aubrey ★ ▲ 1626–71

Calne
Samuel Taylor Coleridge

Marlborough

Yattendon
Robert Bridges ▲ 1882–1904 ■ □

Samuel Taylor Coleridge

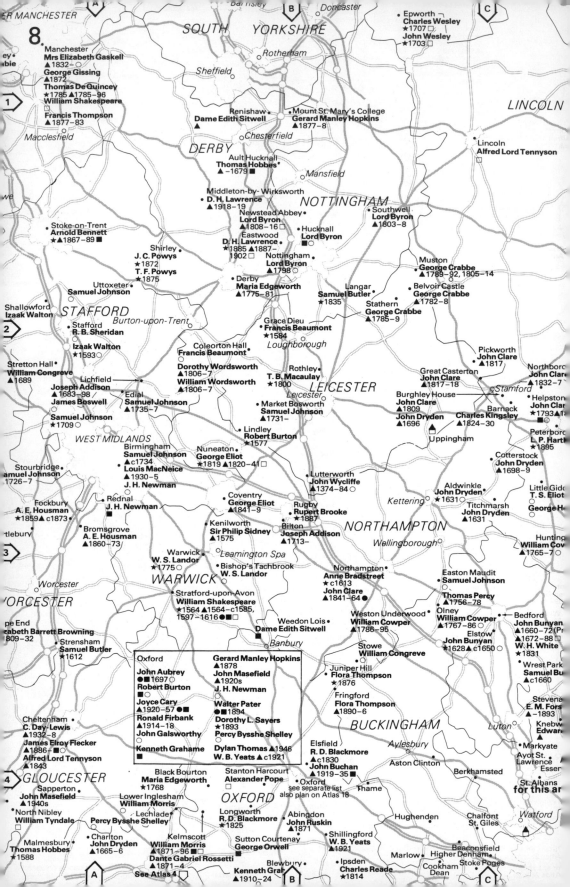

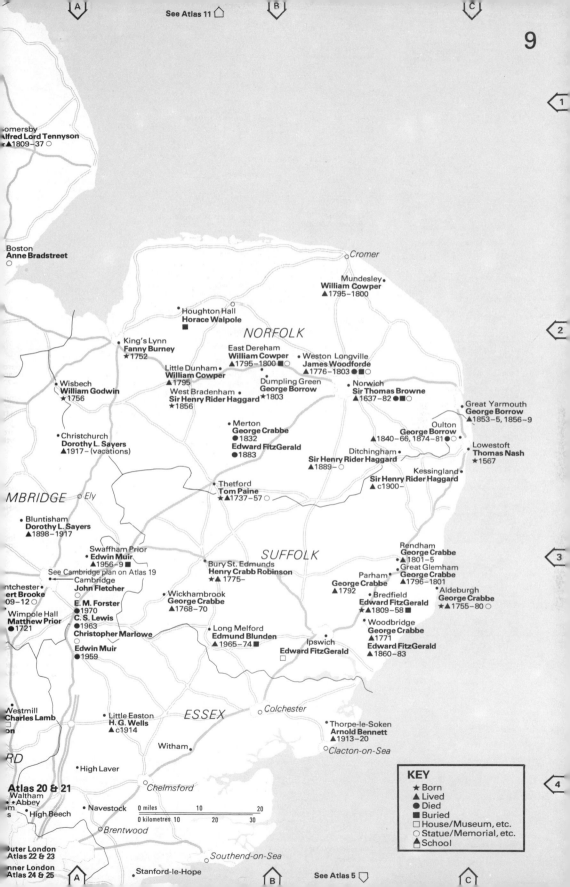

A   B   C

1

omersby
Alfred Lord Tennyson
★▲1809–37 ○

Boston
Anne Bradstreet
○

○ Cromer

Mundesley
William Cowper
▲1795–1800

NORFOLK

Houghton Hall
Horace Walpole
■

King's Lynn
Fanny Burney
★1752

East Dereham
William Cowper
▲1795–1800 ■

Weston Longville
James Woodforde
▲1776–1803 ● ■ ○

Little Dunham
William Cowper
★1795

Dumpling Green
George Borrow
★1803

Norwich
Sir Thomas Browne
▲1637–82 ● ■ ○

Wisbech
William Godwin
★1756

West Bradenham
Sir Henry Rider Haggard
★1856

Great Yarmouth
George Borrow
▲1853–5, 1856–9

Christchurch
Dorothy L. Sayers
▲1917– (vacations)

Merton
George Crabbe
● 1832
Edward FitzGerald
● 1883

Oulton
George Borrow
▲1840–66, 1874–81 ● ○

Lowestoft
Thomas Nash
★1567

Ditchingham
Sir Henry Rider Haggard
▲1889– ○

Kessingland
Sir Henry Rider Haggard
● c1900–

Thetford
Tom Paine
★▲1737–57 ○

2

MBRIDGE ○ Ely

Bluntisham
Dorothy L. Sayers
▲1898–1917

Swaffham Prior
Edwin Muir
▲1956–9 ■

SUFFOLK

Rendham
George Crabbe
▲1801–5

See Cambridge plan on Atlas 19
Cambridge
John Fletcher

ntchester
ert Brooke
09–12 ○

E. M. Forster
● 1970
C. S. Lewis
● 1963
Christopher Marlowe

Wimpole Hall
Matthew Prior
● 1721

Edwin Muir
● 1959

Bury St. Edmunds
Henry Crabb Robinson
★▲1775–

Great Glemham
George Crabbe
▲1796–1801

Parham
George Crabbe
▲1792

Bredfield
Edward FitzGerald
★▲1809–58 ■

Aldeburgh
George Crabbe
★▲1755–80 ○

Wickhambrook
George Crabbe
▲1768–70

Woodbridge
George Crabbe
▲1771
Edward FitzGerald
▲1860–83

Long Melford
Edmund Blunden
▲1965–74 ■

Ipswich
Edward FitzGerald
□

3

Westmill
Charles Lamb
○

ESSEX ○ Colchester

Little Easton
H. G. Wells
▲ c1914

Thorpe-le-Soken
Arnold Bennett
▲1913–20

Witham ●

○ Clacton-on-Sea

High Laver

Atlas 20 & 21
Waltham
Abbey
s

○ Chelmsford

Navestock

High Beech

0 miles   10   20
0 kilometres 10   20   30

Brentwood

4

KEY
★ Born
▲ Lived
● Died
■ Buried
□ House/Museum, etc.
○ Statue/Memorial, etc.
⌂ School

uter London
Atlas 22 & 23
nner London
Atlas 24 & 25

Southend-on-Sea

Stanford-le-Hope

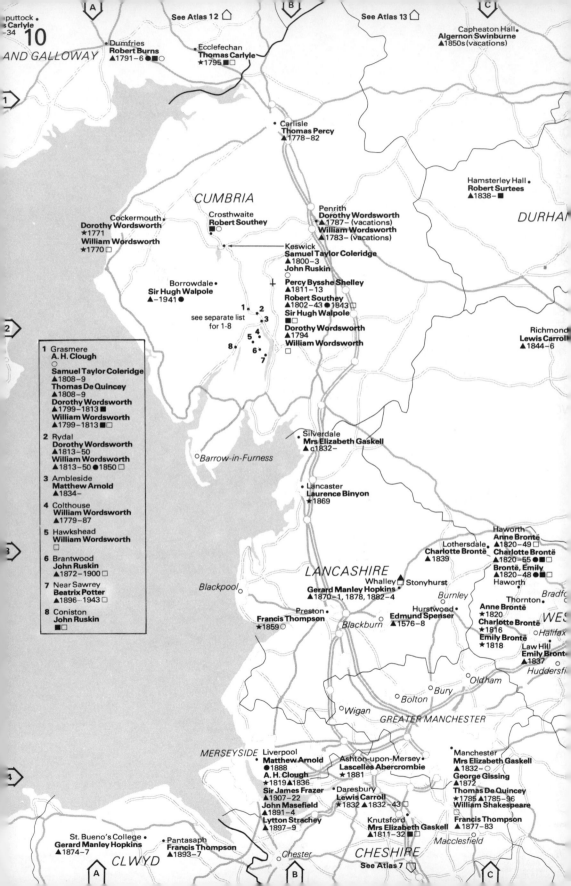

See Atlas 12 ⌂

See Atlas 13 ⌂

C

AND GALLOWAY

A

B

Capheaton Hall •
Algernon Swinburne
▲1850s (vacations)

• Dumfries
Robert Burns
▲1791–6 ●■□

Ecclefechan •
Thomas Carlyle
★1795 ■□

1

• Carlisle
Thomas Percy
▲1778–82

CUMBRIA

Hamsterley Hall •
Robert Surtees
▲1838– ■

DURHAM

Cockermouth •
Dorothy Wordsworth
★1771
William Wordsworth
★1770 □

Crosthwaite •
Robert Southey
■○

Penrith •
Dorothy Wordsworth
▲1787– (vacations)
William Wordsworth
▲1783– (vacations)

Keswick •
Samuel Taylor Coleridge
▲1800–3
John Ruskin
○
Percy Bysshe Shelley
▲1811–13
Robert Southey
▲1802–43 ●1843 □
Sir Hugh Walpole
■○
Dorothy Wordsworth
▲1794
William Wordsworth
□

Borrowdale •
Sir Hugh Walpole
▲–1941 ●

Richmond •
Lewis Carroll
▲1844–6

see separate list
for 1–8

1 • • 2
3 •
4 •
5 •
8 • 6 •
7 •

2

3

1	Grasmere
	A. H. Clough
	○
	Samuel Taylor Coleridge
	▲1808–9
	Thomas De Quincey
	▲1808–9
	Dorothy Wordsworth
	▲1799–1813 ■
	William Wordsworth
	▲1799–1813 ■□
2	Rydal
	Dorothy Wordsworth
	▲1813–50
	William Wordsworth
	▲1813–50 ●1850 □
3	Ambleside
	Matthew Arnold
	▲1834–
4	Colthouse
	William Wordsworth
	▲1779–87
5	Hawkshead
	William Wordsworth
	□
6	Brantwood
	John Ruskin
	▲1872–1900 □
7	Near Sawrey
	Beatrix Potter
	▲1896–1943 □
8	Coniston
	John Ruskin
	■□

Silverdale •
Mrs Elizabeth Gaskell
▲c1832–

○*Barrow-in-Furness*

• Lancaster
Laurence Binyon
★1869

Haworth •
Anne Brontë
▲1820–49 □
Lothersdale •
Charlotte Brontë
▲1839
Charlotte Brontë
▲1820–55 ●■□
Brontë, Emily
▲1820–48 ●■□
Haworth

LANCASHIRE

Whalley □ Stonyhurst
Gerard Manley Hopkins
▲1870–1, 1878, 1882–4

Blackpool ○

Burnley

Thornton •
Anne Brontë
★1820
Charlotte Brontë
★1816
Emily Brontë
★1818

Bradfo

WES

• Preston
Francis Thompson
★1859 ○

Blackburn

Hurstwood •
Edmund Spenser
▲1576–8

Law Hill
Emily Brontë
▲1837

Halifax

Huddersfi

○*Bury*

○*Oldham*

○*Bolton*

○*Wigan*

GREATER MANCHESTER

MERSEYSIDE Liverpool
Matthew Arnold
●1888
A. H. Clough
★1819 ▲1836
Sir James Frazer
▲1907–22
John Masefield
▲1891–4
Lytton Strachey
▲1897–9

Ashton-upon-Mersey •
Lascelles Abercrombie
★1881

• Manchester
Mrs Elizabeth Gaskell
▲1832– ○
George Gissing
▲1872
Thomas De Quincey
★1785 ▲1785–96
William Shakespeare

Francis Thompson
▲1877–83

Daresbury •
Lewis Carroll
★1832 ▲1832–43 □

St. Bueno's College •
Gerard Manley Hopkins
▲1874–7

• Pantasaph
Francis Thompson
▲1893–7

Knutsford •
Mrs Elizabeth Gaskell
▲1811–32 ■□

Macclesfield

CLWYD

Chester ○

CHESHIRE

See Atlas 7 ⌂

4

A B C

1

Newcastle-upon-Tyne

• Jarrow
The Venerable Bede
▲c673–735 ●

YNE AND WEAR

Durham
The Venerable Bede
■ (bones interred) 1020
● **Christopher Smart**
▲c1730
Robert Surtees
▲c1819 • Kelloe
Elizabeth Barrett Browning
★1806○
• Hartlepool
Sir Compton Mackenzie
★1883

○*Darlington*

Middlesborough
CLEVELAND

2

• Croft-on-Tees
Lewis Carroll
▲1843○

NORTH YORKSHIRE

Scarborough•
Anne Brontë
●■1849
Dame Edith Sitwell
★1887□
Sir Osbert Sitwell
□

• Coxwold
Laurence Sterne
▲1760–8■
(reinterred 1969)□

• Sutton-on-the-Forest
Laurence Sterne
▲1741–59
• Foston-le-Clay
Sydney Smith
▲1814–28○

•Thorpe Green Hall
Anne Brontë
▲1841–5
○*Harrogate*
York•
W. H. Auden
★1907
Percy Bysshe Shelley
▲1811

3

• Appleton Roebuck
Andrew Marvell
▲1650–2

HUMBERSIDE

○*Leeds*

Kingston-upon-Hull
• **Andrew Marvell**
▲1624–

YORKSHIRE

• Winestead
Andrew Marvell
★1621

Wakefield
George Gissing
★1857○

...field
...ne Brontë
1830
...arlotte Brontë
...31–2, 1835–7

Scunthorpe

○*Grimsby*

○*Barnsley*

Doncaster

SOUTH YORKSHIRE

• Epworth
Charles Wesley
★1707□
John Wesley
★1703□

Rotherham

...heffield

0 miles   10   20
0 kilometres 10   20   30

4

LINCOLN

• Renishaw
...me Edith Sitwell
Mount St. Mary's College
Gerard Manley Hopkins
▲1877–8

○*Chesterfield*

Somersby •
Alfred Lord Tennyson
★1809▲1809–37○

...RBY   *NOTTINGHAM*
See Atlas 8 ▱
Lincoln
Alfred Lord Tennyson

Ault Hucknall
Thomas Hobbes•
▲–1679■   A
Mansfield   B   C

KEY
★ Born
▲ Lived
● Died
■ Buried
□ House/Museum, etc.
○ Statue/Memorial, etc.
◬ School

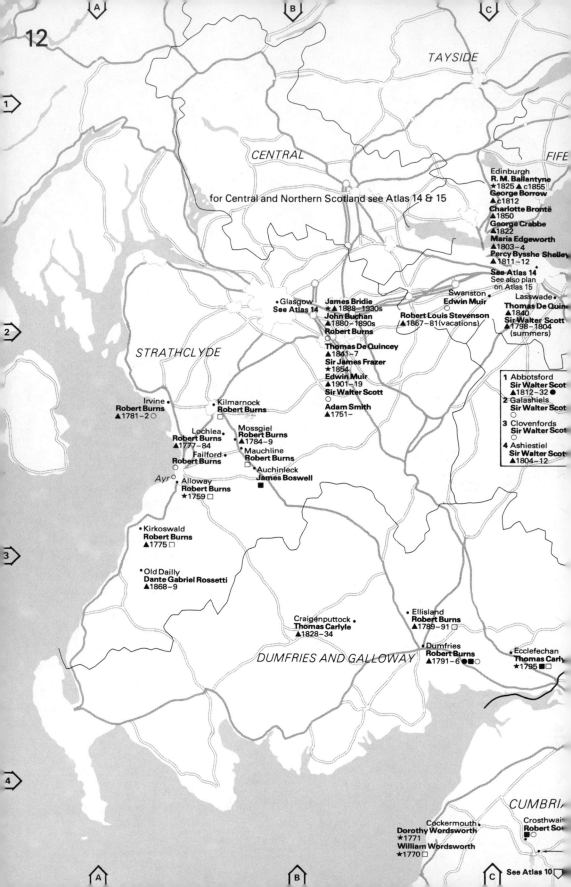

TAYSIDE

CENTRAL

for Central and Northern Scotland see Atlas 14 & 15

FIFE

Edinburgh
R. M. Ballantyne
★1825 ▲ c1855
George Borrow
▲ c1812
Charlotte Brontë
▲1850
George Crabbe
▲1822
Maria Edgeworth
▲1803–4
Percy Bysshe Shelley
▲1811–12

See Atlas 14
See also plan
on Atlas 15

Swanston
Edwin Muir ○

Lasswade
Thomas De Quin
▲1840
Sir Walter Scott
▲1798–1804
(summers)

• Glasgow
See Atlas 14

James Bridie
★▲1888–1930s
John Buchan
▲1880–1890s
Robert Burns

Robert Louis Stevenson
▲1867–81 (vacations)

STRATHCLYDE

Thomas De Quincey
▲1841–7
Sir James Frazer
★1854
Edwin Muir
▲1901–19
Sir Walter Scott
○
Adam Smith
▲1751–

```
1 Abbotsford
  Sir Walter Scot
  ▲1812–32 ●
2 Galashiels
  Sir Walter Scot
  ○
3 Clovenfords
  Sir Walter Scot
  ○
4 Ashiestiel
  Sir Walter Scot
  ▲1804–12
```

Irvine •
Robert Burns
▲1781–2 ○

• Kilmarnock
Robert Burns
□

Lochlea •
Robert Burns
▲1777–84

Mossgiel •
Robert Burns
▲1784–9
Mauchline •
Robert Burns
□

Failford •
Robert Burns
○

Ayr ○
• Alloway
Robert Burns
★1759 □

• Auchinleck
James Boswell ■

• Kirkoswald
Robert Burns
▲1775 □

• Old Dailly
Dante Gabriel Rossetti
▲1868–9

Craigenputtock •
Thomas Carlyle
▲1828–34

• Ellisland
Robert Burns
▲1789–91 □

• Dumfries
Robert Burns
▲1791–6 ● ■ ○

• Ecclefechan
Thomas Carly
★1795 ■ □

DUMFRIES AND GALLOWAY

CUMBRI

Cockermouth •
Dorothy Wordsworth
★1771
William Wordsworth
★1770 □

Crosthwai
Robert So
■ ○

See Atlas 10

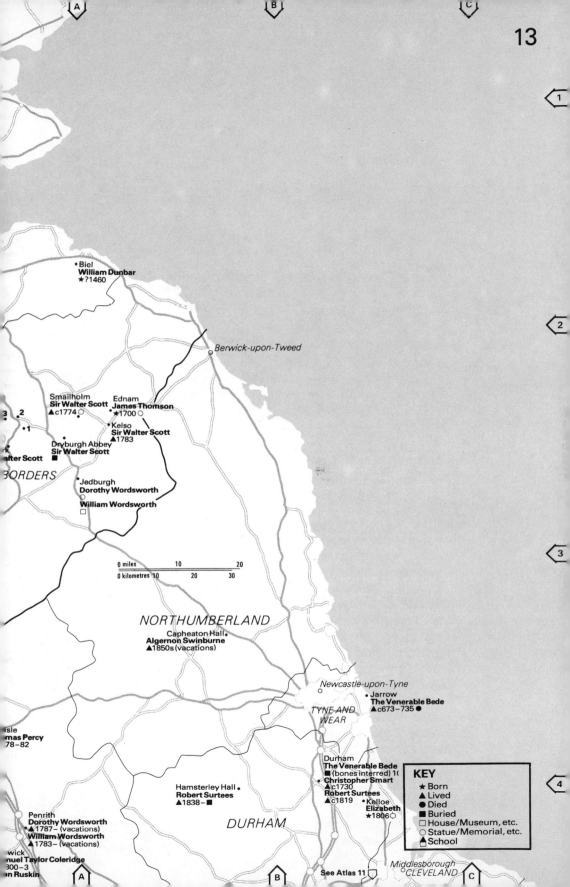

A

B

C

1

2

• Biel
William Dunbar
★?1460

Berwick-upon-Tweed

3 • 2

Smailholm
Sir Walter Scott
▲c1774 ○

• 1

Ednam
James Thomson
★1700 ○

alter Scott

• Kelso
Sir Walter Scott
▲1783

Dryburgh Abbey
Sir Walter Scott
■

BORDERS

• Jedburgh
Dorothy Wordsworth
○

William Wordsworth
□

0 miles   10   20

0 kilometres 10   20   30

NORTHUMBERLAND

Capheaton Hall •
Algernon Swinburne
▲1850s (vacations)

Newcastle-upon-Tyne
○

• Jarrow
The Venerable Bede
▲c673–735 ●

TYNE AND WEAR

isle
mas Percy
78–82

Durham
The Venerable Bede
■ (bones interred) 1(
• **Christopher Smart**
▲c1730
Robert Surtees
▲c1819

Hamsterley Hall •
Robert Surtees
▲1838– ■

• Kelloe
Elizabeth
★1806 ○

DURHAM

Penrith
Dorothy Wordsworth
▲1787– (vacations)
William Wordsworth
▲1783– (vacations)

wick
nuel Taylor Coleridge
300–3
n Ruskin

KEY
★ Born
▲ Lived
● Died
■ Buried
□ House/Museum, etc.
○ Statue/Memorial, etc.
▲ School

4

Middlesborough
○ *CLEVELAND*

See Atlas 11

A

B

C

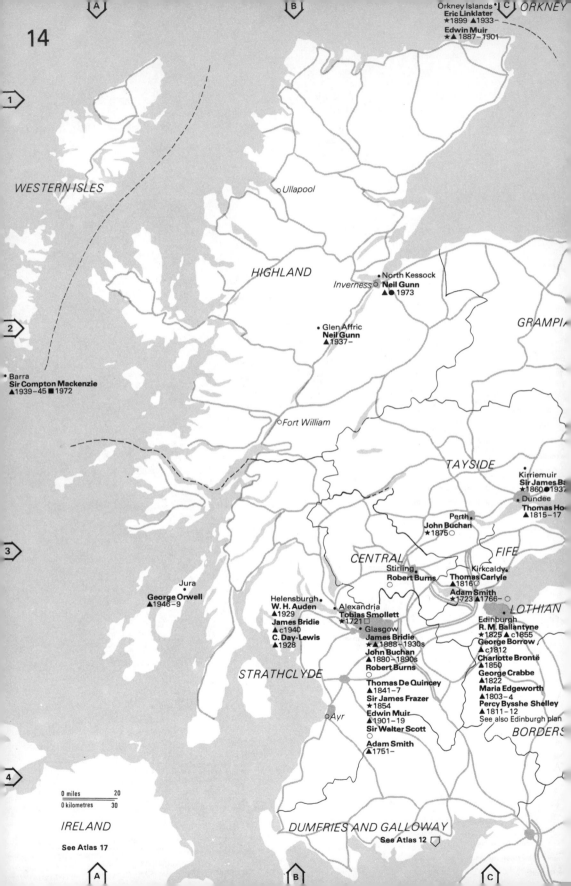

A

B

C

ORKNEY

Orkney Islands
Eric Linklater
★1899 ▲1933–
Edwin Muir
★▲ 1887–1901

1

WESTERN ISLES

○ Ullapool

HIGHLAND

Inverness ○ • North Kessock
Neil Gunn
▲●1973

GRAMPIA

2

• Glen Affric
Neil Gunn
▲1937–

• Barra
Sir Compton Mackenzie
▲1939–45 ■1972

○ Fort William

TAYSIDE

• Kirriemuir
Sir James Ba
★1860●1937

• Dundee
Thomas Ho
▲1815–17

• Perth
John Buchan
★1875○

3

CENTRAL

FIFE

Stirling •
Robert Burns

Kirkcaldy •
Thomas Carlyle
▲1816○

Adam Smith
★1723▲1766○

LOTHIAN

Jura
• **George Orwell**
▲1946–9

Helensburgh •
W. H. Auden
▲1929
James Bridie
▲c1940
C. Day-Lewis
▲1928

• Alexandria
Tobias Smollett
★1721□

○ Glasgow
James Bridie
★▲1888–1930s
John Buchan
▲1880–1890s
Robert Burns

Edinburgh
R. M. Ballantyne
★1825 ▲ c1855
George Borrow
▲c1812
Charlotte Brontë
▲1850
George Crabbe
▲1822
Maria Edgeworth
▲1803–4
Percy Bysshe Shelley
▲1811–12
See also Edinburgh plan

STRATHCLYDE

Thomas De Quincey
▲1841–7
Sir James Frazer
★1854
Edwin Muir
▲1901–19
Sir Walter Scott
○
Adam Smith
▲1751–

○ Ayr

BORDERS

4

0 miles   20
0 kilometres   30

IRELAND

See Atlas 17

DUMFRIES AND GALLOWAY

See Atlas 12 ⬡

A

B

C

Edinburgh Gazetteer

Barrie, Sir James
1 ▲1878–△: 3 Great King St.

Boswell, James
2 ★▲1740–9: Blair's Land, Parliament Sq.
3 ▲——: James Court (gone)
4 ▲——: 15A Meadow Pl. (S of city, off map)

Burns, Robert
5 ▲1786△: Baxter's Close (house gone)
6 ▲——: St. James's Sq.
7 ○Regent Rd.

Carlyle, Thomas
8 ▲1826–8△: 21 Comely Bank (W of city, off map)

De Quincey, Thomas
9 ▲——: Great King St.
10 ▲——: Forres St.
11 ▲——: 42 Lothian St. (gone)
12 ▲——: 29 Ann St.
13 ■St. Cuthbert's churchyard

Doyle, Sir Arthur Conan
14 ★1859: 11 Picardy Pl. (gone)

Gay, John
15 ▲1729: Queensberry House

Grahame, Kenneth
16 ★1859△: 30 Castle St.

Hume, David
17 ▲1751: Riddle's Close, 322 High St.
18 ▲——: Jack's Land (now 229), Canongate
19 ▲1762: James Court (gone)
20 ▲——: St. Andrew Sq./St. David St.
21 ■1776: Calton Old Burial Ground

Johnson, Samuel
22 ▲1773△: White Horse Inn, Boyd's Close (gone), (now St. Mary's St.)

Mackenzie, Sir Compton
23 ▲1962–72: 31 Drummond Pl.

Scott, Sir Walter
24 ★1771: College Wynd (now Guthrie St.)
25 ▲1774–97△: 25 George Sq.
26 ▲1797: 108 George St.
27 ▲——: 10 South Castle St.
28 ▲1798–1826△: 39 Castle St.
29 ○East Princes St. Gardens
30 △8 Chambers St.

Smollett, Tobias
31 ▲1776△: Canongate (now 22 St. John St.)

Stevenson, Robert Louis
32 ★1850△: 8 Howard Pl.
33 ▲1857–: 17 Heriot Row
34 ○St. Giles's Cathedral

KEY
★ Born
▲ Lived
● Died
■ Buried
□ House/Museum, etc.
○ Statue/Memorial, etc.
△ Plaque

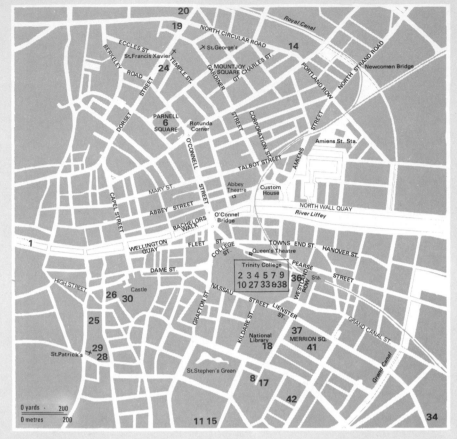

Dublin Gazetteer

Burke, Edmund
1 ★1729: 12 Arran Quay (gone)
2 ▲———: Trinity College
3 ○Trinity College

Congreve, William
4 ▲1686–9: Trinity College

Farquhar, George
5 ▲1694–: Trinity College

Gogarty, Oliver St John
6 ★1878△: 5 Parnell Sq.
7 ▲———: Trinity College
8 ▲———: 25 Ely Pl.

Goldsmith, Oliver
9 ▲1744—: Trinity College
10 ○Trinity College

Hopkins, Gerard Manley
11 ▲1884–9●: University College

Joyce, James
12 ★1882△: 41 Brighton Sq. (S. of city, off map)
13 ▲1884–7: 23 Castlewood Ave., Rathmines (S. of city, off map)
14 ▲———: 17 North Richmond St.
15 ▲–1902: University College, Dublin
16 ▲———: 8 Royal Ter. (now Inverness Ter.), Fairview (NE of city, off map)

Moore, George
17 ▲———: 4 Ely Pl.
18 ▲———: 4 Upper Merrion St.

O'Casey, Sean
19 ★1880△: 85 Upper Dorset St.
20 ▲c1881–2: 9 Innisfallen Parade
21 ▲1889: 25 Hawthorne Ter. (E of city, off map)
22 ▲1897–9: 18 Abercorn Rd. (E of city, off map)

Shaw, George Bernard
23 ★1856△: 3 (now 33) Synge St. (S of city, off map)

Sheridan, Richard Brinsley
24 ★1751△: 12 Upper Dorset St.

Steele, Sir Richard
25 ★1672: Bull Alley

Swift, Jonathan
26 ★1667: 7 Hoey's Court (gone)
27 ▲———: Trinity College
28 ▲1713–45●: St. Patrick's Deanery
29 ■1745: St. Patrick's Cathedral
30 △Ship Street

Synge, J. M.
31 ★1871: 2 Newton Villas, Rathfarnham (S of city, off map)
32 ▲———: 4 Orwell Park, Rathgar (S of city, off map)
33 ▲1888–92: Trinity College
34 ●1909: 130 Northumberland Rd.

Trollope, Anthony
35 ▲1854–9: 5 Seaview Ter., Donnybrook (SE of city, off map)

Wilde, Oscar
36 ★1854△: 21 Westland Row
37 ▲———△: 1 Merrion Sq.
38 ▲———: Trinity College

Yeats, W. B.
39 ★1865: Georgeville, 5 Sandymount Ave. (SE of city, off map)
40 ▲———: 10 Ashfield Terrace, Harold's Cross (S of city, off map)
41 ▲1922–△: 82 Merrion Sq.
42 △: 42 Fitzwilliam Sq.
43 △: Riversdale House, Rathfarnham (S of city, off map)

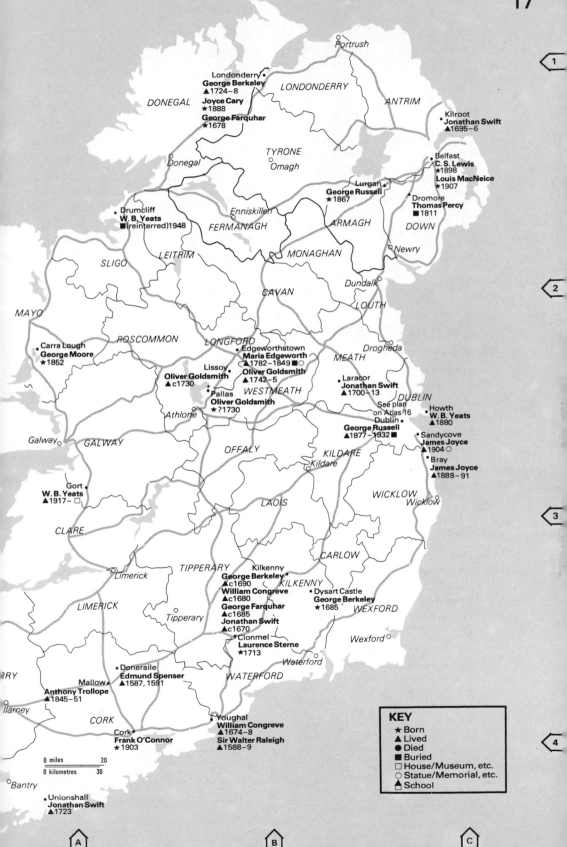

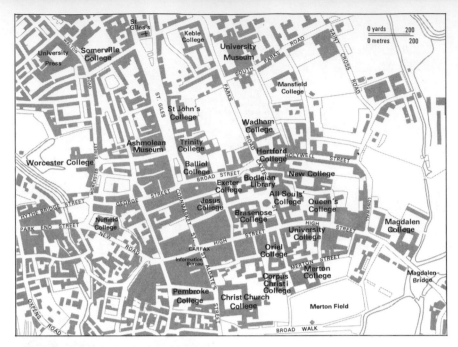

Oxford University

All Souls
T. E. Lawrence (F) 1919

Balliol
John Wycliffe (F) (M) 1361
John Evelyn 1637–40
Adam Smith c1744
Robert Southey 1792→
Matthew Arnold 1841→
A. H. Clough →1841
Algernon Swinburne 1856–9
J. A. Symonds 1860s
Gerard Manley Hopkins
   1863→
Hilaire Belloc 1890s
L. P. Hartley c1914
Aldous Huxley c1914

Brasenose
Robert Burton 1593–9
Thomas Traherne →1656
Walter Pater (F) 1864→
John Buchan 1897–9
J. Middleton Murry c1909–12

Christ Church
Sir Thomas More 1492–4
Philip Sidney 1568–71
Robert Burton 1599–1640
John Locke →1658, 1680–4
Thomas Otway →1672
Richard Steele 1690–1
Thomas Percy c1749
John Ruskin c1837–42
Lewis Carroll 1851–5, 1855→
W. H. Auden 1925–8, 1972–3

Corpus Christi
John Ruskin (Hon. F.) 1871
Robert Bridges c1864,
   1907–30

Exeter
R. D. Blackmore 1844–7
William Morris 1853–5
J. R. R. Tolkien (Hon. F.) c1914

Hertford
John Donne 1584→
Evelyn Waugh 1920s

Jesus
T. E. Lawrence 1906–10

Magdalen
Joseph Addison (F)
   1698–1711
Edward Gibbon 1752–3
Charles Reade 1831–5, (F)
   1838→
J. A. Symonds (F) 1862→
Oscar Wilde 1874–8
T. E. Lawrence 1910–14
Compton Mackenzie c1900
C. S. Lewis (F) 1924–54

(Magdalen Hall) Thomas
   Hobbes 1603–8

Merton
Richard Steele 1691–2
Max Beerbohm 1891–4
T. S. Eliot 1914–15, (Hon. F.)
   1949
Louis MacNeice 1926–30
Edmund Blunden (F) 1931–44
J. R. R. Tolkien (F) 1945–59

New College
James Woodforde 1759–63,
   (F)1773
Sydney Smith 1789→
   (F)1791→
John Galsworthy 1880s

Oriel
Walter Raleigh 1568–9
Gilbert White 1740–3, (F)
   1744–55
J. H. Newman (F) 1822
A. H. Clough (F) 1841–8
Matthew Arnold (F) 1845–7

Pembroke
Francis Beaumont 1597–8
Thomas Browne →1629
Samuel Johnson 1728→
J. R. R. Tolkien (F) 1926–45

Queen's
Thomas Middleton 1598
William Wycherley 1659
Joseph Addison c1688
Walter Pater →1862
Edmund Blunden 1919–23
Thomas Hardy (Hon. F.) 1922

St. John's
Abraham Cowley 1644–6
A. E. Housman 1877–81

Somerville
Dorothy L. Sayers 1912→

Trinity
John Aubrey c1643
W. S. Landor 1793
J. H. Newman 1816–20
Richard Burton 1840–2
Sir Arthur Quiller-Couch
   1882–6
Laurence Binyon 1887–90
James Elroy Flecker 1902→
Joyce Cary 1909–12

University
Percy Bysshe Shelley 1810
C. S. Lewis 1917, 1919→

Wadham
C. Day-Lewis 1923→

Worcester
Richard Lovelace 1634–9
Thomas De Quincey 1803–8

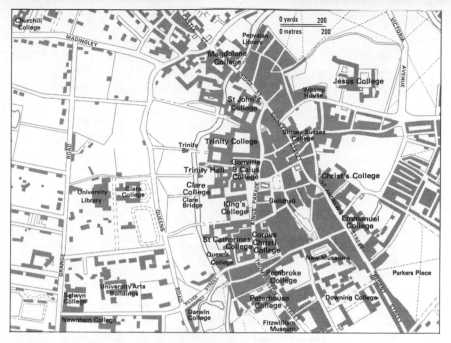

Cambridge University

Christ's
John Milton 1625–32

Clare
Siegfried Sassoon 1904–8

Corpus Christi
Christopher Marlowe c1578
John Fletcher 1593
J. C. Powys c1900

Emmanuel
Hugh Walpole 1902–5

Gonville & Caius
James Elroy Flecker 1908–10

Jesus
Laurence Sterne 1733→
Samuel Taylor Coleridge
    1791–4
Sir Arthur Quiller-Couch (F)
    1912

King's
Horace Walpole 1735–9
Rupert Brooke 1906→, (F)
    1913
E. M. Forster 1897–1901, (F)
    1927, In residence 1946–70

Magdalene
Samuel Pepys 1651–3
Charles Kingsley 1838–42,
    (Prof. of Mod. History)
    1860–9
C. S. Lewis (F) 1954

Pembroke
Edmund Spenser c1566
Lancelot Andrewes (M)
    1589–1605
Richard Crashaw 1632–4
Christopher Smart c1742, (F)
    1745–9
Thomas Gray 1756–71

Peterhouse
John Skelton c1484
Richard Crashaw (F) 1637–43
Thomas Gray 1734–8,
    1743–56

St. Catherine's
Malcolm Lowry 1929–32

St. John's
Thomas Wyatt c1518
Thomas Nash (?) 1581–7
Robert Herrick 1613–16
Matthew Prior 1682–6, (F)
    1688
William Wordsworth
    1787–90
Samuel Butler 1854→

Trinity
Francis Bacon 1573–5
George Herbert 1609→, (F)
    1616
Andrew Marvell 1633–8
Abraham Cowley 1637–44
John Dryden c1654
Lord Byron 1805→
T. B. Macaulay 1818→, (F)
    1824
W. M. Thackeray 1829–30
Edward FitzGerald 1827–30
Alfred Tennyson c1829
James Frazer 1875–1907, (F)
    1879, 1922–41
Lytton Strachey 1899–1903
A. E. Housman (F) 1911

Trinity Hall
Edward Bulwer-Lytton c1825
Ronald Firbank 1907–9

KEY
(F) Fellow
(M) Master

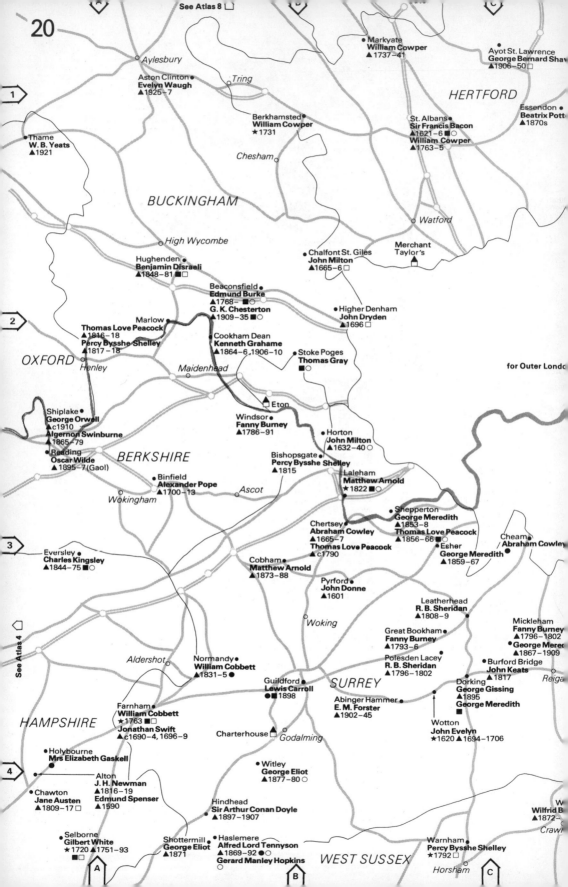

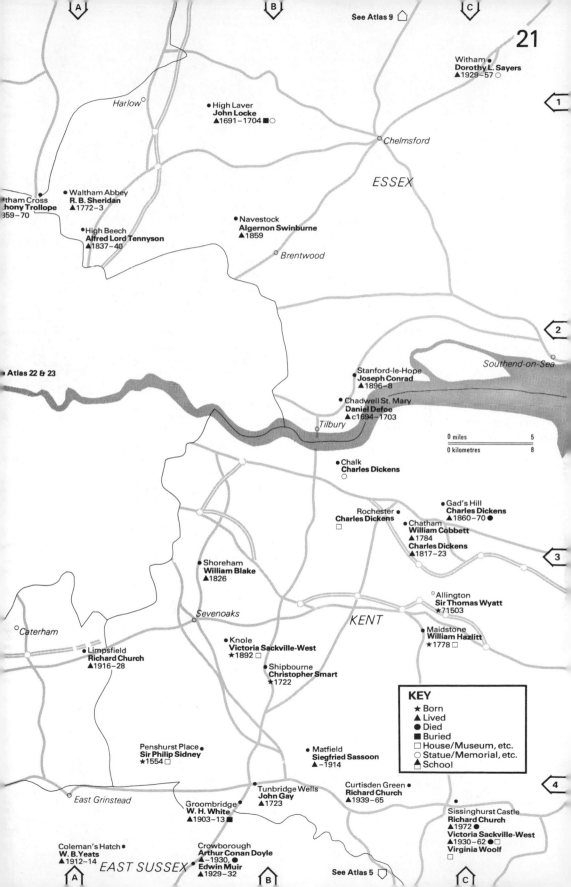

See Atlas 9

A **B** **C**

Witham
Dorothy L. Sayers
▲1929–57 ○

Harlow

● High Laver
John Locke
▲1691–1704 ■○

○ *Chelmsford*

ESSEX

1

●tham Cross
●hony Trollope
359–70

● Waltham Abbey
R. B. Sheridan
▲1772–3

● Navestock
Algernon Swinburne
▲1859

●High Beech
Alfred Lord Tennyson
▲1837–40

Brentwood

Atlas 22 & 23

2

Southend-on-Sea

Stanford-le-Hope
Joseph Conrad
▲1896–8

● Chadwell St. Mary
Daniel Defoe
▲c1694–1703

Tilbury

0 miles 5
0 kilometres 8

● Chalk
Charles Dickens
○

● Gad's Hill
Charles Dickens
▲1860–70 ●

Rochester ●
Charles Dickens
□

Chatham
William Cobbett
▲1784
Charles Dickens
▲1817–23

3

● Shoreham
William Blake
▲1826

○ Allington
Sir Thomas Wyatt
★?1503

Sevenoaks

KENT

● Maidstone
William Hazlitt
★1778 □

○ *Caterham*

● Limpsfield
Richard Church
▲1916–28

● Knole
Victoria Sackville-West
★1892 □

● Shipbourne
Christopher Smart
★1722

KEY
★ Born
▲ Lived
● Died
■ Buried
□ House/Museum, etc.
○ Statue/Memorial, etc.
▲ School

Penshurst Place ●
Sir Philip Sidney
★1554 □

● Matfield
Siegfried Sassoon
▲–1914

○ *East Grinstead*

Curtisden Green ●
Richard Church
▲1939–65

4

● Tunbridge Wells
John Gay
▲1723

Groombridge ●
W. H. White
▲1903–13 ■

● Sissinghurst Castle
Richard Church
▲1972 ●
Victoria Sackville-West
▲1930–62 ●□
Virginia Woolf
□

Coleman's Hatch ●
W. B. Yeats
▲1912–14

Crowborough ●
Arthur Conan Doyle
▲–1930, ●
Edwin Muir
▲1929–32

EAST SUSSEX

See Atlas 5

A **B** **C**

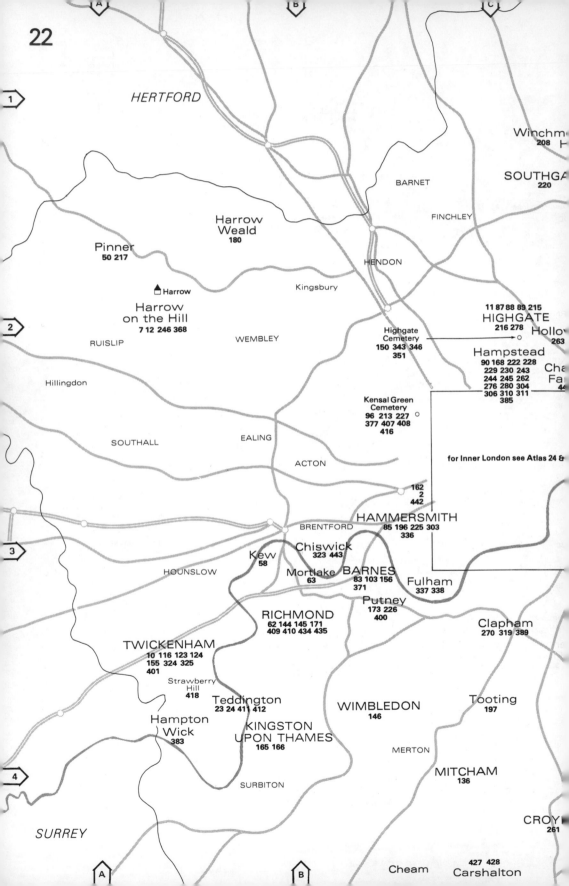

A
B
C

1

HERTFORD

Winchm
208

BARNET

SOUTHGA
220

FINCHLEY

Harrow
Weald
180

Pinner
50 217

HENDON

Kingsbury

⌂ Harrow

11 87 88 89 215

Harrow
on the Hill
7 12 246 368

2

HIGHGATE
216 278

Hollo
263

RUISLIP

WEMBLEY

Highgate
Cemetery
150 343 346
351

Hampstead
90 168 222 228
229 230 243
244 245 262
276 280 304
306 310 311
385

Cha
Fa
44

Hillingdon

Kensal Green
Cemetery
96 213 227
377 407 408
416

SOUTHALL

EALING

ACTON

for Inner London see Atlas 24 &

3

162
2
442

HAMMERSMITH
85 196 225 303
336

Chiswick
323 443

BRENTFORD

Kew
58

Mortlake
63

BARNES
83 103 156
371

Fulham
337 338

HOUNSLOW

Putney
173 226
400

Clapham
270 319 389

RICHMOND
62 144 145 171
409 410 434 435

TWICKENHAM
10 116 123 124
155 324 325
401

Strawberry
Hill
418

Teddington
23 24 411 412

WIMBLEDON
146

Tooting
197

Hampton
Wick
383

KINGSTON
UPON THAMES
165 166

MERTON

MITCHAM
136

4

SURBITON

CROY
261

SURREY

A
B

Cheam

427 428
Carshalton

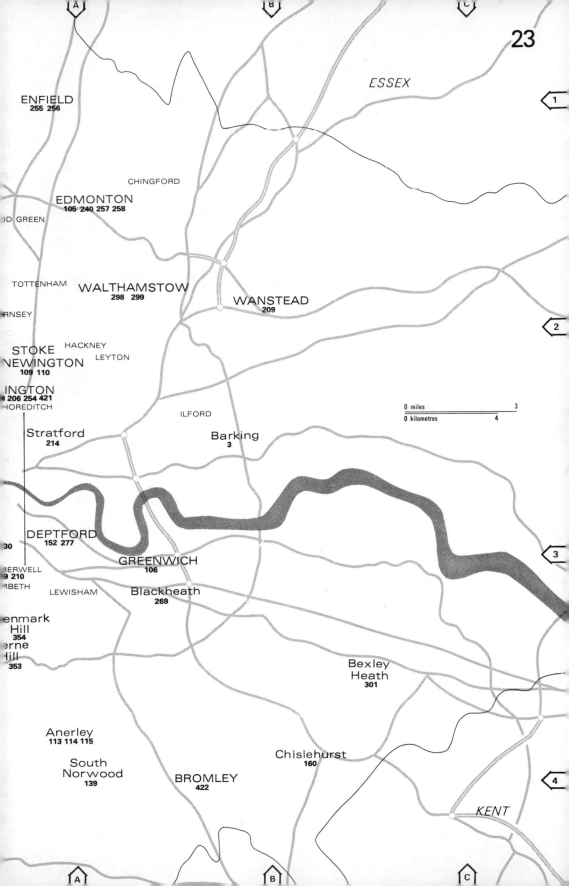

A

B

C

ESSEX

ENFIELD
255 256

1

CHINGFORD

EDMONTON
105 240 257 258

OD GREEN

TOTTENHAM

WALTHAMSTOW
298 299

WANSTEAD
209

2

RNSEY

STOKE
NEWINGTON
109 110

HACKNEY

LEYTON

INGTON
206 254 421

HOREDITCH

ILFORD

0 miles   3

0 kilometres   4

Stratford
214

Barking
3

DEPTFORD
152 277

30

GREENWICH
106

3

BERWELL
210

LEWISHAM

Blackheath
269

MBETH

enmark
Hill
354

erne
Hill
353

Bexley
Heath
301

Anerley
113 114 115

South
Norwood
139

Chislehurst
160

BROMLEY
422

4

KENT

A

B

C

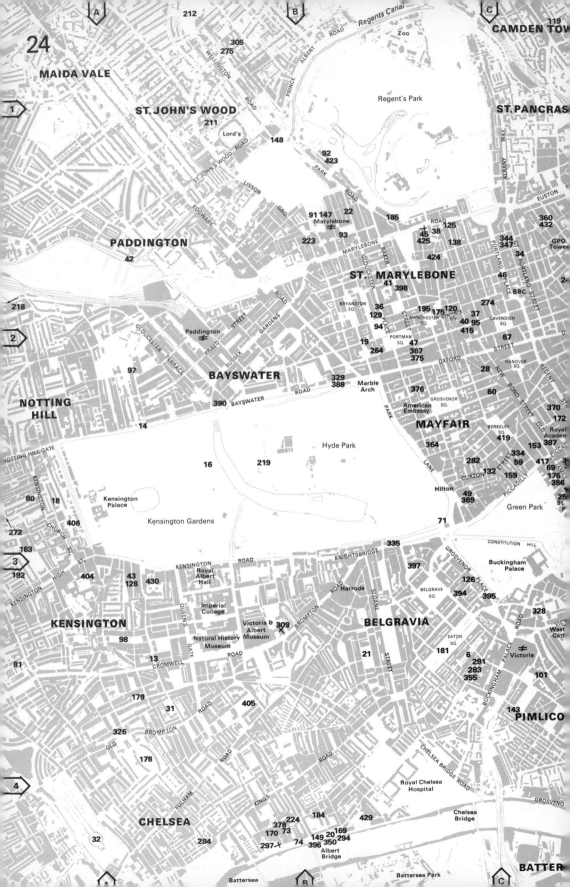

General Gazetteer

Abercrombie, Lascelles
(1881–1938)
★ Ashton-upon-Mersey
10.*C4*
▲ 1911–14 Dymock 7.*B3*

Addison, Joseph (1672–1719)
★ Milston 4.*B3*
▲ 1683–98 Lichfield 8.*A2*
▲ 1710, 1716–19 ● London
▲ 1713— Bilton 8.*B3*
See also London, Schools,
Oxford

Andrewes, Lancelot
(1555–1626)
★●■ London
See also London,
Cambridge

Arnold, Matthew (1822–1888)
★■○ Laleham 20.*B3*
▲ 1834–Ambleside 10.*B2*
▲ 1858–73 London
▲ 1873–88 Cobham 20.*B3*
● Liverpool 10.*B4*
See also London, Schools,
Oxford

Aubrey, John (1626–1697)
★▲ 1626–71 Kington St.
Michael (Easton Piercy)
3.*C1*
▲ c1650 Broad Chalke 3.*C2*
●■○ Oxford 4.*B2*
See also London, Oxford

Auden, W. H. (1907–1973)
★ York 11.*A3*
▲ 1929 Helensburgh 14.*B3*
See also London, Oxford

Austen, Jane (1775–1817)
★▲ 1775–1801 ○ Steventon
4.*B3*
▲ 1801–6 Bath 3.*C2*
▲ 1806–9 Southampton
4.*B4*
▲ 1809–17 □ Chawton
20.*A4*
▲ 1813 London
▲ 1817 ●■○ Winchester
4.*B3*
□ Lyme Regis 3.*B3*
See also London

Bacon, Sir Francis
(1561–1626)
★ 1561 ▲ 1595–1605
● 1626 London
▲ 1621–6 ■○ St. Albans
20.*C1*
See also London,
Cambridge

Ballantyne, R. M. (1825–1894)
★ 1825 ▲ c1855 Edinburgh
12.*C2*
See also London

Barrett, Elizabeth,
See Browning, Elizabeth
Barrett

Barrie, Sir James (1860–1937)
★●□ Kirriemuir 14.*C3*
▲ 1878–82 ○ Edinburgh
12.*C2*
▲ 1895–1937 London
See also London,
Edinburgh

Beaumont, Francis
(1584–1616)
★ Grace Dieu 8.*B2*
○ Coleorton Hall 8.*B2*
See also London, Oxford

Beckford, William
(1759–1844)
★ London
▲ 1807–22 Fonthill Abbey
3.*C2*
▲ 1822–44 ■ Bath 3.*C2*
See also London

Bede, The Venerable
(673–735)
▲ c673–735 ● Jarrow 11.*A1*
■ (bones interred) 1020
Durham 11.*A1*

Beerbohm, Sir Max
(1872–1956)
★ 1872 ▲ 1893–1910 London
See also London, Schools,
Oxford

Behn, Aphra (1640–1689)
See London

Belloc, Hilaire (1870–1953)
▲ c1900–9 London
▲ 1906–53 ■ Shipley 5.*A3*
■ West Grinstead 5.*A3*
See also London, Oxford

Bennett, Arnold (1867–1931)
★▲ 1867–89 ■ Stoke-on-
Trent 7.*A1*
▲ 1913–20 Thorpe-le-Soken
9.*C4*
▲ 1923–31 ● London
See also London

Berkeley, George (1685–1753)
★ Dysart Castle 17.*B3*
▲ c1690 Kilkenny 17.*B3*
▲ 1724–8 Londonderry 17.*B1*

Binyon, Laurence
(1869–1943)
★ Lancaster 10.*B3*
See also Schools, Oxford

Blackmore, R. D. (1825–1900)
★ Longworth 4.*B2*
▲ c1830 Elsfield 4.*C2*
▲ c1830 Newton Nottage
6.*C4*

▲ 1831 Culmstock 3.*A2*
▲ 1860–1900 ■ London
○ Charles 2.*C2*, Exeter 3.*A3*,
Oare 3.*A2*
See also London, Oxford

Blake, William (1757–1827)
★ 1757 ▲ 1771–8, 1785–91,
1804–27 ●■ London
▲ 1800–4 Felpham 4.*C4*
▲ 1826 Shoreham 21.*B3*
See also London

Blunden, Edmund
(1896–1974)
▲ 1965–74 ■ Long Melford
9.*B3*
See also Schools, Oxford

Blunt, Wilfrid (1840–1922)
▲ 1872–Worth 20.*C4*
▲ 1895–1922 ■○ Shipley
5.*A3*
See also Schools

Borrow, George (1803–1881)
★ Dumpling Green 9.*B2*
▲ c1812 Edinburgh 12.*C2*
▲ 1840–66, 1874–81
●○ Oulton 9.*C2*
▲ 1853–5, 1856–9 Great
Yarmouth 9.*C3*
▲ 1860–74 ■ 1881 London
○ Glyn Ceiriog 7.*A2*
See also London

Boswell, James (1740–1795)
★▲ 1740–Edinburgh 12.*C2*
▲ 1763, 1790–5 ● London
■ Auchinleck 12.*B3*
○ Lichfield 8.*A2*
See also London,
Edinburgh

Bradstreet, Anne
(c1613–1672)
★ Northampton 8.*C3*
○ Boston, Lincs. 8.*C1*

Bridges, Robert (1844–1930)
★ Walmer 5.*C3*
▲ 1869–81 London
▲ 1882–1904
■○ Yattendon 4.*B2*
See also London, Schools,
Oxford

Bridie, James (1888–1951)
★▲ 1888–1930s Glasgow
12.*B2*
▲ c1940 Helensburgh 14.*B3*

Brontë, Anne (1820–1849)
★ Thornton 10.*C3*
▲ 1820–49 □ Haworth 10.*C3*
▲ c1830 Mirfield 10.*C3*
▲ 1841–5 Thorpe Green Hall
11.*A3*

●■ Scarborough *11.B2*
See also London

Brontë, Charlotte (1816–1855)
★ Thornton *10.C3*
▲ 1820–55 ●■□ Haworth
10.C3
▲ 1831–2, 1835–7 Mirfield
10.C3
▲ 1839 Lothersdale *10.C3*
▲ 1850 Edinburgh *12.C2*
See also London

Brontë, Emily (1818–1848)
★ Thornton *10.C3*
▲ 1820–48 ●■□ Haworth
10.C3
▲ 1837 Law Hill *10.C3*
See also London

Brooke, Rupert (1887–1915)
★ Rugby *8.B3*
▲ 1909–12 ○ Grantchester
9.A3
▲ 1913 Dymock *7.B3*
See also Schools,
Cambridge

Browne, Sir Thomas
(1605–1682)
▲ 1637–82 ●■○ Norwich
9.C2
See also Schools, Oxford

Browning, Elizabeth Barrett
(1806–1861)
★○ Kelloe *11.A1*
▲ 1809–32 Hope End *7.B3*
▲ 1832–5 Sidmouth *3.A3*
▲ 1835–46, 1852, 1855
London
▲ 1838–41 ○ Torquay *3.A3*
See also London

Browning, Robert
(1812–1889)
★ 1812 ▲ 1852, 1855,
1861–89 ■ London
▲ 1886 Llangollen *7.A1*
○ Llantysilio *7.A1*
See also London

Buchan, John (1875–1940)
★○ Perth *14.C3*
▲ 1880–1890s Glasgow
12.B2
▲ 1913–19 London
▲ 1919–35 ■ Elsfield *4.C2*
See also London, Oxford

Bulwer-Lytton, Edward
(1803–1873)
★ 1803 ▲ 1831–2 ■ 1873
London
▲ Knebworth *5.A2*
▲ 1873 ● Torquay *3.A3*
See also London,
Cambridge

Bunyan, John (1628–1688)
★▲ c1650 ○ Elstow *8.C3*
▲ 1660–72 Bedford (Prison)
8.C3
▲ 1672–88 □ Bedford

●■ London
See also London

Burke, Edmund (1729–1797)
★ Dublin *17.B3*
▲ 1768– ■○ Beaconsfield
20.B2
▲ 1787–94 London
See also London, Dublin

Burney, Fanny (1752–1840)
★ King's Lynn *9.A2*
▲ 1770–86, 1818–28
● 1840 London
▲ 1786–91 Windsor *20.B2*
▲ 1793–6 Great Bookham
20.C3
▲ 1796–1802 Mickleham
20.C3
▲ 1815–18 ■ Bath *3.C2*
See also London

Burns, Robert (1759–1796)
★□ Alloway *12.A3*
▲ 1775 □ Kirkoswald *12.A3*
▲ 1777–84 Lochlea *12.B3*
▲ 1781–2 ○ Irvine *12.A2*
▲ 1784–9 Mossgiel *12.B2*
▲ 1786–9 ○ Edinburgh
12.C2
▲ 1789–91 □ Ellisland *12.B3*
▲ 1791–6 ●■○ Dumfries
12.C3
○ Failford *12.B3*
○ Glasgow *12.B2*
□ Kilmarnock *12.A2*
□ Mauchline *12.B2*
○ Stirling *14.C3*
See also London,
Edinburgh

Burton, Sir Richard
(1821–1890)
★ Torquay *3.A3*
▲■ 1890 London
See also London, Oxford

Burton, Robert (1577–1640)
★ Lindley *8.B2*
■○ Oxford *4.B2*
See also Oxford

Butler, Samuel (1612–1680)
★ Strensham *7.B3*
▲ c1660 Wrest Park *4.C1*
▲ 1661–2 Ludlow *7.A3*
▲■ 1680 London
See also London

Butler, Samuel (1835–1902)
★ Langer *8.C2*
▲ 1864–1902 London
See also London, Schools,
Cambridge

Byron, Lord (1788–1824)
★ 1788 ▲ 1812–14 London
▲ 1798 ○ Nottingham *8.B2*
▲ 1803–8 Southwell *8.C1*
▲ 1808–16 □ Newstead
Abbey *8.B1*
■○ Hucknall *8.B2*
See also London, Schools,
Cambridge

Carlyle, Thomas (1795–1881)
★ 1795 ■□ Ecclefechan
12.C4
▲ 1809–13, 1817, 1826–8
Edinburgh *12.C2*
▲ 1816 ○ Kirkcaldy *14.C3*
▲ 1828–34 Craigenputtock
12.B3
▲ 1831–2, 1834–81 ●
London
See also London,
Edinburgh

Carroll, Lewis (1832–1898)
★▲ 1832–43 □ Daresbury
10.B4
▲ 1843 ○ Croft-on-Tees
11.A2
▲ 1844–6 Richmond (Yorks)
10.C2
▲ 1877–87 Eastbourne
(vacations) C *5.B4*
●■ Guildford *20.B4*
See also Schools, Oxford

Cary, Joyce (1888–1957)
★ Londonderry *17.B3*
▲ 1920–57 ●■ Oxford *4.B2*
See also Schools, Oxford

Chapman, George
(?1559–1634)
■ London
See also London

Chatterton, Thomas
(1752–1770)
★▲ 1752–68 ○ Bristol *3.B1*
▲ 1770 ●■ London
See also London

Chaucer, Geoffrey
(?1345–1400)
★ (?)1345 ▲ 1374–86
■ 1400 London
▲ 1360–1 Canterbury *5.C3*
See also London

Chesterton, G. K. (1874–1936)
★ 1874 ▲ 1879–99 London
▲ 1909–35 ■○ Beaconsfield
20.B2
See also London, Schools

Church, Richard
(1893–1972)
▲ 1916–28 Limpsfield *21.A3*
▲ 1939–65 Curtisden Green
21.C4
▲ 1972 ● Sissinghurst Castle
21.C4

┌─────────────────────────┐
│ **KEY**
│ ★ Born
│ ▲ Lived
│ ● Died
│ ■ Buried
│ □ House/Museum, etc.
│ ○ Statue/Memorial, etc.
│ △ Plaque
└─────────────────────────┘

263

Clare, John (1793–1864)
★ 1793 ▲ 1820– ■○ Helpston
8.C2
▲ 1809 Burghley House 8.C2
▲ 1817 Pickworth 8.C2
▲ 1817–18 Great Casterton
8.C2
▲ 1832–7 Northborough
8.C2
▲ 1841–64 ● Northampton
8.C3

Clough, A. H. (1819–1861)
★ 1819 ▲ 1836 Liverpool
10.B4
○ Grasmere 10.B2
See also Schools, Oxford

Cobbett, William (1763–1835)
★■□ Farnham 20.A3
▲ 1784 Chatham 21.C3
▲ c1800–3, 1828–30 London
▲ 1804–17 Botley 4.B4
▲ 1831–5 ● Normandy
(Surrey) 20.A4
See also London

Coleridge, Samuel Taylor
(1772–1834)
★▲ 1772–81 Ottery St. Mary
3.A3
▲ 1795–6 Clevedon 3.B1
▲ 1796 Bristol 3.B1
▲ 1796–8 □ Nether Stowey
3.A2
▲ 1797 Porlock 3.A2
▲ 1799, 1811–13, 1818–34
●■ London
▲ 1800–3 Keswick 10.B2
▲ 1808–9 Grasmere 10.B2
▲ 1814–16 Calne 3.C1
See also London, Schools,
Cambridge

Collins, Wilkie (1824–1889)
★ 1824 ▲ 1840–59, 1864–8
●■ 1889 London
See also London

Compton-Burnett, Ivy
(1884–1969)
▲ 1892–1916 Brighton 5.A4
▲ 1916–29, 1934–69 London
See also London

Congreve, William
(1670–1729)
▲ 1674–8 Youghal 17.A4
▲ c1680 Kilkenny 17.B3
▲ 1686–9 Dublin 17.B3
▲ 1689 Stretton Hall 7.B2
▲■ London
○ Stowe 4.C1
See also London, Dublin

Conrad, Joseph (1857–1924)
▲ 1889–90, 1893–6 London
▲ 1896–8 Stanford-le-Hope
21.B2
▲ 1898–1907 Postling 5.C3
▲ 1909–10 Aldington 5.C3
▲ 1910–19 Orlestone 5.B3
▲ 1920–4 Bishopsbourne
5.C3

■○ Canterbury 5.C3
See also London

Cowley, Abraham
(1618–1667)
★ 1618 ▲ 1663–5 ■ 1667
London
▲ 1665–7 Chertsey 20.B3
● Cheam 20.C4
See also London, Schools,
Cambridge, Oxford

Cowper, William (1731–1800)
★ Berkhamsted 20.B1
▲ 1737–41 Markyate 20.B1
▲ 1750s London
▲ 1763–5 St. Albans 20.C1
▲ 1765–7 ○ Huntingdon
9.A3
▲ 1767–86 ○ Olney 8.C3
▲ 1786–95 Weston
Underwood 4.C1
▲ 1795 Little Dunham 9.B2
▲ 1795–1800 ■○ East
Dereham 9.B2
▲ 1795–1800 Mundesley
9.C2
See also London, Schools

Crabbe, George (1755–1832)
★▲ 1755–80 ○ Aldeburgh
9.C3
▲ 1768–70 Wickhambrook
9.B3
▲ 1771 Woodbridge 9.C3
▲ 1782–8 Belvoir Castle
8.C2
▲ 1785–9 Stathern 8.C2
▲ 1789–92, 1805–14 Muston
8.C2
▲ 1792 Parham 9.C3
▲ 1796–1801 Great
Glemham 9.C3
▲ 1801–5 Rendham 8.C2
▲ 1814–32 ■○ Trowbridge
3.C2
▲ 1822 Edinburgh 12.C2
● Merton 9.B2

Crashaw, Richard
(?1612–1649)
See Schools, Cambridge

Day-Lewis, Cecil (1904–1972)
▲ 1928 Helensburgh 14.B3
▲ 1932–8 Cheltenham 7.B4
▲ 1938– Musbury 3.B3
▲ 1954–72 London
■ Stinsford 4.A4
See also London, Schools,
Oxford

Defoe, Daniel (?1660–1731)
★ (?)1660 ▲ 1703–31 ●■
London
▲ c1694–1703 Chadwell St
Mary 21.B2
See also London

de la Mare, Walter
(1873–1956)
▲ 1899–1925, 1950–6
● London
See also London

De Quincey, Thomas
(1785–1859)
★▲ 1785–96 Manchester
10.C4
▲ 1796–9 Bath 3.C2
▲ 1802, 1824 London
▲ 1808–9 Grasmere 10.B2
▲ 1822–59 ●■ Edinburgh
12.C2
▲ 1840 Lasswade 12.C2
▲ 1841–7 Glasgow 12.B2
See also London, Oxford,
Edinburgh

Dickens, Charles (1812–1870)
★□ Portsmouth 4.C4
▲ 1817–23 Chatham 21.C3
▲ 1823–4, 1833–4, 1836–60,
1862, 1865 London
▲ 1836–50 Broadstairs
(vacations) 5.C3
▲ 1849 Bonchurch 4.C4
▲ 1855 Folkestone 5.C3
▲ 1860–70 ● Gad's Hill 21.C3
○ Canterbury 5.C3, ○ Chalk
21.C3,
□ Rochester 21.C3, ○ Ross-
on-Wye 7.A4
See also London

Disraeli, Benjamin
(1804–1881)
★● London
▲ 1848–81 ■□ Hughenden
20.A1
See also London

Donne, John (1571/2–1631)
★ 1572 ▲ 1596–1601,
1606–10, 1624–31 ●
London
▲ 1601 Pyrford 20.B3
See also London, Oxford

Doyle, Sir Arthur Conan
(1859–1930)
★▲ 1859–82 Edinburgh
12.C2
▲ 1882–9 Portsmouth 4.C4
▲ 1890–4 London
▲ 1897–1907 Hindhead
20.A4
▲ –1930 ● Crowborough
21.B4
■ Minstead 4.B4
See also London, Schools,
Edinburgh

Dryden, John (1631–1700)
★○ Aldwinkle 8.C3
▲ 1631 Titchmarsh 4.C2
▲ 1665–6 Charlton 3.C1
▲ 1673–82, 1686–1700
● London
▲ 1696 □ Higher Denham
20.B2
▲ 1696 Burghley House 8.C2
▲ 1698–9 Cotterstock 8.C3
See also London, Schools,
Cambridge

Dunbar, William
(?1460–?1530)
★ Biel 13.A2

264

Edgeworth, Maria
(1768–1849)
★ Black Bourton *4.B2*
▲ 1775–81 Derby *8.B2*
▲ 1782–1849
◼○ Edgeworthstown
17.B2
▲ 1803–4 Edinburgh *12.C2*

Eliot, George (1819–1880)
★ 1819 ▲ 1820–41
☐ Nuneaton *8.B3*
▲ 1841–9 Coventry *8.B3*
▲ 1853–80 ●◼ London
▲ 1871 Shottermill *20.A4*
▲ 1877–80 ○ Witley *20.B4*
See also London

Eliot, T. S. (1888–1965)
◼ East Coker *3.B2*
○ Little Gidding *8.C3*
See also London, Oxford

Evelyn, John (1620–1706)
★ 1620 ▲ 1694–1706 Wotton
20.C4
▲ c1630 Lewes *5.A4*
▲ 1640, 1653–94 ● 1706
London
See also London, Oxford

Farquhar, George (1678–1707)
★ Londonderry *17.B1*
▲ c1685 Kilkenny *17.B3*
▲ 1694– Dublin *17.B3*
▲ 1705 Shrewsbury *7.A2*
◼ 1707 London
See also London, Dublin

Fielding, Henry (1707–1754)
★ Sharpham *3.B2*
▲ 1734 East Stour *3.C2*
▲ 1743–4, 1748–53 London
▲ 1748 Widcombe *3.C2*
See also London, Schools

Firbank, Ronald (1886–1926)
★▲ 1886 London
▲ 1914–18 Oxford *4.B2*
○ Newport *7.A4*
See also London, Schools,
Cambridge

FitzGerald, Edward
(1809–1883)
★▲ 1809–58 ◼ Bredfield *9.C3*
▲ 1860–83 Woodbridge *9.C3*
● Merton 1883 *9.B2*
☐ Ipswich *9.B3*
See also Cambridge

Flecker, James Elroy
(1884–1915)
▲ 1886– ◼○ Cheltenham
7.B4
See also Schools,
Cambridge, Oxford

Fletcher, John (1579–1625)
★○ Rye *5.B3*
○ Cambridge *9.A3*
◼ 1625 London
See also London,
Cambridge

Ford, Ford Madox
(1873–1939)
▲ 1890s Aldington *5.C3*
▲ 1908–10, c1912–15
London
See also London

Forster, E. M. (1879–1970)
▲ –1893 Stevenage *5.A2*
▲ 1902–45 Abinger Hammer
20.B4
▲ 1929–39 London
● Cambridge *9.A3*
See also London,
Cambridge

Frazer, Sir James (1854–1941)
★ Glasgow *12.B2*
▲ 1907–22 Liverpool *10.B4*
See also Cambridge

Galsworthy, John
(1867–1933)
★ 1867 ▲ 1875–8, 1881–6,
1912–33 ● London
▲ 1904–1919 Manaton
(vacations) *3.A3*
▲ 1920–33 Bury, W. Sussex
(partly) *4.C4*
○ Oxford *4.B2*
See also London, Schools,
Oxford

Gaskell, Elizabeth
(1810–1865)
★ London
▲ 1811–32 ◼☐ Knutsford
10.C4
▲ 1832– ○ Manchester
10.C4
▲ c1832– Silverdale *10.B2*
● Holybourne *20.A4*
See also London

Gay, John (1685–1732)
★ Barnstaple *2.C2*
▲ c1714, 1720– ● 1732
London
▲ 1723 Tunbridge Wells
21.B4
See also London,
Edinburgh

Gibbon, Edward (1737–1794)
★ 1737 ▲ 1769, 1773–83
● 1794 London
▲ 1758–72 Buriton *4.C3*
▲ 1793 ◼ Fletching *5.A3*
See also London, Schools,
Oxford

Gilbert, W. S. (1836–1911)
★ 1836 ▲ 1876–1911
●◼ London
See also London

Gissing, George (1857–1903)
★○ Wakefield *11.A3*
▲ 1872 Manchester *10.C4*
▲ 1882–90 London
▲ 1891–3 Exeter *3.A3*
▲ 1895 Dorking *20.C4*
See also London

Godwin, Mary (1759–1797)
◼ (reinterred) 1851
Bournemouth *4.B4*

Godwin, William (1756–1836)
★ Wisbech *9.A2*
◼ (reinterred) 1851
Bournemouth *4.B4*

Gogarty, Oliver St John
(1878–1957)
★ Dublin *17.B3*
See also Dublin

Goldsmith, Oliver
(?1730–1774)
★ Pallas *17.B2*
▲ c1730 Lissoy *17.A2*
▲ 1742–5 Edgeworthstown
17.B2
▲ 1744– Dublin *17.B3*
▲ 1759–74 ● London
See also London, Dublin

Grahame, Kenneth
(1859–1932)
★ Edinburgh *12.C2*
▲ 1864–6, 1906–10
Cookham Dean *20.B2*
▲ 1899– Fowey (vacations)
2.B4
▲ 1901–8 London
▲ 1910–24 Blewbury *4.B2*
▲ 1924–32 ○ Pangbourne
4.C2
◼ Oxford *4.B2*
See also London,
Edinburgh

Gray, Thomas (1716–1771)
★ 1716 ▲ 1759–61 London
◼○ Stoke Poges *20.B2*
See also London, Schools,
Cambridge

Grossmith, George
(1847–1912)
▲ London
See also London

Gunn, Neil (1891–1973)
▲ 1937– Glen Affric *14.B2*
▲● 1973 North Kessock
14.B2

Haggard, Sir Henry Rider
(1856–1925)
★ West Bradenham *9.B2*
▲ 1885–88 London
▲ 1889– ○ Ditchingham *9.C3*
▲ c1900– Kessingland *9.C2*
▲ 1918– Hastings *5.B4*
See also London

KEY
★ Born
▲ Lived
● Died
◼ Buried
☐ House/Museum, etc.
○ Statue/Memorial, etc.
△ Plaque

Hardy, Thomas (1840–1928)
★▲ 1840–70 ☐ Higher
Bockhampton *3.C3*
▲ 1870 St. Juliot *2.B3*
▲ 1876 Sturminster Newton
3.C2
▲ 1878–81 London
▲ 1881–3 Wimborne *3.C3*
▲ 1885–1928 ☐○ Dorchester
3.B3
■ (heart) ○ Stinsford *4.A4*
☐ Easton *4.A4*
See also London, Oxford

Hartley, L. P. (1895–1972)
★ Peterborough *9.A2*
See also Schools, Oxford

Hazlitt, William (1778–1830)
★☐ Maidstone *21.C3*
▲ c1786 Wem *7.A2*
▲ 1808–12 Winterslow *4.B3*
▲ 1812–19, 1820, 1829
●■ 1830 London
See also London

Herbert, George (1593–1633)
★ Montgomery *7.A2*
▲ 1630–2 ■○ Bemerton *4.B3*
○ Little Gidding *8.C3*
See also Schools,
Cambridge

Herrick, Robert (1591–1674)
▲ c1604–14, 1647–62
London
▲ 1629–47, 1662–74
●■○ Dean Prior *2.C3*
See also London,
Cambridge

Hobbes, Thomas (1588–1679)
★ Malmesbury *3.C1*
▲ –1679 ■ Ault Hucknall
11.A4
See also Oxford

Hood, Thomas (1799–1845)
★ 1799 ▲ 1824–27, 1829–35,
1840–45 ●■ London
▲ 1815–17 Dundee *14.C2*
See also London

Hopkins, Gerard Manley
(1844–1889)
★ 1844 ▲ 1856–63 London
▲ 1870–1, 1878, 1882–4
Whalley *10.C3*
▲ 1874–7 St. Bueno's
College *6.C1*
▲ 1877–8 Mount St. Mary's
College *11.A4*
▲ 1878 Oxford *4.B2*
▲ 1884–9 ● Dublin *17.B3*
○ Haslemere *20.A4*
See also London, Schools,
Oxford, Dublin

Housman, A. E. (1859–1936)
★ 1859 ▲ c1873 Fockbury
7.B3
▲ 1860–73 Bromsgrove *7.B3*
▲ 1886–1911 London

■○ Ludlow *7.A3*
See also London,
Cambridge, Oxford

Hudson, W. H. (1841–1922)
▲ 1886–1922 London
▲ 1903 Brockenhurst *4.B4*
▲ 1906–7 ○ Zennor *2.A4*
■ Worthing *5.A4*
See also London

Hume, David (1711–1776)
★▲ 1711–76 ●■ Edinburgh
12.C2
See also Edinburgh

Hunt, Leigh (1784–1859)
★ 1784 ▲ 1812–17, 1833–40,
1853–59 ●■ London
See also London, Schools

Huxley, Aldous (1894–1963)
▲ 1917, 1919–20 London
See also London, Schools,
Oxford

Johnson, Dr. Samuel
(1709–1784)
★○ Lichfield *8.A2*
▲ 1726–7 Stourbridge 7.B3
▲ 1731– Market Bosworth
8.B2
▲ c1734 Birmingham *8.A3*
▲ 1735–7 Edial *8.A2*
▲ 1745, 1749–60, 1765–76,
1784 ●■ London
○ Easton Maudit *4.C1*
○ Uttoxeter *8.A2*
See also London, Oxford,
Edinburgh

Jonson, Ben (1572–1637)
★ 1573 ▲ 1605, 1607–16
■ London
See also London, Schools

Joyce, James (1882–1941)
★▲☐ Dublin *17.B3*
▲ 1888–91 Bray *17.C3*
▲ 1904 ○ Sandycove *17.C3*
See also Dublin

Keats, John (1795–1821)
★ 1795 ▲ 1811–20 London
▲ 1817 Burford Bridge
20.C4
▲ 1819 ○ Bedhampton
4.C4
▲ 1819 Winchester *4.B3*
▲ 1819 ○ Shanklin *4.C4*
▲ 1819 ○ Chichester *4.C4*
See also London

Kingsley, Charles (1819–1875)
★○ Holne *3.A3*
▲ 1824–30 Barnack *8.C2*
▲ 1830–6 ○ Clovelly *2.C2*
▲ 1844–75 ■○ Eversley
20.A3
▲ 1853–4 Torquay *3.A3*
▲ 1873 London
○ Bideford *2.C2*
See also London,
Cambridge

Kipling, Rudyard (1865–1936)
▲ 1874–7 Portsmouth *4.C4*
▲ 1889–91 ●■ 1936 London
▲ 1896–7 Maidencombe
3.A3
▲ 1897–1902
☐ Rottingdean *5.A4*
▲ 1902–36 ☐ Burwash *5.B3*
○ Westward Ho! *2.C2*
See also London

Kyd, Thomas (?1558–?1594)
See Schools

Lamb, Charles (1775–1834)
★▲ 1775–96, 1809–47
●■ London
☐ Westmill *5.A2*
See also London, Schools

Lamb, Mary (1764–1847)
★ 1764 ▲●■ London
See also London

Landor, W. S. (1775–1864)
★○ Warwick *8.B3*
▲ 1798 Swansea *6.C4*
▲ c1807–14 Llanthony *7.A4*
▲ 1838–58 Bath *3.C2*
○ Bishop's Tachbrook *8.B3*
See also Schools, Oxford

Langland, William
(?1330–?1400)
★ Cleobury Mortimer *7.B3*

Lawrence, D. H. (1885–1930)
★ 1885 ▲ 1887–1902
☐ Eastwood *8.B2*
▲ 1908–12, 1915 London
▲ 1915–16 Padstow *2.B3*
▲ 1916–17 Zennor *2.A4*
▲ 1918–19 Middleton-by-
Wirksworth *8.B1*
See also London

Lawrence, T. E. (1888–1935)
★○ Tremadoc *6.B2*
▲ 1923–35 ☐ Cloud's Hill
3.C3
■ Moreton *3.C3*
○ Wareham *3.C3*
See also London, Oxford

Lear, Edward (1812–1888)
★▲ 1812–22 London
See also London

Lewis, C. S. (1898–1963)
★ Belfast *17.C1*
● Cambridge *9.A3*
See also Cambridge,
Oxford

Linklater, Eric (1899–1974)
★ Orkney Islands *14.C1*
▲ 1919–, 1927–8 Aberdeen
15.A2
▲ 1933– Orkney Islands
14.C1

Locke, John (1632–1704)
★ Wrington *3.B2*
▲ c1690 London

▲ 1691–1704 ■○ High Laver
21.*B1*
See also London, Schools,
Oxford

Lovelace, Richard
(1618–1658)
▲ 1642 ●■ 1658 London
▲ 1650s Canterbury 5.*C3*
See also London, Schools,
Oxford

Lowry, Malcolm (1909–1957)
▲ 1928 London
▲ 1956–7 ■ Ripe 5.*A4*
See also London,
Cambridge

Macaulay, Thomas Babington
(1800–1859)
★ Rothley 8.*B2*
▲ 1800–23, 1841–59 ●■
London
See also London,
Cambridge

Machen, Arthur (1863–1947)
★ Caerleon 7.*A4*

Mackenzie, Sir Compton
(1883–1972)
★ Hartlepool 11.*A1*
▲ 1896–1900 Beech 4.*C3*
▲ 1939–45 ■ Barra 14.*A2*
▲ 1962–72 Edinburgh 12.*C2*
See also London, Oxford,
Edinburgh

MacNeice, Louis (1907–1963)
★ Belfast 17.*C1*
▲ 1930–5 Birmingham 8.*A3*
See also Schools, Oxford

Malory, Sir Thomas (d.1471)
▲ 1471 ● London
See also London

Mansfield, Katherine
(1888–1923)
▲ 1903–06, 1915, 1918
London
▲ 1916 Mylor 2.*B4*
See also London

Marlowe, Christopher
(1564–1593)
★○ Canterbury 5.*C3*
●■ London
○ Cambridge 9.*A3*
See also London, Schools,
Cambridge

Marvell, Andrew (1621–1678)
★ Winestead 11.*C3*
▲ 1624–Kingston-upon-Hull
11.*B3*
▲ 1650–2 Appleton Roebuck
11.*A3*
See also London,
Cambridge

Masefield, John (1878–1967)
★ Ledbury 7.*B3*
▲ 1891–4 Liverpool 10.*B4*

▲ 1913–16 London
▲ 1920s Oxford 4.*B2*
▲ 1940s Sapperton 3.*C1*
See also London

Maugham, W. Somerset
(1874–1965)
▲ 1880s Whitstable 5.*C3*
▲ 1895, 1911–19 London
See also London, Schools

Meredith, George
(1828–1909)
★▲ 1828–40 Portsmouth
4.*C4*
▲ 1849, 1858–9 London
▲ 1859–67 Esher 20.*C3*
▲ 1867–1909 Mickleham
20.*C3*
■ Dorking 20.*C4*
See also London

Middleton, Thomas
(1570–1627)
▲ 1609–27 London
See also London, Oxford

Milton, John (1608–74)
★ 1608 ▲ 1652–60, 1662–74
■ London
▲ 1632–40 ○ Horton 20.*B2*
▲ 1665–6 □ Chalfont St.
Giles 20.*B2*
See also London, Schools,
Cambridge

Moore, George (1852–1933)
★ Carra Lough 17.*A2*
▲ 1901–11 Dublin 17.*B3*
▲ 1911–33 ● London
See also London, Dublin

More, Sir Thomas
(1478–1535)
★ 1478 ▲ 1511–35 ●■
London
See also London, Oxford

Morris, William (1834–96)
★▲ 1834–40, 1848–72,
1878–96 ● London
▲ 1871–96 ■□ Kelmscott
4.*B2*
○ Lower Inglesham 4.*B2*
See also London, Schools,
Oxford

Muir, Edwin (1887–1959)
★▲ 1887–1901 Orkney
Islands 14.*C1*
▲ 1901–19 Glasgow 12.*B2*
▲ 1929–32 Crowborough
21.*B4*
▲ 1930s London
▲ 1956–9 ■ Swaffham Prior
9.*A3*
● Cambridge 9.*A3*
○ Swanston 12.*C2*
See also London

Murry, J. Middleton
(1889–1957)
▲ 1915, 1918 London
▲ 1916 Mylor 2.*B4*

See also London, Schools,
Oxford

Nash, Thomas (1567–1601)
★ Lowestoft 9.*C3*
▲ 1597 London
See also London,
Cambridge

Newman, John Henry
(1801–1890)
★○ London
▲ 1816–19 Alton 20.*A4*
■ Rednal 7.*B3*
○ Birmingham, ○ Oxford
4.*B2*
See also London, Oxford

O'Casey, Sean (1880–1964)
★▲○ Dublin 17.*B3*
▲ 1938–55 Totnes 3.*A3*
▲ 1955–64 Torquay 3.*A3*
See also Dublin

O'Connor, Frank (1903–1966)
★ Cork 17.*A4*

Orwell, George (1903–1950)
▲ c1910 Shiplake 20.*A2*
▲ 1934–5, 1943–4 London
▲ 1946–9 Jura 14.*A3*
■ Sutton Courtenay 4.*B2*
See also London, Schools

Otway, Thomas (1652–1685)
★○ Milland 4.*C3*
▲ 1652–Woolbeding 4.*C3*
■ London
See also London, Schools,
Oxford

Owen, Wilfred (1893–1918)
★▲ 1893–7 Oswestry 7.*A2*

Paine, Tom (1737–1809)
★▲ 1737–57 ○ Thetford 9.*B3*
▲ 1759 ○ Sandwich 5.*C3*
▲ –1774 Lewes 5.*A4*

Pater, Walter (1839–1894)
●■ Oxford 4.*B2*
See also Oxford

Patmore, Coventry
(1823–1896)
▲ 1848–62 London
▲ 1865–75 Temple Grove
5.*A3*
▲ 1875–91 Hastings 5.*B4*
▲ 1891–6 Lymington 4.*B4*
See also London

KEY	
★	Born
▲	Lived
●	Died
■	Buried
□	House/Museum, etc.
○	Statue/Memorial, etc.
△	Plaque

Peacock, Thomas Love
(1785–1866)
★ Weymouth *3.B3*
▲ c1790 Chertsey *20.B3*
▲ 1816–18 Marlow *20.A2*
▲ 1856–66 ■○ Shepperton
20.B3

Pepys, Samuel (1633–1703)
★ 1633 ▲ 1659–73,
1679–1703 ●■ London
See also London, Schools,
Cambridge

Percy, Thomas (1729–1811)
★ Bridgnorth *7.B2*
▲ 1756–78 Easton Maudit
4.C1
▲ 1760s, 1770s London
▲ 1778–82 Carlisle *10.C1*
■ Dromore *17.C1*
See also London, Oxford

Pope, Alexander (1688–1744)
★ 1688 ▲ 1716–44 ■ London
▲ 1700–13 Binfield
20.A3
▲ 1712 West Grinstead
5.A3
□ Stanton Harcourt *4.B2*
See also London

Potter, Beatrix (1866–1943)
★▲ 1886–1913 London
▲ 1870s Essendon *20.C1*
▲ 1896–1943 □ Near Sawrey
10.B2
See also London

Powys, J. C. (1872–1963)
★ Shirley *8.B2*
▲ 1934 Dorchester *3.B3*
▲ 1934–55 Corwen *6.C2*
▲ 1955–63 Blaenau
Ffestiniog *6.C1*
See also Schools,
Cambridge

Powys, T. F. (1875–1953)
★ Shirloy *8.B2*
▲ 1905–40 Chaldon Herring
3.C3
▲ 1940–53 ■ Mappowder
3.C3

Prior, Matthew (1664–1721)
★ Wimborne *3.C3*
▲ 1706–11 ■ London
● Wimpole Hall *5.A1*
See also London, Schools,
Cambridge

Quiller-Couch, Sir Arthur
(1863–1944)
★○ Bodmin *2.B3*
▲ 1892–1944 ○ Fowey
2.B4
○ Truro *2.B4*
See also Schools,
Cambridge, Oxford

Radcliffe, Anne (1764–1823)
▲ 1815–23 ■ London
See also London

Raleigh, Sir Walter
(?1552–1618)
★□ East Budleigh *3.A3*
▲ 1588–9 Youghal *17.A4*
▲ 1592–ⓈSherborne *3.B2*
▲ 1592, 1603–16 ●■ 1618
London
See also London, Oxford

Reade, Charles (1814–1884)
★ Ipsden *4.C2*
▲ 1856–79, 1882–4
●■ London
See also London, Oxford

Richardson, Samuel
(1689–1761)
▲ 1739–61 ●■ London
See also London, Schools

Robinson, Henry Crabb
(1775–1867)
★▲ 1775– Bury St.
Edmunds *9.B3*
▲ 1805–10, 1839–67
■ London
See also London

Rossetti, Christina
(1830–1894)
★▲ 1830–31, 1876–94
●■ London
See also London

Rossetti, Dante Gabriel
(1828–1882)
★ 1828 ▲ 1851–82
●■ London
▲ 1868–9 Old Dailly *12.A3*
▲ 1871–4 Kelmscott *4.B2*
▲ 1882 ●■○ Birchington
5.C3
○ Hastings *5.B4*
See also London

Ruskin, John (1819–1900)
★▲ 1819–72 London
▲ 1871 Abingdon *4.B2*
▲ 1872–1900 □ Brantwood
10.B2
■□ Coniston *10.B2*
○ Keswick *10.B2*
See also London, Oxford

Russell, George (AE)
(1867–1935)
★ Lurgan *17.B1*
▲ 1877–1932 Dublin *17.B3*
▲ –1935 ● Bournemouth
4.B4
■ Dublin *17.B3*

Sackville-West, Victoria
(1892–1962)
★ Knole □ *21.B3*
▲ 1920s London
▲ 1930–62 ●○ Sissinghurst
Castle *21.C4*
See also London

Sassoon, Siegfried
(1886–1967)
▲ –1914 Matfield *21.B4*
▲ –1967 ● Heytesbury *3.C2*

See also Schools,
Cambridge

Sayers, Dorothy L.
(1893–1957)
★ Oxford *4.B2*
▲ 1898–1917 Bluntisham
9.A3
▲ 1917– Christchurch,
Cambs. (vacations) *9.A2*
▲ London
▲ 1929–57 ○ Witham *21.C1*
See also London, Oxford

Scott, Sir Walter (1771–1832)
★▲ 1771–1826 ○ Edinburgh
12.C2
▲ c1774 ○ Smailholm *13.A2*
▲ 1783 Kelso *13.A2*
▲ 1798–1804 Lasswade
(summers) *12.C2*
▲ 1804–12 Ashiestiel *13.A2*
▲ 1812–32 ● Abbotsford
13.A2
■ Dryburgh Abbey *13.A2*
○ Clovenfords *13.A2*
○ Galashiels *13.A2*
○ Glasgow *12.B2*
○ Selkirk *13.A3*
See also London,
Edinburgh

Shakespeare, William
(1564–1616)
★ 1564 ▲ 1564–c1585,
1597–1616 ●■□ Stratford-
upon-Avon *8.A3*
▲ 1604, 1613– London
□ Manchester
See also London

Shaw, George Bernard
(1856–1950)
★○ Dublin *17.B3*
▲ 1887–1950 London
▲ 1906–50 □ Ayot St.
Lawrence *20.C1*
See also London, Dublin

Shelley, Percy Bysshe
(1792–1822)
★□ Warnham *20.C4*
▲ 1811 York *11.A3*
▲ 1811, 1814–15 London
▲ 1811–12 Elan Valley *6.C3*
▲ 1811–12 Edinburgh *12.2C*
▲ 1811–13 Keswick *10.B2*
▲ 1812 Lynmouth *3.A2*
▲ 1812–13 Tremadoc *6.B2*
▲ 1815 Bishopsgate *20.B3*
▲ 1816 Bath *3.C2*
▲ 1817–18 Marlow *20.A2*
■ (heart) Bournemouth *4.B4*
○ Christchurch, Dorset *4.B4*
○ Lechlade *4.B2*
○ Oxford *4.B2*
See also London, Schools,
Oxford

Sheridan, R. B. (1751-1816)
★○ Dublin *17.B3*
▲ 1770–2 Bath *3.C2*
▲ 1772–3 Waltham Abbey
21.A1

268

▲ 1773, c1778, 1795, 1811–16
● London
▲ 1796–1802 Polesden Lacey
20.C4
▲ 1808–9 Leatherhead 20.B3
○ Stafford 7.B2
See also London, Schools,
Dublin

Sidney, Sir Philip (1554–1586)
★□ Penshurst Place 21.B4
▲ 1575 Kenilworth 8.B3
▲ 1583–5 ■ London
○ Shrewsbury 7.A2
See also London, Schools,
Oxford

Sitwell, Dame Edith
(1887–1964)
★□ Scarborough 11.B2
▲ Renishaw 11.A4
■ Weedon Lois 8.B3

Sitwell, Sir Osbert
(1892–1969)
□ Scarborough 11.B2

Skelton, John (?1460–1529)
■ 1529 London
See also London,
Cambridge

Smart, Christopher
(1722–1771)
★ Shipbourne 21.B4
▲ c1730 Durham 11.A1
▲ 1769–71 London
See also London,
Cambridge

Smith, Adam (1723–1790)
★ 1723 ▲ 1766– ○ Kirkcaldy
14.C3
▲ 1751– Glasgow 12.B2
See also Oxford

Smith, Sydney (1771–1845)
▲ 1794 Netheravon 4.B3
▲ 1803–09, 1839–45
■ London
▲ 1814–28 ○ Foston-le-Clay
11.A3
▲ 1828 Bristol 3.B1
▲ 1829–45 ○ Combe Florey
3.A2
See also London, Schools,
Oxford

Smollett, Tobias (1721–1771)
★□ Alexandria 14.B3
▲ 1750–62 London
▲ 1766 Edinburgh 17.C2
See also London,
Edinburgh

Southey, Robert (1774–1843)
★ 1774 ▲ 1794–5, 1798
Bristol 3.B1
▲ 1792–5 Bath 3.C2
▲ 1797 Burton 4.B4
▲ 1799 Porlock 3.A2
▲ 1802–43 ●□ Keswick
10.B2
■○ Crosthwaite 10.B2

See also London, Schools,
Oxford

Spenser, Edmund
(?1552–1599)
★ (?)1552 ▲ 1578–80, 1596–9
●■ London
▲ 1576–8 Hurstwood 10.C3
▲ 1587, 1591 Doneraile 17.A4
▲ 1590 Alton 20.A4
See also London, Schools,
Cambridge

Steele, Sir Richard
(1672–1729)
★ Dublin 17.B3
▲ 1707–12, 1714–16 London
▲ 1724– ●■ Carmarthen
6.C4
▲ c1724 ○ Llangunnor 6.B4
See also London, Schools,
Oxford, Dublin

Sterne, Laurence (1713–1768)
★ Clonmel 17.B3
▲ 1741–59 Sutton-on-the-
Forest 11.A3
▲ 1760–8 ■ (reinterred 1969)
□ Coxwold 11.A2
●■ 1768 London
See also London,
Cambridge

Stevenson, Robert Louis
(1850–1894)
★▲ 1850–, 1880 ○ Edinburgh
12.C2
▲ 1867–81 Swanston
(vacations) 12.C2
▲ 1884–7 □ Bournemouth
4.B4
See also Edinburgh

Strachey, Lytton (1880–1932)
★ 1880 ▲ 1884–1909 London
▲ 1897–9 Liverpool 10.B4
▲ 1917–24 Tidmarsh 4.C2
▲ 1924–32 Ham, Wilts. 4.B3
See also London,
Cambridge

Surtees, Robert (1803–1864)
▲ c1819 Durham 11.A1
▲ 1838– ■ Hamsterley Hall
10.C1
● Brighton 5.A4

Swift, Jonathan (1667–1745)
★ 1667 ▲ 1713–45 ●■○
Dublin 17.B3
▲ c1670 Kilkenny 17.B3
▲ c1690–4, 1696–9 Farnham
20.A3
▲ 1695–6 Kilroot 17.C1
▲ 1700–13 Laracor 17.B2
▲ 1710, 1711, 1713, 1726
London
▲ 1723 Unionshall 17.A4
See also London, Dublin

Swinburne, Algernon
(1837–1909)
★ 1837 ▲ 1860–70,
1872–1909 ● London

▲ 1837– Bonchurch 4.C4
▲ 1850s Capheaton Hall
(vacations) 10.C1
▲ 1859 Navestock 21.B2
▲ 1864 Tintagel 2.B3
▲ 1865–79 Shiplake 20.A2
See also London, Schools,
Oxford

Symonds, J. A. (1840–1893)
★ 1840 ▲ 1868–80 Bristol
3.B1
▲ 1864– Hastings 5.B4
See also Schools, Oxford

Synge, J. M. (1871–1909)
★▲●■ Dublin 17.B3
See also Dublin

Tennyson, Alfred Lord
(1809–1892)
★▲ 1809–37 ○ Somersby
9.A1
▲ 1837–40 High Beech 21.A2
▲ 1843 Cheltenham 7.B4
▲ 1851–53 ■ 1892 London
▲ 1853–69 Farringford 4.B4
▲ 1869–92 ●○ Haslemere
20.A4
○ Freshwater 4.B4
□ Lincoln 8.C1
See also London,
Cambridge

**Thackeray, William
Makepeace** (1811–1863)
▲ 1837, 1840–63 ●■ London
See also London, Schools,
Cambridge

Thomas, Dylan (1914–1953)
★▲ 1914–36 ○ Swansea 6.C4
▲ 1938, 1949–53 ■
Laugharne 6.B4
▲ 1946 Oxford 4.B2

Thompson, Flora (1876–1947)
★ Juniper Hill 4.C1
▲ 1890–6 Fringford 4.C1
▲ 1928–40 Dartmouth 3.A4
▲ 1940–7 ● Brixham 3.A3

Thompson, Francis
(1859–1907)
★○ Preston 10.B3
▲ 1877–83 Manchester 10.C4
▲ 1893–7 Pantasaph 7.A1
■ 1907 London
See also London

KEY	
★	Born
▲	Lived
●	Died
■	Buried
□	House/Museum, etc.
○	Statue/Memorial, etc.
△	Plaque

Thomson, James (1700–1748)
★○ Ednam *13.A2*
▲ 1736–48 ■ London
See also London

Tolkien, J. R. R. (1892–1973)
See Oxford

Traherne, Thomas
(?1638–1674)
★ Hereford *7.A3*
▲ 1661–7 Credenhill *7.A3*
▲ 1669–74 ●■ London
See also London, Oxford

Trollope, Anthony
(1815–1882)
★ 1815 ▲ 1872–80 ●■ 1882
London
▲ 1845–51 Mallow *17.A4*
▲ 1854–9 Dublin *17.B3*
▲ 1859–70 Waltham Cross
21.A1
▲ 1880–2 ○ South Harting
4.C3
See also London, Schools,
Dublin

Tyndale, William (d.1536)
□ North Nibley *3.C1*
See also London

Walpole, Horace (1717–1797)
★ 1717 ▲ 1745–97 ● London
■ Houghton Hall *9.C2*
See also London, Schools,
Cambridge

Walpole, Sir Hugh
(1884–1941)
▲ –1941 ● Borrowdale *10.B2*
■□ Keswick *10.B2*
See also Schools,
Cambridge

Walton, Izaak (1593–1683)
★○ Stafford *7.B2*
▲ 1660–2 Hartlebury *7.B3*
▲□ Shallowford *7.B2*
▲ 1678–83 ●■○ Winchester
4.B3
See also London

Waugh, Evelyn (1903–1966)
▲ 1925–7 Aston Clinton
20.A1
▲ 1928 London
▲ 1937–56 Stinchcombe
3.C1
▲ 1956–66 Combe Florey
3.A2
See also London, Oxford

Wells, H. G. (1866–1946)
★ 1866 ▲ 1937–46

● London
▲ c1879 Uppark *4.C3*
▲ 1881–3 Portsmouth *4.C4*
▲ 1881, 1882–94 Midhurst
4.C3
▲ 1900–□ Folkestone *5.C3*
▲ c1914 Little Easton *21.B2*
See also London

Wesley, Charles (1707–1788)
★□ Epworth *11.B4*
▲● London
See also London, Schools

Wesley, John (1703–1791)
★□ Epworth *11.B4*
▲ London
See also London, Schools

White, Gilbert (1720–1793)
★ 1720 ▲ 1751–93
■□ Selborne *20.A4*
See also Oxford

White, W. H. (Mark
Rutherford) (1831–1913)
★ Bedford *8.C3*
▲ 1865–66, 1868–89 London
▲ 1892–1900 Hastings *5.B4*
▲ 1903–13 ■ Groombridge
21.B4
See also London

Wilde, Oscar (1854–1900)
★▲○ Dublin *17.B3*
▲ 1884–95 London
▲ 1895–7 Reading (Gaol)
20.A3
See also London, Oxford,
Dublin

Woodforde, James
(1740–1803)
★ 1740 ▲ 1771 Ansford *3.B2*
▲ 1776–1803 ●■○ Weston
Longville *9.B2*
See also Oxford

Woolf, Virginia (1882–1941)
★ 1882 ▲ 1905–15, 1924–40
London
▲ 1912–17 Asheham *5.A4*
▲ 1926 St. Ives *2.A5*
▲ 1939–41 ● Rodmell *5.A4*
□ Sissinghurst Castle *21.C4*
See also London

Wordsworth, Dorothy
(1771–1855)
★ Cockermouth *10.A1*
▲ 1787–Penrith (vacations)
10.B1
▲ 1794 Keswick *10.B2*
▲ 1795–7 Racedown Lodge
3.B3

▲ 1797 Porlock *3.A2*
▲ 1797–8 Alfoxton Park
3.A2
▲ 1799–1813 ■ Grasmere
10.B2
▲ 1806–7 Coleorton Hall
8.B2
▲ 1813–50 Rydal *10.B2*
○ Jedburgh *13.A3*

Wordsworth, William
(1770–1850)
★□ Cockermouth *10.A1*
▲ 1779–87 Colthouse *10.B2*
▲ 1783–Penrith (vacations)
10.B1
▲ 1795–7 Racedown Lodge
3.B3
▲ 1797 Porlock *3.A2*
▲ 1797–8 Alfoxton Park *3.A2*
▲ 1799–1813 ■□ Grasmere
10.B2
▲ 1806–7 Coleorton Hall
8.B2
▲ 1813–50 ●□ Rydal *10.B2*
□ Hawkshead *10.B2*
□ Jedburgh *13.A3*
□ Keswick *10.B2*
See also London,
Cambridge

Wyatt, Sir Thomas
(?1503–1542)
★ Allington *21.C3*
▲ 1536, 1540–1 London
●■ Sherborne *3.B2*
See also London,
Cambridge

Wycherley, William
(1640–1716)
★ Preston Brockhurst *7.A2*
●■ 1716 London
See also London, Oxford

Wycliffe, John (?1320–1384)
▲ 1374–84 ○ Lutterworth
8.B3
See also Oxford

Yeats, W. B. (1865–1939)
★▲○ Dublin *17.B3*
▲ 1867–80, 1895–1919
London
▲ 1880 Howth *17.C2*
▲ 1912–14 Coleman's Hatch
21.A4
▲ 1917–□ Gort *17.A3*
▲ c1921 Oxford *4.B2*
▲ 1921 Shillingford *4.C2*
▲ 1921 Thame *20.A1*
▲ 1930s ○ Steyning *5.A4*
■ (reinterred) 1948 Drumcliff
17.A2
See also London, Dublin

London Gazetteer

Addison, Joseph
1 ▲1710: St. James's Pl. *24.C3*
2 ▲1716–19●: Holland House *22.C3*
See also Westminster Abbey

Andrewes, Lancelot
3 ★1555: All Hallows, Barking *23.B2*
4 ●1626: Winchester Palace, Southwark *24.C3*
5 ■Southwark Cathedral *25.C3*

Arnold, Matthew
6 ▲1858–68△: 2 Chester Sq. *24.C3*
7 ▲1868–73: Byron Hill, Harrow on the Hill *22.A2*

Aubrev, John
See Inns of Court

Auden, W. H.
See Westminster Abbey

Austen, Jane
8 ▲1813: 10 Henrietta St. *25 (inset)*

Bacon, Sir Francis
9 ★1561: Strand *25.A2*
10 ▲1595–1605: Twickenham Park *22.A3*
11 ●1626: St. Michael's, Highgate (site of Arundel House) *22.C2*
See also Inns of Court

Ballantyne, R. M.
12 ▲1880–93: Mount Park Rd., Harrow on the Hill *22.A2*

Barrie, Sir James
13 ▲1895–98: 133 Gloucester Rd. *24.A3*
14 ▲1902–9△: 100 Bayswater Rd. *24.A2*
15 ▲1909–37△: 1–3 Robert St. *25 (inset)*
16 ○Kensington Gdns. *24.A3*

Beaumont, Francis
See Westminster Abbey, Inns of Court

Beckford, William
17 ★1759: 22 Soho Sq. *25.A2*

Beerbohm, Sir Max
18 ★1872△: 57 Palace Gardens Ter. *24.A3*
19 ▲1893–1910: 48 Upper Berkeley St. *24.B2*
See also St. Paul's Cathedral

Belloc, Hilaire
20 ▲c1900–5△: 104 Cheyne Walk *24.B4*

Behn, Aphra
See Westminster Abbey

Bennett, Arnold
21 ▲1923–30△: 75 Cadogan Sq. *24.B3*
22 ▲1930–1●: Chiltern Ct. Mansions *24.B1*

Blackmore, R. D.
23 ▲1860–1900: Doone Close, Teddington *22.B4*
24 ■1900: Teddington Cemetery *22.B4*

Blake, William
25 ★1757△: 74 Broadwick St. *24.C2*
26 ▲1771–8: 31 Great Queen St. *25 (inset)*
27 ▲1785–91: 28 Poland St. *24.C2*
28 ▲1804–21△: 17 South Molton St. *24.C2*
29 ▲1821–7●: Fountain Ct., Strand *25 (inset)*
30 ■Bunhill Fields *25.C1*
See also Westminster Abbey, St. Paul's Cathedral

Borrow, George
31 ▲1860–74△: 22 Hereford Sq. *24.A4*
32 ■1881: Brompton Cemetery *24.A4*

Boswell, James
33 ▲1763: Downing St. *25.A3*
34 ▲1790–9●△: 122 Gt. Portland St. *24.C2*
See also Inns of Court

Bridges, Robert
35 ▲1869–81: St. Barthomew's Hospital *25.A2*

Brontë sisters
See Westminster Abbey

Browning, Elizabeth Barrett
36 ▲1835–8△: 99 (prev. 74) Gloucester Pl. *24.B2*
37 ▲1838–46△: 50 Wimpole St. *24.C2*
38 ○Marylebone Parish Church *24.C2*
See also Robert Browning (*below*)

Browning, Robert (* with Elizabeth)
39 ★1812: Southampton St., Camberwell *23.A3*
40 *▲ 1852: 58 Welbeck St. *24.C2*
41 *▲ 1855: 13 Dorset St. *24.C2*
42 ▲1861–87: 19 Warwick Crescent *24.A2*
43 ▲1888–9△: 22 De Vere Gdns. *24.A3*
44 △179 Southampton Way *25.C4*
45 ○Marylebone Parish Church *24.C2*
See also Westminster Abbey

Buchan, John
46 ▲1913–19: 76 Portland Pl. *24.C2*

Bulwer-Lytton, Edward
47 ★1803: 31 Baker St. *24.C2*
48 ▲——: Albany *24.C2*
49 ▲——: 36 Hertford St. *24.C3*
50 ▲1831–2: Albury Dr., Pinner *22.A2*
See also Westminster Abbey

Bunyan, John
51 ●1688: Snow Hill *25.B2*
52 ■Bunhill Fields *25.C1*
53 ○Southampton Row *25.A2*
See also Westminster Abbey

Burke, Edmund
54 ▲1787–93△: 37 Gerrard St. *25.A2*
55 ▲1793–4: Duke St., St. James's *24.C3*
See also Inns of Court

Burney, Fanny
56 ▲1770–4: Queen's Sq. *25.A2*

KEY
★ Born
▲ Lived
● Died
■ Buried
□ House/Museum, etc.
○ Statue/Memorial, etc.
△ Plaque

57 ▲1774–86: St. Martin's
St. *25.A2*
58 ▲c1786: Kew Palace *22.B3*
59 ▲1818–28△: 11 Bolton
St. *24.C3*
60 ●1840: Grosvenor St.
24.C3

Burns, Robert
61 ○Victoria Embankment
Gardens *25 (inset)*
See also Westminster
Abbey

Burton, Sir Richard
62 ▲——: Little Green,
Richmond *22.B3*
63 ■1890: St. Mary
Magdalen, Mortlake
22.B3

Butler, Samuel
(1612–1680)
64 ▲——: Rose Alley (now
Rose St.) *25 (inset)*
65 ■1680: St. Paul's, Covent
Garden *25 (inset)*
See also Westminster
Abbey

Butler, Samuel
(1835–1902)
66 ▲1864–1902: 15
Cliffords Inn, Fetter
Lane *25 (inset)*

Byron, Lord
67 ★1788: Holles St. *24.C2*
68 ▲1812△: 8 St. James's
St. *24.C3*
69 ▲1813–14: 4 Bennet St.
24.C3
70 ▲——: Albany *24.C2*
71 ○Hyde Park *24.C3*
See also Westminster
Abbey

Carlyle, Thomas
72 ▲1831–2△: 33 (prev. 4)
Ampton St. *25.A1*
73 ▲1834–81●□: 24
Cheyne Row *24.B4*
74 ○Chelsea Embankment
24.C4

Chapman, George
75 ■1634○: St. Giles-in-the-
Fields *25.A2 (inset)*

Chatterton, Thomas
76 ▲1770●△: 39 Brooke St.
25.B2
77 ■Shoe Lane Workhouse
25.B2

Chaucer, Geoffrey
78 ★1345(?): Upper
Thames St. (site of)
25.B2
79 ▲1374–86△: 2 Aldgate
High St. (then Aldgate,
removed 1760) *25.C2*
See also Westminster
Abbey

Chesterton, G. K.
80 ★1874△: 32 Sheffield
Ter. *24.A3*
81 ▲1879–99△: 11 Warwick
Gdns. *24.A3*

Cobbett, William
82 ▲c1800–3: Fleet St. *25
(inset)*
83 ▲1828–30: Barn Elms
Estate, Barnes *22.B3*

Coleridge, Samuel Taylor
84 ▲1799: 21 Buckingham
St. *25 (inset)*
85 ▲1811–12△: 7 Addison
Bridge Pl.,
Hammersmith *22.C2*
86 ▲1812–13△: 71 Berners
St. *24.C2*
87 ▲1818–23: Highgate
22.C2
88 ▲1823–34●△: 3 The
Grove, Highgate *22.C2*
89 ■△: St. Michael's,
Highgate *22.C2*
See also Westminster
Abbey

Collins, Wilkie
90 ★1824: North End,
Hampstead *22.C2*
91 ▲1840s: 38 Blandford
Sq. *24.B1*
92 ▲1850–9: 17 Hanover
Ter. *24.B1*
93 ▲1864–7: 9 Melcombe
Pl. *24.B2*
94 ▲1867–8△: 65 (prev. 90)
Gloucester Pl. *24.B2*
95 ▲1889●: 32 Wimpole St.
24.C2
96 ■Kensal Green
Cemetery *22.C2*

Compton-Burnett, Ivy
97 ▲1916–29: 59 Leinster
Sq. *24.A2*
98 ▲1934–69△: Cornwall
Gdns. *24.A3*

Congreve, William
99 ▲——: Surrey St. (now
Arundel Great Ct.) *25
(inset)*
See also Westminster
Abbey, Inns of Court

Conrad, Joseph
100 ▲1889–90:
Bessborough Gdns.
25.A4
101 ▲1893–6: 17 Gillingham
St. *24.C3*

Cowley, Abraham
102 ★1618: Fleet St. *25 (inset)*
103 ▲1663–5: Barn Elms
Park, Barnes *22.B3*
See also Westminster
Abbey

Cowper, William
104 ▲1750s: 62 Russell Sq.
25.A2

105 ○Edmonton Church
23.A1
See also Inns of
Court

Day-Lewis, Cecil
106 ▲1954–72: Crooms Hill,
Greenwich *23.B3*

Defoe, Daniel
107 ★c1660: Cripplegate
25.B2
108 ▲1703: Newgate St.
(then prison) *25.B2*
109 ▲1709: Stoke Newington
Church St. *23.A2*
110 ▲——△: 95 Stoke
Newington Church St.
23.A2
111 ●1731: Ropemaker St.
(then Ropemaker's
Alley) *25.C2*
112 ■○ Bunhill Fields
25.C1

de la Mare, Walter
113 ▲1899–1908: 195
Mackenzie Rd., Anerley
23.A4
114 ▲1908–12: Worbeck Rd.,
Anerley *23.A4*
115 ▲1912–25: 14 Thornsett
Rd., Anerley *23.A4*
116 ▲1950–6●: 4 South End
House, Twickenham
23.A4
See also St. Paul's
Cathedral

De Quincey, Thomas
117 ▲1802: 61 Greek St.
25.A2
118 ▲1824: Tavistock St. (site
of 4 York St.) *25 (inset)*

Dickens, Charles
119 ▲1823–4: 16 Bayham St.
(gone) *24.C1*
120 ▲1833–4: 18 Bentinck St.
24.C2
121 ▲1836○: Furnival's Inn
(gone; now Prudential
Building) *25.B2*
122 ▲1837–9□△: 48
Doughty St. *25.A1*
123 ▲1838–9: 2 Ailsa Park
Villas, Twickenham
22.A3
124 ▲1839: Petersham Rd.
22.B3
125 ▲1839–51○: 1
Devonshire Ter. (site
of) *24.C2*
126 ▲1846: 1 Chester Row
24.C3
127 ▲1851–60: Tavistock Sq.
25.A1
128 ▲1862: 16 Hyde Park
Gate (gone) *24.A3*
129 ▲1865: 57 Gloucester Pl.
24.B2
130 □ New Kent Rd. *23.A3*
See also Westminster
Abbey

Disraeli, Benjamin
131 ★1804△: 22 Theobald's Rd. (then 6 King's Rd., Bedford Row) *25.A2*
132 ●1881△: 19 Curzon St. *24.C3*
See also Inns of Court

Donne, John
133 ★1572(?): Bread St. *25.B2*
134 ▲1596–1601: Strand *25 (inset)*
135 ▲1601: Farringdon St. (Fleet Prison) *25.B2*
136 ▲1606–10: Whitford Lane (gone), Mitcham *22.C4*
137 ▲1624–31: St. Dunstan-in-the-West (rector) *25 (inset)*
See also St. Paul's Cathedral, Inns of Court

Doyle, Sir Arthur Conan
138 ▲1890: 2 Devonshire Pl. *24.C2*
139 ▲1891–4△: 12 Tennison Rd., South Norwood *23.A4*
140 ○Northumberland St. *25.A3*

Dryden, John
141 ▲1673–82: Fleet St. *25 (inset)*
142 ▲1686–1700●△: 43 Gerrard St. *25.A2*
See also Westminster Abbey

Eliot, George
143 ▲1853–4: 21 Cambridge St., Pimlico *24.C4*
144 ▲1855: 7 Clarence Row, Richmond *22.B3*
145 ▲1855–9: 8 Park Shot, Richmond *22.B3*
146 ▲1859–60△: Holly Lodge, Southfields (now 31 Wimbledon Park Rd.) *22.B4*
147 ▲1860–6: 16 Blandford Sq. *24.B1*
148 ▲1863–80: 21 North Bank (gone; off Lodge Rd.) *24.B1*
149 ▲1880●△: 4 Cheyne Walk *24.B4*
150 ■Highgate Cemetery *22.C2*

Eliot, T. S.
See Westminster Abbey

Evelyn, John
151 ▲1640: Essex Ct. *25 (inset)*
152 ▲1653–94: Sayes Ct., Deptford *23.A3*
153 ●1706: Dover St. *24.C2*
See also Inns of Court

Farquhar, George
154 ■1707: St. Martin-in-the-Fields *25.A2*

Fielding, Henry
155 ▲1743–4: Back Lane (now Holly Rd.), Twickenham *22.A3*
156 ▲1748–53: Barnes Green (Milburne House) *22.B3*
157 ▲——△: 19–20 Bow St. *25 (inset)*
158 ▲——△: Essex St. *25 (inset)*
See also Inns of Court

Firbank, Ronald
159 ★1886: 40 Clarges St. *24.C3*
160 ▲1886: Hawkwood Lane, Chislehurst *23.B4*

Fletcher, John
161 ■1625: Southwark Cathedral *25.C3*

Ford, Ford Madox
162 ▲1908–10: 84 Holland Park Avenue *22.C3*
163 ▲c1912–15△: 80 Campden Hill Rd. *24.A3*

Forster, E. M.
164 ▲1929–39: 26 Brunswick Sq. *25.A1*

Galsworthy, John
165 ★1867: Parkfield, Kingston Hill *22.B4*
166 ▲1875–8, 1881–6: Coombe Leigh (now Coombe Ridge), Kingston Hill *22.B4*
167 ▲1912–18△: 1–3 Robert St. *25 (inset)*
168 ▲1918–33△: Grove Lodge, Hampstead Grove *22.C2*
See also Inns of Court

Gaskell, Elizabeth
169 ★1810△: 93 Cheyne Walk *24.B4*

Gay, John
170 ▲c1714: 16 Lawrence St., Chelsea *22.B4*
171 ▲1720–: Petersham Rd., Richmond *22.B3*
172 ●1732: Old Burlington St., Burlington Gdns. (gone) *24.C2*
See also Westminster Abbey

Gibbon, Edward
173 ★1737: Lime Grove, Putney *22.A2*
174 ▲1769: 29 Pall Mall *25.A3*
175 ▲1773–83△: 7 Bentinck St. *24.C2*
176 ●1794: 76 St. James's St. *24.C3*

Gilbert, W. S.
177 ★1836: 17 Southampton St. *25 (inset)*
178 ▲1876–82: 24 The Boltons *24.A4*
179 ▲1883–90△: 39 Harrington Gdns. *24.A4*
180 ▲1890–1911●■: Harrow Weald *22.B1*
181 ▲1907–11: 90 Eaton Sq. *24.C3*
182 ○Victoria Embankment *25.A3*

Gissing, George
183 ▲1878: 22 Colville Pl. *25.A2*
184 ▲1882–4△: 33 Oakley Gdns., Chelsea *24.B4*
185 ▲1884–90: 7K Cornwall Residences, Baker St. *24.B1*

Goldsmith, Oliver
186 ▲1759–60: Green Arbour Ct. *25.B2*
187 ▲1760–2: 6 Wine Office Ct. *25 (inset)*
188 ▲1762–7: Canonbury Tower *22.A2*
189 ▲1764: Garden Ct., Temple *25 (inset)*
190 ▲1765, 1767–74●: 2 Brick Ct. (gone), Temple *25 (inset)*
191 ■Temple Church (graveyard) *25 (inset)*
See also Westminster Abbey

Grahame, Kenneth
192 ▲1901–8△: 16 Phillimore Pl. *24.A3*

Gray, Thomas
193 ★1716: 39 Cornhill (rebuilt) *25.C2*
194 ▲1759–61: Russell Sq. *25.A2*
See also Westminster Abbey

Grossmith, George
195 ▲——△: 28 Dorset Square *24.C2*

KEY
★ Born
▲ Lived
● Died
■ Buried
□ House/Museum, etc.
○ Statue/Memorial, etc.
△ Plaque

Haggard, Sir Henry Rider
196 ▲1885–8: 69 Gunterstone Rd. *22.C2*
See also Inns of Court

Hardy, Thomas
197 ▲1878–81△: 172 Trinity Rd., Tooting *23.C4*
See also Westminster Abbey

Hazlitt, William
198 ▲1812–19: Petty France (gone) *25.A3*
199 ▲1820: Chancery Lane *25 (inset)*
200 ▲1829: Bouverie St. *25 (inset)*
201 ●1830△: 6 Frith St. *25.A2*
202 ■St. Anne's, Soho *25.A2*

Herrick, Robert
203 ▲c1604–14: Wood St., Cheapside *25.B2*
204 ▲1647–62: St. Anne's St., Westminster *25.A3*

Hood, Thomas
205 ★1799△: 31 Poultry (now Midland Bank) *25.C2*
206 ▲1824–7: 50 Essex Rd. *22.C2*
207 ▲1827△: 2 Robert St. *25 (inset)*
208 ▲1829–32: Vicars Moor La., Winchmore Hill *22.C1*
209 ▲1832–5: Lake House (gone), Wanstead *23.B2*
210 ▲1840: 8 South Pl. (now 181 Camberwell New Rd.) *23.A3*
211 ▲1841–5: 17 Elm Tree Rd, St. John's Wood *24.B1*
212 ●1845△: 28 Finchley Rd. *24.B1*
213 ■Kensal Green Cemetery *22.C2*

Hopkins, Gerard Manley
214 ★1844: Stratford *23.A3*
215 ▲1856–63: High St., Highgate *22.C2*
See also Westminster Abbey

Housman, A. E.
216 ▲1886–1905△: 17 North Rd., Highgate *22.C2*
217 ▲1905–11: Devonshire Rd. (gone), Pinner *22.A2*

Hudson, W. H.
218 ▲1886–1922△: 40 St. Luke's Rd., Westbourne Park *24.A2*
219 ○Hyde Park *24.B3*

Hunt, Leigh
220 ★1784: High St., Southgate *22.C1*
221 ▲1812–14: Horsemonger La. (prison) (gone) *25.B3*
222 ▲1815: Vale of Health *22.C2*
223 ▲c1815–17: 15 Lisson Grove (gone) *24.B2*
224 ▲1833–40△: 22 Upper Cheyne Row *24.B4*
225 ▲1853–9△: 7 (now 16) Rowan Rd. (formerly Cornwall Rd.), Hammersmith *22.C2*
226 ●1859: Putney High St. *22.B3*
227 ■Kensal Green Cemetery *22.C2*

Huxley, Aldous
228 ▲1917: 16 Bracknell Gdns., Hampstead *22.C2*
229 ▲1919–20: 18 Hampstead Hill Gdns. *22.C2*

Johnson, Samuel
230 ▲1745: Frognal (gone) *22.C2*
231 ▲1749–59□: 17 Gough Sq. *25 (inset)*
232 ▲1759–60: 2 Staple Inn *25.B2*
233 ▲1765–76△: Johnson's Ct. *25 (inset)*
234 ▲1784●: Bolt Ct. (gone) *25 (inset)*
235 ○St. Clement Danes Church *25 (inset)*
See also Westminster Abbey, St. Paul's Cathedral

Jonson, Ben
236 ★1573: Northumberland St. *25 (inset)*
237 ▲1605: Old Marshalsea Prison (near Mermaid Ct.) *25.C3*
238 ▲1607–16: Blackfriars *25.B2*
See also Westminster Abbey

Keats, John
239 ★1795△: 85 Moorgate (site) *25.C2*
240 ▲1811–15△: Keats Parade (site of), Edmonton *23.A1*
241 ▲1816: 8 Dean St. (now Stainer St.) *25.C3*
242 ▲1816–17: 76 Cheapside *25.C2*
243 ▲1818: Well Walk *22.C2*
244 ▲1818–20□△: Keats Grove *22.C2*
245 ○Hampstead Parish Church *22.C2*
See also Westminster Abbey

Kingsley, Charles
246 ▲1873: London Rd., Harrow on the Hill *22.A2*

Kipling, Rudyard
247 ▲1889–91△: 43 Villiers St. *25 (inset)*
248 ●1936: Middlesex Hospital *24.C2*
See also Westminster Abbey

Lamb, Charles (* with Mary)
249 ★▲1775–95△: 2 Crown Office Row (rebuilt) *25 (inset)*
250 *▲1795–6△: 7 Little Queen St. (now Holy Trinity, Kingsway), *25.A2*
251 *▲1809: Chancery La. *25 (inset)*
252 *▲1809–17: Hare Ct., Inner Temple La. *25 (inset)*
253 *▲1817–21: 20 Russell Ct. *24.C3*
254 *▲1823–7△: 64 Duncan Ter. (then Colebrook Cottage), Islington *22.A2*
255 *▲1827–9△: 85 Chase Side (now Clarendon Cottage), Enfield *23.A1*
256 *▲1829–33: Westwood Cottage, Enfield *23.A1*
257 *▲1833–4△: Lamb's Cottage, Edmonton *23.A1*
258 ■1834 *■1847 ○Edmonton Churchyard *23.A1*
259 ○△St. Sepulchre's *25.B2*
260 ○Inner Temple Gardens *25 (inset)*

Lawrence, D. H.
261 ▲1908–12: 12 Colworth Rd., Croydon *22.C2*
262 ▲1915△: 1 Byron Villas, Hampstead

Lawrence, T. E.
See St. Paul's Cathedral

Lear, Edward
263 ★▲1812–22: Bowman's Lodge (gone), Holloway *22.C2*
264 ▲——△: 30 Seymour St. *24.B2*

Locke, John
265 ▲c1690: Strand *25 (inset)*

Lovelace, Richard
266 ▲1642: Westminster Abbey Gatehouse (prison) (gone) *25.A3*
267 ●1658: Shoe La. (then Gunpowder Alley) *25 (inset)*

268 ■ St. Bride's Church (old) 25.B2

Lowry, Malcolm
269 ▲ 1928: 5 Woodville Rd. 23.A3

Macaulay, Thomas Babington
270 ▲ 1803–23△: 5 The Pavement, Clapham Common 22.C3
271 ▲ 1841–56: Albany 24.C2
272 ▲ 1856–9: Holly Lodge (gone, now part of Queen Elizabeth College), Campden Hill 24.A3
See also Westminster Abbey, Inns of Court

Mackenzie, Sir Compton
See Inns of Court

Malory, Sir Thomas
273 ▲–1471●: Newgate St. (then prison) 25.B2

Mansfield, Katherine
(*with J. Middleton Murry)
274 ▲ 1903–6: 41 Harley St. 24.C2
275 *▲ 1915: 5 Acacia Rd. 24.B1
276 *▲ 1918△: 17 East Heath Rd. 22.C2

Marlowe, Christopher
277 ■ 1593○: St Nicholas's Church, Deptford 23.A3

Marvell, Andrew
278 ▲——: Waterlow Park, Highgate 22.C2
279 ■ 1678○: St. Giles-in-the-Fields 25.A2

Masefield, John
280 ▲ 1913–16: 14 Well Walk 22.C2
See also Westminster Abbey

Maugham, W. Somerset
281 ▲ 1895: 11 Vincent Sq. 25.A3
282 ▲ 1911–19△: 6 Chesterfield St. 24.C2

Meredith, George
283 ▲ 1849: 153 Ebury St. (gone) 24.C3
284 1858–9△: 8 Hobury St. 24.A4

Middleton, Thomas
285 ▲ 1607–27●■: Newington Butts 25.B3
See also Inns of Court

Milton, John
286 ★ 1608: Bread St. 25.B2
287 ▲ 1652–60: Petty France

(gone) 25.A3
288 ▲ 1662–74: Bunhill Row (then Artillery Row) 25.C1
289 ■ 1674○: St. Giles, Cripplegate 25.B2
290 ○ St. Margaret's, Westminster 25.A3

Moore, George
291 ▲ 1911–33●△: 121 Ebury St. 24.C3

More, Sir Thomas
292 ★ 1478: Milk St. 25.B2
293 ▲ 1516–24: Crosby Sq., Bishopsgate 25.C2
294 ▲ c1524–34: Cheyne Walk 24.B4
295 ▲ 1534–5●■: Tower of London 25.C2
296 ○ St. Lawrence Jewry 25.B2
297 ○ Chelsea Old Church 24.B4
See also Inns of Court

Morris, William
298 ★▲ 1834–40△: Elm House (gone), Walthamstow 23.A2
299 ▲ 1848–56: The Water House (now Lloyd Park), Walthamstow 23.A2
300 ▲ 1856–9△: 17 Red Lion Sq. 25.A2
301 ▲ 1860–65□△: Red House La., Bexleyheath 23.C3
302 ▲ 1865–72: 26 Queen Sq. 25.A2
303 ▲ 1878–96●○△: 26 Upper Mall, Hammersmith 22.C2

Muir, Edwin
304 ▲ 1930s: 7 Downshire Hill 22.C2

Murry, J. Middleton
(*with Katherine Mansfield)
305 *▲ 1915: 5 Acacia Rd. 24.B1
306 *▲ 1918△: 17 East Heath Rd. 22.C2

Nash, Thomas
307 ▲ 1597: Farringdon St. (Fleet Prison) 25.B2

Newman, John Henry
308 ★ 1801: Old Broad St. 25.C2
309 ○ Brompton Oratory 24.B3

Orwell, George
310 ▲ 1934–5△: South End Green, Hampstead 22.C2
311 ▲ 1943–4: 10A Mortimer Crescent 22.C2

Otway, Thomas
312 ■ 1685: St. Clement Dane's 25 (inset)

Patmore, Coventry
313 ▲ 1863–4△: 14 Percy St. 25.A2

Pepys, Samuel
314 ★ 1633△: Salisbury Ct. 25 (inset)
315 ▲ 1659–73: Seething La. 25.C2
316 ▲ 1660: Axe Yd. 25.A3
317 ▲ 1679–88△: 12 Buckingham St. 25 (inset)
318 ▲ 1688–1700△: 14 Buckingham St. 25 (inset)
319 ▲ 1700–3●: 29 North Side (site of), Clapham Common 22.C3
320 ■ St. Olave's Church, Hart St. 25.C2

Percy, Thomas
321 ▲ 1760s, 1770s: St. Martins le Grand (then Northumberland House) 25.B2

Pope, Alexander
322 ★ 1688△: Plough Ct., Lombard St. (house gone) 25.C2
323 ▲ 1716–18: Chiswick La. South (now Fox and Hounds) 22.B3
324 ▲ 1719–44: Crossdeep, Twickenham 22.A3
325 ■ 1744△: Twickenham Parish Church 22.A3

Potter, Beatrix
326 ★▲ 1886–1913: Bolton Gdns. (gone) 24.A4

Prior, Matthew
327 ▲ 1706–11: Gt. George St. 25.A3
See also Westminster Abbey

Radcliffe, Anne
328 ▲ 1815–23: 5 Stafford Row (now Bressendon Pl.) 24.C3
329 ■ 1823: Hyde Park Pl. (disused graveyard, now a school) 24.B2

Raleigh, Sir Walter
330 ▲ 1592, 1603–16: Tower of London 25.C2

┌─────────────────────────┐
KEY
★ Born
▲ Lived
● Died
■ Buried
□ House/Museum, etc.
○ Statue/Memorial, etc.
△ Plaque
└─────────────────────────┘

331 ●1618: Old Palace Yd.
25.A3
332 ■○ St. Margaret's,
Westminster *25.A3*
333 ○ Whitehall *25.A3*
See also Inns of Court

Reade, Charles
334 ▲1856–68: 6 Bolton Row
(gone) *24.C3*
335 ▲1869–79: 2 Albert Ter.,
Hyde Park *24.B3*
336 ▲1882–4●: 3 Blomfield
Villas, Uxbridge Rd.,
Hammersmith *22.C2*
See also St. Paul's
Cathedral, Inns of
Court

Richardson, Samuel
337 ▲1739–54: 40 North End
Crescent, Fulham
22.C3
338 ▲1754–61●: Parsons
Green *22.C2*
339 ■ St. Bride's Church
(Wren) *25.B2*

Robinson, Henry Crabb
340 ▲1805–10: Little Smith
St. *25.A3*
341 ▲1810: 56 Hatton Gdn.
25.B2
342 ▲1839–67: 30 Russell
Sq. (gone) *25.A2*
343 ■1867: Highgate
Cemetery *22.C2*

Rossetti, Christina
344 ★▲1830–1: 106–110
Hallam St. (then 38
Charlotte St.) *24.C2*
345 ▲1876–94●△: 30
Torrington Sq. *25.A2*
346 ■ Highgate Cemetery
22.C2

Rossetti, Dante Gabriel
347 ★1828△: 106–110
Hallam St. (then 38
Charlotte St.) *24.C2*
348 ▲1851△: 17 Red Lion Sq.
25.A2
349 ▲1852–62: 14 Chatham
Pl. (gone) *25 (inset)*
350 ▲1862–82●△: 16
Cheyne Walk *24.B4*
351 ■ Highgate Cemetery
22.C2

Ruskin, John
352 ★▲1819–23: 54 Hunter
St. (gone), Holborn
25.A1
353 ▲1823–42△: 28 Herne
Hill *25.A1*
354 ▲1842–72: 163 Denmark
Hill (gone) *23.A3*
See also Westminster
Abbey

Sackville-West, Victoria
355 ▲1920s: 182 Ebury St.
(gone) *24.C3*

Sayers, Dorothy L.
356 ▲——: 24 Gt. James St.
25.A2

Scott, Sir Walter
See Westminster
Abbey

Shakespeare, William
357 ▲(?)1604: Silver St.
(gone) *25.B2*
358 ▲1613–: Blackfriars
25.A2
359 ○ Aldermanbury *25.C2*
Leicester Sq. *25.A2*
Southwark Cathedral
25.C3
See also Westminster
Abbey

Shaw, George Bernard
360 ▲1887–98△: 29 Fitzroy
Sq. *24.C2*
361 ▲1899–1906, 1906–50
(partly)△: 10 Adelphi
Ter. *25 (inset)*
362 ▲1928–45 (partly): 4
Whitehall Ct. *25.A3*

Shelley, Percy Bysshe
363 ▲1811: 11 Poland St.
24.C2
364 ▲1811: 23 Aldford St.
24.C2
365 ▲1814–15: 26 Nelson
Sq., Blackfriars *25.A1*
366 ▲1815: 26 Marchmont
St. *25.A1*
See also Westminster
Abbey

Sheridan, R. B.
367 ▲1773–: 22 Orchard St.
24.C2
368 ▲c1778: The Grove,
Harrow on the Hill
22.A1
369 ▲1795–1802△: 10
Hertford St. *24.C3*
370 ▲1811–16●△: 14 Savile
Row *24.C2*
See also Westminster
Abbey

Sidney, Sir Philip
371 ▲1583–85: Barn Elms
Park, Barnes *22.B3*
See also St. Paul's
Cathedral

Skelton, John
372 ■1529: St. Margaret's,
Westminster *25.A3*

Smart, Christopher
373 ▲1769–71: King's Bench
Prison (gone), Scovell
Rd., Southwark *25.B3*

Smith, Sydney
374 ▲1803–6△: 14 (then 8)
Doughty St. *25.A2*
375 ▲1806–9: 18 Orchard St.
24.C2

376 ▲1839–45: 56 Green St.
24.C2
377 ■1845: Kensal Green
Cemetery *22.C2*
See also St. Paul's
Cathedral

Smollett, Tobias
378 ▲1750–62△: 16
Lawrence St. (gone)
24.B4
379 ▲1759: King's Bench
Prison (gone), Scovell
Rd., Southwark *25.B3*

Southey, Robert
See Westminster
Abbey, Inns of Court

Spenser, Edmund
380 ★1552: East Smithfield
25.C2
381 ▲1578–80, 1596–7:
Essex St. *25 (inset)*
382 ▲1598–9●: King St.,
Westminster *25.A2*
See also Westminster
Abbey

Steele, Sir Richard
383 ▲1707: Hampton Wick
22.A4
384 ▲1707–12: Bury St., St.
James's *24.C3*
385 ▲1712: Steele's Rd.
(site), Hampstead *22.C2*
386 ▲1714–16: St. James's
St. *24.C3*

Sterne, Laurence
387 ●1768: 39B Old Bond St.
24.C2
388 ■ Hyde Park Pl. (disused
graveyard, now a
school) *24.B2*

Strachey, Lytton
389 ★1880: Stowey House,
Clapham Common
22.C3
390 ▲1884–1909: 69
Lancaster Gate *24.B2*
391 ▲1909–△: 51 Gordon
Sq. *25.A1*

Swift, Jonathan
392 ▲1710, 1713, 1726: Bury
St., St. James's *24.C3*
393 ▲1711: Leicester Sq.
25.A2

Swinburne, Algernon
394 ★1837: 7 Chester St.
24.C3
395 ▲1860–1: 18 Grosvenor
Pl. *24.C3*
396 ▲1862–4: 16 Cheyne
Walk *24.B4*
397 ▲1865: 36 Wilton
Crescent *24.C3*
398 ▲1865–70: 22 Dorset St.
24.C2
399 ▲1872–5, 1877–8: 3 Gt.
James St. *25.A2*

400 ▲1879–1909△: The
Pines, 11 (then 2)
Putney Hill 22.B3

Tennyson, Alfred Lord
401 ▲1851–3: Montpelier,
Row, Twickenham
22.A3
See also Westminster
Abbey

**Thackeray, William
Makepeace**
402 ▲1837–: 13 (Gt.) Coram
St. 25.A1
403 ▲1840s: 88 St. James's
St. 24.C3
404 ▲1846–53△: 13 (now 16)
Young St. 24.A3
405 ▲1854–62△: 36 Onslow
Sq. 24.B4
406 ▲1861–3●△: 2 Palace
Green 24.A3
407 ■Kensal Green
Cemetery 22.C2
See also Westminster
Abbey, Inns of Court

Thompson, Francis
408 ■1907: Kensal Green
Cemetery 22.C2

Thomson, James
409 ▲1736–48: Kew Foot La.,
Richmond 22.B3
410 ■1748△: Richmond
Parish Church 22.B3
See also Westminster
Abbey

Traherne, Thomas
411 ▲1669–74●:
Teddington 22.B4
412 ■1664: St. Mary's,
Teddington 22.B4

Trollope, Anthony
413 ★1815: 6(?) Keppel St.
(gone) 25.A2
414 ▲1872–80△: 39
Montagu Sq. 25.A2

415 ●1882: 33 Welbeck St.
24.C2
416 ■1882: Kensal Green
Cemetery 22.C2

Tyndale, William
See Westminster
Abbey

Walpole, Horace
417 ★1717 ▲ 1745–79:
Arlington St. (gone)
24.C3
418 ▲1747–97: Strawberry
Hill 22.A3
419 ▲1779–97 (partly) ●: 11
Berkeley Sq. (gone)
24.C2

Walton, Izaak
420 ○St. Dunstan in the West
25 (inset)

Waugh, Evelyn
421 ▲1928: Canonbury Sq.
22.C2

Wells, H. G.
422 ★1866: 47 High St.,
Bromley 23.B4
423 ▲1937–46●△: 13
Hanover Ter. 24.B1

Wesley, Charles
424 ▲–1788●△: 1 Wheatley
St. 24.C2
425 ■○ Marylebone Parish
Church 24.C2

Wesley, John
426 ▲——△: 47 City Rd.
25.C1

White, W. H. (Mark
Rutherford)
427 ▲1865–6: Stream or
Spring House (now
Honeywood),
Carshalton 22.C4
428 ▲ 1868–9: Park Hill (now
19), Carshalton 22.C4

Wilde, Oscar
429 ▲1884–95△: 34 Tite St.
24.B4

Woolf, Virginia
430 ★1882: Hyde Park Gate
24.A3
431 ▲1905–7: 46 Gordon Sq.
25.A1
432 ▲1907–11△: 29 Fitzroy
Sq. 24.C2
433 ▲1911–12: 38
Brunswick Sq. (gone)
25.A1
434 ▲1914: 17 The Green,
Richmond 22.B3
435 ▲1915–24: Paradise Rd.,
Richmond 22.B3
436 ▲1924–39: 52 Tavistock
Sq. (gone) 25.A1
437 ▲1939–40: 37
Mecklenburgh Sq.
(gone) 25.A1

Wordsworth, William
See Westminster
Abbey

Wyatt, Sir Thomas
438 ▲ 1536, 1540–1: Tower
of London 25.C2

Wycherley, William
439 ●1716△: 19–20 Bow St.
25 (inset)
440 ■St. Paul's, Covent Gdn.
25 (inset)
See also Inns of Court

Yeats, W. B.
441 ▲1867–74△: 23 Fitzroy
Rd., Chalk Farm
22.C2
442 ▲1874–6: 14 Edith Rd.,
West Kensington
22.C3
443 ▲1876–80: 8 Woodstock
Rd., Chiswick 22.B3
444 ▲1895–1919: 5 Woburn
Pl. (then 18 Woburn
Buildings) 25.A1

KEY
★ Born
▲ Lived
● Died
■ Buried
□ House/Museum, etc.
○ Statue/Memorial, etc.
△ Plaque

Westminster Abbey 25.A3

St. Paul's Cathedral 25.B2

Inns of Court

Schools

(Qualification: 2 or more
  literary figures)

Charterhouse *20.B4*
Joseph Addison
Max Beerbohm
Richard Crashaw
Richard Lovelace
Richard Steele
W. M. Thackeray
John Wesley

Christ's Hospital *5.A4*
Edmund Blunden
Samuel Taylor Coleridge
Leigh Hunt
Charles Lamb
J. Middleton Murry
Samuel Richardson

Clifton *3.B1*
Joyce Cary
Arthur Quiller-Couch

Eton *20.B2*
Robert Bridges
Henry Fielding
Thomas Gray
Aldous Huxley
George Orwell
Percy Bysshe Shelley
Algernon Swinburne
Horace Walpole

Harrow *22.B2*
Lord Byron
John Galsworthy
L. P. Hartley
R. B. Sheridan
J. A. Symonds
Anthony Trollope

King's Canterbury *5.C2*
Christopher Marlowe
W. Somerset Maugham
Hugh Walpole

Marlborough *4.B3*
Louis MacNeice
William Morris
Siegfried Sassoon

Merchant Taylor's *20.C2*
Thomas Kyd
Edmund Spenser

Rugby *8.B3*
Matthew Arnold
Rupert Brooke
Lewis Carroll
A. H. Clough
W. S. Landor

Sherborne *4.A3*
Cecil Day-Lewis
J. C. Powys

Shrewsbury *7.A2*
Samuel Butler (19th century)
Sir Philip Sydney

St. Paul's *25.B2*
Laurence Binyon
G. K. Chesterton
John Milton
Samuel Pepys

Stonyhurst *10.B3*
Wilfrid Blunt
Arthur Conan Doyle
Gerard Manley Hopkins

Uppingham *8.C2*
Ronald Firbank
James Elroy Flecker

Westminster *25.A3*
Abraham Cowley
William Cowper
John Dryden
Edward Gibbon
George Herbert
Ben Jonson
John Locke
Matthew Prior
Robert Southey
Charles Wesley

Winchester *4.B3*
Matthew Arnold (before
  move to Rugby 1837)
Sir Thomas Browne
Thomas Otway
Sydney Smith
Anthony Trollope (before
  move to Harrow 1827)

KEY
★ Born
▲ Lived
● Died
■ Buried
□ House/Museum, etc.
○ Statue/Memorial, etc.
△ Plaque

Geographical Index

INDEX

This is an index of names and places appearing in the narrative section on pages 7–234 and excludes the Atlas and Gazetteer material on pages 235–281. For Atlas references to specific towns, consult the Geographical Index.

ATLAS AND GAZETTEER SOURCES

The following publications have proved extremely useful in the preparation of the Atlas and Gazetteer section:

The Oxford Literary Guide to the British Isles, eds. Dorothy Eagle and Hilary Correll (Oxford University Press, 1977).
Blue Plaques on Houses of Historical Interest (Greater London Council, n.d.)
A Literary Atlas and Gazetteer of the British Isles by Michael Hardwick (David and Charles, 1973).

All errors and omissions are, however, the responsibility of the authors and publishers of this volume.

MAJOR CARTOGRAPHICAL REFERENCES AND ACKNOWLEDGEMENTS

London chapters, generally: Philippa Glanville and staff at the Museum of London Library; *Growth of Stuart London* by N.G. Brett James.
London, early 1870s: *Baedeker's Guide to London* (1878).
London, early 20th century: *Guide to London* (1907), published by Ward Lock & Co.
City of Bath (early 19th century): adapted from a map by Thomas Moule.
City of Bath (present day): *Blue Guide to England*, published by Ernest Benn Ltd.
The Lake District: relief drawing by Tom Stalker Miller.
Thomas Hardy maps, generally: pamphlets issued by the Thomas Hardy Society.
Brontë Country: Brontë Parsonage Museum, Haworth.
Wuthering Heights—Fiction and Fact: "Emily Brontë: *Wuthering Heights*" by Frank Goodridge in *Studies in English Literature*, no. 20 (1964); and 1:25,000 Ordnance Survey Map.
The Blackening of England: Local History Department, Manchester Central Library; *A New Historical Geography of England* by H.C. Darby, published by Cambridge University Press, 1973.
Atlas map of Edinburgh: *Blue Guide to Scotland*, published by Ernest Benn Ltd.
Atlas maps of Oxford and Cambridge: *Blue Guide to England*, published by Ernest Benn Ltd.
Atlas map of Central London: *Blue Guide to London*, published by Ernest Benn Ltd.

PICTURE CREDITS

The authors and publishers wish to thank the following for giving permission to reprint material from their collections:
Barnaby Picture Library, London: *159, 164, 165*; British Museum, London: *71*; Brontë Parsonage Museum, Haworth, Yorkshire: *147, 152*; Dorset County Museum, Dorchester: *167*; Mary Evans Picture Library, London: *62, 127, 137, 175, 189, 200*; Greater London Council Map Collection, London: *54, 57, 60*; Inglis and Stephenson Ltd., Edinburgh: *207*; London Transport Executive, London: *87*; Mansell Collection, London: *31, 36, 88, 96, 116, 122, 123, 221*; Museum of London, London: *32, 44, 46, 51, 68, 76, 184*; John Murray Publishers Ltd., London: *134, 143*; Phyllis Murray Hill, London: *201*; Popperfoto, London: *215, 217, 225*; Radio Times Hulton Picture Library, London: *11, 12, 17, 19, 20, 29 (both), 37, 47, 93, 150, 182–3*; Victoria and Albert Museum, London: *119*; Victoria Art Gallery, Bath City Council, Bath: *92, 101*; Mrs. Edwin Smith, Saffron Walden, Essex: *209*